# Trailblazing in Entrepreneurship

Dean A. Shepherd • Holger Patzelt

# Trailblazing in Entrepreneurship

Creating New Paths for Understanding the Field

Dean A. Shepherd  
Indiana University  
Bloomington, Indiana, USA

Holger Patzelt  
School of Management  
Technical University of Munich  
School of Management  
München, Germany

ISBN 978-3-319-48700-7     ISBN 978-3-319-48701-4  (eBook)  
DOI 10.1007/978-3-319-48701-4

Library of Congress Control Number: 2016956561

© The Editor(s) (if applicable) and The Author(s) 2017  
**Open Access** This book is distributed under the terms of the Creative Commons Attribution 4.0 International License (http://creativecommons.org/licenses/by/4.0/), which permits use, duplication, adaptation, distribution and reproduction in any medium or format, as long as you give appropriate credit to the original author(s) and the source, provide a link to the Creative Commons license and indicate if changes were made.  
The images or other third party material in this chapter are included in the work's Creative Commons license, unless indicated otherwise in the credit line; if such material is not included in the work's Creative Commons license and the respective action is not permitted by statutory regulation, users will need to obtain permission from the license holder to duplicate, adapt or reproduce the material.  
The use of general descriptive names, registered names, trademarks, service marks, etc. in this publication does not imply, even in the absence of a specific statement, that such names are exempt from the relevant protective laws and regulations and therefore free for general use.  
The publisher, the authors and the editors are safe to assume that the advice and information in this book are believed to be true and accurate at the date of publication. Neither the publisher nor the authors or the editors give a warranty, express or implied, with respect to the material contained herein or for any errors or omissions that may have been made.

Cover illustration: © Digital Vision iii / Alamy Stock Photo; all rights reserved, used with permission.

Printed on acid-free paper

This Palgrave Macmillan imprint is published by Springer Nature  
The registered company is Springer International Publishing AG  
The registered company address is: Gewerbestrasse 11, 6330 Cham, Switzerland

# Contents

1 The Importance of Trailblazing Scholarship for
  Understanding Entrepreneurship                                    1

2 Researching the Generation, Refinement, and
  Exploitation of Potential Opportunities                          17

3 Researching Entrepreneurial Failures                             63

4 Researching at the Intersection of Innovation,
  Operations Management, and Entrepreneurship                     103

5 Researching Entrepreneurships' Role in Sustainable
  Development                                                     149

6 Researching at the Intersection of Family Business
  and Entrepreneurship                                            181

7 Researching the Inter-Relationship of Health
  and Entrepreneurship                                            209

| | | |
|---|---|---|
| 8 | **Researching Entrepreneurial Decision Making** | 257 |
| 9 | **Conclusion** | 287 |
| **Index** | | 291 |

# List of Figures

| | | |
|---|---|---|
| Fig. 1.1 | A sketch of the topics of the book | 10 |
| Fig. 2.1 | A sketch of a more interaction-based perspective of entrepreneurial opportunities | 27 |
| Fig. 2.2 | A sketch of research that is more activity based as a micro-foundation of entrepreneurial action | 33 |
| Fig. 2.3 | A sketch of a more cognitively hot perspective of the entrepreneurial process | 41 |
| Fig. 2.4 | A sketch of entrepreneurial research that is more compassionate and more prosocial | 49 |
| Fig. 3.1 | A sketch of a model of the implications of failure as part of the entrepreneurial process | 89 |
| Fig. 4.1 | A sketch of absorptive capacity in the entrepreneurial process | 112 |
| Fig. 4.2 | A sketch of a different stage-gate process for evaluating entrepreneurial projects | 121 |
| Fig. 4.3 | A sketch of the role of operations management in the formation of opportunity beliefs | 131 |
| Fig. 5.1 | A sketch of entrepreneurial action linking sustainability and development | 162 |
| Fig. 5.2 | A sketch of entrepreneurial action linking scientific and user communities for sustainable development | 169 |
| Fig. 6.1 | A sketch of an opportunity-based perspective of family business interactions | 189 |
| Fig. 6.2 | A sketch of an emotion-based entrepreneurial process in a family business | 195 |
| Fig. 6.3 | A sketch of a prosocially based entrepreneurial process in a family business | 200 |

| | | |
|---|---|---|
| Fig. 7.1 | A sketch of the role of health in the pursuit of an entrepreneurial career | 231 |
| Fig. 7.2 | A sketch of the role of entrepreneurial action in enhancing others' health | 239 |
| Fig. 8.1 | A sketch of a model of the nested nature of data captured by conjoint analysis (and other experimental techniques); cross-level effects in dashed arrows | 276 |

CHAPTER 1

# The Importance of Trailblazing Scholarship for Understanding Entrepreneurship

> "Do not go where the path may lead; go instead where there is no path and leave a trail."
> —*Ralph Waldo Emerson*

Recently, the co-authors of this book met in Blairgowrie, Australia. Dean Shepherd showed Holger Patzelt the Back Beach where he had spent much of his youth. Dean recalled his childhood taking the trek from his house along the path through the coastal reserve to the rock pool and surf:

> Although the path made the trip relatively quick, easy, and safe, it was a somewhat boring walk. Sometimes my brother and I took a narrower path to see a less populated section of the beach, and other times, we created our own path—a route that no one else had taken. We called it "bushwhacking" because we had to beat our way through the dense tea-tree. We did this to explore. This new path was always slower than the normal route as well as less comfortable (with branches scratching and long grasses poking) and less safe (with the chance of coming across poisonous snakes and/or spiders), but we did it anyway. We held out hope this new path would lead to a new sand dune we could tumble down, a new vista we could appreciate, a cave to hide in, or a rock pool within which we could dive and swim. But even when we did not find one of these desirable outcomes and spent hours walking only to find that we had returned to our original starting point, we had enjoyed every minute of it.

This description of bushwhacking is the Australian version of trailblazing, and metaphorically, entrepreneurs can also be **trailblazers**—*make a path through new or unsettled terrain upon which others may follow.* That is, rather than follow the established path created by others, entrepreneurs often challenge the status quo by attempting to chart a new direction through the creation of new products, services, and/or processes. However, this book is not about trailblazing in coastal reserves or in product markets but about trailblazing in the field of entrepreneurship. We believe that scholars can be trailblazers, and in doing so, they can create new knowledge that others can build on to create additional knowledge and inform practice. Although this trailblazing may not have to deal with the poisonous snakes and spiders of Australia, it certainly has its fair share of obstacles, requires considerable effort, and may also lead to dead ends. Along with the challenges of creating a new trail are the intrinsic rewards from the process and the extrinsic rewards from the outcomes of making substantial contributions to knowledge. For scholars traveling along a well-worn path or a semi-worn path, the research outcomes are replication and incremental research, whereas trailblazing creates new knowledge through more radical ideas. Important in trailblazing is knowing where to start and having some knowledge about the terrain to be covered, the tools to help clear the path, and the potential "gems" that might be encountered along the way. The purpose of this book is to provide some insights into where trailblazing may be best directed, how, and with what potential outcomes. Specifically, this book offers a series of frameworks from which or within which we believe important research will emerge—research that will have a substantial impact on our understanding of an entrepreneurial phenomenon and, thus, on the way we progress with subsequent entrepreneurship research.

We emphasize trailblazing (as opposed to taking existing paths) because we strongly believe that the future of the entrepreneurship field is promising but only if our research itself continues to be entrepreneurial. That being said, continuing to be entrepreneurial in our research may be more difficult than it initially appears. The success we have had thus far may lead us into a competency trap (Levitt & March, 1988) that rewards us in the short term but is detrimental to the field in the long term. That is, entrepreneurship researchers sometimes decide to "play it safe," using "accepted" theories and methods to answer progressively narrower research questions that are of interest to smaller and smaller audiences (i.e., taking the known path). By no means are we arguing that this type of incremental research does not make important contributions to the field. Rather, we are suggesting that if incremental research starts to dominate and overtake more trailblazing research, the field could begin to stagnate and lose the essence that makes it special—namely, the very real and pervasive willingness to accept substantial novelty in the way we question, theorize, and test ideas to develop new and stimulating insights.[1]

As we consider the entrepreneurship field's future, our goal with this book is not to decry or replace Venkataraman's (Shane & Venkataraman, 2000; Venkataraman, 1997) or others' (e.g., Busenitz et al., 2003; Carlsson et al., 2013; Davidsson, 2003; Gartner, 1990; Wiklund, Davidsson, Audretsch, & Karlsson, 2011) description of entrepreneurship's characteristic domain with our own; rather, our goal is to illuminate areas of unsettled terrain worthy of trailblazing work as a basis for the vitality of the field's future. Such trailblazing is likely to continuously alter what is considered to be entrepreneurship. As researchers, we should maybe focus less on whether our current work conforms to published domain statements within the entrepreneurship field because the field itself has likely already shifted. Our current work may make a more substantial contribution to the field by expanding its boundaries further by, for instance, opening up new terrain that then becomes part of the field of entrepreneurship (in retrospect).

Indeed, researchers from a variety of fields tend to focus narrowly on prevailing principles and themes, which can homogenize knowledge creation (in the literature) about the diverse world (Glynn, Barr, & Dacin, 2000). More specifically, Kuhn (2012) classified fields of study based on the extent to which they create paradigms—namely, "shared theoretical structures and methodological approaches about which there is a high level of consensus" (Cole, 1983, p. 112). When a paradigm is more developed, there is less uncertainty about knowledge production as well as less fragmentation, both of which appear to lead to growth in a field (Pfeffer, 1993). That is, agreement about core assumptions—namely, of the nature of "knowledge [ontology], the nature of knowledge about those phenomena [epistemology], and the nature of ways of studying those phenomena [methodology]" Gioia & Pitre, 1990, p. 585)—can result in more knowledge accumulation (Pfeffer, 1993). Stemming from these ideas, Davidsson (2003) bemoaned that entrepreneurship research occasionally suffers from an abundance of studies articulated on different core principles and assumptions—a practice that has resulted in slow knowledge accumulation in the field. These arguments are consistent with those for the benefits of well-established paths.

While there is a great deal of value in knowledge-accumulation arguments, this paradigm-development approach seems to prefer parsimony and consistency above depth and diversity. As a result, this approach has the potential to generate an exceedingly narrow view (Burrell & Morgan, 1979), particularly considering the rich nature of entrepreneurial phenomena. Indeed, as researchers, we need to keep up with the intricacies of the phenomena we explore, which we can begin doing by taking an array of perspectives to develop an assortment of interpretations (Glynn et al., 2000). Namely, the "paradigm mentality simultaneously proliferates and polarizes perspectives, often inhibiting discourse across paradigms, biasing theorists against opposing explanations and fostering development of provincial theories" (Lewis & Grimes, 1999, p. 672)—all with the aim of winning the "paradigm war." In this context, the more exploratory is overtaken by the more exploitive. Indeed, this mindset is like putting up wire fences to dissuade people from leaving the path to create their own.

## Entrepreneurship and Beyond

Although our primary intent with this book is to advance the field of entrepreneurship (without specifying the domain of entrepreneurship), we are conscious that in doing so, we have an opportunity to make contributions to knowledge that also advance other fields. Indeed, in many instances throughout the book, we focus our attention at the boundaries of current entrepreneurship theories, particularly constructs and relationships in the gray area between overlapping paradigms, levels of analysis, and fields of knowledge. This focus provides a systematic search, "the search of known information sources" (see Fiet, 2007, p. 595), for potential opportunities to advance our understanding of entrepreneurial phenomena—that is, to blaze a new trail. In particular, we start with topics we have some knowledge about and considerable interest in (i.e., familiar paths) to begin to search for and explore potential research opportunities (i.e., from which to trailblaze). Therefore, in justifying the basis for our search, we end up citing a number of our previous studies—not because we are so arrogant to believe that they represent the only basis upon which future contributions can be made to the field of entrepreneurship but because they represent "known information sources" (consistent with systematic search [Fiet, 2007]).

## POTENTIAL RESEARCH OPPORTUNITIES AND RESEARCH METHODS

The precursor to this book was the "Party On" paper (Shepherd, 2015), which challenged us, as scholars, to remain entrepreneurial and pursue areas of vitality (largely recounted in Chap. 2). We built on these notions to explore other areas that could be trailblazed to provide further vitality to the field. Although we discuss the content of research opportunities that we believe can advance our knowledge, we do not investigate the research methods necessary to empirically pursue these potential opportunities (with the possible exception of a brief discussion of conjoint analysis in Chap. 8). We are agnostic about research methods. Rather, we are pluralistic. We believe that the appropriateness of a particular research method depends on the research question and likely the knowledge and motivation of the researcher. It could be that multiple methods could be used to approach the same research opportunity, although it is likely that the operationalizations, sample context, and so forth may be so different such that they represent a different (but related) research opportunity; one that may be complementary in knowledge production. This is a good thing. Consistent results provide confidence in our knowledge based on replication. Differences in results signal the need for additional theorizing—a win-win.

Although the above assumes that the new content of our theorizing on an entrepreneurial phenomenon can be tested using (multiple) established research methods, we recognize that some research questions and/or conjectures may require the creation of new methods—new to entrepreneurship but established elsewhere, new combinations of multiple methods, or the creation of "new to the world" methods. However, the creative process does not necessarily need to be from content to method; it could be the other way around. As new methods are developed and introduced, we believe that they will open up new conceptual domains—new methods lead to new content. Therefore, although we focus on the importance of being entrepreneurial in our theorizing for advancing the field, we also recognize the importance of being entrepreneurial in our methods and welcome such advancements.

## Assumptions and Boundary Conditions

Just as we do not focus on a particular research method, we also do not focus on one particular philosophical perspective. We realize that people may be able to read into this book a philosophical perspective that we have applied subconsciously. However, we wish to point out that we believe that it is perfectly fine for people to approach their research from different philosophical perspectives. Indeed, it is better than fine because these different lenses can provide deeper insight into entrepreneurial phenomena and advance the field (even this statement is replete with unintended philosophical undertones). We like to think of different philosophical perspectives as enabling diverse knowledge creation, which is important for the vitality of the field. However, we realize that it can also constrain our thinking. To avoid constraining our thinking about research, we try to use the following rules of thumb in writing this book (and in writing and reviewing papers as well as making editorial decisions on papers) as the primary purpose is not to make a philosophical contribution:

1. We try to acknowledge the key assumptions and boundary conditions of our theorizing for the focal work.
2. We build on and direct our contributions of the focal work to the ongoing scholarly conversation that has similar assumptions and boundary conditions.
3. We allow others to use different philosophical perspectives in their papers and try to be aware of our potential biases (if any) in reading those papers.
4. We allow ourselves to use one philosophical perspective in one paper and a different philosophical perspective in a different paper (i.e., philosophically consistent within a paper but not necessarily across papers).
5. We do not acknowledge a "debate" about philosophical differences that may exist in the literature unless the specific purpose of the paper is to add something substantial to that debate.
6. We do not try to interpret a study as supporting one philosophical perspective over another nor suggest that one philosophical perspective is superior to another.
7. We do not re-interpret the findings of the study from a different philosophical perspective.
8. We realize that we are highly fallible in all of the above but dedicated to open mindedness.

These are the rules that we try to follow. We find that they help us keep an open mind about research and avoid being pulled into endless discussions that seem to go nowhere other than around and around and around again. Like a merry-go-round, we realize that the circles, the ups and downs, the lights, and the bells and whistles of philosophical debates are enticing (like moths drawn to a flame), but because we are unwilling to spend a career trying to gain (and probably never fully achieving) an understanding of these deep and complicated issues, we avoid the temptation of "dabbling" (or at least we try). We also realize that contributions can be made by trained philosophers in exploring these issues.

## IMPLICATIONS FOR ENTREPRENEURIAL SCHOLARS

While trailblazing can sound exciting, as we mentioned above, it is more likely that incremental (i.e., exploitation) research has begun to crowd out trailblazing (i.e., exploration) research to the detriment of the field. This crowding out can be caused by individual scholars who want to take advantage of the legitimacy and popularity of the entrepreneurship field to focus on providing many incremental contributions, for instance, by adding another moderator to an extensive list of moderators of an existing main-effect relationship. This may seem to be a prudent research approach for a sole scholar, and it does contribute to the literature; however, if the majority of scholars use this strategy and are rewarded for doing so, we run into the "crowding-out effect" that we are worried about.

While it is understandable why some scholars, especially junior scholars, might take this approach, we put forth two cautionary observations and a challenge. First, the biggest risk when attempting to publish work in prestigious journals is using a conservative research strategy. Similar to the higher outcome variance in more entrepreneurial organizations (McGrath, 1999), entrepreneurial scholars are also likely to experience greater variance in research outcomes. Totally mixing metaphors, we argue that some trailblazing projects are likely to completely "bomb," whereas other projects could end up being "home runs" (i.e., they are able to capture editors', reviewers', and audiences' attention). Scholars who are organizing new research projects often use these "home run" entrepreneurial papers to develop their own stories. Thus, entrepreneurial scholars' published papers are likely to influence the development of the field (as well as other fields) more significantly than less entrepreneurial scholars' papers (even though entrepreneurial scholars are likely to experience higher project failure rates).

Second, researchers can consider taking a portfolio approach with their projects, combining more radical research projects with "safer" projects. As entrepreneurial scholars, we can build a portfolio of projects that includes a few studies we believe are trailblazing (i.e., are odd, peculiar, and/or challenge the status quo). This approach is in line with the real options reasoning approach many organizations take to deal with the uncertainty underlying potential opportunities (McGrath, 1999).

Third, the challenge we present herein is to broaden the array of research questions, theories, and methods and to look to the "flipside" of prominent research streams for inspiration. For instance, entrepreneurship researchers trust there are benefits resulting from entrepreneurial action, so they generally focus on exploring those benefits. However, only studying benefits may lead to an incomplete picture. Different research questions and theories may be necessary to fully comprehend the costs associated with entrepreneurial action. For instance, why do some individuals undertake entrepreneurial action to destroy value, take advantage of the susceptible, and/or damage nature? Why does entrepreneurial action sometimes lead to physical, psychological, and/or emotional suffering? Is there a motivation that is the antithesis to prosocial motivation? That is, how do we examine the motivations of individuals who want to take entrepreneurial action to hurt or weaken other people or the natural environment (if such individuals exist)? These thought experiments may be useful in finding a terrain through which to begin to try to blaze a new trail.

New research questions, theories, and topics are also likely to broaden the range of research methods and vice versa. In the past, entrepreneurial scholars have broadened the range of research methods by taking methodological developments from other fields and applying them in the entrepreneurial context. However, similar to borrowing theories for application in the field of entrepreneurship, employing methods from other fields will likely necessitate some re-working, which may in itself contribute back to the initial source. Researchers also have the chance to engage in bricolage by considering the methods currently available and combining them in new ways to reveal novel grounds for theorizing and empirical testing. For example, we (along with Robert Baron) attempted bricolage by combining three basic methodological approaches—a conjoint study, an experimental manipulation, and an "intercepts-only" model—to help us better understand an issue that would have been challenging to test otherwise (see Shepherd et al., 2013).

## Implications for Entrepreneurial Journals

Crowding out also happens during the journal review process when editors and reviewers take a more conservative approach because they are more concerned with errors of commission (i.e., publishing a paper that lessens the journal's legitimacy) than with errors of omission (i.e., turning down a paper that is riskier but could be very impactful). As a result, editors and reviewers often decide to "play it safe," deciding to accept only papers that fit their particular mold and are "done well" regardless of misgivings about the size of the work's contribution. While this conservative approach may work out in the short term, it is likely to lead to a stagnant field with inflexible borders, narrow questions, and tricky turf battles. If this occurs in entrepreneurship, we, as entrepreneurship scholars, will become the exact opposite of what we study.

So where is the field headed? Well, that depends on changes in the phenomena (which are difficult to predict) and where we, as a community of scholars, blaze new trails through publishing high-quality research papers. In this book, we focus on the latter—where we, as a community of scholars, can take the field through trailblazing—because scholarly knowledge is within our control. In this book, we present some trailblazing possibilities, possibilities that we believe hold great promise for future research to make important contributions to the continued development of the field. These possibilities are by no means an exhaustive list. Indeed, even within a particular topic of interest, there is almost an infinite array of research questions possible. It is our sincere hope that this book stimulates new exploratory research whether or not it is along the lines outlined herein.

In Fig. 1.1, we illustrate the framework for the book. In the next chapter (Chap. 2), we lay out the basis for trailblazing in terms of the generation, refinement, and exploitation of potential opportunities and the benefits generated for the entrepreneur (and/or the entrepreneurial firm) and/or others. In Chap. 3, we extend the notion of the "potential" opportunity to recognize that failure is a frequent outcome of entrepreneurial action that can also benefit the entrepreneur (and/or the entrepreneurial firm) and/or others primarily through learning from the experience. In Chap. 4, we describe how trailblazing can involve combining the operational processes of innovation and the various aspects of the entrepreneurial process to provide a deeper explanation of entrepreneurial activities and outcomes (including failure). The entrepreneurial process is (or micro-entrepreneurial processes are) embedded in a number of environments that

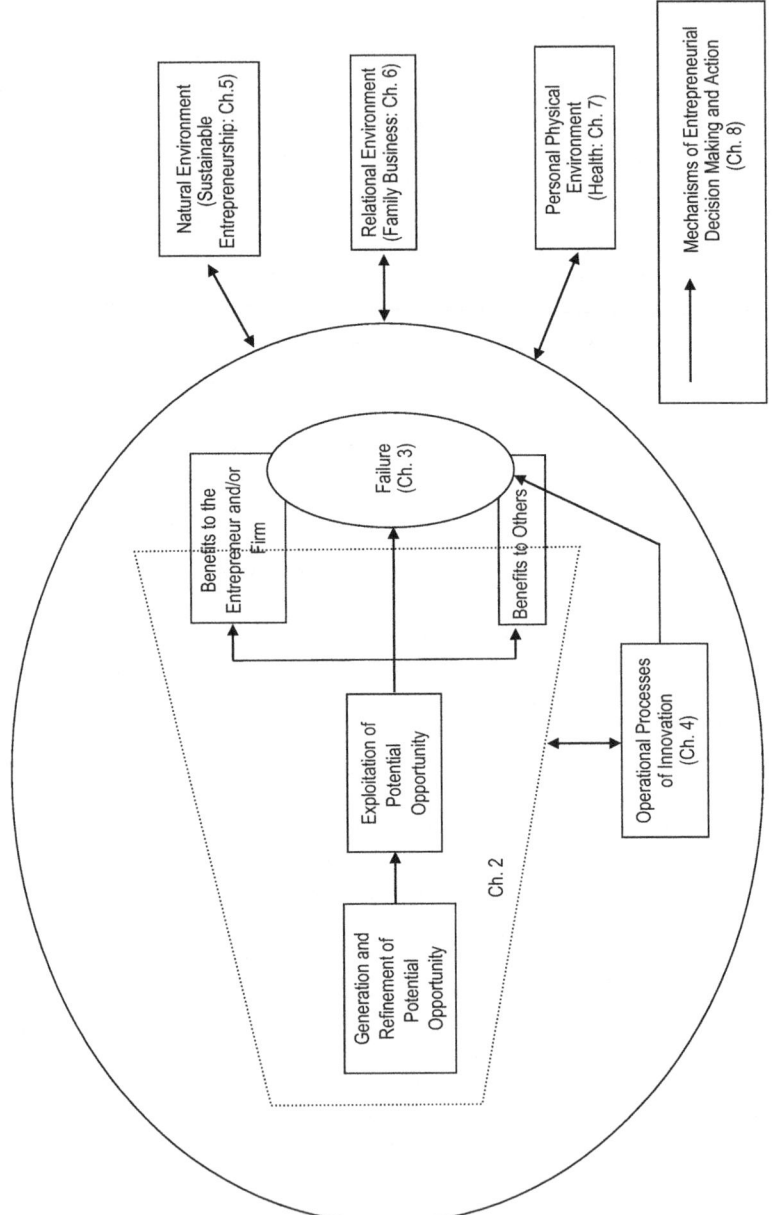

**Fig. 1.1** A sketch of the topics of the book

can trigger new paths of knowledge creation. Specifically, by exploring the entrepreneurial process in the natural environment, we can advance our understanding of sustainable entrepreneurship (Chap. 5); in the relational environment, we can advance our understanding of the family's role in entrepreneurial businesses (Chap. 6); and in the personal physical environment, we can gain a deeper understanding of how health impacts entrepreneurial action and how entrepreneurial action impacts health (of the entrepreneur and/or others) (Chap. 7). Although each chapter details the possible mechanisms underlying the proposed relationships (e.g., emotion, cognition, and motivation), we recognize that a central core assumption is that entrepreneurial actions are largely driven by decision making. In Chap. 8, we make explicit the role of decision making by explaining how entrepreneurial decision-making research can help blaze new trails in the field of entrepreneurship. Next, we describe each chapter in more detail.

In Chap. 2, we build on previous work (e.g., Shepherd, 2015) to investigate the central aspect of entrepreneurship—the opportunity—and build a deeper understanding of the possibilities of research from exploring (1) how the entrepreneurial process involves the mutual adjustment of the entrepreneur, a community of practice, and the nature of the potential opportunity over time; (2) how entrepreneurial activities inform and motivate opportunity beliefs as a micro-foundation of entrepreneurial action; (3) how entrepreneurial cognitions influence emotions and vice versa as a basis for a more dynamic and "hot" perspective of entrepreneurial thinking; and (4) how idiosyncratic motivations and knowledge can lead to entrepreneurial action that "does good" for others.

In Chap. 3, we build on our previous work (e.g., Shepherd, 2003; Shepherd, Patzelt, Williams, & Warnecke, 2014; Shepherd, Patzelt, & Wolfe, 2011) to acknowledge the frequency of failure given the uncertainty of the entrepreneurial process—failure of projects within an established firm and the failure of entrepreneurial firms. We then highlight how future research can make an important contribution to knowledge and open up new ground for subsequent research by exploring (1) the financial, social, and psychological consequences of failure; (2) the inter-relationships between the financial, social, and/or psychological outcomes of experiencing failure, including magnifying and dampening effects; and (3) the processes of sensemaking and learning from failure, especially those related to developing plausible stories of failure.

In Chap. 4, we highlight the importance of managing the entrepreneurial process and discuss how building on the innovation and operations management literatures provides a strong foundation from which numerous explorations can take place. In particular, although knowledge is central to the generation and refinement of a potential opportunity, we do not have a good understanding of how to manage that knowledge and, for that matter, what motivations lead to entrepreneurial actions. In this chapter, we describe the stepping stones of absorptive capacity, stage gates, and operations management more generally and start to lay them out in unsettled terrain in the field of entrepreneurship to provide an indication of the vitality generated by future trailblazing work in this area. Such trailblazing not only creates vitality to the field of entrepreneurship but also has the potential to revitalize these topics in the fields of innovation and operations management.

In Chap. 5, we build on our previous work (e.g., Patzelt & Shepherd, 2011; Shepherd & Patzelt, 2011) to offer sustainable entrepreneurship as the link between what is to be sustained (i.e., nature, life support, and community) and what is to be developed (broadly construed to include economic and non-economic gains to individuals, the economy, and society) through entrepreneurial actions. We explore the possibilities of research questions related to what is to be sustained and what is to be developed in sustainable entrepreneurship. We also explore entrepreneurs as a link between the scientific community and the end-user community. This is important because scientists' research-based knowledge has the potential to influence the sustainability of end users' development behaviors, but there are numerous obstacles to this occurring. Entrepreneurial action is a mechanism for overcoming some of these obstacles and thereby linking the scientific and user communities for sustainable development outcomes.

In Chap. 6, we build on our previous work (e.g., Shepherd, 2016) to begin to establish a stronger link between entrepreneurship and family business to build knowledge in both fields. Specifically, we explore (1) how a potential opportunity for a family business changes as a result of the interactions between sub-communities of inquiry inside and outside the family, the business, and the family business as well as how these sub-communities can be transformed by the entrepreneurial process; (2) how the entrepreneurial process and the notion of socio-emotional wealth intertwine to provide the possibilities for new insights into the entrepreneurial action and performance of family businesses; and (3) how family businesses have the capability and motivation for compassion organizing to alleviate the suffering of people inside and outside the family and inside and outside the business.

In Chap. 7, we build on our previous work (Shepherd & Patzelt, 2015) to highlight the need for research linking entrepreneurial action to health outcomes and health to entrepreneurial outcomes. Such future research could have a substantial impact on the health of individuals. This approach suggests a number of terrains for which trailblazing could be highly beneficial. We believe that future entrepreneurship research should explore how health influences the decision to pursue an entrepreneurial career—the creation of a new organization and/or the pursuit of a potential opportunity. However, there is also likely a reciprocal relationship. We identify a number of research opportunities to explore how an entrepreneurial career can influence health through stress, emotional reactions, and socioeconomic status. In addition, as a consistent theme throughout the book, we believe that by considering entrepreneurial action as a tool that can be used for good, researchers need to investigate the path between entrepreneurial action and the health of others.

In Chap. 8, we build on our previous work (e.g., Shepherd, 2011; Shepherd, Williams, & Patzelt, 2015) to point out that entrepreneurial decision making represents an extreme decision-making context faced by many corporate and independent entrepreneurs, a context high in uncertainty, time pressure, emotions, and consequential extremes. We explore research possibilities on the topics of opportunity-assessment decisions, entrepreneurial career decisions, decisions on funding entrepreneurial action, and biases and heuristics in entrepreneurial decision making. We also acknowledge a foundation of multi-level research on decision making in the entrepreneurial context and explore future research opportunities to build upon it. This exploration is organized conceptually as a hierarchy of levels below and above the level of the individual, and we use conjoint analysis as a methodological framework to keep these ideas anchored in what is empirically possible.

## Conclusion

Through this book, we present a challenge (to ourselves and anyone else who will listen) for future research to build a stronger, more complete understanding of entrepreneurial phenomena. To achieve this strength and completeness, researchers (and journals) must accept that there is not one correct approach or answer in this field, and they must welcome numerous viewpoints, including those from different paradigms and multi-paradigms. Indeed, scholars have begun to recognize a "post-paradigm war" approach to building fields of knowledge (Romani, Primecz, & Topçu, 2011)—a multi-paradigm perspective (e.g., Gioia & Pitre, 1990)—that emphasizes a more complete picture of the phenomena at hand. This more complete picture of entrepreneurial phenomena will likely come from scholars who undertake at least some trailblazing projects; from scholars who broaden the range of research questions, the potential outcomes of entrepreneurial action, and the selection and combination of research methods; and from researchers who avoid the endless debates about the margins of the field and its sub-fields or about whether one theoretical or philosophical lens is superior to another.

## Note

1. We acknowledge that some scholars may argue that we are lacking enough incremental research (e.g., there are calls for more replication studies). However, thinking about the future of the field of entrepreneurship, we are far more worried about "exploitation" overtaking "exploration" (consistent with March, 1991) than vice versa.

## References

Burrell, G., & Morgan, G. (1979). *Sociological paradigms and organisational analysis* (Vol. 248). London: Heinemann.

Busenitz, L. W., West, G. P., Shepherd, D., Nelson, T., Chandler, G. N., & Zacharakis, A. (2003). Entrepreneurship research in emergence: Past trends and future directions. *Journal of Management, 29*, 285–308.

Carlsson, B., Braunerhjelm, P., McKelvey, M., Olofsson, C., Persson, L., & Ylinenpää, H. (2013). The evolving domain of entrepreneurship research. *Small Business Economics, 41*, 913–930.

Cole, S. (1983). The hierarchy of the sciences? *American Journal of Sociology, 89*(1), 111–139.

Davidsson, P. (2003). The domain of entrepreneurship research: Some suggestions. *Advances in Entrepreneurship, Firm Emergence and Growth, 6*(3), 315–372.

Fiet, J. O. (2007). A prescriptive analysis of search and discovery. *Journal of Management Studies, 44*(4), 592–611.

Gartner, W. B. (1990). What are we talking about when we talk about entrepreneurship? *Journal of Business Venturing, 5*(1), 15–28.
Gioia, D. A., & Pitre, E. (1990). Multiparadigm perspectives on theory building. *Academy of Management Review, 15*(4), 584–602.
Glynn, M. A., Barr, P. S., & Dacin, M. T. (2000). Pluralism and the problem of variety. *Academy of Management Review, 25*(4), 726–734.
Kuhn, T. S. (2012). *The structure of scientific revolutions.* Chicago, IL: University of Chicago Press.
Levitt, B., & March, J. G. (1988). Organizational learning. *Annual Review of Sociology, 14,* 319–340.
Lewis, M. W., & Grimes, A. I. (1999). Metatriangulation: Building theory from multiple paradigms. *Academy of Management Review, 24*(4), 672–690.
McGrath, R. G. (1999). Falling forward: Real options reasoning and entrepreneurial failure. *Academy of Management Review, 24*(1), 13–30.
Patzelt, H., & Shepherd, D. A. (2011). Recognizing opportunities for sustainable development. *Entrepreneurship Theory and Practice, 35*(4), 631–652.
Pfeffer, J. (1993). Barriers to the advance of organizational science: Paradigm development as a dependent variable. *Academy of Management Review, 18*(4), 599–620.
Romani, L., Primecz, H., & Topçu, K. (2011). Paradigm interplay for theory development: A methodological example with the Kulturstandard method. *Organizational Research Methods, 14*(3), 432–455.
Shane, S., & Venkataraman, S. (2000). The promise of entrepreneurship as a field of research. *Academy of Management Review, 25*(1), 217–226.
Shepherd, D. A. (2003). Learning from business failure: Propositions of grief recovery for the self-employed. *Academy of Management Review, 28*(2), 318–328.
Shepherd, D. A. (2011). Multilevel entrepreneurship research: Opportunities for studying entrepreneurial decision making. *Journal of Management, 37*(2), 412–420.
Shepherd, D. A. (2015). Party on! A call for entrepreneurship research that is more interactive, activity based, cognitively hot, compassionate, and prosocial. *Journal of Business Venturing, 30*(4), 489–507.
Shepherd, D. A. (2016). An emotions perspective for advancing the fields of family business and entrepreneurship: Stocks, flows, reactions, and responses. *Family Business Review,* 1–8.
Shepherd, D. A., & Patzelt, H. (2011). The new field of sustainable entrepreneurship: Studying entrepreneurial action linking "what is to be sustained" with "what is to be developed". *Entrepreneurship Theory and Practice, 35*(1), 137–163.
Shepherd, D. A., Patzelt, H., & Baron, R. A. (2013). "I care about nature, but ...": Disengaging values in assessing opportunities that cause harm. *Academy of Management Journal, 56*(5), 1251–1273.

Shepherd, D. A., & Patzelt, H. (2015). The "heart" of entrepreneurship: The impact of entrepreneurial action on health and health on entrepreneurial action. *Journal of Business Venturing Insights, 4,* 22–29.

Shepherd, D. A., Patzelt, H., Williams, T. A., & Warnecke, D. (2014). How does project termination impact project team members? Rapid termination, 'creeping death', and learning from failure. *Journal of Management Studies, 51*(4), 513–546.

Shepherd, D. A., Patzelt, H., & Wolfe, M. (2011). Moving forward from project failure: Negative emotions, affective commitment, and learning from the experience. *Academy of Management Journal, 54*(6), 1229–1259.

Shepherd, D. A., Williams, T. A., & Patzelt, H. (2015). Thinking about entrepreneurial decision making: Review and research agenda. *Journal of Management, 41*(1), 11–46.

Venkataraman, S. (1997). The distinctive domain of entrepreneurship research. In J. Katz (Ed.), *Advances in entrepreneurship, firm emergence, and growth* (pp. 119–138). Greenwich: JAI Press.

Wiklund, J., Davidsson, P., Audretsch, D. B., & Karlsson, C. (2011). The future of entrepreneurship research. *Entrepreneurship Theory and Practice, 35*(1), 1–9.

**Open Access** This chapter is distributed under the terms of the Creative Commons Attribution 4.0 International License (http://creativecommons.org/licenses/by/4.0/), which permits use, duplication, adaptation, distribution and reproduction in any medium or format, as long as you give appropriate credit to the original author(s) and the source, provide a link to the Creative Commons license and indicate if changes were made.

The images or other third party material in this chapter are included in the work's Creative Commons license, unless indicated otherwise in the credit line; if such material is not included in the work's Creative Commons license and the respective action is not permitted by statutory regulation, users will need to obtain permission from the license holder to duplicate, adapt or reproduce the material.

CHAPTER 2

# Researching the Generation, Refinement, and Exploitation of Potential Opportunities

## INTRODUCTION

Most research opportunities are characterized by uncertainty, and scholars generally have numerous options when thinking about how to contribute to and energize a field of study. In this chapter, we argue that future contributions to the field of entrepreneurship will stem from considering the entrepreneurial process as a series of steps to generate and refine opportunities through developing, engaging, and transforming communities of inquiry. In addition, this process involves a dynamic and recursive pattern of activities immersed in entrepreneurial practice that goes beyond financial goals and engages the heart as much as the mind. We believe viewing the entrepreneurial process in this way will help researchers gain a deeper understanding of how entrepreneurial action can meet some of the most challenging issues of our time, thereby enabling important contributions to the field of entrepreneurship.

First, scholars have contributed significantly to the body of research on entrepreneurial cognition focusing on individuals' beliefs about whether a specific situation is (or is not) an opportunity (e.g., Autio Dahlander, & Fredrickson, 2013; Cornelissen & Clarke, 2010; Gregoire, Barr, & Shepherd, 2010; Grégoire & Shepherd, 2012; Gruber, Macmillan, & Thompson, 2013; Keh, Foo, & Lim, 2002; McMullen & Shepherd,

---

This chapter is based on Shepherd (2015).

© The Author(s) 2017
D.A. Shepherd, H. Patzelt, *Trailblazing in Entrepreneurship*,
DOI 10.1007/978-3-319-48701-4_2

2006; Tang, Kacmar, & Busenitz, 2012). Unsurprisingly, given its roots in cognitive psychology, most of this research has focused on individual-level characteristics (Baron & Ensley, 2006; Mitchell et al., 2002; Shane, 2000; Shepherd & DeTienne, 2005) or cognitive processes (Bryant, 2007; Busenitz & Barney, 1997; Cornelissen & Clarke, 2010; Grégoire et al., 2010) when explaining how people detect, understand, and/or assess possible opportunities. Future research can extend this body of research as well as enhance our understanding of entrepreneurial phenomena by taking a more interactive view of the entrepreneurial process and investigating how a community of inquiry influences the refinement of a possible opportunity and changes in the entrepreneur's mind, how potential opportunities alter a community of inquiry, and how an evolving opportunity can lead to the mutual adjustment between the entrepreneur's mind and the community of inquiry.

Second, previous research has significantly deepened our knowledge of the outcomes (Bornstein, 2004; Dean & McMullen, 2007; Foss, Foss, Klein, & Klein, 2007; Roberts & Woods, 2005) and antecedents of entrepreneurial action (Krueger, 2007; McMullen & Shepherd, 2006; Meek, Pacheco, & York, 2010; Mitchell & Shepherd, 2010). Scholars can further complement this research by exploring the numerous sub-activities associated with a single entrepreneurial action. More specifically, by focusing on activity as the key unit of analysis, future research can extend the literature on nascent entrepreneurship that emphasizes the series of activities involved in new venture emergence (Delmar & Shane, 2004; Gartner, 1985; Lichtenstein, Carter, Dooley, & Gartner, 2007) rather than the solitary act of exploiting an opportunity. Such research will help separate entrepreneurial action into its basic sub-activities and elucidate the interrelationships between activities, between an activity (or sequence of activities) and an individual's *motivation* to form an opportunity belief, and between an activity (or sequence of activities) and the *knowledge* needed to form an opportunity belief. With this research, scholars will be able to begin constructing a theory of the micro-foundations of entrepreneurial action.

Third, research has already provided strong evidence of the role cognition plays in individuals' execution of tasks essential to the entrepreneurial process, including identifying (e.g., Ardichvili, Cardozo, & Ray, 2003; Corbett, 2005; Grégoire et al., 2010), assessing (e.g., Haynie, Shepherd, & McMullen, 2009; Keh et al., 2002), and acting on (e.g., Autio, Dahlander, & Frederiksen, 2013; Hmieleski & Baron, 2008; McMullen & Shepherd,

2006) potential opportunities. In addition, research has begun to reveal how emotion influences entrepreneurs' cognitive information processing for important tasks (e.g., Baron, 2008; Foo, 2011; Shepherd, 2003; Welpe, Spörrle, Grichnik, Michl, & Audretsch, 2012). Along these lines, research could make important contributions by building on the concept of "hot cognition" (i.e., the notion that emotions affect cognitive processing in the entrepreneurial context [Cardon, Foo, Shepherd, & Wiklund, 2012]) to study the opposite relationship—namely, how entrepreneurial activity affects the way individuals generate emotions (both positive and negative) as they engage in challenging entrepreneurial tasks (see Gielnik, Spitzmuller, Schmitt, Klemann, & Frese, 2015). As this research evolves, scholars can begin to investigate the reciprocal relationship between cognitions and emotions as individuals engage in entrepreneurial tasks over time.

Finally, scholars have made recent progress in the field of entrepreneurship by investigating the outcomes of entrepreneurial actions benefitting others—for instance, research on social entrepreneurship (e.g., Dacin, Dacin, & Tracey, 2011; Dees, 1998; Mair & Marti, 2006; McMullen, 2011; Peredo & Chrisman, 2006), environmental entrepreneurship (e.g., Dean & McMullen, 2007; Meek et al., 2010; Shepherd, Patzelt, & Baron, 2013; York & Venkataraman, 2010), and sustainable development (e.g., Hall, Daneke, & Lenox, 2010; Shepherd & Patzelt, 2011). Future scholarship that develops and extends the compassion organizing (e.g., Dutton, 2003; Dutton, Worline, Frost, & Lilius, 2006; George, 2013; Kanov et al., 2004; Lilius et al., 2008) and prosocial motivation (e.g., Batson, 1998; De Dreu, 2006; Grant, 2007, 2008; Grant & Berry, 2011; Grant & Sumanth, 2009) literatures is likely to contribute significantly to these previous research lines by exploring the distinct role of entrepreneurial actions and their underlying sub-activities. More specifically, entrepreneurship researchers are particularly well suited to study how individuals can alleviate others' suffering by going beyond depending on established organizations' normal routines and developing new routines within these organizations or creating new organizations, how organizational members can alleviate non-organizational members' suffering, and how people can build new organizations in resource-devastated environments to help others. Going beyond investigating individuals' ability to act entrepreneurially to help others overcome suffering, future scholarship will likely progress this line of research by adding to and extending the concept of prosocial motivation to entrepreneurs' compassionate venturing.

Throughout the rest of this chapter, we discuss each of these research streams in more detail. Of course, these streams are not the only potential sources of continued vitality in the field of entrepreneurship. However, we chose to focus on four sources of vitality as the foundation for future research for four primary reasons. First, the four potential sources of vitality are not inconsistent with the current entrepreneurship literature, thus enabling us to build on past research while also overcoming current and future difficulties in existing research streams. Second, irrespective of how the field is defined, opportunities and individuals' actions are essential concepts in entrepreneurship research discussions, and the focus of this chapter is in line with these critical components. Third, each source of vitality is grounded in fruitful scholarship from another field (e.g., with established theories, methods, techniques, etc.), thus enabling us to extend both the field of entrepreneurship and outside fields through combination, recombination, and creativity. Finally, research has shown that the nature of a potential opportunity is related to an individual's (or a firm's) prior knowledge. The same notion applies to us as we begin to think about future research paths and opportunities. While we will likely need to venture into unknown territory, these themes are still very much in line with the distinct knowledge of the psychology of entrepreneurship, and there are doubtless many significant opportunities within and outside these areas.

## A More Interactive Perspective of Entrepreneurial Opportunity

### *The Dominant Cognitive Psychology Perspective*

Although scholars have yet to agree on the exact nature and definition of opportunities (e.g., Davidsson, 2003, 2015; Dimov, 2011; Gartner, Carter, & Hills, 2003; McMullen, Plummer, & Acs, 2007; Short, Ketchen, Shook, & Ireland, 2009), most agree that opportunities are uncertain ex-ante (Knight, 1921) and can only really be determined post hoc. As a result, recent research on entrepreneurial opportunities has generally centered on an individual's assessment of whether a particular situation signifies an opportunity for someone (i.e., third-person opportunity) (e.g., Cornelissen & Clarke, 2010; Grégoire et al., 2010; Grégoire & Shepherd, 2012; Gruber et al., 2013; Shepherd & DeTienne, 2005) and then whether it signifies an opportunity for him or her personally (i.e., first-person opportunity) (e.g., Autio et al., 2013; Fitzsimmons & Douglas,

2011; Haynie et al., 2009; Keh et al., 2002; Mitchell & Shepherd, 2010; Tang et al., 2012). Most researchers explain the formation of opportunity beliefs (first- and/or third-person) (McMullen & Shepherd, 2006) in terms of cognitive attributes, such as prior knowledge (e.g., Shane, 2000; Shepherd & DeTienne, 2005) and expert prototypes (Baron & Ensley, 2006) and explore this belief formation using cognitive processes, such as heuristics (Bryant, 2007; Busenitz & Barney, 1997), metaphors (Cornelissen & Clarke, 2010), and structural alignments (Grégoire et al., 2010; Grégoire & Shepherd, 2012), as the foundation. It is not surprising—given this cognitive foundation—that researchers' focus has recently centered on how individuals detect and try to decipher indicators of a potential opportunity (with social resources occasionally supporting this effort). This line of cognitive research on opportunity beliefs can likely be supplemented and extended by future research that takes a more interactive view and contributes additional insights into the refinement of potential opportunities, the transformations of communities through potential opportunities, and the mutual adjustment of both.

### *An Interactive Perspective of the Identification and Refinement of a Potential Opportunity*

There are obviously quite a few social perspectives that could contribute to research on the formation of opportunity beliefs (e.g., collective cognition [Shalley & Perry-Smith, 2008; West, 2007], relational capital [Hite, 2005; Yli-Renko, Autio, & Sapienza, 2001], brokerage [Burt, 2005; Stinchfield, Nelson, & Wood, 2013], crescive conditions [Dorado & Ventresca, 2013], and social structure [Sorenson & Audia, 2000]); however, particularly fruitful research is likely to come from viewing a potential opportunity as a process of social interaction between an entrepreneur and a community as opposed to an outcome of thinking on behalf of the entrepreneur. Nonetheless, if we move away from focusing on knowledge structures (e.g., schema [e.g., Corbett & Hmieleski, 2007; Krueger, 2003], mental models [e.g., Hill & Levenhagen, 1995; Krueger, 2007], scripts [e.g., Mitchell, Smith, Seawright, & Morse, 2000; Smith, Mitchell, & Mitchell, 2009], or prototypes [Baron & Ensley, 2006]) and begin to focus on the embodiment of knowledge between an entrepreneur and a community, we are likely to gain deeper insights into the mutual adjustment between these two actors as well as the ways potential opportunities are cultivated and refined.

While a potential opportunity can arise through an abductive process in an individual's mind (Swedberg, 2009), the idea underlying that potential opportunity is likely to stem from experiences the individual has had in the world, which must then be tested back in that context. That is, ideas "must be tested against the phenomena they are intended to unpack" (Prawat, 1995, p. 17). This testing requires a potential opportunity to be exposed "to a community whose standards allow us to correct and revise our ideas" (Pardales & Girod, 2006, p. 302). A community of inquiry for a potential opportunity could comprise potential stakeholders who are able to comment on the potential opportunity's promise and validity (Autio et al., 2013). For instance, a community made up of other entrepreneurs, financiers, technologists, consumers, and suppliers is likely to provide a sound "reality check" for an entrepreneur pursuing a possible opportunity (Bruner, 1986; Klofsten, 2005; Kloppenberg, 1989; Seixas, 1993; Wilson, 1990). If the entrepreneur faces criticism from such a community, it is likely to raise some doubt in his or her mind, thus informing and motivating the entrepreneur to alter the potential opportunity or discard it altogether. Assuming the entrepreneur decides to continue to pursue the potential opportunity, he or she must further test it against socially verifiable facts.

Furthermore, the community of inquiry may also be transformed by interacting with the potential opportunity. For example, an entrepreneur's communication and explanation of an opportunity may alter a community member's knowledge (e.g., provide new insights into technological developments), which can influence how that member judges the opportunity (and other opportunities in the future). Alternatively, those community members who discarded the opportunity in the first place might not be available to the entrepreneur (or approached by him or her) to judge future developments of the opportunity. In contrast, when members of a community of inquiry come to the same conclusions about a potential opportunity's promise (and those conclusions are positive), there is belief in the potential opportunity (Autio et al., 2013).

### *Potential Opportunity of the Mind* and *of the World*

A more interactive perspective of opportunity is in line with pragmatism and a number of associated key assumptions. First, pragmatism is characterized by a world independent of individuals' minds about which people can form beliefs (Peirce, 1955). Second, in this belief system, individuals are only able to access the real world through their mental world (Peirce, 1955), thus meaning the two worlds are entwined (Gergen, 1994). Finally, the pragmatic perspective argues that while people search for truth, they can never truly find it. Thus, what the community of inquiry deems is truth is merely the current best opinion and is itself only temporary (Haskel, 1984; Seixas, 1993). This perspective has implications for entrepreneurship.

Namely, research on opportunities has often taken the view that opportunities are discovered or created and that creation dominates discovery in certain contexts and vice versa in other contexts (Alvarez & Barney, 2007). An interaction perspective of opportunity, however, provides an alternative path for future studies (consistent with Dewey's [1939] characterization of mind–world dualism). Under this perspective, potential opportunities do not belong exclusively to the domain of the mind or of the world; rather, they involve the inter-relationship (i.e., mutual adjustment) of both. Indeed, as Gergen (1994, p. 129) pointed out, a vexing problem can arise when there is division and isolation between the mind and the world: "When a real world is to be reflected by a mental world and the only means of determining the match is via the mental world, the real world will always remain opaque and the relationship between the two inexplicable." Scholars can make future contributions to our understanding of opportunity by viewing potential opportunities as a conceivable means to think about and discuss the world that proves useful (through action) while simultaneously recognizing that opportunities are only tentatively held and are subject to modification as they enter and re-enter the environment.

### *Research Opportunities from a More Interactive Perspective of Entrepreneurial Opportunity*

**Community contributions to potential opportunity refinement.** Following this line of thinking (i.e., viewing opportunity detection and refinement in an interactive manner), the notion of a potential opportunity should not only be considered as part of the initial creator's mind but also grounded in a community. For example, a potential opportunity that is not fully formed is likely to change after being presented to a community of inquiry as a result of that community's social forces, feedback, and criticism. In this context, many questions surrounding the community arise. What comprises a community member for a specific potential opportunity, including who is involved in this community, how and when do members of the community interact (if they do), how does the community come about in the first place, and how does it transform (in composition and in mind) as time passes? It could be that the nature of the community depends on the nature of the opportunity (and its dynamics), and perhaps certain communities have more success in "changing" a potential opportunity than others. It then becomes important to explore what strategies entrepreneurs use to construct, engage, and learn from communities of inquiry and why and when certain entrepreneurs are more effective in conducting these activities than others.

It is clear that a potential opportunity is likely to change after the entrepreneur has received feedback from the community; however, our understanding of the nature of this feedback and the resulting changes is still opaque. In particular, how much does a potential opportunity change after interacting with the community of inquiry and why? Perhaps the amount of change in a potential opportunity depends on the personal relationship between the entrepreneur and the community member(s) (e.g., feedback from some community members is incorporated more in the opportunity change than feedback from others). Further, it could be that the amount of opportunity change lessens over time (consistent with the notion of refinement), but perhaps changes to the potential opportunity follow a different pattern (e.g., a punctuated equilibrium model characterized by periods of incremental refinement followed by substantial change). It is interesting to consider whether opportunity changes are ever so extensive that the eventual opportunity only vaguely resembles its initial form. As with most change, perhaps there is resistance by the entrepreneur to the changes community members suggest. If so, it would be interesting to gain a deeper understanding of what effect (if any) the entrepreneur's resistance to change has on the development, refinement, and/or transformation of the potential opportunity.

**Potential opportunities transforming communities of inquiry.** Thus far, our discussion implies a uni-directional information flow from the community to the entrepreneur, with only the entrepreneur's mind changing from feedback about the potential opportunity. However, it is likely that the community of inquiry—and more generally the external environment—will also change from exposure to the potential opportunity. That is, as a potential opportunity is vetted, not only is there a change in the creator's mind about the potential opportunity, but there is also a change in the environment in which the potential opportunity is positioned. Thus, from an interaction-based view, the research challenge in this context is not determining whether or when a potential opportunity is in the entrepreneur's mind versus in the world; rather, the challenge is considering both sides of the interaction at once—namely, the mind and the world are inseparably connected as a "functional unit" through a process of mutual adjustment (Dewey, 1939).

Future research can further contribute to this discussion by extending, for example, the notion of user innovation to user entrepreneurship (Shah & Tripsas, 2007). For instance, the individual who discovered rodeo kayaking saw a potential opportunity to adapt his kayak so he could perform various tricks (e.g., enter waves in the river sideways and backwards). When others saw him doing these tricks, they asked the rider whether he could make them special kayaks as well. The potential opportunity for rodeo kayaks was further refined to include the creation of plastic hulls and center-buoyant squirt boats, which enabled "flashier tricks on steeper and more dangerous runs" and "brought media attention to the sport and a growing number of people [trying] out rodeo kayaking" (Baldwin, Hienerth, & Von Hippel, 2006, p. 1295). Not only did the idea of rodeo kayaking change the way others viewed the sport, it also altered where the sport could take place (e.g., steeper rivers). The potential opportunity behind rodeo kayaking began in one individual's mind; however, the idea was further refined by a community of users, which itself changed because the potential opportunity was developed. This example clearly demonstrates the concept of mutual adjustment: the continual modification of a potential opportunity between the mind of the creator(s) (which changed over time) and the community of users and spectators (which also changed over time).

In line with our call for research on the ways a potential opportunity is altered through interactions with a community of inquiry, future research can significantly contribute to the field of entrepreneurship by more thoroughly investigating how and why a potential opportunity changes a community. More specifically, we can explore how changes in the nature of a potential opportunity change the associated community of inquiry in terms of its composition, collective mind, collective actions, and so on. What if we contest the implied notion that only one community exists or that the community is similar in the ways it is altered by a potential opportunity? The community may morph in one direction, but it could also split in two (perhaps based on competing opinions about the opportunity), forcing the entrepreneur to choose which branch to take (which in turn alters the community). If there are numerous communities for one potential opportunity, would each community be transformed differently by the opportunity, or would the potential opportunity itself become two different potential opportunities—one for each community—or both? Before we begin unpacking these questions and explore different communities or sub-communities, researchers will need to clearly define and operationalize what is meant by a community (or communities) for a potential opportunity.

**Mutual adjustment between the entrepreneur's mind and the community.** Fruitful research is also likely to come from the exploration of mutual adjustment—the continuous reciprocal relationship between changes in the individual's mind and transformations of the community through the development and refinement of a potential opportunity. Such research is likely to delve into the mechanisms that begin and continue the reciprocal relationship underlying the development and refinement of a potential opportunity. It is also important to explore the point at which the process of developing a potential opportunity stops such that the entrepreneur can fully exploit the refined opportunity; alternatively, perhaps, the potential opportunity continues to be changed during full exploitation (further transforming the entrepreneur's mind and the community). It could be that both alternatives are possible. That is, certain entrepreneurs and certain communities in certain situations may constantly be "updating," whereas this may not happen for other entrepreneurs, communities, and/or situations. Indeed, one could also imagine the existence of escalating "adjustment spirals" such that a change in the opportunity causes a change in the community, which triggers further changes in the opportunity and so on. Research then needs to explore how these spirals are started, perpetuated, and stopped. It will take a great deal of scholarly work to gain a deeper understanding of how this "interaction" process of developing a potential opportunity is initiated, perpetuated, and terminated. Nevertheless, we believe such research could greatly benefit the entrepreneurship field.

### *Future Research*

Figure 2.1 provides an overview of the more interaction-based perspective of entrepreneurial opportunities we have described thus far. This interaction-based view provides countless research opportunities; however, we argue that important future research avenues worth pursuing include

RESEARCHING THE GENERATION, REFINEMENT, AND EXPLOITATION... 27

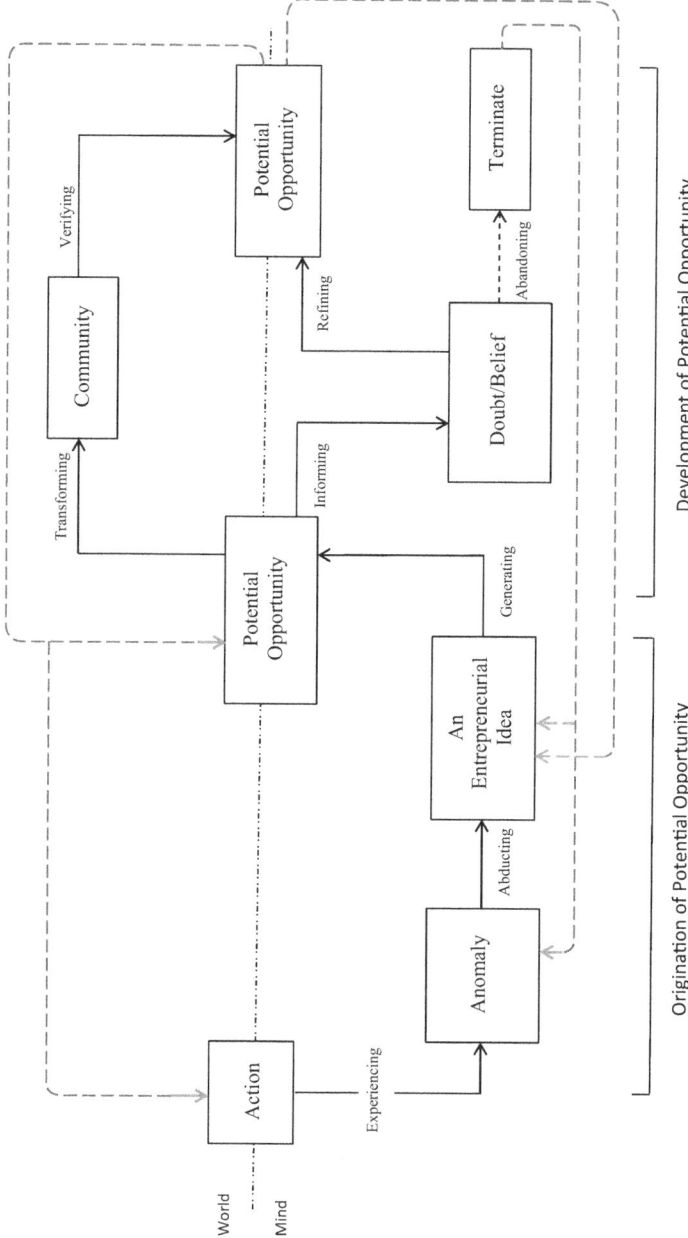

**Fig. 2.1** A sketch of a more interaction-based perspective of entrepreneurial opportunities. Source: This figure is from Shepherd (2015)

the following: (1) how does experiencing the world (through actions) lead to the creation of an entrepreneurial idea, (2) how does an entrepreneurial idea cause one to act on a potential opportunity, (3) how does acting on a potential opportunity inform an individual's opportunity belief (or reduce doubt) about the existence of an opportunity, (4) how does a community of inquiry validate a potential opportunity, (5) how does validation from a community of inquiry alter a potential opportunity and an individual's experience of the world, (6) how do changes in an individual's beliefs/doubts refine a potential opportunity and affect the decision to abandon it, and (7) how does a potential opportunity alter a community of inquiry.

## ACTIVITY-BASED ENTREPRENEURSHIP

### *Toward a Theory of the Micro-Foundations of Entrepreneurial Action*

Researchers continue to have considerable interest in entrepreneurial action (Autio et al., 2013; Brettel, Mauer, Engelen, & Kupper, 2012; McKelvie, Haynie, & Gustavsson, 2011; Meek et al., 2010; Mitchell & Shepherd, 2010)—or "behavior in response to a judgmental decision under uncertainty about a possible opportunity for profit" (McMullen & Shepherd, 2006, p. 134). Such actions can lead to a variety of outcomes, including generating economic gains and/or losses for the entrepreneur (Foss et al., 2007; Klein, 2008), preserving (Dean & McMullen, 2007) and/or destroying the natural environment (Dorfman & Dorfman, 1993; Tietenberg, 2000), upholding (Bornstein, 2004; Roberts & Woods, 2005) and/or ruining community culture (Schuler, Hashemi, & Badal, 1998), and creating (Bornstein, 2004; Dacin et al., 2011) and/or destroying (Khan, Munir, & Willmott, 2007) value for society.

The examples above demonstrate researchers' interest in the ultimate consequences of entrepreneurial action; however, scholars interested in nascent entrepreneurship tend to focus less on the *single act* of opportunity exploitation and more on the *series of actions* in new venture emergence (Delmar & Shane, 2004; Gartner, 1985; Kim, Longest, & Lippmann, 2015; Lichtenstein et al., 2007). Indeed, nascent entrepreneurs undertake numerous entrepreneurial activities, including actions that make their businesses more concrete to themselves and others. For instance, nascent entrepreneurs often look for and purchase facilities and equipment; seek and obtain financial backing, form legal entities, organize teams; and dedicate all their time and energy to their business (Carter, Gartner, & Reynolds, 1996, p. 151). However, further research is needed to uncover why and when entrepreneurs undertake these activities when developing their ventures (Davidsson & Gordon, 2012) as well as how these activities are inter-related and mutually dependent on each other.

To begin this research, it may be useful to view entrepreneurial action as a dynamic, highly iterative process of engaging in activities and experiences that both inform and are informed by a potential opportunity. When thinking of *entrepreneuring* as a series of activities in the entrepreneurial process, *activity* is the key unit of analysis. Along this line of thinking, scholars could begin to uncover the micro-foundations of entrepreneurial action by exploring key activities and their outcomes. The overall picture of the entrepreneurial process without this more detailed understanding of the micro-foundations of entrepreneurial action is more linear, granular, and disconnected from everyday life, shedding little light onto the practice of entrepreneurship. However, when the emphasis is placed on activities, the picture of the entrepreneurial process becomes more dynamic, fine grained, and immersed in everyday occurrences.

As we described in our call for an interaction-based perspective to entrepreneurship research, when a potential opportunity is refined, it produces (and reflects) changes in the entrepreneur's mind and in the community of inquiry. These changes are caused by a series of inter-related activities. For instance, if an entrepreneur is left with some level of doubt (i.e., a feeling of not knowing [Locke, Golden-Biddle, & Feldman, 2008]) about the veracity of a potential opportunity after interacting with the community of inquiry, the entrepreneur would be motivated to inquire further. In this context, inquiry is the "activity of resolving genuine doubt in order to arrive at stable beliefs" (Locke et al., 2008, p. 908). In other words, doubt inspires the entrepreneur to undertake activities that inform (through changes in his or her mind) the refinement of the entrepreneurial idea. Thus, doubt can be seen as "nothing less than an opportunity to re-enter the present" (Shanley, 2005, p. viii) to help create a more fertile idea (Paavola, 2004).

### *Future Research on the Micro-Foundations of Entrepreneurial Action*

**Breaking down entrepreneurial action into constituent activities.** Substantial contributions to the field of entrepreneurship are likely to come from research investigating the numerous activities that make up entrepreneurial action because it will provide the foundation for theorizing about and testing micro-foundation models of entrepreneurial action. For example, as Lumpkin and Dess (1996, p. 136) noted, the "essential act of entrepreneurship is new entry. New entry can be accomplished by entering new or established markets with new or existing goods or services. New entry is the act of launching a new venture, either by a start-up firm, through an existing firm, or via internal corporate venturing." Future scholarship can complement this research on new entry by focusing on the series of activities that lead to new entry—activities that start with a notion of a potential opportunity (i.e., a conjecture)—and activities that refine and transform that potential opportunity with the hope of eventual exploitation (including, in some contexts, activities associated with new venture creation). For example, the Panel Study of Entrepreneurial Dynamics (PSED) lists about 30 different activities entrepreneurs pursue at different stages of the venture-development process. In addition, future research can explore the more nuanced activities that make up broader entrepreneurial action and the connections between these activities. Doing so could have an important impact on the field because although some scholars have recognized that a potential opportunity may change over time (e.g., Dimov, 2007; McMullen & Dimov, 2013; Sarasvathy, 2001), the activities surrounding these changes have largely been neglected. Thus far, the scholarly focus has either been on a rather fully formed entrepreneurial idea (with only minor changes, if any [Gruber et al., 2013]) or on a mindset as a precursor to these activities (e.g., effectual logic [Sarasvathy, 2001]). Shane (2000), for example, studied eight entrepreneurial individuals and teams who had discovered different opportunities to exploit three-dimensional printing. The underlying assumption in this particular research context is that individuals/teams recognize opportunities in a more or less fully formed state that is ready for exploitation. Specifically, when an entrepreneur talks about *the* opportunity to members of a community of inquiry, this sole explanation not only relates to what the entrepreneur initially recognized but also to what he or she assessed (Gruber et al., 2013).

Future research can further develop our understanding of the activities involved once a potential opportunity is identified throughout its continuous evaluation and refinement up to final exploitation. This approach acknowledges that a potential opportunity begins as a tentative conjecture and develops and evolves based on the entrepreneur's activities. In turn, these activities alter the nature of the initial potential opportunity. It seems likely that in many cases, a potential opportunity will change frequently and substantially (as opposed to infrequently and/or minimally). One way we can more fully understand these changes is by focusing on the activities that together shape the potential opportunity as well as the entrepreneur's (and the community's) belief in it. In addition, the entrepreneur's (and the community's) doubts and beliefs related to the opportunity are likely to influence these activities (and thus a theory of the micro-foundations of entrepreneurial action), to which we now turn.

**The role of opportunity doubt and belief in entrepreneurial activities.** Both doubt and belief are likely to stimulate entrepreneurial activities. However, we currently have a limited understanding of the roles doubt and belief play in this process. What activities are stimulated by doubt? It is important to understand what is activated to resolve doubt and how entrepreneurial activities change as doubt is settled and a first-person opportunity belief forms. It is likely that certain activities are more likely than others to negate a belief (and possibly additional refinement of the potential opportunity) by re-introducing uncertainty and that some individuals or teams are more likely than others to undertake these activities. It could be that the pursuit of some activities is like a "double-edged sword" because they relieve doubt about some aspects of the opportunity (e.g., the market) but enhance doubt about other aspects (e.g., technological feasibility). Thus, we need to explore how certain combinations of activities help resolve doubt more effectively than other combinations or the activities independently. Moreover, a community of inquiry may impact the relationship between the pursuit of activities and the resolution of doubt about an opportunity (e.g., the community might communicate to the entrepreneur that some activities are more or less valuable for opportunity development).

As these conjectures reveal, this interaction-based view of entrepreneurship shifts the focus to the numerous activities comprising the entrepreneurial process, including those associated with probing an uncertain environment (Brown & Eisenhardt, 1997; McGrath, 1999), combining and recombining resources to create potential opportunities (Baker, Miner, & Eesley, 2003; Baker & Nelson, 2005), engaging the community and responding to that engagement (Chandra & Coviello, 2010; Haefliger, Jäger, & Von Krogh, 2010; Shah & Tripsas, 2007), testing a potential opportunity's validity and probability of success (Shane & Eckhardt, 2003; Shepherd, Haynie, & McMullen, 2012), exploiting a potential opportunity through new venture creation (Carter et al., 1996; Davidsson & Honig, 2003; Lichtenstein et al., 2007), and so on. As the previous citations illustrate, entrepreneurship scholars have already blazed the initial trail in investigating some of these activities. However, in many ways, the work has only begun; we still have much to accomplish in this area.

## Future Research

Figure 2.2 builds on the basic model of entrepreneurial action (McMullen & Shepherd, 2006) to provide a sketch of a more activity-based perspective of entrepreneurial action, highlighting some of the significant elements of the discussion above. Future research on the activities underlying the materialization of opportunity beliefs will likely help scholars build a theory of the micro-foundations of entrepreneurial action. While many research paths open up by taking a more activity-based perspective of entrepreneurship, valuable future research questions worthy of exploration include the following: (1) what activities lead an individual to identify what he or she believes (or doubts) to be a third- and/or first-person opportunity, (2) how and why does an individual's prior knowledge affect the types of activities he or she engages in to form a third- and/or first-person opportunity belief, (3) how and why does the nature of an individual's motivation impact the types of activities he or she undertakes to form a third- and/or first-person opportunity belief, (4) how does the interconnection between activities affect a third- and/or first-person opportunity belief, (5) how and why do certain activities shape an individual's prior knowledge and motivation (which can then shape ensuing activities), (6) how and why does altered knowledge in the evaluation stage influence knowledge in the attention stage for the detection of later potential third-person opportunities, and (7) how and why does the altered motivation of the evaluation stage influence motivation in the attention stage for the detection of later third-person opportunities.

## ENTREPRENEURSHIP THAT IS MORE COGNITIVELY HOT

### Entrepreneurial Cognition and Emotion's Effect on These Cognitive Processes

Researchers have long believed that individuals' cognitive abilities play an important role in driving entrepreneurial action (for reviews, see Gregoire, Corbett, & McMullen, 2011; Mitchell et al., 2002). More specifically,

RESEARCHING THE GENERATION, REFINEMENT, AND EXPLOITATION... 33

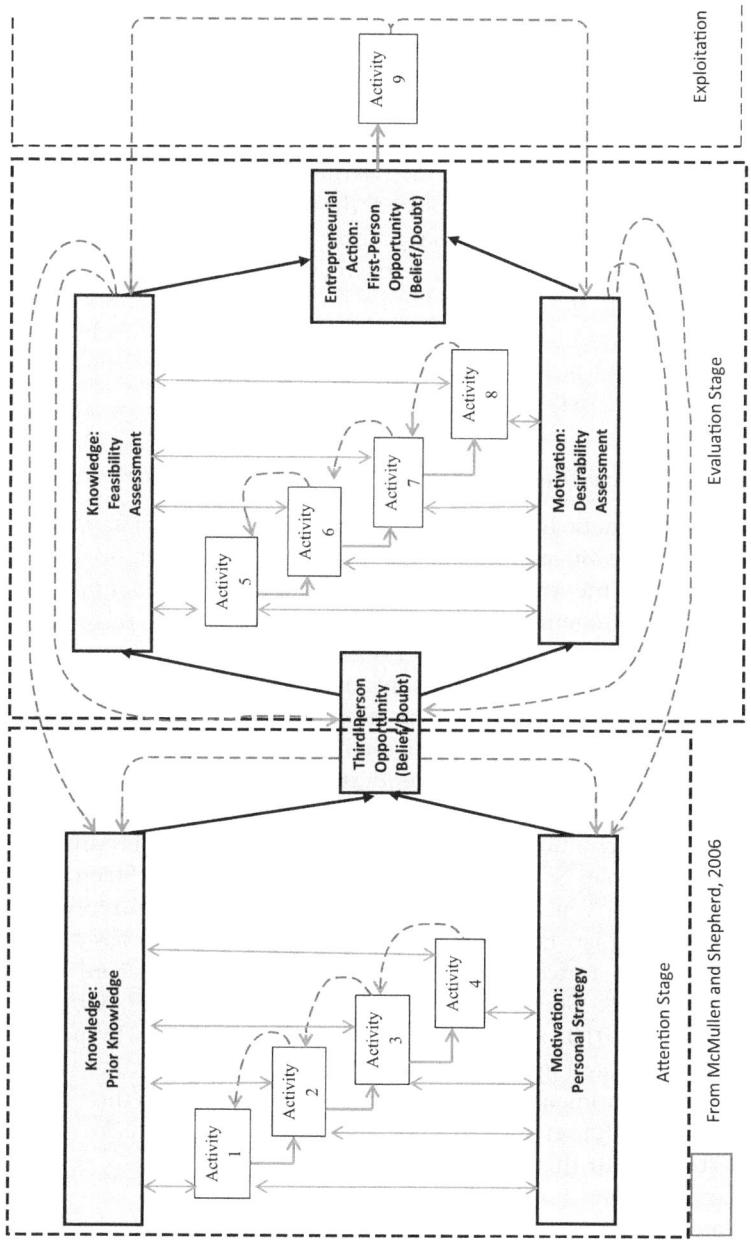

**Fig. 2.2** A sketch of research that is more activity based as a micro-foundation of entrepreneurial action. Source: This figure is from Shepherd (2015)

scholars hold that people are better able to navigate the entrepreneurial process (i.e., recognize, evaluate, and act on opportunities) when they have substantial knowledge (Davidsson & Honig, 2003; Shane, 2000), have access to information (Fiet, 2007; Hoang & Antoncic, 2003), can quickly make decisions (Eisenhardt, 1989; Forbes, 2005), and are cognitively flexible (Haynie, Shepherd, Mosakowski, & Earley, 2010). More recently, researchers have also explored the role emotions play in the entrepreneurial process, finding that positive emotions tend to facilitate the process (Baron, 2008; Cardon, Wincent, Singh, & Drnovsek, 2009) whereas negative emotions tend to hinder it (Shepherd, 2003; Shepherd, Patzelt, & Wolfe, 2011). However, even with this past work, substantial opportunities remain in the field of entrepreneurship to investigate the inter-relationship between emotion and cognition.

### The Role of Entrepreneurial Activity in Emotions

As a field, entrepreneurship continues to gain a deeper understanding of emotion's influence on entrepreneurial cognition. However, so far, we know little about the reverse situation—namely, entrepreneurial cognition's influence on emotions—as well as the reciprocal relationship between cognition and emotions. As a result, there are numerous opportunities for entrepreneurial scholars to make significant contributions by developing and empirically testing new theoretical perspectives that enhance our understanding of cognitive-emotion processes.

**Entrepreneurial activities that generate positive emotions.** Positive psychology research has shown that generating positive emotions is vital for individuals as they adjust and grow throughout their lives (Fredrickson, 1998, 2001; Seligman & Csikszentmihalyi, 2000; Seligman, Steen, Park, & Peterson, 2005), which has important implications for entrepreneurship research. Thus far, however, extant research in this area has primarily centered on the outcomes of positive emotions (e.g., Baron, 2008; Brundin, Patzelt, & Shepherd, 2008; Cardon et al., 2009; Grichnik, Smeja, & Welpe, 2010) while relatively ignoring how and why positive emotions are generated in the entrepreneurial context. Indeed, the benefits of positive emotions are likely to be especially important in this context (Baron, 2008; Cardon et al., 2012), so future research will make significant contributions to the field by investigating how individuals generate positive emotions and how these positive emotions impact ensuing cognitions, emotions, and activities throughout the entrepreneurial process.

For example, how do the (more or less successful) development of an entrepreneurial opportunity, experiences in the entrepreneurial team, and interactions with investors and other stakeholders influence entrepreneurs' positive emotions? It could be that an entrepreneur's private and family life impact positive emotions, which in turn spill over to and influence his or her entrepreneurial activities. Moreover, as entrepreneurial action entails various different activities (Kim et al., 2015), the experience of positive emotions may serve as a trigger for the start, execution, and completion of specific entrepreneurial activities. These are only a few conjectures that scholars can address when viewing entrepreneurship through the lens of positive emotions.

Furthermore, researchers have often characterized entrepreneurs based on their emotions (e.g., highly passionate) (Cardon, Zietsma, Saparito, Matherne, & Davis, 2005; Cardon et al., 2009) or cognitive abilities (Alvarez & Busenitz, 2001; Ardichvili et al., 2003; Corbett, 2005; Ucbasaran, Westhead, & Wright, 2008), and differences among individuals have been used to explain entrepreneurial action and performance. Complementing these *between*-individual differences, researchers can explore *within*-individual variance—more specifically, the ways emotions and cognitive processing change over time throughout the entrepreneurial process (for a good example, see Foo, Uy, & Baron, 2009). For example, to what extent are positive emotions generated through positive feedback from stakeholders or the successful execution of a specific entrepreneurial activity (e.g., passing a milestone in product development, finding an attractive location for the business) sustainable over time? Research can then explore the circumstances under which entrepreneurs generate more of these positive emotions and the circumstances under which they generate fewer positive emotions.

**Challenging entrepreneurial tasks and the generation of positive emotions.** Changes in the environment can indicate possible opportunities (Dutton & Duncan, 1987; Grégoire & Shepherd, 2012; Shane, 2000). However, for entrepreneurial action to actually unfold, an individual must first respond to these signals (Dutton, 1993; Shepherd, McMullen, & Jennings, 2007; Tripsas & Gavetti, 2000) and then recognize that they represent a potential opportunity (Ardichvili et al., 2003; Gaglio & Katz, 2001; Grégoire et al., 2010; Ucbasaran et al., 2008). Because opportunities are seldom overly obvious (like finding $20 on the pavement), recognizing a possible opportunity can be quite challenging. Opportunities require one to connect a new means of supply with an existing (yet occasionally latent) market demand, a developing market demand with a current means of supply, or a new market demand with a new means of supply (Sarasvathy, Dew, Velamuri, & Venkataraman, 2010). At the individual level, this requires a willing and able entrepreneur "to make sense of signals of change (e.g., new information about new conditions) to form beliefs regarding whether or not enacting a course of action could lead to net benefits (for instance, in terms of profit, growth, competitive jockeying, and/or other forms of individual or organizational gains)" (Grégoire et al., 2010, p. 415). For instance, researchers have found that the cognitive processes of structural alignment have been used in the formation of opportunity beliefs (Grégoire et al., 2010), and even though they are cognitively demanding (Blanchette & Dunbar, 2001; Catrambone & Holyoak, 1989; Holland, Holyoak, Nisbett, & Thagard, 1986; Keane, Ledgeway, & Duff, 1994), they can result in *mental leaps* (Holyoak & Thagard, 1995). Interestingly, when one is able to successfully finish a cognitively demanding task, he or she is likely to have positive emotions (Blood & Zatorre, 2001; Maffei & Fiorentini, 1995; Russell, 2003; Russell & Milne, 1997). This discussion leads to several stimulating research questions on the role of emotions: when do entrepreneurs think that identifying potential opportunities is more or less challenging, to what extent does this opportunity identification generate positive emotions, what types of positive emotions result from identifying a potential opportunity, and how do these positive emotions (and perhaps some types of positive emotions more than others) affect ensuing cognitions and activities?

Research in the positive psychology tradition has also shown that positive emotions improve an individual's performance at cognitive tasks as well as extend individuals' scope of attention (Derryberry & Tucker, 2006; Fredrickson & Branigan, 2005; Isen & Daubman, 1984); improve openness to new information (Estrada, Isen, & Young, 1997); facilitate cognitive processes that are more creative (Isen, Daubman, & Nowicki, 1987) and flexible (Baumann & Kuhl, 2005; Isen & Daubman, 1984); and produce more physical, intellectual, and social resources (Fredrickson, 2000), including generating new relationships and improving existing relationships (Fredrickson, Cohn, Coffey, Pek, & Finkel, 2008; Waugh & Fredrickson, 2006). If positive emotions stemming from completing a challenging entrepreneurial task improve an individual's attention, cognition, and access to resources, it is important to explore how these resulting benefits influence later activities in the entrepreneurial process. Indeed, it could be that certain types of positive emotions influence certain types of activities.

Further, perhaps early progress in entrepreneurial activities can even lead to a spiral of positive emotions and subsequent progress through the underlying mechanisms of increased attention, cognitive flexibility, and social resources. Under what conditions would such a spiral begin? Perhaps individuals need to complete a certain number of challenging entrepreneurial tasks (i.e., meet a specific threshold) or a certain type of task (e.g., secure funding) before generating positive emotions. If this is the case, what is that threshold or type, does it differ across individuals (and if so, how), and does it change for an individual depending on the entrepreneurial task at hand? Perhaps the threshold needed to generate positive emotions has to increase with each successive task to perpetuate a spiral, for example, to overcome habituation effects (Ashforth & Kreiner, 2002; Belschak, Verbeke, & Bagozzi, 2006). On the other hand, generating positive emotions may come with limitations, such as escalation of commitment, reluctance to receive community feedback, and so on.

In addition to understanding what begins and perpetuates these spirals of positive emotions and entrepreneurial progress, it is also important to explore what stops them (or perhaps even reverses them such that fewer positive emotions slow down progress, which further lowers positive emotions and so on). Certain factors may hinder progress—for example, a surprise (e.g., a negative environmental jolt); bad luck; or another task requiring immediate attention, cognition, and other resources. There could also be factors that reduce or destroy the generation of positive emotions. For instance, outside events (work or non-work related) that cause negative emotions may outweigh positive emotions in cognitive processing, such as a serious injury, the loss of a loved one, or marital problems. On the other hand, non-work–related events that generate positive emotions (e.g., marital bliss, sports team success, positive recreational experiences, etc.) could negate negative emotions at work, thus improving progress on entrepreneurial tasks.

**A reciprocal relationship between challenging entrepreneurial tasks and positive emotions.** By studying how different positive emotions (e.g., curiosity versus happiness) influence the mechanisms underlying progress (e.g., the ability to structurally align new means of supply with potential markets), future research can provide a deeper understanding of the reciprocal relationship between progress and positive emotions. Maybe certain positive emotions (e.g., curiosity) influence individuals' attention to a greater degree than the other mechanisms (e.g., creativity and building social resources), or perhaps there is another set of reciprocal relationships: as positive emotions generate a greater scope of attention, this scope of attention in turn positively influences cognitive processes (e.g., creativity, flexibility, and the generation of diverse alternatives or the identification of alternative opportunities) and access to social resources. As these conjectures reveal, there are fruitful research prospects to explore the inter-relationships between progress in entrepreneurial tasks and positive emotions as well as between the attentional, cognitive, and resource mechanisms resulting from positive emotions following progress on entrepreneurial tasks.

**Challenging entrepreneurial tasks and the generation of negative emotions.** As discussed above, making progress on challenging tasks tends to lead to positive emotions. However, entrepreneurs may not always feel like they are making progress (Kim et al., 2015; Kuratko, Hornsby, & Covin, 2014). When this occurs, it is important to explore the emotional consequences that result from this lack of progress. It could be that the individual simply does not generate positive emotions, in which case the advantages of positive emotions (i.e., broadened attention, greater creativity, and enhanced access to social resources) for effectively engaging in entrepreneurial tasks do not materialize. Further, perhaps experiencing high levels of certain positive emotions has negative performance implications. For example, when entrepreneurs feel high levels of satisfaction about progress already made, they might become reluctant to invest additional effort and "lay back" and bask in achieved glory, which can diminish future progress and performance. Moreover, feelings of hope might result in over-optimism and biased evaluations of a product or venture's future potential, leading to inappropriate investment and resource-allocation decisions.

However, a lack of progress on entrepreneurial tasks can also generate negative emotions (Shepherd, Patzelt, Williams, & Warnecke, 2014), which likely has detrimental effects on attention, cognitive flexibility, and creativity as well as socially isolates the individual (Fredrickson, 2001; Fredrickson, Mancuso, Branigan, & Tugade, 2000; Shepherd et al., 2011). This type of situation could trigger a negative spiral such that the lack of progress leads to negative emotions that in turn hinder progress, which then generates further negative emotions and so on. While entrepreneurship scholars are generally interested in exploring success (and thus tend to concentrate on positive spirals of positive emotions), it is also important to study individuals' failure to progress on important entrepreneurial tasks. For instance, scholars could investigate the inter-relationship between negative emotions and attentional scope, creativity, and social resources. Perhaps certain negative emotions or levels of specific negative emotions can facilitate progress on an entrepreneurship task. If so, what are the mechanisms underlying this relationship, and under what conditions do they operate? For example, it could be that some negative emotions (e.g., fear of failure) are needed to make an entrepreneur pay attention to a focal task and act on it. If this is the case, then we need to understand how much attention is necessary, and how much is too much. Also, assuming individuals are heterogeneous, some people are likely more able to function at a certain level of negative emotion while others become dysfunctional at the same level. Thus, how does the "maximum" tolerable level of certain negative emotions differ across entrepreneurs?

Some argue that positive emotions negate negative emotions (Fredrickson, 2001; Fredrickson et al., 2000), but research has shown that people can experience both highly positive and highly negative emotions at the same time. What effect does this ambivalence toward a specific entrepreneurial task (experiencing both highly negative and highly positive emotions [Schneider et al., 2013]) have on the cognitions needed for that entrepreneurial task and the task's influence on successive tasks and activities? For example, entrepreneurs exit their businesses for different reasons, one of which could be because they successfully achieved their goals (e.g., selling their business for a large capital gain). While this successful exit is likely to lead to positive emotions, negative emotions are also likely to arise (e.g., having to end relationships with the business and employees). On the other hand, exiting a failing business is likely to cause feelings of grief; however, these negative feelings are likely to coincide with feelings of relief that a troubling situation (giving the business "away") has come to an end. These examples lead to several interesting questions: when can entrepreneurial events lead to highly positive and highly negative emotions at the same time, what combinations of specific positive and negative emotions are possible, how do these (combinations of) emotions evolve independently and conjointly as time passes, and how do the levels and combinations of certain positive and negative emotions depend on the specific situation (e.g., selling a successful business or ending an entrepreneurial project perceived as "creeping death" [cf. Shepherd et al., 2014])? Entrepreneurship scholars can also explore why some entrepreneurs (more than others) are able to exploit the benefits of both positive and negative emotions while reducing their costs.

## Future Research

Figure 2.3 offers an overview of a more cognitively hot perspective of entrepreneurship. Like the previous research streams we have discussed, there are many possible opportunities from taking a more cognitively hot perspective. However, the following are particularly important future research avenues worth investigating: (1) how does cognitive functioning influence progress on a challenging entrepreneurial task; (2) how and why does progress on a challenging task lead to positive and/or negative emotions, and how are the levels of those reactions affected; (3) how and why do emotional reactions to progress on an entrepreneurial task affect continued cognitive functioning on that task and/or other tasks; (4) how do emotional reactions to progress on an entrepreneurial task influence one's choice to undertake challenging tasks; and (5) beyond progress on a challenging task, what other factors (work and non-work related) cause positive and/or negative emotional reactions, and what impact do they have on the entrepreneurial process?

# ENTREPRENEURSHIP RESEARCH THAT IS MORE COMPASSIONATE AND PROSOCIAL

## *Heterogeneous Motivations to Investigate Entrepreneurially Generated Gains*

People are motivated to engage in the entrepreneurial process for different reasons, which is important when determining the suitability of a study's outcomes. For example, people more or less want to "do good," and entrepreneurship scholars are no exception. Using a liberal interpretation of what "gain" means, entrepreneurship scholars have conducted research that deepens our understanding of how entrepreneurial action can help individuals and communities (e.g., Dacin et al., 2011; Dees, 1998; Mair & Marti, 2006; McMullen, 2011; Peredo & Chrisman, 2006). Some scholars are particularly interested in the natural environment and have investigated why some entrepreneurs create products and technologies that conserve the natural world (Dean & McMullen, 2007; Meek et al., 2010; York & Venkataraman, 2010) while others opt to pursue opportunities that harm nature (Shepherd et al., 2013). As we continue to explore social and sustainable entrepreneurship, we will uncover new ways entrepreneurial action *helps* and also *hurts* people, communities, and the natural envi-

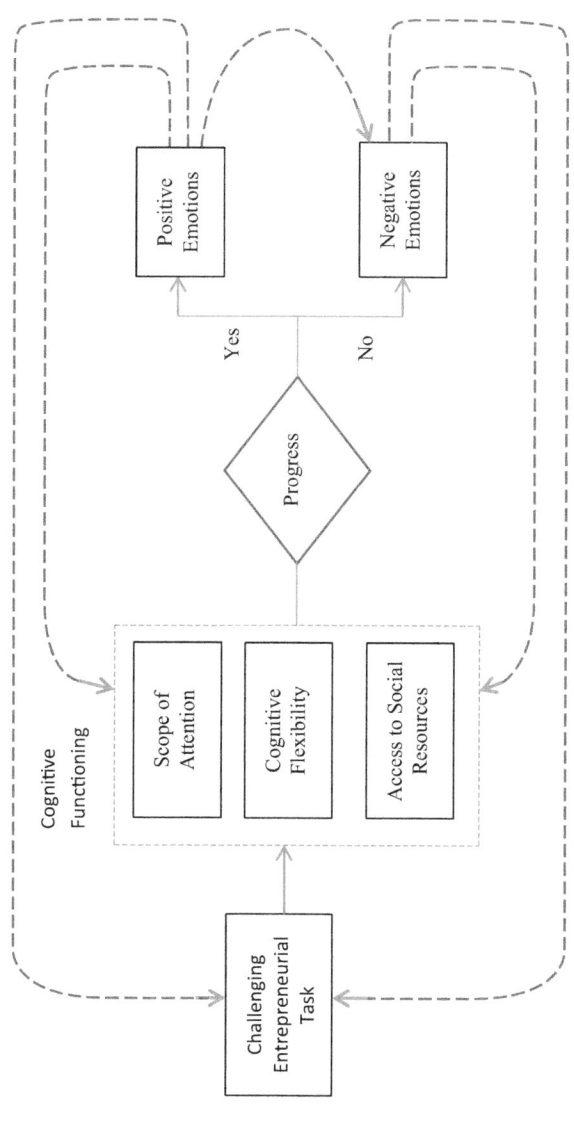

**Fig. 2.3** A sketch of a more cognitively hot perspective of the entrepreneurial process. Source: This figure is from Shepherd (2015)

ronment. In line with our comments earlier regarding the unique domain of entrepreneurship, although discussions about the specific definitions of "social entrepreneurship," "sustainable entrepreneurship," and "environmental entrepreneurship" are stimulating (as an example, see a review of multiple definitions of social entrepreneurship by Zahra, Rawhouser, Bhawe, Neubaum, & Hayton, 2008), these discussions should not become a perpetual debate that restricts or destroys interesting research because a study does not correspond to a pre-specified category of "sustainable," "social," or "environmental" entrepreneurship. By being more flexible about the boundaries of topics within the entrepreneurship field, we provide the space for scholars to explore these themes more freely, thus opening up the field to contributions that can expand our understanding of entrepreneurial phenomena (which, over time, might also converge into a commonly accepted definition of the field of interest).

## *Compassion Organizing*

Positive psychology research has improved our understanding of how to alleviate people's suffering (e.g., Dutton, 2003; Dutton, Workman, & Hardin, 2014; Dutton et al., 2006; George, 2013; Kanov et al., 2004; Lilius et al., 2008). A subset of this research has studied *compassion organizing*, "a collective response to a particular incident of human suffering that entails the coordination of individual compassion" and recognizes that the structures and routines an organization uses for normal work can be repurposed to alleviate a member's suffering (Dutton et al., 2006, p. 62). Suffering, or "the experience of pain or loss that evokes a form of anguish that threatens an individual's sense of meaning about his or her personal existence" (Dutton et al., 2006, p. 60; see also Sutcliffe & Vogus, 2003), can be caused by a number of factors, such as personal tragedies, work-related events, and disasters (Armstrong, 2011; Frost, 2003; Rynes, Bartunek, Dutton, & Margolis, 2012). Organizations are particularly well positioned to respond compassionately to member suffering. More specifically, through existing relationships with organizational members, organizations are able to collectively *identify* a member's suffering, *feel* that member's pain, and *respond* by repurposing current routines to lessen that member's suffering (Dutton et al., 2006; Kanov et al., 2004; Lilius, Worline, Dutton, Kanov, & Maitlis, 2011; Rynes et al., 2012).

While much research has already been done on compassion organizing, scholars can add to and expand positive organizational research to deepen our understanding of how entrepreneurial action can ease human suffering. The majority of research on compassion organizing thus far has taken a positive *organizational* perspective. Unsurprisingly, this research stream has largely assumed the existence of a firm, focusing on the ways firms use normal routines to respond to members' pain (e.g., Dutton et al., 2006). While this research has provided an important foundation, entrepreneurship scholars can make important contributions to this line of work by investigating compassion organizing above and beyond the assumptions of an existing organization and actions limited by existing routines. Indeed, the contexts in which human suffering occurs are likely to be profoundly different from an established organization with normal routines, processes, and procedures. Furthermore, past research on compassion organizing has centered on the alleviation of *human* suffering. However, entrepreneurship scholars (and perhaps compassion organizing scholars) are well positioned to broaden their view and explore suffering in terms of humans, animals, communities, the natural environment, and so on (e.g., Patzelt & Shepherd, 2011; Shepherd & Patzelt, 2011; see also Chap. 5). Taking this broader perspective, scholars can contribute to the current body of knowledge on the alleviation of suffering (broadly defined for the field but specifically defined in a single study) while simultaneously extending the boundaries of both entrepreneurship and positive organizational psychology.

### *Future Research on Entrepreneurial Action to Alleviate the Suffering of Others*

**Beyond the normal routines of established organizations.** Although there are certain circumstances in which adapting an established organization's normal structures and routines can quite effectively alleviate human suffering (Dutton et al., 2006; Kanov et al., 2004), some events are likely to disable or obstruct these normal structures and routines (Drabek & McEntire, 2003; Majchrzak, Jarvenpaa, & Hollingshead, 2007). In this context, entrepreneurship scholars can shed light on the alleviation of suffering by exploring how, when, and why new ventures are created within or outside established organizations for the purpose of easing others' suffering (e.g., Miller, Grimes, McMullen, & Vogus, 2012; Shepherd & Williams, 2014; Williams & Shepherd, 2017). It is important that we gain a deeper understanding of the factors that restrict or block an organization's normal routines from alleviating human suffering and both the motivations and the means some people have to start new ventures to alleviate human suffering. For example, why do some individuals start new ventures within established firms to alleviate others' suffering while others create new organizations to do so, why do these internal ventures emerge in some organizations but not in others, and why do some ventures solely focus on alleviating suffering while others focus on multiple objectives (e.g., earning profit and alleviating suffering) and to what effect? Ultimately, we are interested in why some entrepreneurial activities ease suffering more effectively than others and whose suffering is alleviated. This stream of research has the potential to extend the boundaries of compassion organizing theory and (hopefully) provide practical advice on how to help those who are suffering.

**Alleviating the suffering of non-organizational members.** Scholars have investigated how organizations effectively respond to their own organizational members' suffering (Dutton et al., 2006, p. 59; see also Dutton et al., 2014; Gittell, Cameron, Lim, & Rivas, 2006; Powley, 2009; Rynes et al., 2012) because members of the same organization are more likely to *detect* (Powley, 2009) and *empathize with* a coworker's suffering (Lilius et al., 2011) while being close enough to act to alleviate that suffering (Dutton et al., 2006). Going beyond exploring suffering inside existing organizational boundaries, future research can explore how new ventures (within established organizations or entirely new organizations) are quickly and seemingly spontaneously formed to alleviate the suffering of individuals outside the responder's organization. Although we are beginning to gain a deeper understanding of why some individuals, groups, and/or organizations are capable of detecting and understanding others' (i.e., non-organizational members) suffering (Shepherd & Williams, 2014) and why some are more effective at providing a more long-run solution to suffering (Williams & Shepherd, 2017), we have barely scratched the surface of this important topic. Initial findings hint at the importance of the local community (Shepherd & Williams, 2014; Williams & Shepherd, 2017), but more needs to be done in exploring how to define, form, and lead communities in their compassionate endeavors. Specifically, what is the role of entrepreneurial action (and its underlying activities) in this community-creation process, and how does community formation in turn impact entrepreneurial action (in terms of a co-evolution).

**Spontaneous venturing to alleviate others' suffering.** While it generally takes time for a new organization to emerge (Katz & Gartner, 1988; Liao, Welsch, & Tan, 2005; Reynolds & Miller, 1992), recent research has shown that new ventures can form almost immediately (in only hours or days) after an event that causes human suffering (Shepherd & Williams, 2014; Williams & Shepherd, 2017). Thus, it is important to understand how the venture-creation process is accelerated so quickly in this context. That is, how is the potential opportunity to ease others' suffering refined, what activities are involved in rapidly creating a new venture to alleviate suffering, which (if any) organizational-emergence activities are modified or simply omitted, and how are interactions between the entrepreneur and the various communities associated with the suffering (e.g., victims and suppliers) facilitated in such intense situations? This research is likely to advance our understanding of the many ways entrepreneurial action can ease others' suffering as well as offer a particularly fitting context for investigating organizational-emergence activities as the time required to follow and track those activities is considerably reduced in this context. (We also recognize the challenge of researching ventures formed in the immediate aftermath of a surprising event—the researcher is likely to find him- or herself among human suffering to study these activities.) If researchers can find a viable way to explore these spontaneous ventures, they are likely to uncover findings from these intense contexts that add to our understanding of organizational emergence in more traditional settings. For example, perhaps there are "spontaneous acts" in more traditional settings that precede later activities. If so, what form do these acts take; are such activities meant to be temporary, or are they probe-like actions used to provide immediate feedback; what are the motivations behind these actions, and what are the anticipated results; and what role (if any) does the government play in fostering compassion venturing?

**Resourcefulness for compassionate responding.** While existing conceptions of compassion generally stress that the more fortunate help the less fortunate (Dutton et al., 2006; Lilius et al., 2011), entrepreneurship scholars can add to our understanding of resourcefulness, such as bricolage (Baker & Nelson, 2005), effectuation (Sarasvathy, 2001), improvisation (Baker et al., 2003; Hmieleski & Corbett, 2008), identity (Powell & Baker, 2014), entrepreneurial management (Bradley, Wiklund, & Shepherd, 2011; Stevenson & Jarillo, 1990), and knowledge corridors (Fiet, 2007; Fiet & Samuelsson, 2000; Hayek, 1945), by exploring how resources are obtained, assembled, and recombined to alleviate specific types of suffering. This involves exploring how the less fortunate (i.e., those who are themselves suffering) take entrepreneurial actions to help the unfortunate (i.e., others who are suffering) and to what effect for the actor and the victims helped. How and why are some individuals who are themselves suffering and facing hardship able to act entrepreneurially to help others whereas some individuals are unable to do so? Research has also shown that locals (i.e., those living close to those suffering) are best positioned to help alleviate others' suffering as they are familiar with the region (i.e., Bui & Sebastian, 2011; Quarantelli, 1993; Sebastian & Bui, 2009) and have direct knowledge about the cause of the suffering as well as potential ways to ease it due to their strong understanding of the people involved and the local context (Sebastian & Bui, 2009; Shepherd & Williams, 2014; Waugh & Streib, 2006; Williams & Shepherd, 2017). However, it is likely that these locals are suffering themselves. What impact does helping alleviate others' suffering have on the entrepreneurial actor him- or herself? Interestingly, initial evidence suggests that victims of a natural disaster who act in the aftermath of that natural disaster by creating a new venture to alleviate others' suffering have better personal outcomes than those who do not act and that this gap in personal outcomes from those who create new ventures and those who do not is even greater for those with entrepreneurial experience (Williams & Shepherd, 2016). However, more research is needed. For example, it is important to understand when entrepreneurial action in a disaster context leads to further personal risks and losses that could be detrimental to personal functioning (e.g., the failure of the new venture that creates increased feelings of loss; further shatters the individual's assumptions about the self, the world, and others; and drains all remaining resources) and the conditions under which entrepreneurial action serves as a form of coping for those who suffer (Shepherd, 2003) that leads to recovery (e.g., by distracting from the own suffering) or as the basis for resilience.

**Prosocial motivation to act entrepreneurially to alleviate others' suffering.** Not only do individuals need to be *capable* of acting to alleviate others' suffering, but they must also be *motivated* to do so. What factors motivate people to act entrepreneurially to ease others' suffering? Research grounded in the prosocial motivation literature will likely lead to fruitful explorations that can help answer this question. *Prosocial motivation* refers to individuals' desire to expend effort out of concern for helping or contributing to others (Batson, 1998; De Dreu, 2006; Grant, 2007, 2008; Grant & Berry, 2011; Grant & Sumanth, 2009) and can have numerous benefits for those being helped (Batson et al., 2008). Grant (2008, p. 49) explained that prosocial motivation is "a more temporary psychological state, [and it] involves a momentary focus on the goal of protecting and promoting the welfare of other people." While prosocial motivation is relatively under-researched, it appears to be a particularly important precursor to entrepreneurial actions that alleviate others' suffering (important exceptions include Miller et al., 2012; Renko, 2013).

Future research exploring the role of prosocial motivation compared to other forms of motivation in the compassionate venturing context is likely to make important contributions to the entrepreneurship literature. For example, prosocial motivation could compensate for a lack of intrinsic motivation in the creation of a new venture to alleviate others' suffering. If this is the case, what long-term effects on entrepreneurial activity would result from this motivational state? Perhaps being successful in alleviating others' suffering creates intrinsic motivation for the entrepreneurial tasks required in compassion venturing, or perhaps an initial lack of intrinsic motivation wears the entrepreneurial actor down, thus weakening the effect of prosocial motivation. If a lack of intrinsic motivation does wear the actor down, it is important to investigate what impact this reduced motivation has on the duration or development of compassion-oriented ventures. It could be that individuals need to develop other motivations to continue these ventures.

In addition to exploring these conjectures, investigating the possible shortcomings or boundaries of prosocial motivation in compassionate venturing is also likely to be important. Because prosocially motivated individuals are likely to view their work as a way to help others (Grant, 2007, 2008), this "ends justifies the means" approach to the alleviation of human suffering could have downsides. For example, there could be negative consequences for taking shortcuts to alleviate a particular group of individuals' suffering: maybe this aid comes at the expense of another group's suffering, perhaps it obstructs a greater (and perhaps more successful) effort to alleviate suffering, and/or perhaps it is a temporary solution that proves harmful in the long term. Indeed, perhaps the question is not whether it is good or bad to ignore constraints; rather, the question might be which constraints should be tolerated and which constraints should be overcome. In addition, exploring the ways potential resource providers come to notice, evaluate, and respond to prosocially motivated individuals who strive to alleviate others' suffering is also likely to provide interesting insights. How (if at all) do prosocially motivated entrepreneurial actors who try to alleviate others' suffering attract outside resource providers? What signals (if any) indicate prosocial motivation to outsiders, and how do outsiders respond to such signals?

## Future Research

Figure 2.4 illustrates some of the important aspects discussed above and provides a sketch of more compassionate and prosocial entrepreneurship research. Numerous research opportunities are imaginable from taking a more compassionate and prosocial perspective. However, we believe that exploring the following questions will lead to productive research: (1) how and why does awareness of others' suffering influence the formation of third- and/or first-person opportunity beliefs to do good, (2) how and why does prosocial motivation affect the formation of third- and/or first-person opportunity beliefs to do good, (3) what characterizes entrepreneurial actions that exploit a potential opportunity to do good, (4) how and why do certain types of entrepreneurial action ease different kinds of suffering in others, (5) how and why do different entrepreneurial actions lead to different societal benefits, (6) how does entrepreneurial action to ease suffering and/or improve sustainability influence the entrepreneur him- or herself, (7) how and why does progress in the entrepreneurial process (in terms of gains for others, the entrepreneur, and/or sustainability) influence the entrepreneur's knowledge (particularly knowledge of suffering) and motivation (particularly prosocial motivation and its interactions with intrinsic and extrinsic motivation) to form third- and/or first-person opportunity beliefs, (8) what other entrepreneurial activities influence the success of compassionate and sustainable venturing, and (9) what other forms of suffering can compassion venturing help overcome?

## DISCUSSION AND CONCLUSION

There are inarguably numerous stimulating research opportunities that could advance our understanding of entrepreneurial phenomena, and we will illustrate many of them in the following chapters. In this chapter, we chose to focus on four avenues, offering a subset of potential conjectures within each avenue to inspire future work on the generation, refinement, and exploitation of potential opportunities. In doing so, we purposefully cast a wide net and went beyond what is considered a typical opportunity for profit by many scholars. Specifically, we believe future research can maintain the vitality of the field of entrepreneurship as well as advance knowledge by exploring (1) potential opportunities as social interactions between an entrepreneur's mind and a community of inquiry as well as the mutual adjustment between the two; (2) the antecedents, outcomes, and

RESEARCHING THE GENERATION, REFINEMENT, AND EXPLOITATION... 49

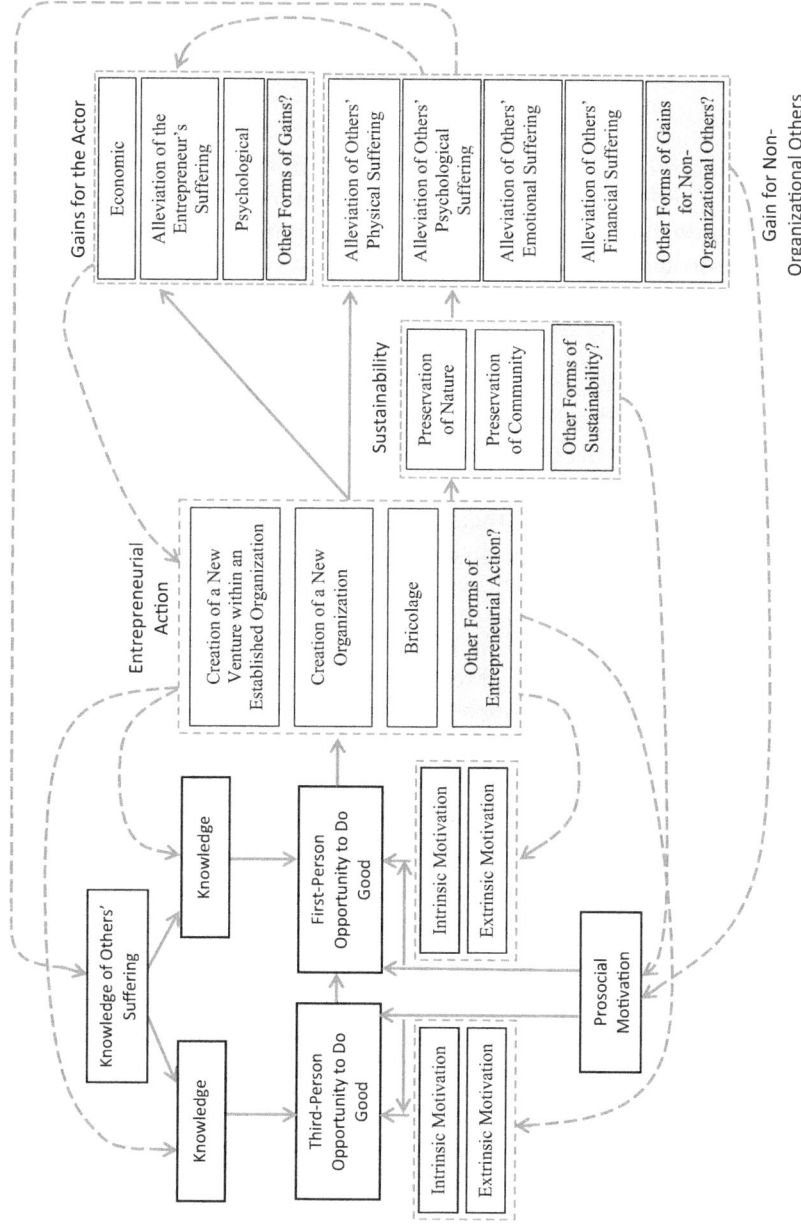

**Fig. 2.4** A sketch of entrepreneurial research that is more compassionate and more prosocial. Source: This figure is from Shepherd (2015)

inter-relationships of activities as a micro-foundation of identifying, evaluating, and exploiting entrepreneurial opportunities; (3) the reciprocal relationships between cognition and emotion that are created, continued, and ended when an individual is engaged in the entrepreneurial process; and (4) the motivations and capabilities behind new venture creation (i.e., new organizations or new ventures in established organizations) that generate, evaluate, and exploit potential opportunities to do good.

Through these opportunities for future entrepreneurship research, we also want to challenge the way scholars engage in research—namely, we want to encourage scholars to go beyond studying entrepreneurial phenomena to engage in entrepreneurship research. Such research is possible when scholars (1) *think entrepreneurially* by keeping an open mind about new topics, methods, and ways of conducting research rather than focusing on one "right" or "traditional" approach; (2) *think about interactions* such that ideas become refined after interactions with communities of inquiry (e.g., colleagues, reviewers, editors, and so on) rather than focusing on the sole domain of their individual creativity; (3) *think about the series of activities* comprising their research by tending to the activities involved in developing a paper (i.e., the micro-foundations of research that we can control) and less on the overall outcomes of single projects or career milestones; (4) *generate cognitive heat* by remaining open to (or otherwise evoking) emotional reactions to interesting research activities and harnessing these emotions to invigorate and inform subsequent activities instead of taking a "cold" calculated approach to research, and (5) *act prosocially to organize compassion venturing* by selecting and exploring topics that will deepen our understanding of entrepreneurial actors who make helpful and/or harmful contributions to society as well as to help develop scholars who want to make a difference and/or are not as fortunate.

## References

Alvarez, S. A., & Barney, J. B. (2007). Discovery and creation: Alternative theories of entrepreneurial action. *Strategic Entrepreneurship Journal, 1*(1–2), 11–26.

Alvarez, S. A., & Busenitz, L. W. (2001). The entrepreneurship of resource-based theory. *Journal of Management, 27*(6), 755–775.

Ardichvili, A., Cardozo, R., & Ray, S. (2003). A theory of entrepreneurial opportunity identification and development. *Journal of Business Venturing, 18*(1), 105–123.

Armstrong, K. (2011). *Twelve steps to a compassionate life*. Random House.
Ashforth, B. E., & Kreiner, G. E. (2002). Normalizing emotion in organizations: Making the extraordinary seem ordinary. *Human Resource Management Review, 12*(2), 215–235.
Autio, E., Dahlander, L., & Frederiksen, L. (2013). Information exposure, opportunity evaluation, and entrepreneurial action: An investigation of an online user community. *Academy of Management Journal, 56*(5), 1348–1371.
Baker, T., Miner, A. S., & Eesley, D. T. (2003). Improvising firms: Bricolage, account giving and improvisational competencies in the founding process. *Research Policy, 32*(2), 255–276.
Baker, T., & Nelson, R. E. (2005). Creating something from nothing: Resource construction through entrepreneurial bricolage. *Administrative Science Quarterly, 50*(3), 329–366.
Baldwin, C., Hienerth, C., & Von Hippel, E. (2006). How user innovations become commercial products: A theoretical investigation and case study. *Research Policy, 35*(9), 1291–1313.
Baron, R. A. (2008). The role of affect in the entrepreneurial process. *Academy of Management Review, 33*(2), 328–340.
Baron, R. A., & Ensley, M. D. (2006). Opportunity recognition as the detection of meaningful patterns: Evidence from comparisons of novice and experienced entrepreneurs. *Management Science, 52*(9), 1331–1344.
Batson, C. (1998). Altruism and prosocial behavior. In J. Y. Shah & W. L. Gardner (Eds.), *The Handbook of Social Psychology, 2*, 463–484.
Batson, C. D., Ahmad, N., Powell, A. A., Stocks, E., Shah, J., & Gardner, W. (2008). Prosocial motivation. *Handbook of Motivation Science*, 135–149.
Baumann, N., & Kuhl, J. (2005). Positive affect and flexibility: Overcoming the precedence of global over local processing of visual information. *Motivation and Emotion, 29*(2), 123–134.
Belschak, F., Verbeke, W., & Bagozzi, R. P. (2006). Coping with sales call anxiety: The role of sale perseverance and task concentration strategies. *Journal of the Academy of Marketing Science, 34*(3), 403–418.
Blanchette, I., & Dunbar, K. (2001). Analogy use in naturalistic settings: The influence of audience, emotion, and goals. *Memory & Cognition, 29*(5), 730–735.
Blood, A. J., & Zatorre, R. J. (2001). Intensely pleasurable responses to music correlate with activity in brain regions implicated in reward and emotion. *Proceedings of the National Academy of Sciences, 98*, 11818–11823.
Bornstein, D. (2004). *How to change the world: Social entrepreneurs and the power of new ideas*. Oxford: Oxford University Press.
Bradley, S. W., Wiklund, J., & Shepherd, D. A. (2011). Swinging a double-edged sword: The effect of slack on entrepreneurial management and growth. *Journal of Business Venturing, 26*(5), 537–554.

Brettel, M., Mauer, R., Engelen, A., & Küpper, D. (2012). Corporate effectuation: Entrepreneurial action and its impact on R&D project performance. *Journal of Business Venturing, 27*(2), 167–184.

Brown, S. L., & Eisenhardt, K. M. (1997). The art of continuous change: Linking complexity theory and time-paced evolution in relentlessly shifting organizations. *Administrative Science Quarterly, 42*, 1–34.

Brundin, E., Patzelt, H., & Shepherd, D. A. (2008). Managers' emotional displays and employees' willingness to act entrepreneurially. *Journal of Business Venturing, 23*(2), 221–243.

Bruner, J. S. (1986). *Actual minds, possible worlds.* Cambridge, MA: Harvard University Press.

Bryant, P. (2007). Self-regulation and decision heuristics in entrepreneurial opportunity evaluation and exploitation. *Management Decision, 45*(4), 732–748.

Bui, T. X., & Sebastian, I. (2011). Beyond rationality: Information design for supporting emergent groups in emergency response. In F. Burstein, P. Brézillon, & A. Zaslavsky (Eds.), *Supporting real time decision-making* (pp. 159–179). Springer.

Burt, R. S. (2005). *Brokerage and closure: An introduction to social capital.* Oxford: Oxford University Press.

Busenitz, L. W., & Barney, J. B. (1997). Differences between entrepreneurs and managers in large organizations: Biases and heuristics in strategic decision-making. *Journal of Business Venturing, 12*(1), 9–30.

Cardon, M. S., Foo, M. D., Shepherd, D., & Wiklund, J. (2012). Exploring the heart: Entrepreneurial emotion is a hot topic. *Entrepreneurship Theory and Practice, 36*(1), 1–10.

Cardon, M. S., Wincent, J., Singh, J., & Drnovsek, M. (2009). The nature and experience of entrepreneurial passion. *Academy of Management Review, 34*(3), 511–532.

Cardon, M. S., Zietsma, C., Saparito, P., Matherne, B. P., & Davis, C. (2005). A tale of passion: New insights into entrepreneurship from a parenthood metaphor. *Journal of Business Venturing, 20*(1), 23–45.

Carter, N. M., Gartner, W. B., & Reynolds, P. D. (1996). Exploring start-up event sequences. *Journal of Business Venturing, 11*(3), 151–166.

Catrambone, R., & Holyoak, K. J. (1989). Overcoming contextual limitations on problem-solving transfer. *Journal of Experimental Psychology: Learning, Memory, and Cognition, 15*(6), 1147.

Chandra, Y., & Coviello, N. (2010). Broadening the concept of international entrepreneurship: 'Consumers as international entrepreneurs'. *Journal of World Business, 45*(3), 228–236.

Corbett, A. C. (2005). Experiential learning within the process of opportunity identification and exploitation. *Entrepreneurship Theory and Practice, 29*(4), 473–491.

Corbett, A. C., & Hmieleski, K. M. (2007). The conflicting cognitions of corporate entrepreneurs. *Entrepreneurship Theory and Practice, 31*(1), 103–121.

Cornelissen, J. P., & Clarke, J. S. (2010). Imagining and rationalizing opportunities: Inductive reasoning and the creation and justification of new ventures. *Academy of Management Review, 35*(4), 539–557.

Dacin, M. T., Dacin, P. A., & Tracey, P. (2011). Social entrepreneurship: A critique and future directions. *Organization Science, 22*(5), 1203–1213.

Davidsson, P. (2003). The domain of entrepreneurship research: Some suggestions. *Advances in Entrepreneurship, Firm Emergence and Growth, 6*(3), 315–372.

Davidsson, P. (2015). Entrepreneurial opportunities and the entrepreneurship nexus: A re-conceptualization. *Journal of Business Venturing, 30*(5), 674–695.

Davidsson, P., & Gordon, S. R. (2012). Panel studies of new venture creation: A methods-focused review and suggestions for future research. *Small Business Economics, 39*(4), 853–876.

Davidsson, P., & Honig, B. (2003). The role of social and human capital among nascent entrepreneurs. *Journal of Business Venturing, 18*(3), 301–331.

De Dreu, C. K. (2006). When too little or too much hurts: Evidence for a curvilinear relationship between task conflict and innovation in teams. *Journal of Management, 32*(1), 83–107.

Dean, T. J., & McMullen, J. S. (2007). Toward a theory of sustainable entrepreneurship: Reducing environmental degradation through entrepreneurial action. *Journal of Business Venturing, 22*(1), 50–76.

Dees, J. G. (1998). *The meaning of social entrepreneurship*. Working paper.

Delmar, F., & Shane, S. (2004). Legitimating first: Organizing activities and the survival of new ventures. *Journal of Business Venturing, 19*(3), 385–410.

Derryberry, D., & Tucker, D. (2006). Motivation, self-regulation, and self-organization. *Developmental Psychopathology, 2*, 502–532.

Dewey, J. (1939). Theory of valuation. *International Encyclopedia of Unified Science, 2*(4), vii–v67.

Dimov, D. (2007). Beyond the single-person, single-insight attribution in understanding entrepreneurial opportunities. *Entrepreneurship Theory and Practice, 31*(5), 713–731.

Dimov, D. (2011). Grappling with the unbearable elusiveness of entrepreneurial opportunities. *Entrepreneurship Theory and Practice, 35*(1), 57–81.

Dorado, S., & Ventresca, M. J. (2013). Crescive entrepreneurship in complex social problems: Institutional conditions for entrepreneurial engagement. *Journal of Business Venturing, 28*(1), 69–82.

Dorfman, R., & Dorfman, N. S. (1993). *Economics of the environment: Selected readings*. WW Norton & Company.

Drabek, T. E., & McEntire, D. A. (2003). Emergent phenomena and the sociology of disaster: Lessons, trends and opportunities from the research literature. *Disaster Prevention and Management, 12*(2), 97–112.

Dutton, J. E. (1993). Interpretations on automatic: A different view of strategic issue diagnosis. *Journal of Management Studies, 30*(3), 339–357.
Dutton, J. E. (2003). Breathing life into organizational studies. *Journal of Management Inquiry, 12*(1), 5–19.
Dutton, J. E., & Duncan, R. B. (1987). The creation of momentum for change through the process of strategic issue diagnosis. *Strategic Management Journal, 8*(3), 279–295.
Dutton, J. E., Workman, K. M., & Hardin, A. E. (2014). Compassion at work. *Annual Review of Organizational Psychology and Organizational Behavior, 1*, 277–304.
Dutton, J. E., Worline, M. C., Frost, P. J., & Lilius, J. (2006). Explaining compassion organizing. *Administrative Science Quarterly, 51*(1), 59–96.
Eisenhardt, K. M. (1989). Making fast strategic decisions in high-velocity environments. *Academy of Management Journal, 32*(3), 543–576.
Estrada, C. A., Isen, A. M., & Young, M. J. (1997). Positive affect facilitates integration of information and decreases anchoring in reasoning among physicians. *Organizational Behavior and Human Decision Processes, 72*(1), 117–135.
Fiet, J. O. (2007). A prescriptive analysis of search and discovery. *Journal of Management Studies, 44*(4), 592–611.
Fiet, J. O., & Samuelsson, M. (2000). Knowledge-based competencies as a platform for firm formation. *Frontiers of Entrepreneurship Research*, 166–178.
Fitzsimmons, J. R., & Douglas, E. J. (2011). Interaction between feasibility and desirability in the formation of entrepreneurial intentions. *Journal of Business Venturing, 26*(4), 431–440.
Foo, M. D. (2011). Emotions and entrepreneurial opportunity evaluation. *Entrepreneurship Theory and Practice, 35*(2), 375–393.
Foo, M.-D., Uy, M. A., & Baron, R. A. (2009). How do feelings influence effort? An empirical study of entrepreneurs' affect and venture effort. *Journal of Applied Psychology, 94*(4), 1086.
Forbes, D. P. (2005). Are some entrepreneurs more overconfident than others? *Journal of Business Venturing, 20*(5), 623–640.
Foss, K., Foss, N. J., Klein, P. G., & Klein, S. K. (2007). The entrepreneurial organization of heterogeneous capital. *Journal of Management Studies, 44*, 1165–1186.
Fredrickson, B. L. (1998). What good are positive emotions? *Review of General Psychology, 2*(3), 300–319.
Fredrickson, B. L. (2000). Cultivating positive emotions to optimize health and well-being. *Prevention & Treatment, 3*(1), 1a.
Fredrickson, B. L. (2001). The role of positive emotions in positive psychology: The broaden-and-build theory of positive emotions. *American Psychologist, 56*(3), 218–226.
Fredrickson, B. L., & Branigan, C. (2005). Positive emotions broaden the scope of attention and thought-action repertoires. *Cognition & Emotion, 19*(3), 313–332.

Fredrickson, B. L., Cohn, M. A., Coffey, K. A., Pek, J., & Finkel, S. M. (2008). Open hearts build lives: Positive emotions, induced through loving-kindness meditation, build consequential personal resources. *Journal of Personality and Social Psychology, 95*(5), 1045.

Fredrickson, B. L., Mancuso, R. A., Branigan, C., & Tugade, M. M. (2000). The undoing effect of positive emotions. *Motivation and Emotion, 24*(4), 237–258.

Frost, P. J. (2003). *Toxic emotions at work: How compassionate managers handle pain and conflict.* Boston, MA: Harvard Business School Publishing.

Gaglio, C. M., & Katz, J. A. (2001). The psychological basis of opportunity identification: Entrepreneurial alertness. *Small Business Economics, 16*(2), 95–111.

Gartner, W. B. (1985). A conceptual framework for describing the phenomenon of new venture creation. *Academy of Management Review, 10*(4), 696–706.

Gartner, W. B., Carter, N. M., & Hills, G. E. (2003). The language of opportunity. In C. Steyaert & D. Hjorth (Eds.), *New movements in entrepreneurship* (pp. 103–124). Edward Elgar Publishing Limited.

Gergen, K. J. (1994). *Realities and relationships: Soundings in social construction.* Cambridge, MA: Harvard University Press.

George, J. M. (2013). Compassion and capitalism implications for organizational studies. *Journal of Management.* Advance online publication.

Gielnik, M. M., Spitzmuller, M., Schmitt, A., Klemann, D. K., & Frese, M. (2015). "I put in effort, therefore I am passionate": Investigating the path from effort to passion in entrepreneurship. *Academy of Management Journal, 58*(4), 1012–1031.

Gittell, J. H., Cameron, K., Lim, S., & Rivas, V. (2006). Relationships, layoffs, and organizational resilience airline industry responses to September 11. *Journal of Applied Behavioral Science, 42*(3), 300–329.

Grant, A. M. (2007). Relational job design and the motivation to make a prosocial difference. *Academy of Management Review, 32*(2), 393–417.

Grant, A. M. (2008). Does intrinsic motivation fuel the prosocial fire? Motivational synergy in predicting persistence, performance, and productivity. *Journal of Applied Psychology, 93*(1), 48.

Grant, A. M., & Berry, J. W. (2011). The necessity of others is the mother of invention: Intrinsic and prosocial motivations, perspective taking, and creativity. *Academy of Management Journal, 54*(1), 73–96.

Grant, A. M., & Sumanth, J. J. (2009). Mission possible? The performance of prosocially motivated employees depends on manager trustworthiness. *Journal of Applied Psychology, 94*(4), 927.

Grégoire, D. A., Barr, P. S., & Shepherd, D. A. (2010). Cognitive processes of opportunity recognition: The role of structural alignment. *Organization Science, 21*(2), 413–431.

Grégoire, D. A., & Shepherd, D. A. (2012). Technology-market combinations and the identification of entrepreneurial opportunities: An investigation of the opportunity-individual nexus. *Academy of Management Journal, 55*(4), 753–785.

Gregoire, D. A., Corbett, A. C., & McMullen, J. S. (2011). The cognitive perspective in entrepreneurship: An agenda for future research. *Journal of Management Studies, 48*(6), 1443–1477.

Grichnik, D., Smeja, A., & Welpe, I. (2010). The importance of being emotional: How do emotions affect entrepreneurial opportunity evaluation and exploitation? *Journal of Economic Behavior & Organization, 76*(1), 15–29.

Gruber, M., MacMillan, I. C., & Thompson, J. D. (2013). Escaping the prior knowledge corridor: What shapes the number and variety of market opportunities identified before market entry of technology start-ups? *Organization Science, 24*(1), 280–300.

Haefliger, S., Jäger, P., & Von Krogh, G. (2010). Under the radar: Industry entry by user entrepreneurs. *Research Policy, 39*(9), 1198–1213.

Hall, J. K., Daneke, G. A., & Lenox, M. J. (2010). Sustainable development and entrepreneurship: Past contributions and future directions. *Journal of Business Venturing, 25*(5), 439–448.

Haskel, T. (1984). Professionalism versus capitalism: R. H. Tawney, Emile Durkheim, and C. S. Pierce on the disinterestedness of professional communities. In T. Haskel (Ed.), *The authority of experts: Studies in history and theory* (pp. 180–225). Bloomington, IN: Indiana University Press.

Hayek, F. A. (1945). The use of knowledge in society. *The American Economic Review, 35*, 519–530.

Haynie, J. M., Shepherd, D. A., & McMullen, J. S. (2009). An opportunity for me? The role of resources in opportunity evaluation decisions. *Journal of Management Studies, 46*(3), 337–361.

Haynie, J. M., Shepherd, D. A., Mosakowski, E., & Earley, P. C. (2010). A situated metacognitive model of the entrepreneurial mindset. *Journal of Business Venturing, 25*(2), 217–229.

Hill, R. C., & Levenhagen, M. (1995). Metaphors and mental models: Sensemaking and sensegiving in innovative and entrepreneurial activities. *Journal of Management, 21*(6), 1057–1074.

Hite, J. M. (2005). Evolutionary processes and paths of relationally embedded network ties in emerging entrepreneurial firms. *Entrepreneurship Theory and Practice, 29*(1), 113–144.

Hmieleski, K. M., & Baron, R. A. (2008). Regulatory focus and new venture performance: A study of entrepreneurial opportunity exploitation under conditions of risk versus uncertainty. *Strategic Entrepreneurship Journal, 2*(4), 285–299.

Hmieleski, K. M., & Corbett, A. C. (2008). The contrasting interaction effects of improvisational behavior with entrepreneurial self-efficacy on new venture performance and entrepreneur work satisfaction. *Journal of Business Venturing, 23*(4), 482–496.

Hoang, H., & Antoncic, B. (2003). Network-based research in entrepreneurship: A critical review. *Journal of Business Venturing, 18*(2), 165–187.

Holland, J., Holyoak, K., Nisbett, R., & Thagard, P. (1986). *Process of inference, learning, and discovery*. Cambridge, MA: MIT Press.

Holyoak, K. J., & Thagard, P. (1995). *Mental leaps*. Cambridge, MA: MIT Press.

Isen, A. M., & Daubman, K. A. (1984). The influence of affect on categorization. *Journal of Personality and Social Psychology, 47*(6), 1206.

Isen, A. M., Daubman, K. A., & Nowicki, G. P. (1987). Positive affect facilitates creative problem solving. *Journal of Personality and Social Psychology, 52*(6), 1122–1131.

Kanov, J. M., Maitlis, S., Worline, M. C., Dutton, J. E., Frost, P. J., & Lilius, J. M. (2004). Compassion in organizational life. *American Behavioral Scientist, 47*(6), 808–827.

Katz, J., & Gartner, W. B. (1988). Properties of emerging organizations. *Academy of Management Review, 13*(3), 429–441.

Keane, M. T., Ledgeway, T., & Duff, S. (1994). Constraints on analogical mapping: A comparison of three models. *Cognitive Science, 18*(3), 387–438.

Keh, H. T., Foo, M. D., & Lim, B. C. (2002). Opportunity evaluation under risky conditions: The cognitive processes of entrepreneurs. *Entrepreneurship Theory and Practice, 27*(2), 125–148.

Khan, F. R., Munir, K. A., & Willmott, H. (2007). A dark side of institutional entrepreneurship: Soccer balls, child labour and postcolonial impoverishment. *Organization Studies, 28*(7), 1055–1077.

Kim, P. H., Longest, K. C., & Lippmann, S. (2015). The tortoise versus the hare: Progress and business viability differences between conventional and leisure-based founders. *Journal of Business Venturing, 30*(2), 185–204.

Klein, P. G. (2008). Opportunity discovery, entrepreneurial action, and economic organization. *Strategic Entrepreneurship Journal, 2*(3), 175–190.

Klofsten, M. (2005). New venture ideas: An analysis of their origin and early development. *Technology Analysis and Strategic Management, 17*(1), 105–119.

Kloppenberg, J. T. (1989). Objectivity and historicism: A century of American historical writing. *American Historical Review, 94*(4), 1011–1030.

Knight, F. H. (1921). *Risk, uncertainty and profit*. New York: Hart, Schaffner and Marx.

Krueger Jr., N. F. (2003). *The cognitive psychology of entrepreneurship, Handbook of entrepreneurship research* (pp. 105–140). New York: Springer.

Krueger, N. F. (2007). What lies beneath? The experiential essence of entrepreneurial thinking. *Entrepreneurship Theory and Practice, 31*(1), 123–138.

Kuratko, D. F., Hornsby, J. S., & Covin, J. G. (2014). Diagnosing a firm's internal environment for corporate entrepreneurship. *Business Horizons, 57*(1), 37–47.

Liao, J., Welsch, H., & Tan, W.-L. (2005). Venture gestation paths of nascent entrepreneurs: Exploring the temporal patterns. *Journal of High Technology Management Research, 16*(1), 1–22.

Lichtenstein, B. B., Carter, N. M., Dooley, K. J., & Gartner, W. B. (2007). Complexity dynamics of nascent entrepreneurship. *Journal of Business Venturing, 22*(2), 236–261.

Lilius, J. M., Worline, M. C., Dutton, J. E., Kanov, J. M., & Maitlis, S. (2011). Understanding compassion capability. *Human Relations, 64*(7), 873–899.

Lilius, J. M., Worline, M. C., Maitlis, S., Kanov, J., Dutton, J. E., & Frost, P. (2008). The contours and consequences of compassion at work. *Journal of Organizational Behavior, 29*(2), 193–218.

Locke, K., Golden-Biddle, K., & Feldman, M. S. (2008). Perspective-making doubt generative: Rethinking the role of doubt in the research process. *Organization Science, 19*(6), 907–918.

Lumpkin, G. T., & Dess, G. G. (1996). Clarifying the entrepreneurial orientation construct and linking it to performance. *Academy of Management Review, 21*(1), 135–172.

Maffei, L., & Fiorentini, A. (1995). *Art and brain*. Bologna: Zanichelli.

Mair, J., & Marti, I. (2006). Social entrepreneurship research: A source of explanation, prediction, and delight. *Journal of World Business, 41*(1), 36–44.

Majchrzak, A., Jarvenpaa, S. L., & Hollingshead, A. B. (2007). Coordinating expertise among emergent groups responding to disasters. *Organization Science, 18*(1), 147–161.

McGrath, R. G. (1999). Falling forward: Real options reasoning and entrepreneurial failure. *Academy of Management Review, 24*(1), 13–30.

McKelvie, A., Haynie, J. M., & Gustavsson, V. (2011). Unpacking the uncertainty construct: Implications for entrepreneurial action. *Journal of Business Venturing, 26*(3), 273–292.

McMullen, J. S. (2011). Delineating the domain of development entrepreneurship: A market-based approach to facilitating inclusive economic growth. *Entrepreneurship Theory and Practice, 35*(1), 185–193.

McMullen, J. S., & Dimov, D. (2013). Time and the entrepreneurial journey: The problems and promise of studying entrepreneurship as a process. *Journal of Management Studies, 50*(8), 1481–1512.

McMullen, J. S., Plummer, L. A., & Acs, Z. J. (2007). What is an entrepreneurial opportunity? *Small Business Economics, 28*(4), 273–283.

McMullen, J. S., & Shepherd, D. A. (2006). Entrepreneurial action and the role of uncertainty in the theory of the entrepreneur. *Academy of Management Review, 31*(1), 132–152.

Meek, W. R., Pacheco, D. F., & York, J. G. (2010). The impact of social norms on entrepreneurial action: Evidence from the environmental entrepreneurship context. *Journal of Business Venturing, 25*(5), 493–509.

Miller, T. L., Grimes, M. G., McMullen, J. S., & Vogus, T. J. (2012). Venturing for others with heart and head: How compassion encourages social entrepreneurship. *Academy of Management Review, 37*(4), 616–640.

Mitchell, J. R., & Shepherd, D. A. (2010). To thine own self be true: Images of self, images of opportunity, and entrepreneurial action. *Journal of Business Venturing, 25*(1), 138–154.

Mitchell, R. K., Smith, J. B., Morse, E. A., Seawright, K. W., Peredo, A. M., & McKenzie, B. (2002). Are entrepreneurial cognitions universal? Assessing entrepreneurial cognitions across cultures. *Entrepreneurship Theory and Practice, 26*(4), 9–32.

Mitchell, R. K., Smith, B., Seawright, K. W., & Morse, E. A. (2000). Cross-cultural cognitions and the venture creation decision. *Academy of Management Journal, 43*(5), 974–993.

Paavola, S. (2004). Abduction as a logic and methodology of discovery: The importance of strategies. *Foundations of Science, 9*(3), 267–283.

Pardales, M. J., & Girod, M. (2006). Community of Inquiry: Its past and present future. *Educational Philosophy and Theory, 38*(3), 299–309.

Patzelt, H., & Shepherd, D. A. (2011). Recognizing opportunities for sustainable development. *Entrepreneurship Theory and Practice, 35*(4), 631–652.

Peirce, C. S. (1955). *Philosophical writings of Peirce.* Courier Dover Publications.

Peredo, A. M., & Chrisman, J. J. (2006). Toward a theory of community-based enterprise. *Academy of Management Review, 31*(2), 309–328.

Powell, E. E., & Baker, T. (2014). It's what you make of it: Founder identity and enacting strategic responses to adversity. *Academy of Management Journal, 7*(5), 1406–1433.

Powley, E. H. (2009). Reclaiming resilience and safety: Resilience activation in the critical period of crisis. *Human Relations, 62*(9), 1289–1326.

Prawat, R. S. (1995). Misreading Dewey: Reform, projects, and the language game. *Educational Researcher, 24*(7), 13–22.

Quarantelli, E. L. (1993). Community crises: An exploratory comparison of the characteristics and consequences of disasters and riots. *Journal of Contingencies and Crisis Management, 1*(2), 67–78.

Renko, M. (2013). Early challenges of nascent social entrepreneurs. *Entrepreneurship Theory and Practice, 37*(5), 1045–1069.

Reynolds, P., & Miller, B. (1992). New firm gestation: Conception, birth, and implications for research. *Journal of Business Venturing, 7*(5), 405–417.

Roberts, D., & Woods, C. (2005). Changing the world on a shoestring: The concept of social entrepreneurship. *University of Auckland Business Review, 7*, 45–51.

Russell, J. A. (2003). Core affect and the psychological construction of emotion. *Psychological Review, 110*(1), 145–172.

Russell, P., & Milne, S. (1997). Meaningfulness and hedonic value of paintings: Effects of titles. *Empirical Studies of the Arts, 15*(1), 61–73.

Rynes, S., Bartunek, J., Dutton, J., & Margolis, J. (2012). Care and compassion through an organizational lens: Opening up new possibilities. *Academy of Management Review, 37*(4), 503–523.

Sarasvathy, S. D. (2001). Causation and effectuation: Toward a theoretical shift from economic inevitability to entrepreneurial contingency. *Academy of Management Review, 26*(2), 243–263.

Sarasvathy, S. D., Dew, N., Velamuri, S. R., & Venkataraman, S. (2010). Three views of entrepreneurial opportunity. In *Handbook of entrepreneurship research* (pp. 77–96). Springer.

Schneider, I. K., Eerland, A., van Harreveld, F., Rotteveel, M., van der Pligt, J., Van der Stoep, N., et al. (2013). One way and the other the bidirectional relationship between ambivalence and body movement. *Psychological Science, 24*(3), 319–325.

Schuler, S. R., Hashemi, S. M., & Badal, S. H. (1998). Men's violence against women in rural Bangladesh: Undermined or exacerbated by microcredit programmes? *Development in Practice, 8*(2), 148–157.

Sebastian, I. M., & Bui, T. X. (2009). Emergent groups for emergency response-theoretical foundations and information design implications. *AMCIS 2009 Proceedings, 638*, 1–9.

Seixas, P. (1993). The community of inquiry as a basis for knowledge and learning: The case of history. *American Educational Research Journal, 30*(2), 305–324.

Seligman, M. E., & Csikszentmihalyi, M. (2000). *Positive psychology: An introduction*. American Psychological Association.

Seligman, M. E., Steen, T. A., Park, N., & Peterson, C. (2005). Positive psychology progress: Empirical validation of interventions. *American Psychologist, 60*(5), 410.

Shah, S. K., & Tripsas, M. (2007). The accidental entrepreneur: The emergent and collective process of user entrepreneurship. *Strategic Entrepreneurship Journal, 1*(1–2), 123–140.

Shalley, C. E., & Perry-Smith, J. E. (2008). The emergence of team creative cognition: The role of diverse outside ties, sociocognitive network centrality, and team evolution. *Strategic Entrepreneurship Journal, 2*(1), 23–41.

Shane, S. (2000). Prior knowledge and the discovery of entrepreneurial opportunities. *Organization Science, 11*(4), 448–469.

Shane, S., & Eckhardt, J. (2003). The individual-opportunity nexus. In *Handbook of entrepreneurship research* (pp. 161–191). Springer.

Shanley, J. P. (2005). *Doubt: A parable*. New York: Dramatists Play Service, Inc.

Shepherd, D. A. (2003). Learning from business failure: Propositions of grief recovery for the self-employed. *Academy of Management Review, 28*(2), 318–328.

Shepherd, D. A., & DeTienne, D. R. (2005). Prior knowledge, potential financial reward, and opportunity identification. *Entrepreneurship Theory and Practice, 29*(1), 91–112.

Shepherd, D. A., Haynie, J. M., & McMullen, J. S. (2012). Confirmatory search as a useful heuristic? Testing the veracity of entrepreneurial conjectures. *Journal of Business Venturing, 27*(6), 637–651.

Shepherd, D. A., McMullen, J. S., & Jennings, P. D. (2007). The formation of opportunity beliefs: Overcoming ignorance and reducing doubt. *Strategic Entrepreneurship Journal, 1*(1–2), 75–95.

Shepherd, D. A., & Patzelt, H. (2011). The new field of sustainable entrepreneurship: Studying entrepreneurial action linking "what is to be sustained" with "what is to be developed". *Entrepreneurship Theory and Practice, 35*(1), 137–163.

Shepherd, D., Patzelt, H., & Baron, R. (2013). "I care about nature, but ...": Disengaging values in assessing opportunities that cause harm. *Academy of Management Journal, 56*(5), 1251–1273.

Shepherd, D. A., Patzelt, H., Williams, T. A., & Warnecke, D. (2014). How does project termination impact project team members? Rapid termination, 'creeping death', and learning from failure. *Journal of Management Studies, 51*(4), 513–546.

Shepherd, D. A., Patzelt, H., & Wolfe, M. (2011). Moving forward from project failure: Negative emotions, affective commitment, and learning from the experience. *Academy of Management Journal, 54*(6), 1229–1259.

Shepherd, D. A. (2015). Party On! A call for entrepreneurship research that is more interactive, activity based, cognitively hot, compassionate, and prosocial. *Journal of Business Venturing, 30*(4), 489–507.

Shepherd, D. A., & Williams, T. A. (2014). Local venturing as compassion organizing in the aftermath of a natural disaster: The role of localness and community in reducing suffering. *Journal of Management Studies, 51*(6), 952–994.

Short, J. C., Ketchen, D. J., Shook, C. L., & Ireland, R. D. (2009). The concept of "opportunity" in entrepreneurship research: Past accomplishments and future challenges. *Journal of Management, 36*(1), 40–65.

Smith, J. B., Mitchell, J. R., & Mitchell, R. K. (2009). Entrepreneurial scripts and the new transaction commitment mindset: Extending the expert information processing theory approach to entrepreneurial cognition research. *Entrepreneurship Theory and Practice, 33*(4), 815–844.

Sorenson, O., & Audia, P. G. (2000). The social structure of entrepreneurial activity: Geographic concentration of footwear production in the United States, 1940–1989. *American Journal of Sociology, 106*(2), 424–462.

Stevenson, H. H., & Jarillo, J. C. (1990). A paradigm of entrepreneurship: Entrepreneurial management. *Strategic Management Journal, 11*, 17–27.

Stinchfield, B. T., Nelson, R. E., & Wood, M. S. (2013). Learning from Levi-Strauss' legacy: Art, craft, engineering, bricolage, and brokerage in entrepreneurship. *Entrepreneurship Theory and Practice, 37*(4), 889–921.

Sutcliffe, K., & Vogus, T. J. (2003). Organizing for resilience. *Positive Organizational Scholarship: Foundations of a New Discipline, 94*, 110.

Swedberg, R. (2009). Schumpeter's full model of entrepreneurship. In R. Ziegler (Ed.), *An introduction to social entrepreneurship: Voices, preconditions, contexts* (pp. 77–106). Cheltenham, UK: Edward Elgar.

Tang, J., Kacmar, K. M., & Busenitz, L. (2012). Entrepreneurial alertness in the pursuit of new opportunities. *Journal of Business Venturing, 27*(1), 77–94.

Tietenberg, T. (2000). *Environmental and natural resource economics*. New York: Addison Wesley.

Tripsas, M., & Gavetti, G. (2000). Capabilities, cognition, and inertia: Evidence from digital imaging. *Strategic Management Journal, 21*(10-11), 1147–1161.

Ucbasaran, D., Westhead, P., & Wright, M. (2008). Opportunity identification and pursuit: Does an entrepreneur's human capital matter? *Small Business Economics, 30*(2), 153–173.

Waugh, C. E., & Fredrickson, B. L. (2006). Nice to know you: Positive emotions, self–other overlap, and complex understanding in the formation of a new relationship. *The Journal of Positive Psychology, 1*(2), 93–106.

Waugh, W. L., & Streib, G. (2006). Collaboration and leadership for effective emergency management. *Public Administration Review, 66*(s1), 131–140.

Welpe, I. M., Spörrle, M., Grichnik, D., Michl, T., & Audretsch, D. B. (2012). Emotions and opportunities: The interplay of opportunity evaluation, fear, joy, and anger as antecedent of entrepreneurial exploitation. *Entrepreneurship Theory and Practice, 36*(1), 69–96.

West, G. P. (2007). Collective cognition: When entrepreneurial teams, not individuals, make decisions. *Entrepreneurship Theory and Practice, 31*(1), 77–102.

Williams, T. A., & Shepherd, D. A. (2016). Victim entrepreneurs doing well by doing good: Venture creation and well-being in the aftermath of a resource shock. *Journal of Business Venturing, 31*(4), 365–387.

Williams, T., & Shepherd, D. (2017). Building resilience or providing sustenance: Different paths of emergent ventures in the aftermath of the haiti earthquake. *Academy of Management Journal.* Forthcoming.

Wilson, E. B. (1990). *An introduction to scientific research.* Courier Dover Publications.

Yli-Renko, H., Autio, E., & Sapienza, H. J. (2001). Social capital, knowledge acquisition, and knowledge exploitation in young technology-based firms. *Strategic Management Journal, 22*(6–7), 587–613.

York, J. G., & Venkataraman, S. (2010). The entrepreneur–environment nexus: Uncertainty, innovation, and allocation. *Journal of Business Venturing, 25*(5), 449–463.

Zahra, S. A., Rawhouser, H. N., Bhawe, N., Neubaum, D. O., & Hayton, J. C. (2008). Globalization of social entrepreneurship opportunities. *Strategic Entrepreneurship Journal, 2*(2), 117–131.

**Open Access** This chapter is distributed under the terms of the Creative Commons Attribution 4.0 International License (http://creativecommons.org/licenses/by/4.0/), which permits use, duplication, adaptation, distribution and reproduction in any medium or format, as long as you give appropriate credit to the original author(s) and the source, provide a link to the Creative Commons license and indicate if changes were made.

The images or other third party material in this chapter are included in the work's Creative Commons license, unless indicated otherwise in the credit line; if such material is not included in the work's Creative Commons license and the respective action is not permitted by statutory regulation, users will need to obtain permission from the license holder to duplicate, adapt or reproduce the material.

CHAPTER 3

# Researching Entrepreneurial Failures

## INTRODUCTION

Due to the highly uncertain nature of pursuing new business opportunities (Knight, 1992; McMullen & Shepherd, 2006), failure is a rather common outcome of entrepreneurial endeavors (Brüderl, Preisendörfer, & Ziegler, 1992; Shane, 2009; Wiklund, Baker, & Shepherd, 2010). Take family businesses as an example. They comprise a significant share of all businesses (up to 90% in the USA [Dumas, 1992; Heck & Trent, 1999; Kets de Vries, 1993]), but nearly 70% of family businesses fail to make it through the second generation, and roughly 90% fail to survive through the third generation (Kets de Vries, 1993). Similarly, established firms often undertake entrepreneurial projects as part of corporate entrepreneurship initiatives to create new products, enter new markets, explore new technologies, and/or build new businesses (Zahra, Jennings, & Kuratko, 1999). Like businesses, however, entrepreneurial projects are basically experiments with unknowable outcomes; there is an air of uncertainty (McGrath, 1999). Thus, sporadic or even repeated entrepreneurial project failure is an inevitability in firms practicing corporate entrepreneurship (Burgelman & Välikangas, 2005). In fact, Boulding, Morgan, & Staelin (1997) estimated that 35–45% of all new products fail (Boulding, Morgan, & Staelin, 1997).

---

In this chapter, we build on Shepherd, Covin, and Kuratko (2009); Shepherd (2009); and Ucbasaran, Shepherd, Lockett, and Lyons (2013).

Further, investigating 95 venturing units in corporations with headquarters in eight countries worldwide, Campbell, Birkinshaw, Morrison, and van Basten Batenburg (2003) reported *no* successful examples among firms exploring "new leg" ventures or among internal corporate ventures started with the sole purpose of pursuing growth opportunities in novel (to the firm) product-market domains.

While being able to successfully exploit entrepreneurial opportunities is the primary aim of all entrepreneurship initiatives, failure is not necessarily a completely negative outcome as some failures can lay the foundation for subsequent success. This path from failure to success has been seen in new product development (Maidique & Zirger, 1985), internal corporate venturing (McGrath, 1995), and joint venturing (Peng & Shenkar, 2002). Although some failures lead to positive outcomes, success is by no means a certain consequence of failure. For success to follow failure, it is essential for the entrepreneur or the organization to *learn* from past mistakes. As such, entrepreneurial failures can actually be potential learning opportunities (Green, Welsh, & Dehler, 2003). By signaling a problem with one's current beliefs or actions (Chuang & Baum, 2003; Sitkin, 1992), failure can motivate individuals to look for solutions (Ginsberg, 1988; McGrath, 2001; Morrison, 2002; Petroski, 1985). Furthermore, failure often triggers sensemaking efforts, thereby serving as a rich source of information for learning. Thus, learning from failure refers to "the sense that one is acquiring, and can apply, knowledge and skills" (Spreitzer, Sutcliffe, Dutton, Sonenshein, & Grant, 2005, p. 538) as a direct result of a failure experience. When entrepreneurs take chances, learn from their failures, and act on the new knowledge they gain from those failures, economies are able to progress (Hoetker & Agarwal, 2007; Knott & Posen, 2005; Mason & Harrison, 2006). Moreover, when entrepreneurs and organizations gain new knowledge from their failures, they are more likely to become involved in future entrepreneurial initiatives (Hayek, 1945). Such initiatives can serve as possible foundations for firm growth and renewal (McGrath, Tsai, Venkataraman, & MacMillan, 1996), thus increasing individuals' odds of succeeding with a new venture after a failure. In a similar way, those who failed in a corporate setting can aid their organizations in improving their innovation "hit rate" by learning from their failures and emotionally committing to later projects.

Because failure can motivate individuals to gain new knowledge or skills, researchers argue that people tend to learn more from their failures than from their successes (Petroski, 1985; Popper, 1959). Sitkin (1992, p. 243) suggested that learning from failure is most likely to occur when failure events "(1) result from thoughtfully planned actions, (2) have uncertain outcomes, (3) are of modest scale, (4) are executed and responded to with alacrity, and (5) take place in domains that are familiar enough to permit effective learning." However, alacrity—namely, "brisk and cheerful readiness" (Concise Oxford Dictionary)—is difficult to maintain when the failure means that the entrepreneur loses something that is important to him or her (i.e., a project or a business). Although most organizations and their members believe that learning from failure is important, they generally find doing so to be difficult (Cannon & Edmondson, 2005), as do entrepreneurs who lose their business (Byrne & Shepherd, 2015; Shepherd, 2003). More specifically, while failure reveals important information, organizations and individuals are frequently unsuccessful at fully processing that information (Weick, 1990; Weick & Sutcliffe, 2006). We need to gain a deeper understanding of the costs of failure (project and business) to the entrepreneur (and by extension the organization) and the ways these costs of failure can create obstacles to achieving the benefits of failure—namely, learning from the experience. However, before we delve into the nuances of advancing knowledge on this important topic, it is important to start with what we mean by failure (in its various forms).

## Defining Entrepreneurial Failures

Failure has been conceptualized in a number of ways, including as the discontinuity of ownership (for a review, see Singh, Corner, & Pavlovich, 2007), bankruptcy (e.g., Shepherd & Haynie, 2011), and discontinuity caused either by insolvency (Coelho & McClure, 2005; Shepherd, 2003) or by performance below the decision makers' threshold (e.g., Ucbasaran, Westhead, Wright, & Flores, 2010). Indeed, Ucbasaran et al. (2013, p. 175) defined **business failure** as "*the cessation of involvement in a venture because it has not met a minimum threshold for economic viability as stipulated by the (founding) entrepreneur.*" Shepherd and colleagues defined **project failure** as *the termination of an initiative to create organizational value that has fallen short of its goals* (Shepherd, Covin, et al., 2009; Shepherd, Patzelt, & Wolfe, 2011; see also Hoang & Rothaermel, 2005; McGrath, 1999). While there are numerous definitions of failure, we believe researchers should utilize the definition that best fits their study's research question. Nevertheless, it is important that the authors offer a clear, explicit definition and a justification for its use. We organize the rest of this chapter based on the major implications arising from the failure of projects or businesses—implications that are financial, social, emotional, or a combination of these implications—and offer various future research opportunities.

## THE FINANCIAL IMPLICATIONS OF ENTREPRENEURIAL FAILURE

The literature captures a long history of scholars focusing on the financial costs of failure. For example, an entrepreneur must often take on personal debt to fund his or her business, which he or she must then bear after business failure (Cope, 2011). However, it appears that the financial costs of failure (project and/or business) for the individual depend on the culture and the broader institutions in which the individual is embedded. For example, bankruptcy laws vary by country, and the "strictness" of these laws has a bearing on the financial costs borne by the entrepreneur from a failed business (Lee, Peng, & Barney, 2007; Lee, Yamakawa, Peng, & Barney, 2011). Although we have gained a substantial understanding of the financial costs of failure (and, for that matter, the financial costs of persisting despite poor performance [Gimeno, Folta, Cooper, & Woo, 1997; Shepherd, Wiklund, & Haynie, 2009]), there is still much to learn.

**Recovering from the financial costs of entrepreneurial failure.** First, we believe it is necessary to gain deeper insights into *how* and *why* some entrepreneurs are able to bounce back from the financial consequences of failure more quickly than others. What actions do such individuals take after a bankruptcy, for example, that help them deal with the financial burden? Moreover, the notion of recovery may be too limiting because it could imply that individuals merely "overcome" the financial costs of failure but does not take into account the possible financial benefits of failure over time. For instance, ultimate financial success after business failure may require individuals to take on traditional employment for a period to restore their financial reserves before entering into business ownership again. Further, those who suffer considerable financial loss after business failure are likely to learn significant lessons in how to manage their subsequent venture's financial resources. What lessons are learned in these difficult contexts, and how do they affect the business model and capital structure of subsequent ventures? Future research can investigate these entrepreneurial career paths (i.e., the sequence of entrepreneurs' career decisions) to help elucidate how entrepreneurs recover from the financial consequences of business failure and capitalize on the benefits of failure to attain financial success in the long term.

Even less clear are the financial costs of project failure within an organization. How does project failure impact the career trajectory of a member of a failed team effort? In some organizations, management may view the leaders of a failed project as lacking leadership, competence, and persistence, which likely obstructs a productive career path for the corporate entrepreneur. In response, the entrepreneur is likely to either leave the organization or stay with the organization but limit entrepreneurial activity (and other organizational members are likely to learn the same behavior vicariously). With either response from the (former) corporate entrepreneur, the organization loses because it kills (or substantially diminishes) the entrepreneurial spirit of the firm. In contrast, there are organizations that are more tolerant of failure and even some that celebrate it. How does a project failure impact the career trajectory of a corporate entrepreneur in such an organization (Farson & Keyes, 2006), especially in contrast to organizations that penalize those associated with a project failure? Perhaps the impact of failure on career trajectory depends on what type of failure occurred, whether the individual learned from the failure, and how that learning can be applied to benefit the organization.

**Entrepreneurial failure and opportunity costs.** Regardless of the direct financial cost of failure (independent or corporate entrepreneur), the failure of a project or a business may lead to the termination of a (insufficiently profitable) track but may also reveal other more profitable entrepreneurial opportunities. More can be done to try to explain how the continued pursuit of one potential opportunity (e.g., persisting with a losing course of action) has an "opportunity" opportunity cost. It could be that the opportunity costs are financial. For example, because the entrepreneur is investing resources (e.g., money) into the current venture, he or she is unable to pursue another potential opportunity. However, the opportunity costs could also be attentional. When focusing attention on the exploitation of a focal potential opportunity, for instance, the entrepreneur may have insufficient attention to notice and/or interpret signals of an alternate potential opportunity. Although these financial and/or attentional constraints could help determine the nature of the opportunity cost, it is important to understand how some are able to reduce these constraints and thus reduce the opportunity costs. This may involve making small investments and rapid terminations (Bakker & Shepherd, 2017;

McGrath, 1999), using a conscious strategy to maintain slack (i.e., cognitive, financial, and time) resources not allocated to the current entrepreneurial endeavor (Bradley, Wiklund, & Shepherd, 2011; George, 2005), and using other means for structuring and/or "freeing up" attentional resources (Ocasio, 1997; Shepherd, McMullen, & Ocasio, 2017).

**Financial costs of entrepreneurial failure at the group level of analysis.** Not only does the entrepreneur take on the financial costs of business failure, his or her family is also likely to feel the consequences. As such, future research on entrepreneurs embedded within a family is likely to provide a more complete picture of the financial costs of business failure for entrepreneurs. For example, while two entrepreneurs may experience the same immediate financial costs after business failure, heterogeneity in each entrepreneur's family wealth may lead to different long-term financial implications. Similarly, the costs of a project failure can more easily be borne by a wealthier organization than a poorer one. How does the wealth of the actor embedded in his or her family or organization influence the nature of the financial costs, the decision to start and to terminate the entrepreneurial endeavor, and the ability and willingness to move on to the next entrepreneurial endeavor? For example, on the surface, it appears that the financial costs of failure will be less damaging to entrepreneurs belonging to wealthier groups (e.g., a corporate entrepreneur embedded in a wealthier organization or an independent entrepreneur embedded in a wealthier family); however, those who belong to less wealthy groups may tend to engage in riskier behavior overall (e.g., believe they are in a loss situation and thus act in ways in line with prospect theory), thus making them more likely to engage in subsequent entrepreneurial actions. Future research can investigate whether those with less family wealth "behind" their entrepreneurial endeavors are more likely to approach a potential opportunity with real options reasoning (for real options reasoning, see McGrath, 1999; McGrath & Nerkar, 2004), have a fundamentally different approach to removing doubt about a potential opportunity and/or exploiting it, or are more willing to "gamble" it all with a "big bet."

**Financial losses from entrepreneurial failure and subsequent entrepreneurial action.** In line with research demonstrating the importance of financial slack for funding both the experimentation needed for successful entrepreneurship (see George, 2005) and start-up costs/early-stage growth (Gilbert, McDougall, & Audretsch, 2006), it may seem like the financial costs of business failure would be a significant barrier to later entrepreneurial activity, especially in the short term. However, the resulting resource scarcity after business failure could create an environment that fosters bricolage (i.e., "making do with whatever is at hand" [Baker & Nelson, 2005, p. 330]), particularly for entrepreneurs in more resource-poor contexts and/or corporate entrepreneurs who find it more difficult to garner resources from management after failure. That is, resource scarcity can trigger entrepreneurial activity, thereby transforming an initial financial cost into a different form of resource advantage (i.e., a valuable resource combination). Are some more able to switch from entrepreneurial activity spurred by slack resources to entrepreneurial activity spurred by resource scarcity? What mechanisms enable people to switch between these two different "sources" of entrepreneurial activity? The answers to these questions likely relate to the mindset triggered (or applied) to the adversity inherent in a resource-scarce environment.

Although we may be first drawn to prospect theory (Kahneman & Tversky, 1979) for answers, there are some other interesting possibilities. For some, this type of adversity likely generates an emphasis on resource protection—a reactive posture that involves consuming some resources to stop further resources from being lost. However, for others, this adversity could lead to an emphasis on resource investment—a proactive posture to replenish and grow resources (Hobfoll, 2001; Hobfoll & Lilly, 1993). Williams and Shepherd (2016) showed that those who engage in resource investment in the form of entrepreneurial action (i.e., the creation of a venture to alleviate the suffering of others in the aftermath of a natural disaster) have superior functioning in that adverse environment than those who do not engage in entrepreneurial action (controlling for a host of factors). Therefore, it may not be whether one fails or how much adversity one experiences when he or she fails; the ultimate net costs (or benefits) of failure may be determined by the mindset one develops regarding whether to protect remaining resources (through conservative action) or to invest those resources in entrepreneurial activity. Shepherd and Williams (2017) also proposed that regulatory focus theory is critical in explaining who escapes an adverse situation by constructing a new work identity (i.e., those with a promotion focus) and who languishes (i.e., those with a prevention focus). As we gain a deeper understanding of how different mindsets influence individuals' reactions, responses, and recovery from failure, attention needs to turn to the antecedents of these mindsets. For example, why do some invest resources under adversity while others protect their remaining resources, and why do some who hit rock bottom after entrepreneurial failure approach the situation with a promotion focus and others with a prevention focus? We need to gain a deeper understanding of the mindsets that reflect the different paths and trajectories of recovery and resilience.

**Entrepreneurial failure and careers.** Since failure can cause an entrepreneur personal financial hardship, end his or her source of income, harm his or her professional reputation, and result in negative financial outcomes for his or her family and/or firm, it is an extreme context that enables researchers to investigate career paths so as to survey the limits of and thus advance theories on careers to reveal the long-term financial implications of failure. This type of research can contribute to and extend current theories by heeding calls for more studies on career constraints (Arnold & Cohen, 2008) and on the ways individuals adapt to new careers (Savickas, 2002), especially when their prior career path has ended (Haynie & Shepherd, 2011; Shepherd & Williams, 2017) and they have financial burdens. As we hinted at earlier, we also suggest that the context of failure (of a project or a business) is ideal for extending theories of bricolage because it involves significant resource scarcity (because of failure's financial costs). Both theories may be further advanced if future research investigates how entrepreneurs who experience failure engage in bricolage to open up new career opportunities. Perhaps by cobbling together different career paths (or elements within those careers), the individual can combine and recombine various work-related aspects in ways that create a new career opportunity.

## THE SOCIAL IMPLICATIONS OF ENTREPRENEURIAL FAILURE

Although failure can have positive consequences for the individual (e.g., learning and personal growth [Cope, 2011; McGrath, 1999; Shepherd, 2003]), others often do not see entrepreneurial failure in such an optimistic light (D'Aveni, 1990; Semadeni, Cannella, Fraser, and Lee, 2008; Sutton & Callahan, 1987). As noted by March and Shapira (1987, p. 1413), "society values risk taking, but not gambling, and what is meant by gambling is risk taking that turns out badly." Oftentimes, the devastation of a business failure on others (e.g., former employees, suppliers, and other stakeholders) is highly salient and immediate, whereas the learning benefits (for the individual and the economy) are more diffuse and take time to develop.

Indeed, there are many reports of entrepreneurs of failed businesses being judged harshly by others. For example, historically, individuals who went bankrupt were subject to punishments that included "forfeiture of all property, relinquishment of spousal consortium, revocation of citizenship, surrendering children as slaves, prohibition from holding public office, imprisonment, and death"; they were required to "bang their buttocks on a rock before a heckling crowd," "wear distinguishing clothes in public," and were subject to other means of degradation and humiliation in public (Efrat, 2006, p. 366). Modern-day equivalents of others' responses to failed (or failing) entrepreneurs include rejection, avoidance, disengagement, and denigration (D'Aveni, 1990; Sutton & Callahan, 1987). These harsh judgments place considerable *blame* (Semadeni, Cannella, Fraser, & Lee, 2008; Sutton & Callahan, 1987) for the failure on the individual, and they suggest that the entrepreneur should be *punished* (Efrat, 2005; Lee et al., 2007) and feel *shame* (Probst & Raisch, 2005; Wiesenfeld, Wurthmann, & Hambrick, 2008). To a greater or lesser extent, these judgments on business failure are reflected in countries' bankruptcy laws (Lee et al., 2011; Lee, Peng, & Barney, 2007), and these judgments on project failure are reflected in an organization's culture (Cannon & Edmondson, 2001; Tucker & Edmondson, 2003). Such harsh judgments and the stress they generate can negatively impact the economic (Semadeni et al., 2008; Sutton & Callahan, 1987), psychological (Byrne & Shepherd, 2015; Shepherd, 2003), and physical (Cope, 2011; Whyley, 1998) well-being of the individual who experiences the failure. We believe that the current literature on this topic has only scratched the surface when it comes to exploring the social costs of business failure for entrepreneurs.

**Relationship ties after entrepreneurial failure.** While we have a strong understanding of relationship ties and the ways they affect entrepreneurial activity within (Kelley, Peters, & O'Connor, 2009; Stam & Elfring, 2008) and outside (Hoang & Antoncic, 2003; Jack, 2005) the organization, we know relatively little about how these ties change (if at all) after failure. Future research has the chance to add to the body of knowledge on this topic by investigating how entrepreneurs' formal (business) relationships change after inter-organizational relationships cease as a result of business failure and when intra-organizational relationships cease due to project failure. Does failure damage these relationships beyond repair, or can they be restored? If these relationship ties are salvageable, what are the mechanisms for rebuilding a relationship tie (or conserving it through the failure) as opposed to creating a new tie? Indeed, the question becomes whether the entrepreneur is better off investing his or her time in rebuilding relationships damaged by failure or creating new relationship ties (i.e., relationships without baggage). How much can entrepreneurs who have experienced failure rely on past relationships to help in the recovery process and/or to provide resources for later entrepreneurial activity? How do the entrepreneur's and others' attributions of the failure impact these relationship ties?

Perhaps external attributions of failure help reduce the number of lost ties, but internal attributions of failure strengthen existing ties. Although the benefits of weak ties are lauded in the literature for their role in the identification of a potential opportunity (Ardichvili, Cardozo, & Ray, 2003; Hoang & Antoncic, 2003), perhaps strong ties are more important in helping reduce the social costs of failure. It could be that strong ties represent surrogates that help repair weak ties damaged by failure or help in the creation of new weak ties necessitated by the loss of previous weak ties through failure. Not only are some ties likely to be damaged and lost as the result of failure, but it could be that some ties change in nature after failure. For example, a failure may serve to strengthen the entrepreneur's relationship with a weak tie (i.e., a weak tie changes to a strong tie) and weaken his or her relationship with a previously strong tie (i.e., a strong tie becomes a weak tie). There are numerous opportunities for future research to explore the termination, use, rebuilding, re-activation, and transformation of relationship ties after a failure.

**Entrepreneurial failure and social stigma.** While we understand how entrepreneurs tend to handle stigmatizing situations (Sutton & Callahan, 1987), we know less about when and why project and business failure represents a stigmatizing event. Beyond entrepreneurs' impression-management strategies, do particular forms of failure and/or types of entrepreneurs cause greater stigma? For instance, Shepherd and Patzelt (2015) found that entrepreneurs who are homosexual are likely to be stigmatized more from business failure than those who are heterosexual (in one region of Germany) and that those who are trying to preserve the environment are stigmatized less for business failure than those who were not trying to preserve the environment. Perhaps female entrepreneurs in supposed "masculine" industries (or masculine organizations or roles) face more stigmatization from failure compared to women in "feminine" industries (or organizations or roles) or men in "masculine" industries (or organizations or roles). That is, when individuals deviate from the norm and fail, they may face greater social costs compared to more "normal failures." If this is the case, however, there is a societal influence that deters the type of novelty that can be highly transformative. What is the impact of stigma for entrepreneurial failures? Perhaps a high stigma for entrepreneurial failure stops some individuals from engaging in entrepreneurial action (as a type of fear of failure), from engaging in certain types of entrepreneurial projects or businesses (i.e., those for which the stigma from failure is the greatest), from terminating a poorly performing project or business (delaying the social costs of failure but increasing the financial costs of failure when it arrives), and/or jumping ship from a failing business in the hope of avoiding stigma. Each alternative represents a host of considerations and implications.

**Entrepreneurial failure role models.** While we have some knowledge on how successful entrepreneurs are viewed and serve as role models (Bosma, Hessels, Schutjens, Van Praag, & Verheul, 2012; Krueger & Brazeal, 1994), we can still learn more about the social signals sent and received from entrepreneurs' business failures. For instance, on the one hand, parents who have entrepreneurial success often serve as role models for their children, not only showing them that entrepreneurship is an achievable and desirable career path but also encouraging their children's entrepreneurial goals and actions (Davidsson & Honig, 2003). On the other hand, how does a parent's business failure influence the "next generation" of potential entrepreneurs? Children who observe and experience (either directly or indirectly) the negative effects of business failure may decide to forgo entrepreneurial careers because they view business failure as a highly prominent possible outcome of entrepreneurial action. However, parents' ability to "bounce back" after failure and show resilience could decrease their children's fear of failure, thereby helping them form more positive beliefs about failure (for initial evidence, see Politis & Gabrielsson, 2009). Perhaps parents who had a business fail (or a mentor who had a project fail) serve as excellent role models for how to face failure, deal with it, recover, learn, and—ultimately—move forward. That is, maybe people can learn how to cope with and benefit from failure vicariously. If this is the case, increases in the saliency of entrepreneurial failure (perhaps through coping self-efficacy or some other mechanism) may make entrepreneurial action more—rather than less—likely.

**The role of social skills in dealing with entrepreneurial failure.** We believe it is valuable to explore the role social skills play in entrepreneurs' responses to failure, including social perception, expressiveness, impression management, and social adaptability. Baron and Tang (2009) highlighted a number of studies establishing the impact these skills have on important outcomes in numerous contexts, including entrepreneurial contexts.

Individuals with strong social skills are likely to be highly skilled at reducing the social costs of business failure (e.g., through shrewd storytelling and sensegiving to others regarding the failure and the role they played in that failure) as well as the associated psychological costs. Additionally, individuals with strong social skills often have wider and more diverse social networks (Diener & Seligman, 2002) with which they can connect to talk about a failure and receive support. Future research can investigate the role social skills play in how entrepreneurs manage the social and psychological costs (and, indirectly, the financial costs, as discussed above) of failure.

There is also an opportunity to gain a deeper understanding of the impact of failure through a fine-grained understanding of an entrepreneur's (corporate or independent) social skills. Which of the social skills—social perception, expressiveness, impression management, and social adaptability—influence which aspect of the failure-resilience/failure-recovery process and to what effect? For example, expressiveness may facilitate a loss orientation, and a loss orientation might help reduce the social costs of the failure as the individual is able to express his or her negative emotions over the failure. However, it appears that having a loss orientation for an extended period can exacerbate negative psychological reactions to the failure (see Shepherd et al., 2011). Therefore, it might not be that greater social skills necessarily lead to better outcomes—there could be tradeoffs, diminishing returns, and even negative returns at high levels. To the extent that there are tradeoffs between different outcomes of a particular social skill, can the downside of that particular social skill be overcome or offset by the activation of a different social skill? It is important to gain a deeper understanding of not only the different social skills and their differential effects on failure outcomes but also the ways these social skills can be combined to reduce the overall costs of failure. With this deeper understanding, we hope that scholars are in a better position to teach students and budding entrepreneurs (whether corporate or independent) the social skills that not only help them succeed with their projects and their businesses but also deal with the possibility (and even the probability) that their entrepreneurial endeavors (projects or businesses) will fail.

**Entrepreneurial failure and work-life balance.** While research has explored work-life balance among entrepreneurs (Shepherd & Haynie, 2009a, 2009b), we know little about how entrepreneurs continue to achieve work-life balance when the work aspect of this relationship has ended in failure. For instance, is an entrepreneur able to compartmentalize a failure into his or her work micro-identity, thus making the failure have minimal effect on other micro-identities (e.g., the "spouse" micro-identity), or does the failure lead to spillover effects? If some are able to compartmentalize the identity experiencing the failure, then it is important to gain an understanding of how the micro-identity experiencing failure is "insulated" from the individual's other micro-identities—that is, how is the "contagion" stopped from affecting other micro-identities and important others (e.g., family members). Although insulation may reduce the extent of failure's harm, perhaps engaging other micro-identities to confront the failure experience (rather than hide from it or insulate it) can provide better outcomes for the entrepreneur (or for some entrepreneurs some of the time). This line of research can be pursued, for example, by finding out whether divorce rates rise after major business or project failures and whether differences in this social cost can be explained by the ways entrepreneurs manage their micro-identities after experiencing failure. Future research addressing these topics will provide deeper insights into failure's social costs and will hopefully enable entrepreneurs to reduce such costs while maximizing the social benefits possible after failure.

## The Emotional Implications of Entrepreneurial Failure

When individuals experience the failure of a business or project that was important to them, they can have a negative emotional reaction—namely, grief (Shepherd, 2003; Shepherd & Cardon, 2009; Shepherd, Covin, et al., 2009; Shepherd et al., 2011). While grief can motivate individuals to seek information about a failure, which is required for learning (Cyert & March, 1963; Kiesler & Sproull, 1982), it often disrupts the attention allocation and information processing entrepreneurs need to learn from their failure experiences (consistent with Bower, 1992; Fredrickson, 2001). Based on previous research, we know that negative emotions can have adverse effects on cognitions. First, negative emotions "narrow individuals' momentary thought-action repertoire by calling forth specific action tendencies (e.g., attack, flee) ... [whereas] many positive emotions broaden individuals' momentary thought-action repertoires, prompting them to pursue a wider range of thoughts and actions than is typical" (Fredrickson & Branigan, 2005, p. 314). Thus, individuals who want to generate original innovations that result in future products should avoid negative emotions (Fredrickson, 1998). Second, research has shown that negative emotions have a harmful effect on individuals' commitment, including on entrepreneurs' motivation to start another venture after previous business failure (Shepherd, 2003) or on team members' desire to put forth personal resources to meet organizational objectives after project failure (Allen & Meyer, 1990; O'Reilly & Chatman, 1986; Shepherd et al., 2011). While being committed to an action can improve performance, this commitment needs to be balanced with learning from failure because learning from failure can also improve performance (McGrath, 1999). Finally, research has found that negative emotions "narrow people's attention, making them miss the forest for the trees" (Fredrickson, 2001, p. 222); disrupt creative and integrative thinking (Estrada, Isen, & Young, 1997; Fredrickson & Branigan, 2005; Isen, Daubman, & Nowicki, 1987); and, ultimately, inhibit learning (Fredrickson & Branigan, 2005; Masters, Barden, & Ford, 1979). As time passes (i.e., after the failure), these negative emotions tend to dissipate (Shepherd et al., 2011), thereby eliminating barriers to learning from failure.

However, it appears that these emotional obstacles to learning from failure can be reduced more quickly for some individuals (e.g., those with learned optimism [Cardon & McGrath, 1999] and self-compassion [Shepherd & Cardon, 2009]) and for those embedded within certain groups (e.g., the family [Shepherd, 2009]) and/or embedded in certain organizations (Shepherd, Covin, & Kuratko, 2009; Shepherd et al., 2011). Previous studies provide a solid foundation for understanding how and why negative emotional reactions are triggered after failure upon which we can build to explore a number of important research topics.

**The emotions that make up grief from entrepreneurial failure.** Previous studies have used the term grief when referring to any of the negative emotions caused by the loss of a business (Byrne & Shepherd, 2015; Shepherd, 2003, 2009) or project (Shepherd & Cardon, 2009; Shepherd, Covin et al., 2009, 2011), and current research has investigated how grief (used as an umbrella term) affects cognitive processes related to learning. However, research on emotions has shown that different forms of negative emotions have distinct sources as well as varying impacts on cognition (Bodenhausen, Sheppard, & Kramer, 1994; Keltner, Ellsworth, & Edwards, 1993). As such, do specific failures result in different psychological outcomes because they cause different forms of negative emotions that in turn affect cognitive processes in distinct ways? Some failures for some people are likely to generate feelings of shame, while other failures may cause feelings of guilt in other individuals. These are related but distinct negative emotions, both of which can contribute to the feeling of grief but can have different effects on cognition. Shame over a failure involves an evaluation of the self such that one feels that he or she is a "bad person," whereas guilt over a failure involves an evaluation of the behavior such that one feels that he or she has done a "bad thing" (Lewis, 1971; Niedenthal, Tangney, & Gavanski, 1994; Tangney, 1989, 1991, 1993). How do these differences between shame and guilt (as contributors to grief over the loss generated by failure) influence the cognitive process of learning from failure and the motivational process of trying again? Additionally, it is important to understand the processes for dealing with shame and distinguish them from the processes of dealing with guilt. Such an understanding of the distinct antecedents, roles, and effects of the different negative emotions that make up grief over failure will not only help explain the psychological implications of failure but will also have some normative implications—namely, we will learn how to facilitate the grief-recovery process to maximize and accelerate learning from the experience and to regain motivation and positive functioning.

Moreover, could a combination of particular negative emotions comprising the entrepreneur's grief (contingent and/or configuration) better explain the psychological costs stemming from failure compared to the impact of each of these emotions separately (main effects)? There is an opportunity to explore the different configurations of negative emotions that make up grief across individuals, failures, and/or situations. What is perhaps even more interesting is to investigate these configurations over time. For example, it could be that for a group of entrepreneurs, a particular negative emotion dominates immediately after the failure (e.g., anger) but then declines shortly after, whereas another negative emotion may have low salience early but comes to dominate later (e.g., guilt). It will be interesting to determine whether entrepreneurs feel a "sequence" of negative emotions; whether different individuals, failures, and/or situations have different sequences; and what psychological implications these different sequences have for the entrepreneurs whose projects or businesses failed.

**Building resources from entrepreneurial failure experiences.** Exploring the psychological costs of the negative emotions associated with business failure is a worthwhile and interesting endeavor, and there is still a great deal of work to be done in this area (see previous point). However, future research should also explore the positive psychological effects of grief after business failure. Research on grief has shown that for some individuals who experience grief after a loved one dies, going through the grieving process leads to personal growth (Hogan, Greenfield, & Schmidt, 2001). Researchers have the opportunity to gain a deeper understanding of this notion of personal growth over and above merely recovering from the experience (Cope, 2011; Shepherd, 2003; Shepherd et al., 2011), which in turn leads to several interesting questions. After business failure, do entrepreneurs realize they have emotional and cognitive resources they did not notice before, and/or does experiencing failure help them build such resources? For instance, handling failure may help entrepreneurs develop coping self-efficacy, emotional intelligence, and other sources of resilience. These resilience resources (and self-knowledge of them) are likely to impact subsequent entrepreneurial thinking in terms of, for example, the willingness to bear uncertainty, which in turn influences the formation of opportunity beliefs. That is, resilience resources can lead to a greater emotional investment in an entrepreneurial course of action given the belief in one's ability to effectively deal with negative emotional reactions if it were to fail. These resources can also result in less reliance on sunk costs and a decreased need to appear consistent, which will help reduce persistence with a poorly performing project or business given the individual's confidence in being able to deal with the consequence of failure.

**Positive emotions in the aftermath of entrepreneurial failure.** Exploring the role of positive emotions and self-regulation is also likely to lead to a deeper understanding of personal growth from business failure. Fredrickson (1998, 2003), for example, showed that positive emotions can counter the influence negative emotions have in limiting attention and information processing and can help develop resources that aid in coping with difficulty. Thus, do entrepreneurs with more dispositional optimism (e.g., see Hmieleski & Baron, 2009) and positive affect (e.g., see Baron, Tang, & Hmieleski, 2011) realize greater advantages from failure experiences (e.g., recover more rapidly, learn more successfully and experience more personal growth)? As opposed to depending on trait affect, maybe entrepreneurs proactively utilize positive emotions to cope with grief resulting from business failure. If they do, however, how are they able to generate such positive emotions after such a significant loss? Perhaps this is where emotional intelligence plays a particularly important role. That is, emotionally intelligent entrepreneurs are likely to be aware of their highly negative emotions from project or business failure, realize that the generation of positive emotions both "undoes" negative emotions and helps build resources (Fredrickson, 1998), and know how to trigger these positive emotions. It is the last of these actions that might be easier said than done—namely, generating positive emotions when one is "feeling blue" from a major failure can be a difficult task. How are some people able to trigger positive emotions after a failure or other form of major loss?

Therefore, understanding the techniques for stimulating positive emotions may be particularly helpful for entrepreneurs who frequently face failures and other major setbacks. Such techniques could include watching a comedy or telling oneself a joke. Alternatively, it may be less about the entrepreneur's possession of emotional intelligence him- or herself but more about having emotionally intelligent individuals in his or her network. For example, individuals who are able to generate positive emotions to remove the obstacles to learning from failure and moving on from the event might be those with friends who (1) recognize that their entrepreneur friend is experiencing negative emotions and has a need for positive emotions and (2) know how to generate those positive emotions in him or her. Again, gaining a deeper understanding of the "who" and the "how" of generating positive emotions in a loss situation is likely to be highly important in advancing our understanding of both the emotional costs and benefits of project and business failure. This stream of research may have an interesting implication for entrepreneurship education—teaching our students how to stimulate positive emotions even in the most adverse of situations.

**Multiple entrepreneurial failures.** While research has begun exploring the "hot cognitions" related to failure for entrepreneurs, there has been limited research exploring the implications of multiple failures (for exceptions, see Shepherd, Haynie, & Patzelt, 2012; Ucbasaran, Westhead, & Wright, 2009; Ucbasaran et al., 2010). For instance, are the psychological costs of a second failure different than those of a first failure, and if so, how? The entrepreneur could be more psychologically equipped to cope with a second failure due to his or her previous failure experience. Alternatively, the entrepreneur could still be dealing with unresolved issues from the first failure that make issues associated with the subsequent failure even worse—a form of accumulated grief (Shepherd et al., 2012). The trial-by-fire model (Swaminathan, 1996) may explain differences between those experiencing their first failure and those experiencing subsequent failure—at least in part. More specifically, among those who experience failure, only those who are "psychologically" strong (through self-selection or learning) will try again and thus suffer fewer psychological consequences from a second failure than those experiencing their first failure.

Also, consistent with the trial-by-fire model, individuals learn from their failures about how best to deal with failure (i.e., build resources and capabilities that promote resilience) and are thus able to more quickly recover, learn, and try again. However, we also know that continual exposure to difficult events can lead to a form of desensitization such that adverse stimuli no longer generate negative emotional reactions (Ashforth & Kreiner, 2002). Do entrepreneurs who have suffered many failures become desensitized to failure such that a failure no longer generates a negative emotional reaction? As authors, we have certainly had so many papers rejected that the "sting" of a rejection is no longer as painful as it once was. If we consider no emotional reaction to be cold cognition, how are the decision-making process and reactions as part of the entrepreneurial process different from a hotter form of cognition? It seems that too much "hot" is detrimental to cognitive performance (e.g., in terms of obstructing learning), but are there negative consequences from the cognition being too cold? May be there is an optimal amount of heat and/or maybe more heat is necessary for some cognitive tasks but less for other cognitive tasks. We believe there is ample opportunity to contribute further insights into the inter-relationship between multiple failure experiences and hot cognition in understanding the costs and benefits for entrepreneurs after failure.

## Multiple and Inter-Related Implications of Entrepreneurial Failure

**The inter-relationship between the financial and social implications of failure.** The more we study the social implications of entrepreneurial failure, the more insights we will gain into its financial implications. For instance, are there financial implications for entrepreneurs after business failure as a result of damage to their ventures or informal networks? The direct financial costs resulting from failure, such as the loss of wealth or remaining debt, may result in less hardship than the indirect financial costs stemming from a damaged reputation and loss of status, which may have a longer-lasting negative impact. If this is the case, initial attempts at recovery are likely to be more successful if they are aimed at maintaining one's network (or rapidly repairing it or developing a new one) as opposed to overcoming direct financial costs. By taking a closer look at the connection between the social and financial costs of business failure for entrepreneurs, we will begin to gain a deeper understanding of why some recovery strategies are more useful than others and perhaps how we can teach entrepreneurs (and budding entrepreneurs) how to "manage" failure to more quickly recover from its negative consequences. Alternatively, it could be the opposite sequence that facilitates recovery—that by recovering financially, the individual then has an easier time regaining and repairing his or her formal business network and creating a new network. We suspect that the process is more iterative and reciprocal—namely, as the entrepreneur starts to financially recover from the failure, his or her network relationships start to be repaired, which helps the entrepreneur recover financially, which helps with social recovery, and so on in the form of a virtuous spiral. The important research questions then become what factors start, perpetuate, and stop these virtual spirals, and are they the same factors that stop or slow a vicious spiral.

**The inter-relationship between the social and emotional/psychological implications of entrepreneurial failure.** Losing a business is often a very personal experience; however, some failures are more public. For instance, in project failure, employees are told the project is terminated, the team is disbanded, and people are redeployed to others projects. When it comes to business failure, the physical business is closed, employees vacate the factory or office, and customers and suppliers eventually find out about the business failure. The extent of the public nature of the failure (and its associated social costs) is likely to impact the entrepreneur's emotional reaction to the failure and its psychological costs. For example, when it comes to project failure, organizational culture can have an important influence on the "social evaluation" of those who fail (Cannon & Edmondson, 2001) and, in doing so, likely has a psychological impact on those who act entrepreneurially, particularly those who experience failure.

Although we expect that the public nature of a failure will increase its social costs, which will in turn exacerbate the psychological costs, perhaps a public failure leads to different social costs such that the psychological costs of a highly public failure are less than the psychological costs of hiding the failure from others (in an attempt to reduce the social costs). It could be that public failures generate unexpected social and psychological benefits, such as support groups being formed to help the entrepreneur deal with the failure that might have otherwise not been available if these others were not aware of the failure. Like for other hidden stigmas (Pachankis, 2007), anxiety and stress about keeping the failure hidden from the public is likely to generate negative psychological and perhaps physical consequences for the entrepreneur. In this way, in terms of failure and its public nature, maybe the entrepreneur is better off disclosing than hiding. Indeed, by disclosing the failure rather than having others find out about it on their own, the entrepreneur can use impression-management strategies to minimize the social (and perhaps also the financial) implications of the failure event (Sutton & Callahan, 1987).

**The inter-relationship between the emotional and cognitive implications of entrepreneurial failure.** Research on bereavement has shown that some losses are more likely than others to result in complicated grief—namely, elevated grief and grief over an extended period of time (Neimeyer, 2006). For instance, parents whose children commit suicide often have complicated grief, and their feelings of grief are frequently made worse by additional feelings of shame and embarrassment, thereby making it more challenging to "talk through their grief" with others (Mitchell, Mitchell, & Smith, 2004). As a result, others may find it more difficult to start discussions as they worry about saying the "wrong thing" (Nolen-Hoeksema & Davis, 1999). Shame and embarrassment are psychological costs caused by the expectation of others' judgments and lead those experiencing such feelings to avoid others and, as a consequence, to incur social costs, such as loneliness. Under what circumstances (i.e., characteristics of the entrepreneur and/or of the social context) can feelings of embarrassment and shame over failure be lessened or even eliminated? We know that grief is lower in environments where failure is normalized (Ashforth & Kreiner, 2002; Shepherd et al., 2011), but perhaps attempts to take emotion out of the entrepreneurial process undermine the emotional commitment necessary to form a strong team, persist through challenges, and make an entrepreneurial endeavor a success. Ironically, by avoiding the negative emotions of failure (by taking emotions out of the process), the entrepreneur may be making failure a more likely outcome for the focal project or business.

**The inter-relationship between the financial and psychological implications of entrepreneurial failure.** There is also an opportunity for future research to further investigate the relationship between the financial costs and the psychological costs of entrepreneurial failure. Do the psychological costs stemming from business failure have financial implications? The psychological costs of business failure may not only be a barrier to learning from failure but could also obstruct the entrepreneur of a failed business from moving on to generate a new income source (the delay of which makes the financial costs of business failure even worse). For example, if the entrepreneur ruminates over his or her business failure, it may inhibit him or her from interviewing for a new job or seeking out new venture opportunities. On the other hand, the psychological costs of the failure could be obvious to potential employers during the interview process (e.g., the person does not demonstrate adequate enthusiasm or self-belief to assure the prospective employer that he or she can successfully take on the new role), ultimately leading to the individual's failure in securing the position. Similarly, the psychological costs of failure may represent an obstacle to the team member of a failed project that prevents him or her from recommitting to the organization and enjoying the financial rewards of those efforts (e.g., promotion and bonus). That is, the psychological costs of project failure mean that the employee is less enthusiastic about subsequent roles and projects, is less committed to the organization, and has less positive interactions with management, all of which can have negative implications for his or her career within the organization.

In terms of individuals' recovery from the financial and psychological costs of entrepreneurial failure, does sequence matter? Perhaps an entrepreneur has to lessen the psychological costs of business failure before trying to recover from the financial costs (i.e., acquiring employment and pursuing his or her next entrepreneurial endeavor), or perhaps he or she needs to reduce the financial costs first, which will diminish one of the major stressors of business failure and thereby help reduce the psychological costs. Likewise, perhaps an employee needs to focus on overcoming the psychological costs of failure before focusing on the financial implications in terms of career progression. By extension, the organization may need to focus on the psychological costs of project failure for its employees first and then the sequence of roles that advance those employees' careers. Alternatively, by fully focusing on the next project as a way to advance one's career, the employee can reduce the financial implications of the loss and thus reduce the failure's psychological costs (there is some evidence of this approach by engineers [Shepherd, Patzelt, Williams, & Warnecke, 2014]). Because there are still so many unknowns regarding this topic, future research on the inter-relationship between the financial and psychological costs (perhaps even the spiral involving a reciprocal relationship between the two) of business failure can make important contributions to our understanding of the consequences of such failure.

**A multi-disciplinary and multi-level approach to understanding the implications of entrepreneurial failure.** Research investigating the inter-connections of the different types of business failure costs has substantial promise, and we believe that such research will likely necessitate multi-disciplinary and/or multi-level theorization and empirical testing. Exploring the inter-relationship between financial and social costs, for instance, may require researchers to build on (and ultimately contribute to) theories of both stigmatization and venture capital markets to provide deeper insights into why some entrepreneurs who have experienced business failure in certain regions are able to obtain the funds required to start a new entrepreneurial venture, whereas other entrepreneurs who have experienced business failure in other regions are unable to obtain such funds. Similarly, investigating the inter-relationship between financial and social costs may require building on (and ultimately making contributions to) theories of both management decision making and organizational culture to gain a deeper understanding of why employees who have experienced project failure in some organizations are celebrated and promoted, whereas employees who have experienced project failure in other organizations are ostracized and demoted. Due to the drastic change in the entrepreneur's social context (for a public failure) and the often extreme feelings accompanying loss after failure, research exploring both the social and psychological costs of failure is likely to make important extensions to current theories of social cognition.

## Sensemaking of Entrepreneurial Failure

Making sense of loss has been found to be critical to recovery efforts (Davis, Nolen-Hoeksema, & Larson, 1998; Park, 2010). A sensemaking perspective argues that learning from failure requires one to continuously develop plausible retrospective accounts that in turn shape current behavior (Weick, Sutcliffe, & Obstfeld, 2005). The changed beliefs that result then alter the actions the individual takes, thereby improving the likelihood of future project/business success. If the individual fails to develop and use increasingly more plausible accounts for the failure, anxiety may paralyze decision making and action (Lüscher & Lewis, 2008; Smircich & Morgan, 1982). The resulting lack of action will decrease the experimentation and social interactions required for successful learning (Balogun & Johnson, 2004; Maitlis, 2005). A few underlying assumptions of the sensemaking perspective are that constraints (e.g., those causing failure) are self-imposed and that the environment is not pre-decided nor is it beyond one's control, both of which are notions in line with the idea of an enacted environment (Daft & Weick, 1984; Gioia & Chittipeddi, 1991; Weick et al., 2005). Future research can add to this body of knowledge by exploring entrepreneurial failure using a sensemaking perspective.

**Sensemaking of entrepreneurial failure involves action.** Because plausibility plays an important role in explaining subsequent action (Weick et al., 2005), we need to better understand the way entrepreneurs create and/or generate plausible accounts of failure. These accounts—namely, the stories we tell ourselves and others—are plausible when the individual thinks they can be true (Epley & Gilovich, 2006), and they become increasingly more plausible as the individual's thoughts and actions to substantiate the proposed story provide satisfactory proof to alter beliefs about why the event at hand (e.g., failure) happened. It could be that entrepreneurs who take more actions are able to create/generate more plausible stories. Indeed, action is an important mechanism of sensemaking as the individual uses the feedback of his or her actions to enhance the plausibility of the enacted and emerging story. What are the initial actions that entrepreneurs take after failure that reflect the initial story of failure and also provide the greatest feedback to enhance the plausibility of that story (without necessarily exacerbating the problems and issues generated by the failure in the first place)? By studying the reciprocal relationship between activities and the development of a plausible story, we can begin to develop a behavioral micro-foundation of learning from failure.

**Individual differences in the sensemaking of entrepreneurial failure.** There are likely to be different individual variables that help explain the extent and/or the speed at which a story for failure becomes plausible and are used to initiate entrepreneurial action. Individuals who have the greatest prior knowledge of a particular domain or of the entrepreneurial process are likely to be those who are best able to combine an emerging story of failure with a subsequent opportunity belief to guide the next step in the entrepreneurial process. Does education or specific experience (e.g., industry-specific experience) play a role here? Perhaps those with greater education and/or experience are better able to think in the abstract to connect the dots of the failure to come up with a plausible story and/or are better able to communicate that story and interpret feedback to improve its plausibility. Furthermore, self-compassion (Neff, 2009; Shepherd & Cardon, 2009) likely helps entrepreneurs disengage ego-protective mechanisms that would otherwise restrict thinking and creativity that could obstruct the construction, revision, and further development of a plausible story. Additionally, analogical thinking facilitates creative thinking and the development of explanations by individuals in novel domains (Dahl & Moreau, 2002; Gick & Holyoak, 1983), including entrepreneurs thinking about potential opportunities (Grégoire, Barr, & Shepherd, 2010; Grégoire & Shepherd, 2012). Perhaps individuals skilled at analogical thinking are better able to connect the dots revealed through entrepreneurial failure to create a plausible story of the past to inform future actions. Similarly, mindfulness relates to a "heightened state of involvement and wakefulness or being in the present" that can be useful in "actively drawing novel distinctions" (Langer & Moldoveanu, 2000, p. 2; see also Brown & Ryan, 2003; Langer, 1989). Mindful individuals have an enhanced quality of attention, which is likely to facilitate sensemaking efforts (Weick & Sutcliffe, 2006). This form of mindfulness may be an important skill that some individuals have (and others can learn) to facilitate the process of failure sensemaking. Finally, it could be that individuals with greater metacognitive awareness—those who think about their thinking (Haynie, Shepherd, Mosakowski, & Earley, 2010; Haynie, Shepherd, & Patzelt, 2012)—are most likely to reflect on the current situation in light of their recent failure to develop a plausible story that informs and motivates entrepreneurial action. All of the above variables deserve additional attention, and we believe that taking a sensemaking perspective of failure is likely to push the theoretical boundaries of story construction after a negative event like failure.

**Sensemaking of entrepreneurial failure over time.** It is important to remember that plausible stories of a failure are temporary outcomes of the sensemaking process. Throughout this process, one plausible story of business failure is exchanged for another "more" plausible story. However, what remains uncertain is how this process unfolds and when it terminates. It could be that immediately after business failure, the entrepreneur creates stories rapidly and then quickly updates those stories as new information provides feedback to improve their plausibility. On the other hand, it could be that the story reaches saturation over time such that additional data provide little useful information. It could also be that sensemaking transforms from making sense of a failure to making sense of one's present situation, which would mean that making sense of the failure becomes less important. Thus, future research is needed to better explain the patterns of plausible stories of failure—specifically, researchers should elucidate the antecedents to and consequences of differences in entrepreneurs' "plausibility updating." That is, why are some quick to update the plausibility of a failure story and others slow to do so, and why do some stop updating when they do?

Not only is it interesting to think about the possible antecedents to the different patterns of failure sensemaking but also to investigate its outcomes. Obviously, one outcome is plausibility, but are there tradeoffs to achieving this plausibility—are financial, emotional, and social costs exacerbated by efforts to quickly develop plausibility? Similarly, perhaps some failure sensemaking patterns magnify the financial, emotional, and social costs of entrepreneurial failure, while other sensemaking patterns diminish them. Moreover, as we discussed above, what may diminish one cost of failure may work in concert with or against other costs of failure. For example, some efforts to enhance the plausibility of the entrepreneurial failure story may help reduce the mental anguish the entrepreneur has over the failure experience but at the same time increase the financial costs of the failure (e.g., because the reflection necessary for enhancing plausibility may take time away from new income-generating actions). There are many opportunities to explore the different patterns, contingencies, and other configurations that involve sensemaking and the implications of failure over time.

**The role of others in the sensemaking of entrepreneurial failure.** After crises, collective sensemaking can enable the development and redevelopment social structure—namely, the social roles and relationships in certain groups of actors (e.g., Weick, 1995). However, what happens when the organization (i.e., in the case of business failure) or the team (i.e., in the case of project failure) around which that social structure was built no longer exists? Do individuals (e.g., entrepreneurs and investors) merely undertake their own sensemaking and carry on, or is there another basis or forum for the collective sensemaking process? When entrepreneurial team members and/or employees take part in collective sensemaking, which aids in learning and recovery, is the likelihood of attribution bias (i.e., developing more plausible stories) reduced, or do these kinds of biases extend to the team? The answers to these questions likely reflect attributes of the team, such as team members' emotional capabilities (see Shepherd, 2009) and/or the cognitive diversity within the group (Kilduff, Angelmar, & Mehra, 2000).

Although team members of a project may feel isolated from others after project failure, which inhibits the opportunity for collective sensemaking, these feelings of isolation and lack of opportunities for collective sensemaking may be particularly pronounced for entrepreneurs of failed businesses. To what extent do members of the founding team come together after a business has failed to engage in collective sensemaking? What about solo entrepreneurs—with whom do they try to engage for the purpose of collective sensemaking? Perhaps these entrepreneurs can try to engage with former stakeholders of the failed business to facilitate failure sensemaking, but it may be a difficult task to engage with previous stakeholders (they have to be found, and the entrepreneur may feel guilty that he or she let them down). On the one hand, it could be that approaching these former stakeholders, despite facilitating sensemaking, may exacerbate the emotional costs of failure—namely, generate additional negative emotions by making others' painful experiences resulting from the business failure more salient. On the other hand, overcoming the anticipation of a negative stakeholder response, the entrepreneur might find it therapeutic to talk with the stakeholders and perhaps find that their response is not as negative as anticipated. Such engagement may also help the stakeholders deal with their negative emotional reaction to the failure. Indeed, helping stakeholders deal with the failure may improve the entrepreneur's own emotional state, and the enhanced sensemaking from engaging these knowledgeable individuals may enhance the plausibility of the failure story, thus helping to break emotional bonds to the lost object (Stroebe & Schut, 2001).

In Fig. 3.1, we offer a sketch of a model of the implications of failure as part of the entrepreneurial process. Entrepreneurial failure (i.e., failure of a project or business) has implications financially (personal and business), socially (e.g., stigma and relationship ties), emotionally (e.g., grief and positive emotions), and psychologically (in terms of the needs for competence, relatedness, and autonomy). The impact of entrepreneurial failure on these implications can be magnified or dampened depending on the culture in which the individual is embedded as well as the attributes of the individual (e.g., social skills, positive emotions, supportive others, and failure role models). The attributes of the individual are inter-related, and some are influenced by culture (and vice versa). The financial, social, emotional, and psychological implications independently and inter-dependently influence entrepreneurs' learning from failure, motivation to try again, and level of resilience resources and capabilities, which in turn influence subsequent entrepreneurial action. Learning, motivation, and resilience influence the culture and the attributes of the individual, and entrepreneurial action can influence individuals' positive emotions.

RESEARCHING ENTREPRENEURIAL FAILURES 89

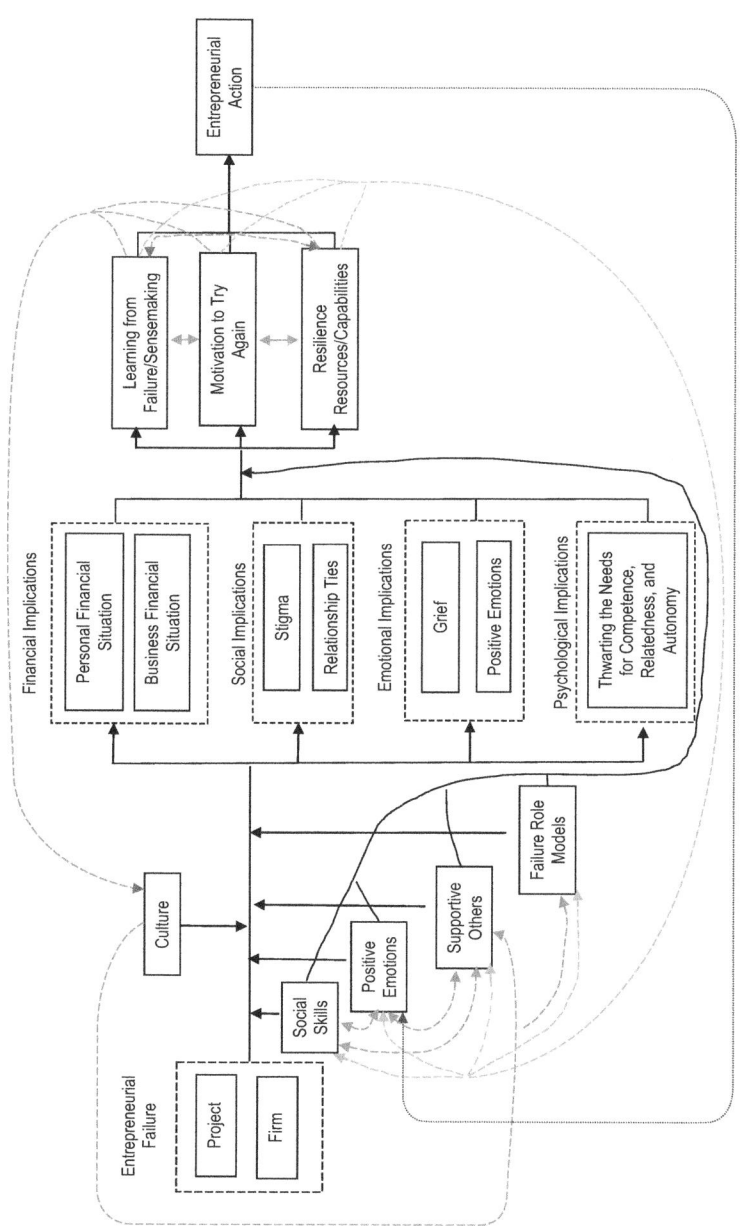

**Fig. 3.1** A sketch of a model of the implications of failure as part of the entrepreneurial process

## Discussion and Conclusion

With the recognition that "opportunity" is central to entrepreneurship and that opportunities are shrouded in uncertainty, a logical next step is to embrace the importance of understanding the implications of entrepreneurial failure. Entrepreneurial action and failure go hand in hand (given the high uncertainty), and we have only scratched the surface of this relationship. Whether exploring the actions of independent entrepreneurs in their newly founded (or emerging) organizations or those of corporate entrepreneurs in their innovative projects within established organizations, the nature of failure and its financial, social, emotional, and psychological implications likely have a critical impact on subsequent entrepreneurial action. However, despite its "criticality," we are just starting to gain an understanding of the complexity of the many interwoven relationships at play for these failure events.

Although it is important to continue to explore main-effect unidirectional causal relationships, it will also be important to progress to multiple contingent/configurational mutually causal relationships of the antecedents and consequences of failure as the basis for a more dynamic micro-foundation theory of entrepreneurial action. That is, scholars need to overcome their anti-failure bias (McGrath, 1999) to better understand the decision making, cognitions, emotions, relationships, and behaviors of those involved in the entrepreneurial process. We believe that such research will help reconcile a number of paradoxes. A paradox involves "contradictory yet inter-related elements that exist simultaneously and persist over time" (Smith & Lewis, 2011, p. 382). Being able to identify the underlying tension between two sets of relationships that seem to make sense when they are viewed individually but appear to be contradictory when viewed at the same time can lead to theorizing as an approach to resolving the paradox (Shepherd & Suddaby, 2017).

Specifically, we can work toward the following:

1. Reconciling the perspective of "fail often and quickly" (e.g., real options reasoning [McGrath, 1999; McGrath & Nerkar, 2004] and design thinking [Brown, 2008; Brown & Wyatt, 2015]) with the perspective that failure "hurts" for those who directly experience it (Byrne & Shepherd, 2015; Shepherd, 2003; Shepherd et al., 2011).
2. Reconciling the perspective that failure is a badge of honor (e.g., Landier, 2004) with the perspective that failure can stigmatize—put a denigrating stain or mark on—those involved with the failure

(Semadeni et al., 2008; Shepherd & Patzelt, 2015; Sutton & Callahan, 1987).
3. Reconciling strategies that try to avoid failure (e.g., risk-reduction strategies [Azadegan, Patel, & Parida, 2013; Shepherd, Douglas, & Shanley, 2000]) with strategies that make failure more likely and frequent (Brown, 2008; Brown & Wyatt, 2015; McGrath, 1999; McGrath & Nerkar, 2004).
4. Reconciling the financial benefits of terminating a poorly performing project (Bakker & Shepherd, 2017; McGrath & Keil, 2007) or firm (Ansic & Pugh, 1999) early with the prevalence of permanently failing projects (Hisrich & Cahill, 1995) and firms (Meyer & Zucker, 1989; van Witteloostuijn, 1998).
5. Reconciling the benefits of a strategy based on a big bet for a big win (Courtney, Kirkland, & Viguerie, 1997; Ireland & Miller, 2004) with the benefits of making numerous small probes and sequential investments with many small failures (Adner & Levinthal, 2004; Brown & Eisenhardt, 1997).
6. Reconciling taking emotions out of project and business failures (e.g., desensitization and normalization of failure [Ashforth & Kreiner, 2002]) with emotional investments that enhance project (Akgün, Keskin, Byrne, & Gunsel, 2011; Rank & Frese, 2008) and business performance (for a meta-analysis, see Meyer, Stanley, Herscovitch, & Topolnytsky, 2002).
7. Reconciling the negative emotions of failure that obstruct learning (Shepherd, 2003; Shepherd et al., 2011) with the negative emotions that capture attention and stimulate sensemaking (Nolen-Hoeksema, 1998; Schwarz, Bless, & Bohner, 1991).
8. Reconciling the opportunity lost as a result of the decision to terminate (Drummond, 2005; Roberts & Weitzman, 1981) with the opportunity cost of missed opportunities caused by delaying termination (Gimeno et al., 1997; Shepherd et al., 2014).
9. Reconciling the use of predetermined stage gates to rapidly terminate a potential opportunity that does not show promise (Cooper, 2008; Cooper & Kleinschmidt, 1993) with the premature termination of a potential opportunity that could otherwise have been changed and refined through learning and adapting the stage-gate criteria (McGrath & Keil, 2007; see also Chap. 4).

So many paradoxes, so many research opportunities, so exciting!

# References

Adner, R., & Levinthal, D. A. (2004). What is not a real option: Considering boundaries for the application of real options to business strategy. *Academy of Management Review, 29*(1), 74–85.

Akgün, A. E., Keskin, H., Byrne, J. C., & Gunsel, A. (2011). Antecedents and results of emotional capability in software development project teams. *Journal of Product Innovation Management, 28*(6), 957–973.

Allen, N. J., & Meyer, J. P. (1990). The measurement and antecedents of affective, continuance and normative commitment to the organization. *Journal of Occupational Psychology, 63*(1), 1–18.

Ansic, D., & Pugh, G. (1999). An experimental test of trade hysteresis: Market exit and entry decisions in the presence of sunk costs and exchange rate uncertainty. *Applied Economics, 31*(4), 427–436.

Ardichvili, A., Cardozo, R., & Ray, S. (2003). A theory of entrepreneurial opportunity identification and development. *Journal of Business Venturing, 18*(1), 105–123.

Arnold, J., & Cohen, L. (2008). The psychology of careers in industrial and organizational settings: A critical but appreciative analysis. In G. Hodgkinson & J. K. Ford (Eds.), *International review of industrial and organizational psychology* (Vol. 23, pp. 1–44). London: John Wiley & Sons Ltd.

Ashforth, B. E., & Kreiner, G. E. (2002). Normalizing emotion in organizations: Making the extraordinary seem ordinary. *Human Resource Management Review, 12*(2), 215–235.

Azadegan, A., Patel, P. C., & Parida, V. (2013). Operational slack and venture survival. *Production and Operations Management, 22*(1), 1–18.

Baker, T., & Nelson, R. E. (2005). Creating something from nothing: Resource construction through entrepreneurial bricolage. *Administrative Science Quarterly, 50*(3), 329–366.

Bakker, R. M., & Shepherd, D. A. (2017). Pull the plug or take the plunge: Multiple opportunities and the speed of venturing decisions in the Australian mining industry. *Academy of Management Journal*, amj-2013.

Balogun, J., & Johnson, G. (2004). Organizational restructuring and middle manager sensemaking. *Academy of Management Journal, 47*(4), 523–549.

Baron, R. A., & Tang, J. (2009). Entrepreneurs' social skills and new venture performance: Mediating mechanisms and cultural generality. *Journal of Management, 35*(2), 282–306.

Baron, R. A., Tang, J., & Hmieleski, K. M. (2011). The downside of being 'up': Entrepreneurs' dispositional affect and firm performance. *Strategic Entrepreneurship Journal, 5*(2), 101–119.

Bodenhausen, G. V., Sheppard, L. A., & Kramer, G. P. (1994). Negative affect and social judgment: The differential impact of anger and sadness. *European Journal of Social Psychology, 24*(1), 45–62.

Bosma, N., Hessels, J., Schutjens, V., Van Praag, M., & Verheul, I. (2012). Entrepreneurship and role models. *Journal of Economic Psychology, 33*(2), 410–424.

Boulding, W., Morgan, R., & Staelin, R. (1997). Pulling the plug to stop the new product drain. *Journal of Marketing Research, 34*(1), 164–176.

Bower, G. H. (1992). How might emotions affect learning. In S. Christianson (Ed.), *The handbook of emotion and memory: Research and theory* (pp. 3–31). New York: Psychology Press.

Bradley, S. W., Wiklund, J., & Shepherd, D. A. (2011). Swinging a double-edged sword: The effect of slack on entrepreneurial management and growth. *Journal of Business Venturing, 26*(5), 537–554.

Brown, T. (2008). Design thinking. *Harvard Business Review, 86*(6), 84–92.

Brown, S. L., & Eisenhardt, K. M. (1997). The art of continuous change: Linking complexity theory and time-paced evolution in relentlessly shifting organizations. *Administrative Science Quarterly, 42,* 1–34.

Brown, K. W., & Ryan, R. M. (2003). The benefits of being present: Mindfulness and its role in psychological well-being. *Journal of Personality and Social Psychology, 84*(4), 822–848.

Brown, T., & Wyatt, J. (2015). Design thinking for social innovation. *Annual Review of Policy Design, 3*(1), 1–10.

Brüderl, J., Preisendörfer, P., & Ziegler, R. (1992). Survival chances of newly founded business organizations. *American Sociological Review, 57*(2), 227–242.

Burgelman, R. A., & Välikangas, L. (2005). Managing internal corporate venturing cycles. *MIT Sloan Management Review, 46*(4), 26–34.

Byrne, O., & Shepherd, D. A. (2015). Different strokes for different folks: Entrepreneurial narratives of emotion, cognition, and making sense of business failure. *Entrepreneurship Theory and Practice, 39*(2), 375–405.

Campbell, A., Birkinshaw, J., Morrison, A., & van Basten Batenburg, R. (2003). The future of corporate venturing. *MIT Sloan Management Review, 45*(1), 30–38.

Cannon, M. D., & Edmondson, A. C. (2001). Confronting failure: Antecedents and consequences of shared beliefs about failure in organizational work groups. *Journal of Organizational Behavior, 22*(2), 161–177.

Cannon, M. D., & Edmondson, A. C. (2005). Failing to learn and learning to fail (intelligently): How great organizations put failure to work to innovate and improve. *Long Range Planning, 38*(3), 299–319.

Cardon, M., & McGrath, R. G. (1999). *When the going gets tough ... Toward a psychology of entrepreneurial failure and re-motivation.* Paper presented at the Frontiers of Entrepreneurship Research Conference. Babson College.

Chuang, Y. T., & Baum, J. A. (2003). It's all in the name: Failure-induced learning by multiunit chains. *Administrative Science Quarterly, 48*(1), 33–59.

Coelho, P. R. P., & McClure, J. E. (2005). Learning from failure. *Mid-American Journal of Business, 20*(1), 13–20.

Cooper, R. G. (2008). Perspective: The stage-gate® idea-to-launch process—Update, what's new, and nexgen systems. *Journal of Product Innovation Management, 25*(3), 213–232.

Cooper, R. G., & Kleinschmidt, E. J. (1993). Major new products: What distinguishes the winners in the chemical industry? *Journal of Product Innovation Management, 10*(2), 90–111.

Cope, J. (2011). Entrepreneurial learning from failure: An interpretative phenomenological analysis. *Journal of Business Venturing, 26*(6), 604–623.

Courtney, H., Kirkland, J., & Viguerie, P. (1997). Strategy under uncertainty. *Harvard Business Review, 75*(6), 67–79.

Cyert, R. M., & March, J. G. (1963). *A behavioral theory of the firm*. Englewood Cliffs, NJ: Prentice-Hall.

Daft, R. L., & Weick, K. E. (1984). Toward a model of organizations as interpretation systems. *Academy of Management Review, 9*(2), 284–295.

Dahl, D. W., & Moreau, P. (2002). The influence and value of analogical thinking during new product ideation. *Journal of Marketing Research, 39*(1), 47–60.

D'Aveni, R. A. (1990). Top managerial prestige and organizational bankruptcy. *Organization Science, 1*(2), 121–142.

Davidsson, P., & Honig, B. (2003). The role of social and human capital among nascent entrepreneurs. *Journal of Business Venturing, 18*(3), 301–331.

Davis, C. G., Nolen-Hoeksema, S., & Larson, J. (1998). Making sense of loss and benefiting from the experience: Two construals of meaning. *Journal of Personality and Social Psychology, 75*(2), 561–574.

Diener, E., & Seligman, M. E. P. (2002). Very happy people. *Psychological Science, 13*(1), 81–84.

Drummond, H. (2005). What we never have, we never miss? Decision error and the risks of premature termination. *Journal of Information Technology, 20*(3), 170–176.

Dumas, B. (1992). Dynamic equilibrium and the real exchange rate in a spatially separated world. *Review of Financial Studies, 5*(2), 153–180.

Efrat, R. (2005). Bankruptcy stigma: Plausible causes for shifting norms. *Emory Bankruptcy Development Journal, 22*, 481–520.

Efrat, R. (2006). The evolution of bankruptcy stigma. *Theoretical Inquiries in Law, 7*(2), 365–393.

Epley, N., & Gilovich, T. (2006). The anchoring-and-adjustment heuristic: Why the adjustments are insufficient. *Psychological Science, 17*(4), 311–318.

Estrada, C. A., Isen, A. M., & Young, M. J. (1997). Positive affect facilitates integration of information and decreases anchoring in reasoning among physicians. *Organizational Behavior and Human Decision Processes, 72*(1), 117–135.

Farson, R., & Keyes, R. (2006). The failure-tolerant leader. In D. Mayle (Ed.), *Managing innovation and change* (pp. 249–257). Thousand Oaks, CA: Sage.

Fredrickson, B. L. (1998). What good are positive emotions? *Review of General Psychology, 2*(3), 300–319.

Fredrickson, B. L. (2001). The role of positive emotions in positive psychology: The broaden-and-build theory of positive emotions. *American Psychologist, 56*(3), 218–226.

Fredrickson, B. L. (2003). Positive emotions and upward spirals in organizations. In K. S. Cameron, J. E. Dutton, & R. E. Quinn (Eds.), *Positive organizational scholarship: Foundations of a new scholarship* (pp. 163–175). San Francisco: Berrett-Kohler.

Fredrickson, B. L., & Branigan, C. (2005). Positive emotions broaden the scope of attention and thought-action repertoires. *Cognition & Emotion, 19*(3), 313–332.

George, G. (2005). Slack resources and the performance of privately held firms. *Academy of Management Journal, 48*(4), 661–676.

Gick, M. L., & Holyoak, K. J. (1983). Schema induction and analogical transfer. *Cognitive Psychology, 15*(1), 1–38.

Gilbert, B. A., McDougall, P. P., & Audretsch, D. B. (2006). New venture growth: A review and extension. *Journal of Management, 32*(6), 926–950.

Gimeno, J., Folta, T. B., Cooper, A. C., & Woo, C. Y. (1997). Survival of the fittest? Entrepreneurial human capital and the persistence of underperforming firms. *Administrative Science Quarterly, 42*, 750–783.

Ginsberg, A. (1988). Measuring and modelling changes in strategy: Theoretical foundations and empirical directions. *Strategic Management Journal, 9*(6), 559–575.

Gioia, D. A., & Chittipeddi, K. (1991). Sensemaking and sensegiving in strategic change initiation. *Strategic Management Journal, 12*(6), 433–448.

Green, S. G., Welsh, M. A., & Dehler, G. E. (2003). Advocacy, performance, and threshold influences on decisions to terminate new product development. *Academy of Management Journal, 46*(4), 419–434.

Grégoire, D. A., Barr, P. S., & Shepherd, D. A. (2010). Cognitive processes of opportunity recognition: The role of structural alignment. *Organization Science, 21*(2), 413–431.

Grégoire, D. A., & Shepherd, D. A. (2012). Technology-market combinations and the identification of entrepreneurial opportunities: An investigation of the opportunity-individual nexus. *Academy of Management Journal, 55*(4), 753–785.

Hayek, F. A. (1945). The use of knowledge in society. *The American Economic Review*, 519–530.

Haynie, J. M., & Shepherd, D. (2011). Toward a theory of discontinuous career transition: Investigating career transitions necessitated by traumatic life events. *Journal of Applied Psychology, 96*(3), 501–524.

Haynie, J. M., Shepherd, D. A., Mosakowski, E., & Earley, P. C. (2010). A situated metacognitive model of the entrepreneurial mindset. *Journal of Business Venturing, 25*(2), 217–229.

Haynie, J. M., Shepherd, D. A., & Patzelt, H. (2012). Cognitive adaptability and an entrepreneurial task: The role of metacognitive ability and feedback. *Entrepreneurship Theory and Practice, 36*(2), 237–265.

Heck, R. K., & Trent, E. S. (1999). The prevalence of family business from a household sample. *Family Business Review, 12*(3), 209–219.

Hisrich, R. D., & Cahill, D. J. (1995). Buried at the crossroads at midnight with an oak stake through its heart: An entrepreneurial replication of Ross and Staw's extended temporal escalation model. *Family Business Review, 8*(1), 41–54.

Hoang, H., & Antoncic, B. (2003). Network-based research in entrepreneurship: A critical review. *Journal of Business Venturing, 18*(2), 165–187.

Hoang, H., & Rothaermel, F. T. (2005). The effect of general and partner-specific alliance experience on joint R&D project performance. *Academy of Management Journal, 48*(2), 332–345.

Hobfoll, S. E. (2001). The influence of culture, community, and the nested-self in the stress process: Advancing conservation of resources theory. *Applied Psychology, 50*(3), 337–421.

Hobfoll, S. E., & Lilly, R. S. (1993). Resource conservation as a strategy for community psychology. *Journal of Community Psychology, 21*(2), 128–148.

Hoetker, G., & Agarwal, R. (2007). Death hurts, but it isn't fatal: The postexit diffusion of knowledge created by innovative companies. *Academy of Management Journal, 50*(2), 446–467.

Hogan, N. S., Greenfield, D. B., & Schmidt, L. A. (2001). Development and validation of the Hogan Grief Reaction Checklist. *Death Studies, 25*(1), 1–32.

Hmieleski, K. M., & Baron, R. A. (2009). Entrepreneurs' optimism and new venture performance: A social cognitive perspective. *Academy of Management Journal, 52*(3), 473–488.

Ireland, R. D., & Miller, C. C. (2004). Decision-making and firm success. *The Academy of Management Executive, 18*(4), 8–12.

Isen, A. M., Daubman, K. A., & Nowicki, G. P. (1987). Positive affect facilitates creative problem solving. *Journal of Personality and Social Psychology, 52*(6), 1122–1131.

Jack, S. L. (2005). The role, use and activation of strong and weak network ties: A qualitative analysis. *Journal of Management Studies, 42*(6), 1233–1253.

Kahneman, D., & Tversky, A. (1979). Prospect theory: An analysis of decision under risk. *Econometrica: Journal of the Econometric Society, 47*(2), 263–291.

Kelley, D. J., Peters, L., & O'Connor, G. C. (2009). Intra-organizational networking for innovation-based corporate entrepreneurship. *Journal of Business Venturing, 24*(3), 221–235.

Keltner, D., Ellsworth, P. C., & Edwards, K. (1993). Beyond simple pessimism: Effects of sadness and anger on social perception. *Journal of Personality and Social Psychology, 64*(5), 740–752.

Kets de Vries, M. F. (1993). The dynamics of family controlled firms: The good and the bad news. *Organizational Dynamics, 21*(3), 59–71.

Kiesler, S., & Sproull, L. (1982). Managerial response to changing environments: Perspectives on problem sensing from social cognition. *Administrative Science Quarterly, 27*(4), 548–570.

Kilduff, M., Angelmar, R., & Mehra, A. (2000). Top management team diversity and firm performance: Examining the role of cognitions. *Organization Science, 11*(1), 21–34.

Knight, J. (1992). *Institutions and social conflict.* Cambridge: Cambridge University Press.

Knott, A. M., & Posen, H. E. (2005). Is failure good? *Strategic Management Journal, 26*(7), 617–641.

Krueger, N. F., & Brazeal, D. V. (1994). Entrepreneurial potential and potential entrepreneurs. *Entrepreneurship Theory and Practice, 18*, 91–91.

Landier, A. (2004). *Entrepreneurship and the stigma of failure.* Paper presented at the MIT Finance, Development and Macro Workshops.

Langer, E. J. (1989). *Mindfulness.* Reading, MA: Addison-Wesley/Addison Wesley Longman.

Langer, E. J., & Moldoveanu, M. (2000). The construct of mindfulness. *Journal of Social Issues, 56*(1), 1–9.

Lee, S. H., Peng, M. W., & Barney, J. B. (2007). Bankruptcy law and entrepreneurship development: A real options perspective. *Academy of Management Review, 32*(1), 257–272.

Lee, S. H., Yamakawa, Y., Peng, M. W., & Barney, J. B. (2011). How do bankruptcy laws affect entrepreneurship development around the world? *Journal of Business Venturing, 26*(5), 505–520.

Lewis, H. B. (1971). Shame and guilt in neurosis. *Psychoanalytic Review, 58*(3), 419–438.

Lüscher, L. S., & Lewis, M. W. (2008). Organizational change and managerial sensemaking: Working through paradox. *Academy of Management Journal, 51*(2), 221–240.

Maidique, M. A., & Zirger, B. J. (1985). The new product learning cycle. *Research Policy, 14*(6), 299–313.

Maitlis, S. (2005). The social processes of organizational sensemaking. *Academy of Management Journal, 48*(1), 21–49.

March, J. G., & Shapira, Z. (1987). Managerial perspectives on risk and risk taking. *Management Science, 33*(11), 1404–1418.

Mason, C. M., & Harrison, R. T. (2006). After the exit: Acquisitions, entrepreneurial recycling and regional economic development. *Regional Studies, 40*(1), 55–73.

Masters, J. C., Barden, R. C., & Ford, M. E. (1979). Affective states, expressive behavior, and learning in children. *Journal of Personality and Social Psychology, 37*(3), 380–390.

McGrath, R. G. (1995). Advantage from adversity: Learning from disappointment in internal corporate ventures. *Journal of Business Venturing, 10*(2), 121–142.

McGrath, R. G. (1999). Falling forward: Real options reasoning and entrepreneurial failure. *Academy of Management Review, 24*(1), 13–30.

McGrath, R. G. (2001). Exploratory learning, innovative capacity, and managerial oversight. *Academy of Management Journal, 44*(1), 118–131.

McGrath, R. G., & Keil, T. (2007). The value captor's process: Getting the most out of your new business ventures. *Harvard Business Review, 85*(5), 128–136.

McGrath, R. G., & Nerkar, A. (2004). Real options reasoning and a new look at the R&D investment strategies of pharmaceutical firms. *Strategic Management Journal, 25*(1), 1–21.

McGrath, R. G., Tsai, M. H., Venkataraman, S., & MacMillan, I. C. (1996). Innovation, competitive advantage and rent: A model and test. *Management Science, 42*(3), 389–403.

McMullen, J. S., & Shepherd, D. A. (2006). Entrepreneurial action and the role of uncertainty in the theory of the entrepreneur. *Academy of Management Review, 31*(1), 132–152.

Meyer, J. P., Stanley, D. J., Herscovitch, L., & Topolnytsky, L. (2002). Affective, continuance, and normative commitment to the organization: A meta-analysis of antecedents, correlates, and consequences. *Journal of Vocational Behavior, 61*(1), 20–52.

Meyer, M. W., & Zucker, L. G. (1989). *Permanently failing organizations*. Thousand Oaks, CA: Sage Publications, Inc.

Mitchell, R., Mitchell, J., & Smith, J. (2004). Failing to succeed: New venture failure as a moderator of startup experience and startup expertise. In W. D. Bygrave (Ed.), *Frontiers of entrepreneurship research*. Wesley, MA: Babson College.

Morrison, E. W. (2002). Newcomers' relationships: The role of social network ties during socialization. *Academy of Management Journal, 45*(6), 1149–1160.

Neff, K. D. (2009). The role of self-compassion in development: A healthier way to relate to oneself. *Human Development, 52*(4), 211–214.

Neimeyer, R. A. (2006). Complicated grief and the reconstruction of meaning: Conceptual and empirical contributions to a cognitive-constructivist model. *Clinical Psychology: Science and Practice, 13*(2), 141–145.

Niedenthal, P. M., Tangney, J. P., & Gavanski, I. (1994). "If only I weren't" versus "If only I hadn't": Distinguishing shame and guilt in conterfactual thinking. *Journal of Personality and Social Psychology, 67*(4), 585–595.

Nolen-Hoeksema, S. (1998). The other end of the continuum: The costs of rumination. *Psychological Inquiry, 9*(3), 216–219.

Nolen-Hoeksema, S., & Davis, C. G. (1999). "Thanks for sharing that": Ruminators and their social support networks. *Journal of Personality and Social Psychology, 77*(4), 801–814.

Ocasio, W. (1997). Towards an attention-based view of the firm. *Strategic Management Journal, 18*(Special), 187–206.

O'Reilly, C. A., & Chatman, J. (1986). Organizational commitment and psychological attachment: The effects of compliance, identification, and internalization on prosocial behavior. *Journal of Applied Psychology, 71*(3), 492–499.

Pachankis, J. E. (2007). The psychological implications of concealing a stigma: A cognitive-affective-behavioral model. *Psychological Bulletin, 133*(2), 328–345.

Park, C. L. (2010). Making sense of the meaning literature: An integrative review of meaning making and its effects on adjustment to stressful life events. *Psychological Bulletin, 136*(2), 257–301.

Peng, M. W., & Shenkar, O. (2002). Joint venture dissolution as corporate divorce. *Academy of Management Executive, 16*(2), 92–105.

Petroski, H. (1985). *To engineer is human: The role of failure in successful design.* New York: St. Martin's Press.

Politis, D., & Gabrielsson, J. (2009). Entrepreneurs' attitudes towards failure. *International Journal of Entrepreneurial Behaviour & Research, 15*(4), 364–383.

Popper, K. R. (1959). *The logic of scientific discovery.* London: Hutchinson.

Probst, G., & Raisch, S. (2005). Organizational crisis: The logic of failure. *The Academy of Management Executive, 19*(1), 90–105.

Rank, J., & Frese, M. (2008). The impact of emotions, moods and other affect-related variables on creativity, innovation and initiative. In N. Ashkanasy & C. Copper (Eds.), *Research companion to emotion in organizations.* Cheltenham: Edward Elgar.

Roberts, K., & Weitzman, M. L. (1981). Funding criteria for research, development, and exploration projects. *Econometrica, 49*(5), 1261–1288.

Savickas, M. L. (2002). Career construction: A developmental theory of vocational behavior. In D. Brown Associates (Ed.), *Career choice and development (4th edition)* (pp. 149–205). San Francisco, CA: Jossey-Bass.

Schwarz, N., Bless, H., & Bohner, G. (1991). Mood and persuasion: Affective states influence the processing of persuasive communications. *Advances in Experimental Social Psychology, 24*, 161–199.

Semadeni, M., Cannella Jr., A. A., Fraser, D. R., & Lee, D. S. (2008). Fight or flight: Managing stigma in executive careers. *Strategic Management Journal, 29*(5), 557–567.

Shane, S. (2009). Why encouraging more people to become entrepreneurs is bad public policy. *Small Business Economics, 33*(2), 141–149.

Shepherd, D. A. (2003). Learning from business failure: Propositions of grief recovery for the self-employed. *Academy of Management Review, 28*(2), 318–328.

Shepherd, D. A. (2009). Grief recovery from the loss of a family business: A multi- and meso-level theory. *Journal of Business Venturing, 24*(1), 81–97.

Shepherd, D. A., & Cardon, M. S. (2009). Negative emotional reactions to project failure and the self-compassion to learn from the experience. *Journal of Management Studies, 46*(6), 923–949.

Shepherd, D. A., Covin, J. G., & Kuratko, D. F. (2009). Project failure from corporate entrepreneurship: Managing the grief process. *Journal of Business Venturing, 24*(6), 588–600.

Shepherd, D. A., Douglas, E. J., & Shanley, M. (2000). New venture survival: Ignorance, external shocks, and risk reduction strategies. *Journal of Business Venturing, 15*(5), 393–410.

Shepherd, D. A., & Haynie, J. M. (2009a). Birds of a feather don't always flock together: Identity management in entrepreneurship. *Journal of Business Venturing, 24*(4), 316–337.

Shepherd, D. A., & Haynie, J. M. (2009b). Family business, identity conflict, and an expedited entrepreneurial process: A process of resolving identity conflict. *Entrepreneurship Theory and Practice, 33*(6), 1245–1264.

Shepherd, D. A., & Haynie, J. M. (2011). Venture failure, stigma, and impression management: A self-verification, self-determination view. *Strategic Entrepreneurship Journal, 5*(2), 178–197.

Shepherd, D. A., Haynie, J. M., & Patzelt, H. (2012). Project failures arising from corporate entrepreneurship: Impact of multiple project failures on employees' accumulated emotions, learning, and motivation. *Journal of Product Innovation Management, 30*(5), 880–895.

Shepherd, D. A., McMullen, J. S., & Ocasio, W. (2017). Is that an opportunity? An attention model of top managers' opportunity beliefs for strategic action. *Strategic Management Journal*.

Shepherd, D. A., & Patzelt, H. (2015). Harsh evaluations of entrepreneurs who fail: The role of sexual orientation, use of environmentally friendly technologies, and observers' perspective taking. *Journal of Management Studies, 52*(2), 253–284.

Shepherd, D. A., Patzelt, H., Williams, T. A., & Warnecke, D. (2014). How does project termination impact project team members? Rapid termination, 'creeping death', and learning from failure. *Journal of Management Studies, 51*(4), 513–546.

Shepherd, D. A., Patzelt, H., & Wolfe, M. (2011). Moving forward from project failure: Negative emotions, affective commitment, and learning from the experience. *Academy of Management Journal, 54*(6), 1229–1259.

Shepherd, D. A., Wiklund, J., & Haynie, J. M. (2009). Moving forward: Balancing the financial and emotional costs of business failure. *Journal of Business Venturing, 24*(2), 134–148.

Shepherd, D. A., & Williams, T. (2017). Hitting rock bottom after job loss: Bouncing back to create a new positive work identity. *Academy of Management Review*. Forthcoming.

Shepherd, D. A., & Suddaby, R. (2017). Theory building: A review and integration. *Journal of Management.* doi:10.1177/0149206316647102.
Singh, S., Corner, P., & Pavlovich, K. (2007). Coping with entrepreneurial failure. *Journal of Management & Organization, 13*(4), 331–344.
Sitkin, S. B. (1992). Learning through failure: The strategy of small losses. *Research in Organizational Behavior, 14,* 231–266.
Smircich, L., & Morgan, G. (1982). Leadership: The management of meaning. *Journal of Applied Behavioral Science, 18*(3), 257–273.
Smith, W. K., & Lewis, M. W. (2011). Toward a theory of paradox: A dynamic equilibrium model of organizing. *Academy of Management Review, 36*(2), 381–403.
Spreitzer, G., Sutcliffe, K., Dutton, J., Sonenshein, S., & Grant, A. M. (2005). A socially embedded model of thriving at work. *Organization Science, 16*(5), 537–549.
Stam, W., & Elfring, T. (2008). Entrepreneurial orientation and new venture performance: The moderating role of intra-and extraindustry social capital. *Academy of Management Journal, 51*(1), 97–111.
Stroebe, M. S., & Schut, H. (2001). Meaning making in the dual process model of coping with bereavement. In R. A. Neimeyer (Ed.), *Meaning reconstruction & the experience of loss* (pp. 55–73). Washington, DC: American Psychological Association.
Sutton, R. I., & Callahan, A. L. (1987). The stigma of bankruptcy: Spoiled organizational image and its management. *Academy of Management Journal, 30*(3), 405–436.
Swaminathan, A. (1996). Environmental conditions at founding and organizational mortality: A trial-by-fire model. *The Academy of Management Journal, 39*(5), 1350–1377.
Tangney, J. P. (1989). *The test of self-conscious affect.* Fairfax, VA: George Mason University Press.
Tangney, J. P. (1991). Moral affect: The good, the bad, and the ugly. *Journal of Personality and Social Psychology, 61*(4), 598–607.
Tangney, J. P. (1993). Shame and guilt. In C. G. Costello (Ed.), *Symptoms of depression* (pp. 161–180). Oxford: John Wiley & Sons.
Tucker, A. L., & Edmondson, A. C. (2003). Why hospitals don't learn from failures: Organizational and psychological dynamics that inhibit system change. *California Management Review, 45*(2), 55–72.
Ucbasaran, D., Shepherd, D. A., Lockett, A., & Lyon, S. J. (2013). Life after business failure: The process and consequences of business failure for entrepreneurs. *Journal of Management, 39*(1), 163–202.
Ucbasaran, D., Westhead, P., & Wright, M. (2009). The extent and nature of opportunity identification by experienced entrepreneurs. *Journal of Business Venturing, 24*(2), 99–115.

Ucbasaran, D., Westhead, P., Wright, M., & Flores, M. (2010). The nature of entrepreneurial experience, business failure and comparative optimism. *Journal of Business Venturing, 25*(6), 541–555.

Van Witteloostuijn, A. (1998). Bridging behavioral and economic theories of decline: Organizational inertia, strategic competition, and chronic failure. *Management Science, 44*(4), 501–519.

Weick, K. E. (1990). The vulnerable system: An analysis of the Tenerife air disaster. *Journal of Management, 16*(3), 571–593.

Weick, K. E. (1995). *Sensemaking in organizations*. Thousand Oaks, CA: Sage.

Weick, K. E., & Sutcliffe, K. M. (2006). Mindfulness and the quality of organizational attention. *Organization Science, 17*(4), 514–524.

Weick, K. E., Sutcliffe, K. M., & Obstfeld, D. (2005). Organizing and the process of sensemaking. *Organization Science, 16*(4), 409–421.

Whyley, C. (1998). *Risky business: The personal and financial costs of small business failure*. London: Policy Studies Institute.

Wiesenfeld, B. M., Wurthmann, K. A., & Hambrick, D. C. (2008). The stigmatization and devaluation of elites associated with corporate failures: A process model. *Academy of Management Review, 33*(1), 231–251.

Wiklund, J., Baker, T., & Shepherd, D. A. (2010). The age-effect of financial indicators as buffers against the liability of newness. *Journal of Business Venturing, 25*(4), 423–437.

Williams, T. A., & Shepherd, D. A. (2016). Victim entrepreneurs doing well by doing good: Venture creation and well-being in the aftermath of a resource shock. *Journal of Business Venturing, 31*(4), 365–387.

Zahra, S. A., Jennings, D. F., & Kuratko, D. F. (1999). The antecedents and consequences of firm-level entrepreneurship: The state of the field. *Entrepreneurship: Theory and Practice, 24*(2), 45–45.

**Open Access** This chapter is distributed under the terms of the Creative Commons Attribution 4.0 International License (http://creativecommons.org/licenses/by/4.0/), which permits use, duplication, adaptation, distribution and reproduction in any medium or format, as long as you give appropriate credit to the original author(s) and the source, provide a link to the Creative Commons license and indicate if changes were made.

The images or other third party material in this chapter are included in the work's Creative Commons license, unless indicated otherwise in the credit line; if such material is not included in the work's Creative Commons license and the respective action is not permitted by statutory regulation, users will need to obtain permission from the license holder to duplicate, adapt or reproduce the material.

CHAPTER 4

# Researching at the Intersection of Innovation, Operations Management, and Entrepreneurship

## Introduction

Although innovation is a critical component of entrepreneurship (e.g., innovation is a dimension of firms' entrepreneurial orientation [Covin & Slevin, 1989]), it seems that the fields of innovation and entrepreneurship run in parallel, with little interaction occurring between the two. While it is unfortunate there has not been more interaction, cross-fertilization, and the co-production of knowledge, the current situation represents a research opportunity—a research opportunity that we begin to explore in this chapter. Innovation refers to the creation of a new product, process, or service that an organization has created for the market; it represents the commercialization of an invention, where invention is an "act of insight" (Li & Atuahene-Gima, 2001, p. 1124). Innovation has been found to lead to enhanced performance in new ventures (Capon, Farley, & Hoenig, 1990; Li & Atuahene-Gima, 2001), superior firm performance (Hull & Rothenberg, 2008; Thornhill, 2006), and dynamic firm capabilities (Eisenhardt & Martin, 2000; Teece, Pisano, & Shuen, 1997). Not surprisingly, innovation scholars have been interested in understanding what makes some firms more innovative than others. Indeed, the innovation literature has produced a long list of antecedents (for a meta-analysis,

---

The link to operations management in this chapter is largely based on Shepherd and Patzelt (2013).

see Damanpour, 1991) including inter-firm cooperation (Shan, Walker, & Kogut, 1994), network position (Tsai, 2001), market orientation (Atuahene-Gima, 1996), and industry structure (Teece, 1996). The corporate entrepreneurship literature has also found that innovation outcomes are associated with growth (Burgelman, 1984), higher profitability (Zahra & Covin, 1995), and competitive advantage (Covin & Miles, 1999). (We note this latter point to reinforce our earlier point that while innovation and corporate entrepreneurship cover much of the same ground, one makes little reference to the other and vice versa [for an exception, see Morris, Kuratko, & Covin, 2010].)

To explore the possibilities at the intersection of innovation and entrepreneurship, we focus on two cornerstones of the innovation literature and start to blend them with those in the entrepreneurship literature to advance our understanding of entrepreneurship (and hopefully also begin to make important contributions to the body of knowledge on innovation). Those cornerstones involve absorptive capacity (ACAP) as a source of potential innovations and stage gates as a process of evaluating potential innovations. In this chapter, we also draw on the field of operations to explain how the entrepreneurial process can be managed more effectively. Therefore, we hope that this chapter generates contributions in the following ways.

First, ACAP is central to capturing and using external information to generate innovations (Cohen & Levinthal, 1990; Zahra & George, 2002). Although ACAP applies to both the individual and organizational levels of analysis (Cohen & Levinthal, 1990), innovation scholars have focused almost exclusively at the firm level of analysis. In this chapter, we explore ACAP at the individual level within the entrepreneurial process to generate ideas for future contributions to knowledge. Specifically, we are interested in the role different dimensions of ACAP play in the identification and exploitation of potential opportunities and the ways the identification and exploitation of potential opportunities can influence ACAP.

Second, although innovation outcomes are often classified as incremental or radical (Dewar & Dutton, 1986; Ettlie, Bridges, & O'keefe, 1984) and perhaps also architectural (Galunic & Eisenhardt, 2001; Henderson & Clark, 1990), with radical innovations representing risky investments, entrepreneurship research focuses on the high uncertainty surrounding potential opportunities (Knight, 1921; McMullen & Shepherd, 2006). In this chapter, we investigate the stage-gate process for evaluating innovations in terms of potential opportunities characterized by high uncertainty.

This "bringing together" of an innovation-evaluation process for the purpose of evaluating a potential entrepreneurial opportunity raises a number of critical issues that, if solved, can make important contributions to both the innovation and the entrepreneurship literatures.

Finally, there is a substantial literature on operations management, which has been developed in the context of managing innovation within established firms (Khazanchi, Lewis, & Boyer, 2007; Sun, Hong, & Hu, 2014; Tatikonda & Rosenthal, 2000; Vickery, Jayaram, Droge, & Calantone, 2003). Thinking about operations management in the context of managing opportunity identification/evaluation within an emerging organization—entrepreneurial operations—provides ample opportunities to contribute to the further development of the operations management, innovation, and entrepreneurship fields.

## ACAP and the Entrepreneurial Process

Central to explanations of innovation and entrepreneurship is the construct of ACAP. ACAP refers to the "ability of a firm to recognize the value of new external information, assimilate it, and apply it to commercial ends" (Cohen & Levinthal, 1990, p. 127); thus, ACAP facilitates the innovation process (Mueller, 1962; von Hippel, 1988). This firm capability is believed to be a function of the firm's prior and related knowledge (Cohen & Levinthal, 1990). That is, the firm's knowledge helps the firm learn about and from external knowledge sources to create new knowledge. This internal knowledge (as the source of ACAP) can be created through research and development (Allen, 1977; Cohen & Levinthal, 1990; Tilton, 1971) and manufacturing operations (Abernathy & Utterback, 1978; Rosenberg, 1982). Therefore, the notion of ACAP rests on the simple generalization that "prior knowledge permits the assimilation and exploitation of new knowledge" (Cohen & Levinthal, 1990, pp. 135–136). However, not all prior knowledge is equally useful. It appears that some of the firm's prior knowledge needs to be related to the new knowledge to enable assimilation, whereas other parts of the firm's prior knowledge need to be different from the new knowledge to facilitate creative use of the new knowledge (Cohen & Levinthal, 1990).

Zahra and George (2002) proposed that ACAP comprises four dimensions that can be categorized into two groups: ACAP is composed of *potential* absorptive capacity (PACAP) (Group 1), which includes the set of organizational routines and processes by which firms (Dimension

1) acquire and assimilate (Dimension 2) new knowledge, and *realized* absorptive capacity (RACAP) (Group 2), which refers to the set of organizational routines and processes by which firms transform (Dimension 3) and exploit (Dimension 4) new knowledge. While PACAP "makes the firm receptive to acquiring and assimilating external knowledge," RACAP "reflects the firm's capacity to leverage knowledge that has been absorbed" (Zahra & George, 2002, p. 190). PACAP provides the basis for adaptation, especially in high-velocity environments, and involves the acquisition and assimilation of new knowledge. Acquisition refers to a firm's ability to identify and obtain external information that is important to its operations (Zahra & George, 2002). It is believed that the greater the firm's acquisition capability, the more quickly it can gather higher-quality information (Kim, 1997a, 1997b). Assimilation refers to a firm's ability to analyze, interpret, and understand the acquired information (Kim, 1997a, 1997b; Szulanski, 1996; Zahra & George, 2002). The greater this assimilation capability, the more comprehensible the acquired external information is and, therefore, the more this external information is internalized—that is, made available for "use" within the organization.

RACAP refers to the firm's "capacity to leverage the knowledge that has been absorbed" (Zahra & George, 2002, p. 190) and involves the transformation and exploitation of external knowledge made available through PACAP. Transformation involves a firm's ability to facilitate the combination (and perhaps recombination) of the firm's prior knowledge with the newly acquired knowledge but may also (or instead) involve interpreting existing knowledge in new ways (Zahra & George, 2002). Exploitation engages the firm's ability to apply the new knowledge in its operations, thereby creating new competences (Zahra & George, 2002).

Research on ACAP has generally focused on external sources of knowledge given a stock of internal knowledge. External knowledge sources include acquisitions (Chaudhuri & Tabrizi, 1999) and other forms of international relationships (Vermeulen & Barkema, 2001), such as alliances (Lane & Lubatkin, 1998). However, exposure to external sources of knowledge is necessary but not sufficient for transfer (Matusik, 2000); transfer also requires an understanding of the breadth and depth of this exposure, the new information's relatedness to prior knowledge, and the extent to which the new knowledge is different from current internal knowledge (Cockburn & Henderson, 1998; Lane & Lubatkin, 1998; Lofstrom, 2000; Matusik & Heeley, 2001; Van Wijk, Van den Bosch, & Volberda, 2001). Indeed, ACAP captures the firm's ability to make the most of these external sources of potential new knowledge, and the motivation to do so may result from an internal trigger (e.g., an organizational crisis) or an external trigger (e.g., an environmental jolt) (Bradley, Aldrich, Shepherd, & Wiklund, 2011).

### ACAP and Opportunity Generation and Refinement

The extant research has focused on the external aspects of ACAP as the source of new information and the focal firm as the recipient. That is, scholarly attention has focused on the uni-directional flow of information, albeit with some firms being better able to capitalize on that flow than others (i.e., those that have higher ACAP). However, there are a number of interesting possibilities when we consider ACAP from an entrepreneurship perspective.

First, from an entrepreneurship viewpoint (in particular, see Shepherd, 2015, and Chap. 2), we investigate the flow of information from outside to inside the firm through the social interactions involved when an entrepreneur tests and refines a potential entrepreneurial opportunity. For example, Domurath and Patzelt (2016) showed that entrepreneurs assess foreign market opportunities based on the nature of their information-providing network in those markets; however, this effect is contingent on entrepreneurs' perceptions of their venture's ACAP being sufficiently developed to acquire, assimilate, transform, and exploit the information received. However, because the concept of ACAP "can best be developed through an examination of the cognitive structures that underlie learning" (Cohen & Levinthal, 1990, p. 129), we start with the mind in which the learning is stored (which can be at the firm or the individual level of analysis [Cohen & Levinthal, 1990, pp. 135–136; Walsh, 1995; Walsh & Ungson, 1991] highlighted that ACAP "applies at both the individual and organizational levels").

Based on prior knowledge or another source of information (e.g., imagination), the mind can generate a potential opportunity. This potential opportunity represents internally generated knowledge, which is often created by experiencing the world. For example, when engaged in a task, an individual can be fully absorbed and make minor adaptations to small perturbations—absorbed coping (Sandberg & Tsoukas, 2011; Weick, 1999). However, when the tools the individual has are insufficient for problem solving, the problem stands out as an anomaly requiring deliberate reasoning to generate a solution. A potential solution in the form of a new product, service, or process presents a potential opportunity. That is, by engaging in activities, the individual comes across new information; an anomaly reflects the acquisition of new information (of a problem), which then triggers efforts to analyze, interpret, and understand the nature of the anomaly (as it does for scholars) (Shepherd & Sutcliffe, 2011).

After beginning to understand the anomaly, the individual is able to generate conjectures of a potential opportunity (i.e., potential solutions to the anomaly) (Shepherd, McMullen, & Ocasio, 2016). The individual forms these conjectures of potential opportunities in his or her mind by combining elements of knowledge as a potential solution; undertaking bisociation, with different perspectives offering new insights; and/or otherwise "tapping into" and challenging existing knowledge. The ability to do this is consistent with "assimilation" and "transformation" and is in line with an entrepreneurial mindset (Grégoire, Barr, & Shepherd, 2010; McGrath & MacMillan, 2000) that informs entrepreneurial action (Baker & Nelson, 2005; Smith & DeGregorio, 2002). The individual can then test the opportunity conjecture in the world—that is, communicate the potential opportunity to a community of inquiry. Although such action is likely to represent probes into an uncertain future (Brown & Eisenhardt, 1997; McGrath, 1999), it can be considered an application of the new knowledge (in the form of a potential opportunity) that has been created and internalized (Lyles & Schwenk, 1992) and therefore represents a form of exploitation (Zahra & George, 2002).

Of course, the process does not stop there. When the entrepreneur releases the potential opportunity from his or her mind into the world, there is an interaction between the community of inquiry and the potential opportunity. This interaction provides new information that reflects how the potential opportunity can be refined, and/or the community of inquiry acts in a way that changes the nature of the potential opportunity. Either way, the community of inquiry, through its interaction with the potential opportunity, generates new information. To the extent that the entrepreneur (i.e., the mind) is able to absorb this new information—namely, acquire, assimilate, transform, and exploit it—he or she can make additional refinements to the potential opportunity. Therefore, there is a mutual adjustment between the mind and the world through a potential opportunity (Shepherd, 2015; Chap. 2). The extent of this mutual adjustment is likely to be higher for those who have high ACAP. However, given the iterative process of generating and refining potential opportunities

**Dimensions of ACAP and the mutual adjustment process of potential opportunities.** Rather than think of ACAP as an aggregation of the four dimensions (or of two groups—PACAP and RACAP), perhaps it is more beneficial to think about the extent of mutual adjustment based on the individual's lowest capability. In other words, if acquisition feeds into assimilation, which feeds into transformation, which feeds into exploitation, and this process is recycled based on engaging a community of inquiry, then it is likely that the process can only proceed as effectively as its lowest capability—it is not the average strength of the links that determines the effectiveness of a chain but the strength of its weakest link. However, perhaps some dimensions are more critical in opportunity refinement than others. For example, after a community of inquiry has been engaged, the ability to acquire information may take on less importance than it did in initial idea generation (perhaps because the source of the information is more apparent), or perhaps transformation, while still important, is not as important when the mind is refining a potential opportunity as opposed to generating one in the first place. How does the importance of the different dimensions of ACAP change throughout the entrepreneurial process, especially as it relates to the mutual adjustment process of opportunity refinement?

**Potential opportunity and transforming ACAP.** As ACAP enables the entrepreneur to refine the potential opportunity, the potential opportunity itself transforms the mind—that is, the idea refined by a community of inquiry transforms the mind of the idea's generator. This transformation is likely to be reflected in the dimensions of ACAP, such as an enhanced ability to acquire, assimilate, transform, and exploit the new knowledge generated by the community of inquiry. Therefore, not only does ACAP facilitate opportunity refinement (and transformation of the community of inquiry), but it also changes as a result of the process. Capturing how the mind is transformed in terms of its ability to acquire, assimilate, transform and exploit knowledge is a critical issue for innovation and entrepreneurship scholars to address. Again, exploring differences in the dimensions of ACAP adds the potential for scope and depth in understanding how a refined opportunity (by the community of inquiry) transforms its originator's mind.

**The dynamism of ACAP as a dynamic capability.** To stretch our own minds, we reflected on Zahra and George's (2002) notion that

ACAP is a dynamic capability—it is a capability that facilitates change in an organization's routines, systems, and processes. However, at least in the mutual adjustment process of developing and refining a potential opportunity, ACAP itself will likely change, making the dynamic capability itself dynamic. It is important to think about the mechanisms of this dynamism. This requires greater theorizing about the form of each capability "housed" in the firm. Specifically, what are the routines of a new information-acquisition capability, assimilation capability, transformation capability, and exploitation capability? Given such an understanding, we are in a position to explore how these capabilities change as part of the mutual adjustment process of potential opportunity refinement. These changes may be reflected in one or many of the capabilities and/or in the routines that connect these capabilities. The entrepreneurial process is a particularly appropriate context to explore these ideas because the potential opportunity is not the sole property of the mind as it changes through social interaction (Shepherd, 2015; see also Chap. 2). While the opportunity, as well as the mind, changes as a result of social interaction, so too does the community of inquiry—it is transformed. This transformation of the community of inquiry (over and above change to the potential opportunity) is also information that, if absorbed, can be useful to the entrepreneurial actor. For example, perhaps two communities arise from one as the potential opportunity changes. Recognizing this transformation of the community of inquiry into two could lead to two different versions of the potential opportunity (different forms of refinement) now representing two potential opportunities—one for each community (e.g., customer target segments). Those with superior ACAP are likely to be in a better position to notice and act upon the new knowledge stemming from the bifurcation of the community and of the opportunity.

**From the individual to the firm level of analysis.** Maintaining a finer-grained treatment of ACAP—considering each of its four dimensions independently—will likely provide greater scope for understanding how a firm generates and refines an opportunity through its interaction with a community (or communities) of inquiry. When investigating the role of ACAP in the generation and refinement of a potential opportunity in the context of an established firm, we need to ask several questions. How does a firm *acquire* information that generates an anomaly? How does the firm *assimilate* new knowledge with existing knowledge to understand the problem and then *transform* prior knowledge of the problem to generate a potential opportunity that is then exploited through interactions with a community of inquiry? To address such questions likely requires an investigation of how ACAP—and thus a series of opportunity-related capabilities—is distributed throughout the firm and coordinated. In other words, how are individuals with the ability to acquire, assimilate, transform, and/or exploit new knowledge positioned within a firm and organized to offer firm-level ACAP for potential opportunity generation and refinement? Further investigations of organizing ACAP for the generation and refinement of potential opportunities will likely benefit from building on the attention-based view of the firm (see Ocasio, 1997; at the individual level for attention and potential opportunity, see Shepherd et al., 2017).

**Potential opportunity as a mechanism for creating firm-level ACAP.** As mentioned above, as the mind (including ACAP) is transformed throughout the process of potential opportunity refinement, we are able to focus on the flow of knowledge and therefore changes in ACAP rather than rely on a relatively static perspective of ACAP as an endowment. As with most research on firms' stocks of resources, researchers who take an entrepreneurial perspective are interested in how these stocks are created as an organization emerges. Before the emergence of an organization, the individual (eventual founder), alone or with others, generates and refines a potential opportunity (as described above), and as this process proceeds, additional steps are taken toward organizing the exploitation of this potential opportunity (Katz & Gartner, 1988; Lichtenstein, Dooley, & Lumpkin, 2006; Tornikoski & Newbert, 2007). As the result of—or in conjunction with—organizational emergence, the firm itself develops ACAP that is distinct and separate from that of the founder(s). How does the pursuit and refinement of a potential opportunity through a de novo venture help explain the development of firm-level ACAP? Because the potential opportunity central to new firm creation contributes to firm-level ACAP, it is likely that a path dependence is created—the potential opportunity generates prior knowledge, which, through ACAP, generates and refines subsequent potential opportunities and so forth. Therefore, the formation of ACAP may be a mechanism by which a new organization's first potential opportunity has an imprinting effect on the identification and exploitation of subsequent potential opportunities.

**Summary**. In Fig. 4.1, we offer a sketch of ACAP's role in the entrepreneurial process. External information can be a source of new knowledge for the identification of a potential opportunity but more so for those with higher ACAP. This ACAP is a function of prior knowledge and is made up of the ability to acquire, assimilate, transform, and exploit information.

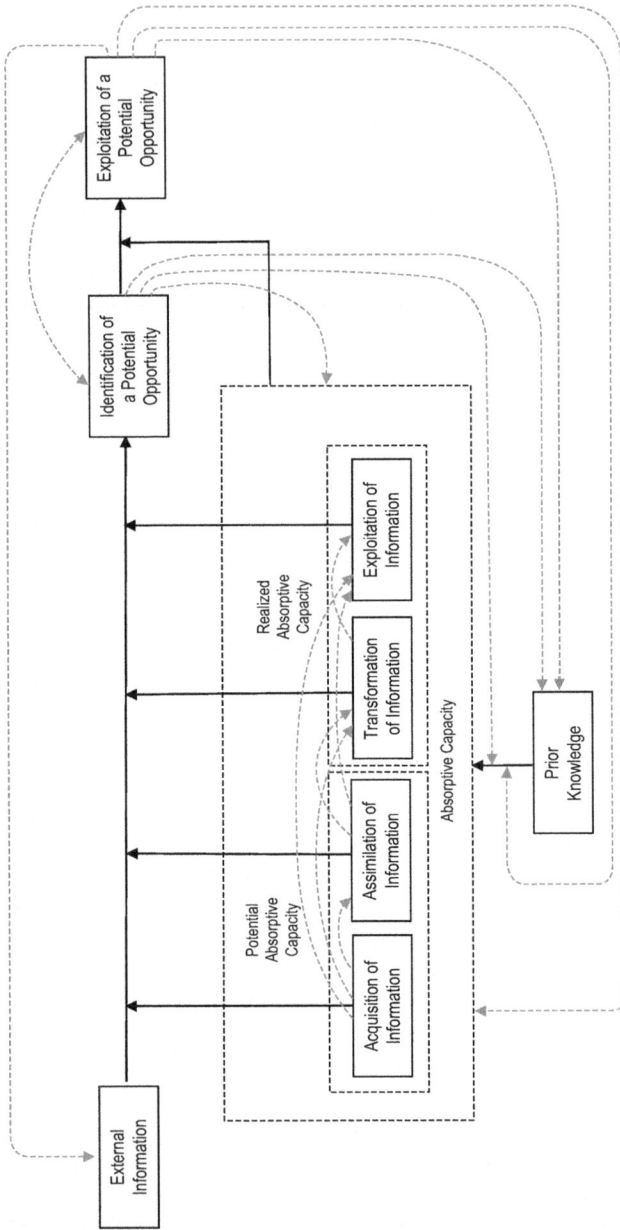

Fig. 4.1 A sketch of absorptive capacity in the entrepreneurial process

ACAP also facilitates the exploitation of an identified potential opportunity. This exploitation can change the nature of the identified opportunity, the external information, the content of prior knowledge, the relationship prior knowledge has with ACAP, and the level of ACAP. Given the interrelated nature of the dimensions of ACAP, information acquisition likely influences the assimilation, transformation, and exploitation of information; assimilation influences the transformation and exploitation of information; and the transformation of information influences the exploitation of information.

## STAGES OF INNOVATION AND ASSESSING ENTREPRENEURIAL PROJECTS

Critical to innovation is the selection process for investing resources—time, energy, and money—into entrepreneurial projects (Cooper, 2008, 2013; Cooper, Edgett, & Kleinschmidt, 2002). This selection process is critical because most organizations have more innovation projects than resources to fund them (Cooper et al., 2002) and because these selection decisions determine the composition of the organization's project portfolio (Behrens & Patzelt, 2017). In turn, portfolio composition has been found to influence (and reflect) business strategy (Bakker & Shepherd, 2017; Cooper et al., 2002), product innovation performance (Klingebiel & Rammer, 2014; van de Vrande, 2013), and—ultimately—firm performance (Salomo, Talke, & Strecker, 2008; Talke, Salomo, & Rost, 2010).

The innovation process is typically represented by a number of stages (Urban & Hauser, 1993; Veryzer, 1998), for example, the stages of (1) idea generation, (2) preliminary assessment, (3) detailed assessment, (4) development, (5) validation, and (6) launch (Cooper & Kleinschmidt, 1993). In each stage, the project team generates, gathers, and analyzes new information to determine whether the innovation project should proceed to the next stage (Cooper, 2008). With each progressive stage, there is a greater need for resource investment. Each (larger) investment becomes less reversible but generally involves less uncertainty (Bakker & Shepherd, 2017; Burgelman, 1983; McGrath, 1999).

To add discipline to the innovation process, many organizations use stage gates—decision points between each stage that present the choice to "go" or "kill" the focal entrepreneurial project (e.g., Behrens & Ernst, 2014). "Go" means the project moves to the next stage of the innovation process, whereas "kill" means the entrepreneurial project is terminated.

The underlying notion is to kill projects that are weak (i.e., those that provide little evidence of viability) and redeploy its resources to projects that show promise. Staging investments provides a mechanism for containing downside losses (Adner & Levinthal, 2004; McGrath, 1999). According to the innovation and project management literatures, it is important that these stage gates are pre-defined in terms of "a set of deliverables" that includes things that must be done and achieved, a list of criteria specifying how the project will be assessed (and how the go/kill decision will be made) for each stage, and outputs in terms of the path by which the innovation should progress (Cooper & Kleinschmidt, 1993). Critical to the stage-gate process is that the gates and their criteria are pre-specified (Boulding, Morgan, & Staelin, 1997; Cooper & Kleinschmidt, 1993; Hart & Milstein, 2003; Schmidt, Sarangee, & Montoya, 2009). This formal planning of the innovation process (Schultz, Salomo, Brentani, & Kleinschmidt, 2013) provides structure and sequence (Tatikonda & Montoya-Weiss, 2001), stabilizes the resource-allocation process (Benner & Tushman, 2003; Christensen & Bower, 1996), provides clarity to those working on different aspects of the project (Tatikonda & Montoya-Weiss, 2001), and reduces—or otherwise manages—risk (Schmidt et al., 2009).

However, one can question whether these entrepreneurial projects involve entrepreneurial risk (as assumed in the go/kill stage-gate process) or uncertainty. Entrepreneurial risk refers to "investments of resources (including the entrepreneur's time and energy) in which the decision maker knows the probability distribution of all possible outcomes from entrepreneurial action, but does not know which outcome will occur," whereas entrepreneurial uncertainty refers to resource investments (again including the entrepreneur's time and energy) in which the decision maker does not know all possible outcomes from entrepreneurial action and does not know the probability distribution of those outcomes but does know that this information is not known by others (Shepherd, McMullen, & Jennings, 2007, p. 77). Learning from one's actions is critical to operating in an environment of uncertainty (McGrath, 1999; see also the interactive perspective in Chap. 2). Indeed, learning is considered to be critical in the innovation process (Brown & Eisenhardt, 1995; Hurley & Hult, 1998; Nonaka & Takeuchi, 1995), yet stage-gate controls are believed to restrict learning (Sethi & Iqbal, 2008). It appears that stage gates are inappropriate for novel or radical innovations (Leifer et al., 2000; McDermott & O'Connor, 2002; Veryzer, 1998). By pre-specifying the criteria to be used for a go/kill decision at each stage, it is assumed that the process planner knows the intended users of the innovation, the benefits the innovation will provide for those users, and ways to competitively position the innovation and the firm (McGrath & Keil, 2007). However, to the extent that the context is uncertain, these aspects are not known and not knowable (Knight, 1921) at the time of formulating and setting the stage gates.

When the innovation is acted upon, further project information is generated and revealed that helps the innovation process by developing and refining—and possibly redirecting—the potential entrepreneurial opportunity (see also Chap. 2). That is, information about the nature of the potential opportunity and thus the appropriate selection criteria emerge as a result of the innovation process; they are not set prior to its beginning. Therefore, when these criteria are pre-defined, learning is constrained to a narrow path, so the value-creation potential of the opportunity could be lost or substantially curtailed. Therefore, potential opportunities that create value in ways not originally conceived are killed by the formal stage-gate process. In this way, decision makers are likely making "premature choices that may not be easily reversible" (Sethi & Iqbal, 2008, p. 120). That is, once a project is killed, it is likely to be difficult to pick up the project again in the future if the decision makers become aware of the error of their "no go" decision.

Recently, the innovation literature has acknowledged the constraints placed on learning (and the deleterious effects on performance) by stage gates and has proposed that the problem is not so much the stage gates themselves but the people enforcing them. Researchers have argued that it is the rigorous use of gates to control the process that likely causes poor innovation outcomes (Sethi & Iqbal, 2008). Rigor in gate control refers to "how strictly, how objectively, and consistently, and how frequently criteria are applied (Cooper, 1998, 2001)" (Sethi & Iqbal, 2008, p. 120). The proposed solution is to make the gates more conditional; with more conditional gates, a project can progress as long as it meets the criteria at the next gate (Cooper, 1994).

However, we know that decision makers are typically biased toward persistence, and the more gates are conditional or malleable, the more decision makers are likely to decide to persist with a poorly performing project. Indeed, there is a substantial literature providing evidence of individuals' (including innovation managers [Patzelt & Shepherd, 2008]) and organizations' persisting with losing courses of action and even escalating commitment to it (Brockner, 1992; Staw, 1981, 1997; Staw, Barsade, & Koput, 1997). Biases toward persistence, especially as it relates to stage gates, mean that decision makers are likely to lower the hurdle of a particular gate (i.e., exercise the condition of a conditional gate) in their mind, for example, to recoup a return on the time, effort, and money already invested in the entrepreneurial project (i.e., a sunk cost effect) (e.g., Pierce, Kostova, & Dirks, 2001; Wagner, Parker, & Christiansen, 2003). Alternatively, they justify the previous decision to start the project, pass it through previous gates, and invest additional resources in its development (i.e., norms for consistency) (Staw, 1981). Finally, there is an expectation that because past projects were successful, the current project will be as well (Audia, Locke, & Smith, 2000), leading decision makers to become over-confident in the project, the team, and the organization and their ability to "turn this thing around" (Forbes, 2005) and/or leading to a pervasive anti-failure bias (McGrath, 1999).

The above pros and cons of a stage-gate process create a paradox that we, as scholars, still need to work through. The paradox is that on the one hand, the tougher the gates of an innovation process, the less likely there will be persistence with a poorly performing entrepreneurial project, thereby reducing the costs of failure when it eventually occurs. On the other hand, the tougher the stage gates, the less learning that takes place and the less adaptation there is to "new" information generated by the actions within a particular stage, resulting in the premature termination of some valuable projects. Strict stage gates reduce type I errors but increase type II errors.

Because the opportunity underlying the innovation is likely shrouded in uncertainty, it would seem that the information generated through the activities of a stage could be used to choose the criteria for the gate. The purpose of the gate is to still weed out weaker projects, but to be effective, the process needs to be less biased toward persistence; otherwise, the criteria will be chosen and set in a way that ensures the entrepreneurial project passes the gate and moves on to the next stage. Therefore, there is a need for two inter-related streams of research based on the following research questions: (1) How can information (generated by stage activities) be used to select and set criteria for terminating weak entrepreneurial projects and progressing strong entrepreneurial projects? (2) How can this selection process be free of biases toward persistence? Perhaps by addressing the second issue (de-biasing the process), we can gain a deeper understanding of how to achieve the first issue. Indeed, research has investigated reducing or eliminating cognitive biases for different decisions in, for example, health-prevention behaviors (Weinstein & Klein, 1995), auditing (Kennedy, 1993), litigation (Babcock, Loewenstein, & Issacharoff,

1997), and laboratories (Arkes, 1991). Perhaps with additional theorizing, these concepts can be applied or blended for the staged decision making involved in the innovation process and in the development of entrepreneurial projects. We offer four examples below.

### *Stage Gates and Real Options Reasoning*

Real options reasoning is an approach to making decisions in a way that manages uncertainty. Under real options reasoning, the decision maker invests in a real option that provides him or her the right but not the obligation to continue investment (McGrath, 1996, 1997; McGrath & Nerkar, 2004). Such an approach requires a mindset that is less focused on achieving success and avoiding failure and more focused on how the two fit together. For example, when one pursues higher-variance entrepreneurial projects, the failure rate will likely increase, but this could lead to highly favorable outcomes if the cost of failure is bounded (McGrath, 1999). When entrepreneurial projects are considered to be a real option, it appears that real options reasoning could be applied to the gate at the end of the first stage of the innovation process. The value of the option is what can be learned at that stage. However, how can real options reasoning be applied to subsequent stages of the innovation process, especially as the investment in the project is greater? Is this greater investment worth it vis-à-vis the project's option value? It would seem that real options reasoning becomes less and less valuable as the entrepreneurial project moves through the stages of innovation because uncertainty is reduced, and option value is lower when uncertainty is lower.

Even if a real options reasoning approach is useful only in the first stage, this first gate is critical to completing the project and reducing the costs of innovation. The mindset underlying real options reasoning fosters learning while preventing a strong commitment to the optioned project. Indeed, this seems to point the way toward a hybrid stage-gate model wherein real options reasoning helps with the go/kill decision at the early stages of the innovation process by enabling learning and flexibility when one makes a decision under high uncertainty. However, for later stages, more focus is given to choosing and setting stage gates because with reduced uncertainty, decision makers are better able to pre-determine the criteria for subsequent gates to manage risk. Further research on this option–stage-gate hybrid will likely make an important contribution to the innovation and entrepreneurship literatures.

### Individuals, Learning, and Stage Gates

Some individuals are better at adapting to changing environments than others. For example, high meta-cognitive awareness—a general level of awareness one has concerning his or her own cognitions focused on a specific entrepreneurial task (Haynie, Shepherd, Mosakowski, & Earley, 2010, p. 221)—has been found to facilitate learning and adaptation in schools (Kamp, Admiraal, Drie, & Rijlaarsdam, 2015; Zohar & Barzilai, 2013) and in the entrepreneurial context (Haynie, Shepherd, & Patzelt, 2012). Indeed, superior learning has been associated with numerous cognitive *attributes* (e.g., learning style [Dunn, Griggs, Olson, Beasley, & Gorman, 1995], higher-order thinking skills [Zohar & Dori, 2003], and age [Cross, 1981]), *processes* (e.g., approaches to learning [Biggs, 1993], spatial transfer [Capello, 1999], and collective learning [Abrahamson & Fairchild, 1999]), and *strategies* (e.g., active learning [Meyers & Jones, 1993], self-regulation [Zimmerman & Pons, 1986], and peer assistance [Fuchs, Fuchs, Mathes, & Simmons, 1997]). However, there has been little discussion about decision makers' learning in the stage-gate process. The more we acknowledge the uncertainty surrounding (some) entrepreneurial projects, the more we recognize the importance of learning and adaptive decision making—in selecting and adjusting the gate criteria. In doing so, more scholarly attention is likely to turn to the cognitive processes underlying gate decisions. Some (or perhaps most) gate decisions are made by a team, and there is a substantial literature on collective cognition upon which future stage-gate research can draw to better understand how stage-gate decisions about entrepreneurial projects are made, under what conditions, and to what effect. Such a cognitive explanation of stage gates can also have normative implications as we link cognitive attributes, processes, strategies, and/or collective cognition to value-creation outcomes from the innovation process.

### Emotions and the Stage-Gate Process

Over and above a cognitive perspective, an emotions perspective provides additional insight into stage-gate decisions. For example, people often fear failure (Cacciotti, Hayton, Mitchell, & Giazitzoglu, 2016; Mitchell & Shepherd, 2010; Tsai, Chang, & Peng, 2016). At times, this fear of failure likely manifests itself in a reluctance to kill an entrepreneurial project despite evidence of its weak viability. On the one hand, it could be that fear of failure leads to persistence despite poor performance and/or a reluctance to start highly uncertain projects in the first place. On the other hand, a high fear of failure may be more concerned with terminating an entrepreneurial project for large losses than terminating a project for small losses, which may equate to the premature termination of projects (even those that show initial promise). If, as we propose, fear of failure impacts stage-gate decisions, the research focus needs to turn to understanding the causes of these fears, the performance implications of these fears for the firm, and the conditions under which they are magnified or dampened.

There are likely a number of emotions (over and above fear) that influence stage-gate decisions, especially for innovation processes characterized by high uncertainty (e.g., entrepreneurial projects), because in such contexts, individuals often use emotion as a form of information to make decisions (i.e., affect as information) (Forgas, 2001; Marroquín, Boyle, Nolen-Hoeksema, & Stanton, 2016). These emotions could be negative—such as anxiety (Reiss, 1991; Taylor, 2014), guilt (Block, 2005), and anticipatory grief (Shepherd, Wiklund, & Haynie, 2009)—and/or positive—such as passion (Cardon, Wincent, Singh, & Drnovsek, 2009; Cardon, Zietsma, Saparito, Matherne, & Davis, 2005), excitement (Klaukien, Shepherd & Patzelt, 2013), and satisfaction (Breugst & Shepherd, 2017; Gimeno, Folta, Cooper, & Woo, 1997). As with the cognitive perspective, scholars can build on emotion research at the individual and team level to better understand the role of collective emotion in the selection and use of stage gates in the termination or progression of entrepreneurial projects through the innovation process.

### *Organizational Climate and Stage-Gate Decisions*

Organizations and teams can create a climate of psychological safety. Psychological safety refers to "a shared belief held by members of a team that the team is safe for inter-personal risk taking" (Edmondson, 1999, p. 354) and can be promoted in an organization by team leader coaching, the development of high-quality relationships, and commitment-based human-resources practices (Edmondson, 1999; Edmondson & Lei, 2014). In a psychologically safe environment, people have greater inter-personal trust and mutual respect (Edmondson, 1999) and are therefore more willing to act creatively (Edmondson & Lei, 2014), report failures (Cannon & Edmondson, 2001; Edmondson, 1996), and learn from their actions (Cannon & Edmondson, 2005; Edmondson, 1999). It is likely that many of the biases that lead to persistence can be reduced or avoided through the creation of a psychologically safe organizational environment such that ego-protective mechanisms are no longer needed. For example, in a psychologically safe environment, there will be less need to justify to others previous decisions to start and progress an entrepreneurial project, thus "freeing" the decision maker to terminate a weak project. Similarly, there will be less need to seem consistent such that the decision maker may be more willing to change the criteria for an upcoming gate. Moreover, as others share this psychologically safe environment, they are likely to be more willing to voice concerns (Edmondson & Lei, 2014) and less likely to penalize those who do, which can have a positive impact on the specifications of stage gates and their use.

We believe that these are conjectures worthy of scholarly investigation. For example, what aspects of a psychologically safe environment reduce the likelihood of persisting with a weak entrepreneurial project? Perhaps the creativity generated in a psychologically safe environment (Gong, Cheung, Wang, & Huang, 2012) enables greater flexibility in generating gate criteria. It could be that the learning facilitated by psychological safety (Edmondson, 1999) informs the formation or refinement of and/or changes the potential opportunity to enable it to exceed the gate criteria. However, is there a downside to a psychologically safe environment for an entrepreneurial project? Furthermore, while we have highlighted the possibilities of psychological safety, there are other aspects of organizational climate and culture. Organizational climate refers to "the meanings people attach to inter-related bundles of experiences they have at work" (Schneider, Ehrhart, & Macey, 2013, p. 361), such as procedural justice climate (Naumann & Bennett, 2000), voice climate (Morrison, Wheeler-Smith, & Kamdar, 2011), and climates for initiative (Baer & Frese, 2003). Organizational culture consists of employees' "basic assumptions about their work and the values that guide life in organizations" (Schneider et al., 2013, p. 361) and includes the notions of clan, adhocracy, market, and hierarchy culture (Hartnell & Walumbwa, 2011)—culture factors that could facilitate the integration of learning into staged decisions in the innovation process.

## *Summary*

In Fig. 4.2, we offer a sketch of a stage-gate process for entrepreneurial projects. At the start, when managers' uncertainty is high, decision makers use their initial conception of the potential opportunity to create an

RESEARCHING AT THE INTERSECTION OF INNOVATION, OPERATIONS... 121

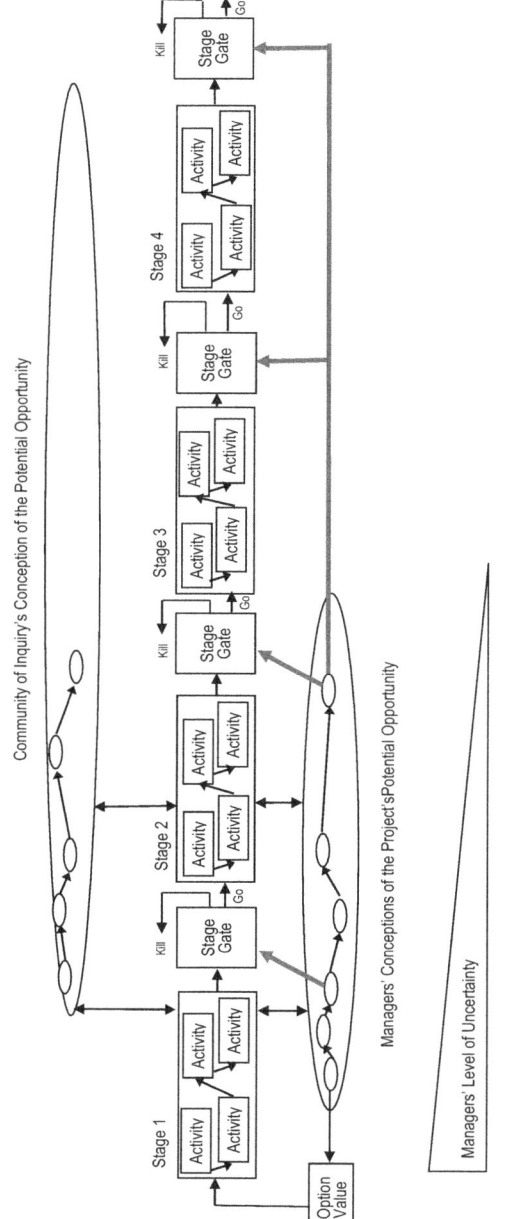

**Fig. 4.2** A sketch of a different stage-gate process for evaluating entrepreneurial projects

option that initiates the innovation and evaluation process. As the team engages in Stage 1 activities, the information generated leads to changes to the decision makers' initial conceived potential opportunity and to the community of inquiry's (e.g., potential users') conception of the potential opportunity. These conceptions (i.e., of the managers and of the community of inquiry) of the potential opportunity influence the stage's activities, and the stage's activities influence these conceptions. The managers use what they have learned to set a gate for the first stage and thus determine whether the entrepreneurial project should proceed to the next stage (go) or be terminated (kill). Stage 2 requires an additional investment of resources but proceeds like Stage 1 in that activities generate information and conceptions of the opportunity change, thus leading to new or revised activities, all of which further reduce uncertainty. Again, decision makers use their most up-to-date conceptualizations of the opportunity to set the criteria and thresholds for the gate, which determines the go/kill decision. Having substantially reduced uncertainty, the decision makers now set the gates for the remaining stages based on the current conceptualization of the potential opportunity. Once these are set, there are unlikely to be major changes to the nature of the potential opportunity.

## USING OPERATIONS TO "MANAGE" THE ENTREPRENEURIAL PROCESS

Production and operations management generally focuses on the opportunity-exploitation stage; however, such management could also directly inform other stages of the entrepreneurial process as well as enable feedback loops. Operations management refers to "the selection and management of transformation processes that create value for society" (Lovejoy, 1998, p. 106). With this definition as a foundation, **operational entrepreneurship** can be defined as *"the selection and management of transformation processes for recognizing, evaluating, and exploiting opportunities for potential value creation"* (Shepherd & Patzelt, 2013, p. 1416). It is important to note that in line with the definitions of both entrepreneurship and operations management, value creation goes beyond the creation of financial value for the entrepreneur and his or her firm and may also entail financial benefits for others in society or non-financial benefits for the natural and communal environments (Shepherd & Patzelt, 2011; see also Chap. 5).

Research on operations management has developed a strong literature on efficient opportunity exploitation in terms of the intermediate and tactical issues related to efficient exploitation. However, we argue that operations management can also be applied to develop a clearer understanding of (1) what knowledge and motivation are needed to identify a potential opportunity, (2) what assessments entrepreneurs make of an identified opportunity to decide whether it represents an opportunity for them specifically, and (3) what influence feedback from the exploitation of a current potential opportunity has on the identification and assessment of subsequent potential opportunities. We now turn to future research paths available at this interface.

### *Operations Management of Opportunity Identification and Evaluation*

The entrepreneurial process begins when the entrepreneur identifies an opportunity for someone, also known as a third-person opportunity (McMullen & Shepherd, 2006; e.g., Grégoire & Shepherd, 2012; Grégoire et al., 2010; Haynie, Shepherd, & McMullen, 2009). This process of identifying a third-person opportunity happens in an environment characterized by high uncertainty (Knight, 1921; McMullen & Shepherd, 2006). For instance, an individual may develop a new technology to detoxify water that helps conserve the natural environment. While knowing this new technology is an opportunity that someone can exploit, the individual must decide whether he or she has the knowledge and motivation to exploit the opportunity, which is the next stage of the entrepreneurial process. The ability to focus (the individual or the firm) is a key mechanism underlying why some people are able to identify opportunities while others are not able to or take longer to do so (Bakker & Shepherd, 2017; Shepherd et al., 2017).

**Managing attention to identify opportunities.** Previous research has established that individuals (Kahneman, Treisman, & Gibbs, 1992) and firms (Ocasio, 1997) have limited attention and that this limited attention can lead individuals to develop blind spots, shielding them from detecting information signals about the environment and causing them to miss opportunities (Shepherd et al., 2007, 2016; Tripsas & Gavetti, 2000; Zahra & Chaples, 1993). While scholars have explored competitive landscapes (Felin, Kauffman, Koppl, & Longo, 2014; Levinthal, 1997; Peteraf & Bergen, 2003) and—to a lesser extent—systematic search for opportunities (Ardichvili, Cardozo, & Ray, 2003; Fiet, 2007; Patel & Fiet, 2009), there is an opportunity to not only gain deeper insights into the ways individuals use attention to detect signals of potential opportunities but also to develop processes that help individuals manage their attention more effectively. These processes, for instance, could include entrepreneurs' building a larger body of prior knowledge that helps them detect environmental signals more readily and, thus, increases their likelihood of identifying an opportunity. In other words, systems that gather, store, and utilize prior market- and technology-related knowledge could improve entrepreneurs' ability to recognize potential opportunities (Grégoire et al., 2010; Shane, 2000; Shepherd & DeTienne, 2005). A firm's knowledge, for instance, is partially embedded in its manufacturing and/or information technologies (Gaimon, 2008, p. 5). Thus, any innovations related to manufacturing or information technologies signify a "process" opportunity. These process opportunities could in turn represent a dynamic capability as they aid the firm in identifying other potential opportunities. Process improvements like these—including potential enhancements in individuals' ability to recognize opportunities to develop a new product, enter a new market, or improve a process—can stem from changes in manufacturing technology (Boyer & Lewis, 2002; Gaimon & Morton, 2005) as well as upgrades in supply chain management systems (Dutta, Lee, & Whang, 2007; Elmaghraby, 2007), service business models (Kastalli & Van Looy, 2013), and workforce management techniques (Gaimon, 1997; Vivares, Sarache Castro, & Naranjo-Valencia, 2016).

Additionally, operational processes could also shed light on why some firms can dedicate more attention to scanning the environment or to initiating creative activities than other firms—that is, the types and nature of their attention structures (Ocasio, 1997). For instance, certain operational processes may be better at facilitating the collection, filtering, and presentation of relevant technology- and market-related information such that decision makers in some firms are given more (or better) opportunity-related information than their counterparts in other firms. Differences in firms' supply chain management (Helmuth, Craighead, Connelly, Collier, & Hanna, 2015; Seshadri & Subrahmanyam, 2005; Tomlin, 2003) could explain why some firms are better at detecting certain environmental signals of potential opportunities; are better at processing information related to a specific technology, market, and/or process challenge; and/or are better at handling the uncertainty and risk inherent in the evaluation and exploitation of potential opportunities. By more deeply exploring the processes related to collecting, storing, filtering, and presenting information, operational entrepreneurship researchers can provide practical contributions to help enterprising individuals and firms identify and exploit more opportunities.

**Managing motivation for attending to signals of a potential opportunity.** Aside from the likely role operational processes play in managing knowledge to increase and focus attentional resources, it is also important to note that motivation has a strong effect on individuals' ability to identify opportunities (Baum & Locke, 2004; Foo, Uy, & Murnieks, 2015; Wood, McKelvie, & Haynie, 2014). Namely, motivation supplies the *criteria* one needs when determining whether environmental signals indicate an opportunity or merely represent noise—a determination that necessitates judgment (McMullen & Shepherd, 2006). An individual who is driven by lax criteria will consider more signals to represent potential opportunities; however, an individual driven by strict criteria will consider fewer signals to represent potential opportunities. By following processes prescribed by operational entrepreneurship (including how strict or lax the criteria), entrepreneurs may be able to identify potential opportunities more effectively.

**Operational entrepreneurship to collect information to distinguish opportunities from noise.** More specifically, to help decide whether a signal represents an opportunity, firms could use operational processes to gather and present information about potential markets, required technologies for the proposed product (e.g., market size, market growth, and technological specifications), and ways to serve customers. For example, knowledge-management systems that assist firms in the creation and storage of technological and market knowledge (Chow, Choy, Lee, & Chan, 2005; Gunasekaran & Ngai, 2007) could collect data on past potential opportunities the firm or other firms in the same industry pursued and the success of those exploitations. Such data can be collected from internal sources, external databases, salespeople, industry experts, and so on. In synthesizing and analyzing the data, the systems could then come up with minimum threshold criteria—for example, for the size and growth of a market for the potential opportunity or for the opportunity's compatibility with the technology available to the firm. Perhaps some firms require a high minimum level of technological compatibility (i.e., strict criteria), whereas others require a low minimum level of technological compatibility (i.e., lax criteria). It could be interesting to explore what types of data should be collected and analyzed (and how) to effectively determine potential criteria for identifying potential opportunities and how they are used to distinguish signals of opportunity from noise.

**Operational entrepreneurship to use motivation to classify what signifies exploitable opportunities and what signifies noise.** There are substantial differences across firms in terms of how much and how effectively knowledge-management systems are applied depending on the firm's culture, leadership, reward and incentive systems, and values and norms (Lai & Chu, 2002). These differences suggest that a match between decision makers' motivation and the results of a system's data analysis is important for decision makers to identify an actionable opportunity rather than an opportunity that they are less motivated to exploit. How can such a match be achieved? For example, decision-support systems based on artificial intelligence, such as those used for location choices (Kuo, Chi, & Kao, 2002) or strategic planning (Pinson, Louçã, & Moraitis, 1997), can learn decision makers' preferences over time, which helps them identify the "right" opportunities that match their motivation and preferences. Interesting research is likely to come from applying such systems and exploring the boundaries of their application (e.g., decision makers' irrational assessments and biases).

**Operational entrepreneurship can help individuals choose and manage processes that regulate the payoffs for entrepreneurial action.** The payoffs for entrepreneurial action include, exploiting a potential opportunity and being right, exploiting a potential opportunity and being wrong, not exploiting a potential opportunity and being right, and not exploiting a potential opportunity and being wrong. For example, operations management research has drawn on simulation techniques for profitability analysis (Montes, Martin, Bayo, & Garcia, 2011; Song & Kim, 2001) and has analyzed the consequences of supply chain failures (Kull & Closs, 2008). Perhaps these systems can serve as a basis for developing simulation processes for the type I and type II errors resulting from exploiting a potential opportunity. Such simulation tools seem to have the potential to substantially improve, advance, change, or supplement the ways individuals and/or organizations assess potential opportunities.

**Operational entrepreneurship to determine the sensitivity of payoffs** by considering (1) the decreased likelihood of errors of commission and omission due to the added information that could be obtained by postponing opportunity exploitation for a period, (2) the likelihood that a window of opportunity will close from a delay in opportunity exploitation, and/or (3) the outcomes that would occur from varying the criteria in terms of being more lax or more strict. Again, building on operations research's tradition of developing and using simulation methods might be a valuable approach. A central strength of these methods is that they allow for experimentation; that is, researchers can systematically vary input opportunity parameters (Davis, Bingham, & Eisenhardt, 2007), such as raw material prices, market size, market growth, lead time, technological developments, prices, and so on. Based on these variations, the simulation can compute the payoffs of pursuing, not pursuing, or postponing the pursuit of a potential opportunity. Moreover, fixing certain parameters to more conservative values (e.g., minimum market size) in a number of simulations might represent a strict criterion that can be relaxed in additional simulations.

**Challenges for operational entrepreneurship in facilitating opportunity identification.** Despite the benefits it is likely to bring, there are several challenges associated with operational entrepreneurship stemming from the uncertainty and complexity inherent in information surrounding potential opportunities (Knight, 1921; McMullen & Shepherd, 2006). For example, entrepreneurs who develop radical innovations often decide not to enter established markets but to instead create new markets (O'Connor, 1998; Santos & Eisenhardt, 2009). Information for these markets is generally not readily available (O'Connor & Veryzer, 2001), thus making it challenging for operational entrepreneurship scholars to create systems that help entrepreneurs identify potential opportunities for radically new technologies. Furthermore, the payoffs of entrepreneurial action vary and include financial costs and benefits as well as non-financial motivational and emotional payoffs. For instance, many entrepreneurs are motivated by independence (McMullen, Bagby, & Palich, 2008), passion (Cardon et al., 2005), and the need for achievement (Shane, Locke, & Collins, 2003), all of which are challenging to quantitatively evaluate. In addition, sustainable and social entrepreneurs frequently have strong environmental and altruistic motivations (Mair & Marti, 2006; Miller, Grimes, McMullen, & Vogus, 2012; Patzelt & Shepherd, 2010; Peredo & Chrisman, 2006), which are, again, challenging to operationalize in quantitative terms.

While such challenges are unlikely to be resolved entirely to the point that "optimal" decisions can be made, operational entrepreneurship research can still be beneficial in this context by clarifying the inputs (e.g., collecting additional information, understanding complexity, and making the criteria and their outcomes clear) entrepreneurs use to form judgments and then communicate those judgments to others. This type of research would likely further develop and expand current operations management research on the various forms of uncertainty entrepreneurs and entrepreneurial firms face in the new product development process (e.g., market, creative, and process uncertainty [Anderson & Joglekar, 2005]) and methods to handle these uncertainties, including, for example, flexible manufacturing capacity (Fine & Freund, 1990), trial-and-error learning or real options reasoning (Sommer & Loch, 2004), supplier selection (Riedl, Kaufmann, Zimmermann, & Perols, 2013; Simangunsong, Hendry, & Stevenson, 2016), and maybe even supply chain management (Seshadri & Subrahmanyam, 2005; Tomlin, 2003).

### *Operations Management of Opportunity Exploitation*

While an individual's identification of a potential opportunity is essential for entrepreneurial action, it is not the only requirement; the entrepreneur or entrepreneurial firm also needs to decide whether the third-person opportunity at hand is a first-person opportunity (i.e., determine that this opportunity for someone is an opportunity for him or her [or the firm]) (McMullen & Shepherd, 2006). This has some interesting implications for blending operations management constructs and new entrepreneurial constructs.

**Operations management when the opportunity is the firm.** The operations management literature includes numerous studies exploring effective and efficient opportunity exploitation in established firms (e.g., Kavadias & Loch, 2003). However, investigating effective and efficient opportunity exploitation becomes more challenging when the particular opportunity necessitates the creation of a new firm. In this case, the potential opportunity is the firm, and the firm is the potential opportunity. Thus, a significant question remains: How is the operations management of the exploitation of a potential opportunity different in new firms than in existing firms? Many important differences are likely to exist between the two types of firms as a new firm is predominately a "blank slate." While new firms can develop operational processes that are tailored to the opportunity at hand, they are unable to take stock of existing operational processes and alter them as needed to act on the opportunity. Thus, starting a new firm necessitates a holistic approach to operations management as opposed to a targeted specialized approach. More specifically, instead of solving *an* operations management problem, operational entrepreneurship for new firms entails finding concurrent solutions for numerous operations challenges. Although operations management scholars are highly skilled at resolving concurrent issues for a problem within one part of an existing firm, operational entrepreneurship scholars who are able to overcome the challenge of simultaneously developing *all* operational processes in a new firm will contribute substantially to the entrepreneurship and operations management literatures.

**Feedback loops arising from the exploitation of a potential opportunity.** Exploiting a specific potential opportunity can reveal information (some of which is only available after action has been taken) that plays a part in altering the existing potential opportunity and/or identifying another potential opportunity. For instance, systems that gather, filter, and store stakeholders' (including customers') feedback on a new product or service and then present that information to decision makers can impact those decision makers' knowledge and desire to direct their attention to particular aspects of their business and/or the natural and communal environments. Feedback from scientific research, for instance, can change an entrepreneur's search processes "by leading them more directly to useful combinations, eliminating fruitless paths of research, and motivating them to continue even in the face of negative feedback [from other sources]" (Fleming & Sorenson, 2004, p. 909). Future operational entrepreneurship research can explore what processes and systems need to be developed to effectively capture and make use of information resulting from the exploitation of potential opportunities and to improve (i.e., inform and/ or motivate) entrepreneurs' ability to refine those potential opportunities and/or act upon subsequent potential opportunities.

Exploiting a potential opportunity has the potential to alter the viability and appeal of that particular potential opportunity or of later potential opportunities. More specifically, opportunity exploitation may modify how entrepreneurs or firms assess third-person opportunities to decide whether they are (or continue to be) first-person opportunities. Exploiting a particular potential opportunity, for instance, may help individuals or firms gain experience, skills, and/or capabilities that must be taken into account when they evaluate the viability of future potential opportunities (e.g., learning's influence on make or buy decisions [Anderson & Parker, 2002]). In a similar way, going through the opportunity-exploitation process and/or having (or not having) success in doing so may alter how appealing one finds the prospect of exploiting future potential opportunities. Such effects have clear implications for the discussion on opportunity evaluation we outlined above. However, if changes like these are expected to be large and occur frequently, a more dynamic system is necessary. Future research in this area can build on the current research stream exploring learning in and about complex dynamic systems (see Rahmandad, 2008; Sterman, 2000a, 2000b) as well as dynamic processes for new product development (Anderson & Joglekar, 2005; Brown & Eisenhardt, 1997).

**Summary.** In Fig. 4.3, we offer a sketch on the role of operations management in the formation of opportunity beliefs. We start with the base model in which (1) knowledge decreases the amount of uncertainty to facilitate the formation of opportunity beliefs (both third- and first-person beliefs) and (2) motivation increases the willingness to bear uncertainty to facilitate the formation of opportunity beliefs (both third- and first-person beliefs). Operations management likely plays a role in this process. More specifically, operations management can enhance information search (i.e., more effective and efficient collection, storage, and use of information) to reduce the level of uncertainty that might have otherwise contributed doubt about a potential opportunity. Decision aids weight criteria as a reflection of the decision makers' motivation, and the decision makers' motivation can influence their willingness to bear uncertainty in the formation of opportunity beliefs (both third- and first-person beliefs). Information systems, decision aids, and other forms of current operations focus decision makers' attention, which in turn impacts the identification and evaluation of potential opportunities. As operations management focuses on decision makers' attention, this will influence their knowledge accumulation and motivation. The identification of a potential opportunity (third-person opportunity belief) and its evaluation (first-person opportunity belief) also influence knowledge accumulation and motivation. Therefore, operations management not only reflects knowledge and motivation but also influences through both decision makers' attentional focus and the formation of opportunity beliefs.

## Discussion and Conclusion

In this chapter, we elaborated on research opportunities emerging from literatures that show considerable similarity to and overlap with the entrepreneurship literature. However, in the past, this overlap has largely been ignored, and thus, a host of research opportunities have gone unheeded.

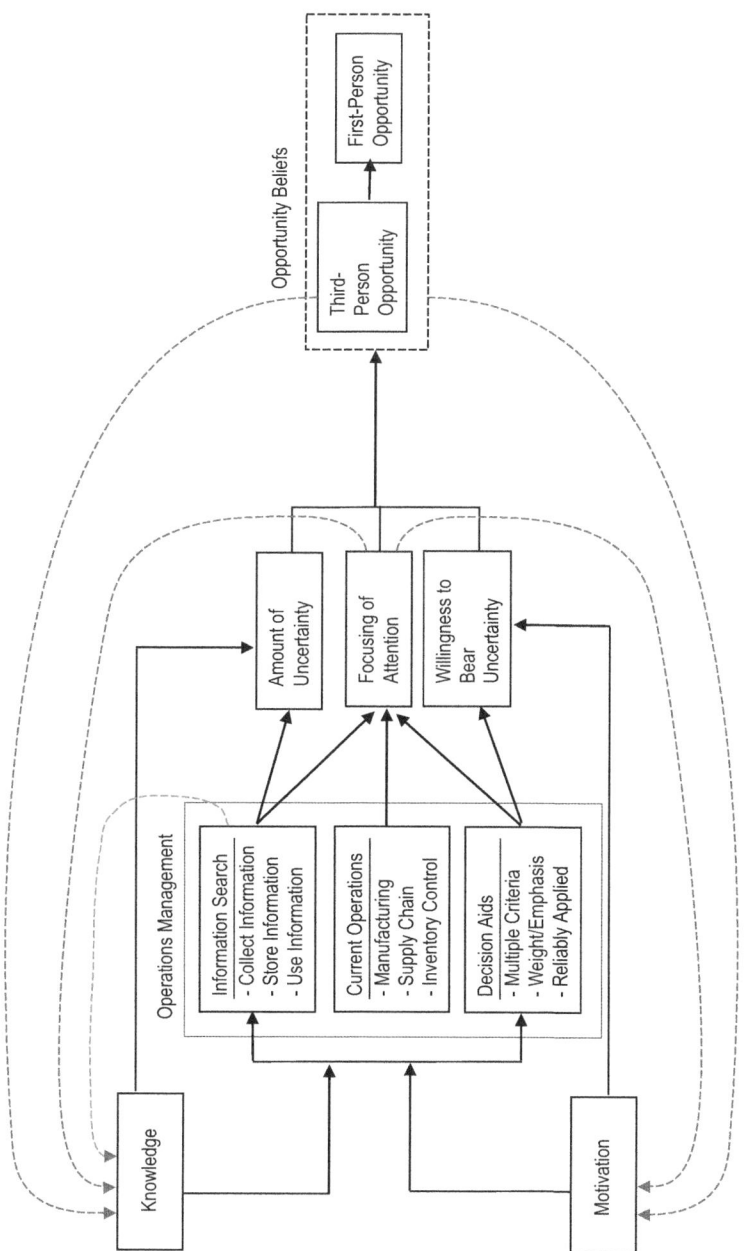

**Fig. 4.3** A sketch of the role of operations management in the formation of opportunity beliefs

Specifically, we believe that research at the intersections of the literatures on ACAP, innovation, and operations research represents substantial potential to advance entrepreneurship theory.

First, our discussion highlights the complementarity between models of entrepreneurial action and the concept of ACAP in terms of the common emphasis on knowledge—either at the individual level or at the organizational level. When potential opportunities are developed and refined based on interactions with a social environment (e.g., Dimov, 2007; Shepherd, 2015), the information received from that environment is "filtered" based on the entrepreneur's or the venture's ACAP, thus influencing the future development of the potential opportunity. In turn, ACAP is developed through knowledge acquired based on feedback on the potential opportunity from the entrepreneurial environment. Given this mutual influence of an entrepreneurial actor's ACAP and opportunity development, it seems surprising that prior research has made little effort to integrate both literatures. We hope that our discussion on the multi-dimensional nature of ACAP in the entrepreneurial context provides a starting point for such efforts.

Second, in the context of innovation, we believe that taking an entrepreneurship perspective on stage-gate processes used to judge projects under development can yield significant new insights. Because entrepreneurial projects are shrouded in uncertainty with little information available about potential outcomes or about the likelihood that these outcomes will be reached, it appears that the stage-gate process as described in the innovation literature might reach its limits when it comes to managing entrepreneurial projects. Specifically, it seems crucial for future research to resolve the paradox of setting tough stage gates to prevent biased decision making (e.g., escalation of commitment) on the one hand and setting less strict stage gates to facilitate learning on the other hand. We offer three potential ways forward: (1) adapting stage gates throughout the innovation process (i.e., more flexible at the beginning and more strict at the end); (2) taking into account individual characteristics that make decision makers more or less prone to biases (i.e., cognitions and emotions); and (3) taking into account organizational characteristics, particularly a climate of psychological safety. We hope scholars will explore how these factors—as well as others (e.g., product characteristics)—can contribute to adapting the stage-gate process so that entrepreneurial (rather than incrementally innovative) projects can be managed effectively for the benefit of the organization as a whole.

Third, the literature on operations management might provide new insights into how to manage the identification and exploitation of entrepreneurial opportunities. This literature has a long tradition of exploring the effective and efficient use of knowledge-management systems (e.g., Chow et al., 2005; Gunasekaran & Ngai, 2007), and given the importance of knowledge for opportunity identification and exploitation, it seems reasonable to assume that such systems can complement the entrepreneurial process. In addition, the more recent development of systems based on artificial intelligence (e.g., Kuo et al., 2002; Pinson et al., 1997) and simulation techniques (e.g., Kull & Closs, 2008; Montes et al., 2011; Song & Kim, 2001) can provide tools that (corporate) entrepreneurs can use to make better decisions in terms of both creating optimal outputs for the firm and matching decision makers' preferences to potential opportunities. However, few entrepreneurship scholars have studied the (potential) role of these computer-based systems in the entrepreneurial process or their complementarities and interactions. Given the increasing digitalization of business and organizational environments, we believe there are many ways future research in this area can advance our understanding of entrepreneurial phenomena.

To conclude, taking a look at neighboring but largely parallel literatures is an important way to extend the boundaries of entrepreneurship theory. We offer three literatures that seem to represent exciting future research opportunities when viewed through an entrepreneurship lens and hope that scholars from either entrepreneurship or one of these disciplines are inspired by our discussion.

## References

Abernathy, W. J., & Utterback, J. M. (1978). Patterns of industrial innovation. *Technology Review, 64*(7), 254–228.

Abrahamson, E., & Fairchild, G. (1999). Management fashion: Lifecycles, triggers, and collective learning processes. *Administrative Science Quarterly, 44*(4), 708–740.

Adner, R., & Levinthal, D. A. (2004). What is not a real option: Considering boundaries for the application of real options to business strategy. *Academy of Management Review, 29*(1), 74–85.

Allen, T. J. (1977). *Managing the flow of technology: Technology transfer and the dissemination of technological information within the R and D organization*. Cambridge, MA: MIT Press.

Anderson, E. G., & Joglekar, N. R. (2005). A hierarchical product development planning framework. *Production and Operations Management, 14*(3), 344–361.

Anderson, E. G., & Parker, G. G. (2002). The effect of learning on the make/buy decision. *Production & Operations Management, 11*(3), 313–339.

Ardichvili, A., Cardozo, R., & Ray, S. (2003). A theory of entrepreneurial opportunity identification and development. *Journal of Business Venturing, 18*(1), 105–123.

Arkes, H. R. (1991). Costs and benefits of judgment errors: Implications for debiasing. *Psychological Bulletin, 110*(3), 486–498.

Atuahene-Gima, K. (1996). Market orientation and innovation. *Journal of Business Research, 35*(2), 93–103.

Audia, P. G., Locke, E. A., & Smith, K. G. (2000). The paradox of success: An archival and a laboratory study of strategic persistence following radical environmental change. *Academy of Management Journal, 43*(5), 837–853.

Babcock, L., Loewenstein, G., & Issacharoff, S. (1997). Creating convergence: Debiasing biased litigants. *Law & Social Inquiry, 22*(4), 913–925.

Baer, M., & Frese, M. (2003). Innovation is not enough: Climates for initiative and psychological safety, process innovations, and firm performance. *Journal of Organizational Behavior, 24*(1), 45–68.

Baker, T., & Nelson, R. E. (2005). Creating something from nothing: Resource construction through entrepreneurial bricolage. *Administrative Science Quarterly, 50*(3), 329–366.

Bakker, R. M., & Shepherd, D. A. (2017). Pull the plug or take the plunge: Multiple opportunities and the speed of venturing decisions in the Australian mining industry. *Academy of Management Journal*.

Baum, J. R., & Locke, E. A. (2004). The relationship of entrepreneurial traits, skill, and motivation to subsequent venture growth. *Journal of Applied Psychology, 89*(4), 587–598.

Behrens, J., & Ernst, H. (2014). What keeps managers away from a losing course of action? Go/stop decisions in new product development. *Journal of Product Innovation Management, 31*(2), 361–374.

Behrens, J., & Patzelt, H. (2017). Corporate entrepreneurship managers' project terminations: Integrating portfolio-level, individual-level, and firm-level effects. *Entrepreneurship Theory and Practice*. Forthcoming.

Benner, M. J., & Tushman, M. L. (2003). Exploitation, exploration, and process management: The productivity dilemma revisited. *Academy of Management Review, 28*(2), 238–256.

Biggs, J. (1993). What do inventories of students' learning processes really measure? A theoretical review and clarification. *British Journal of Educational Psychology, 63*(1), 3–19.

Block, L. G. (2005). Self-referenced fear and guilt appeals: The moderating role of self-construal. *Journal of Applied Social Psychology, 35*(11), 2290–2309.

Boulding, W., Morgan, R., & Staelin, R. (1997). Pulling the plug to stop the new product drain. *Journal of Marketing Research, 34*(1), 164–176.

Boyer, K., & Lewis, M. W. (2002). Competitive priorities: Investigating the need for trade-offs in operations strategy. *Production and Operations Management, 11*(1), 9–20.

Bradley, S. W., Aldrich, H., Shepherd, D. A., & Wiklund, J. (2011). Resources, environmental change, and survival: Asymmetric paths of young independent and subsidiary organizations. *Strategic Management Journal, 32*(5), 486–509.

Breugst, N., & Shepherd, D. A. (2017). If you fight with me, I'll get mad! A social model of entrepreneurial affect. *Entrepreneurship Theory and Practice*.

Brockner, J. (1992). The escalation of commitment to a failing course of action: Toward theoretical progress. *Academy of Management Review, 17*(1), 39–61.

Brown, S. L., & Eisenhardt, K. M. (1995). Product development: Past research, present findings, and future directions. *Academy of Management Review, 20*(2), 343–378.

Brown, S. L., & Eisenhardt, K. M. (1997). The art of continuous change: Linking complexity theory and time-paced evolution in relentlessly shifting organizations. *Administrative Science Quarterly, 42*, 1–34.

Burgelman, R. A. (1983). Corporate entrepreneurship and strategic management: Insights from a process study. *Management Science, 29*(12), 1349–1364.

Burgelman, R. A. (1984). Designs for corporate entrepreneurship in established firms. *California Management Review, 26*(3), 154–166.

Cacciotti, G., Hayton, J. C., Mitchell, J. R., & Giazitzoglu, A. (2016). A reconceptualization of fear of failure in entrepreneurship. *Journal of Business Venturing, 31*(3), 302–325.

Cannon, M. D., & Edmondson, A. C. (2001). Confronting failure: Antecedents and consequences of shared beliefs about failure in organizational work groups. *Journal of Organizational Behavior, 22*(2), 161–177.

Cannon, M. D., & Edmondson, A. C. (2005). Failing to learn and learning to fail (intelligently): How great organizations put failure to work to innovate and improve. *Long Range Planning, 38*(3), 299–319.

Capello, R. (1999). Spatial transfer of knowledge in high technology milieux: Learning versus collective learning processes. *Regional Studies, 33*(4), 353–365.

Capon, N., Farley, J. U., & Hoenig, S. (1990). Determinants of financial performance: A meta-analysis. *Management Science, 36*(10), 1143–1159.

Cardon, M. S., Wincent, J., Singh, J., & Drnovsek, M. (2009). The nature and experience of entrepreneurial passion. *Academy of Management Review, 34*(3), 511–532.

Cardon, M. S., Zietsma, C., Saparito, P., Matherne, B. P., & Davis, C. (2005). A tale of passion: New insights into entrepreneurship from a parenthood metaphor. *Journal of Business Venturing, 20*(1), 23–45.

Chaudhuri, S., & Tabrizi, B. (1999). Capturing the real value in high-tech acquisitions. *Harvard Business Review, 77*(5), 123–130.

Chow, H. K., Choy, K. L., Lee, W. B., & Chan, F. T. (2005). Design of a knowledge-based logistics strategy system. *Expert Systems with Applications, 29*(2), 272–290.

Christensen, C. M., & Bower, J. L. (1996). Customer power, strategic investment, and the failure of leading firms. *Strategic Management Journal, 17*(3), 197–218.

Cockburn, I., & Henderson, R. (1998). Absorptive capacity, co-authoring behavior, and the organization of research in drug discovery. *Journal of Industrial Economics., 46,* 157–183.

Cohen, W. M., & Levinthal, D. A. (1990). Absorptive capacity: A new perspective on learning and innovation. *Administrative Science Quarterly, 35*(1), 128–152.

Cooper, R. G. (1994). Third-generation new product processes. *Journal of Product Innovation Management, 11*(1), 3–14.

Cooper, R. G. (1998). *Product leadership: Creating and launching superior new products.* Reading, MA: Perseus Books.

Cooper, R. G. (2001). *Winning at new products: Accelerating the process from idea to launch.* New York: Perseus Publishing.

Cooper, R. G. (2008). Perspective: The stage-gate® idea-to-launch process—Update, what's new, and nexgen systems. *Journal of Product Innovation Management, 25*(3), 213–232.

Cooper, R. G. (2013). Where are all the breakthrough new products?: Using portfolio management to boost innovation. *Research-Technology Management, 56*(5), 25–33.

Cooper, R. G., Edgett, S. J., & Kleinschmidt, E. J. (2002). Optimizing the stage-gate process: What best-practice companies do. *Research-Technology Management, 45*(5), 21–27.

Cooper, R. G., & Kleinschmidt, E. J. (1993). Major new products: What distinguishes the winners in the chemical industry? *Journal of Product Innovation Management, 10*(2), 90–111.

Covin, J. G., & Miles, M. P. (1999). Corporate entrepreneurship and the pursuit of competitive advantage. *Entrepreneurship Theory and Practice, 23*(3), 47–47.

Covin, J. G., & Slevin, D. P. (1989). Strategic management of small firms in hostile and benign environments. *Strategic Management Journal, 10*(1), 75–87.

Cross, K. P. (1981). *Adults as learners. Increasing participation and facilitating learning. ERIC.* San Francisco, CA: Jossey-Bass, Inc.

Damanpour, F. (1991). Organizational innovation: A meta-analysis of effects of determinants and moderators. *Academy of Management Journal, 34*(3), 555–590.

Davis, J. P., Bingham, C. B., & Eisenhardt, K. M. (2007). Developing theory from simulation models. *Academy of Management Review, 32,* 480–499.

Dewar, R. D., & Dutton, J. E. (1986). The adoption of radical and incremental innovations: An empirical analysis. *Management Science, 32*(11), 1422–1433.

Dimov, D. (2007). Beyond the single-person, single-insight attribution in understanding entrepreneurial opportunities. *Entrepreneurship Theory and Practice, 31*(5), 713–731.

Domurath, A., & Patzelt, H. (2016). Entrepreneurs' assessments of early international entry: The role of foreign social ties, venture absorptive capacity, and generalized trust in others. *Entrepreneurship Theory & Practice, 40*(5), 1149–1177.

Dunn, R., Griggs, S. A., Olson, J., Beasley, M., & Gorman, B. S. (1995). A meta-analytic validation of the Dunn and Dunn model of learning-style preferences. *The Journal of Educational Research, 88*(6), 353–362.

Dutta, A., Lee, H. L., & Whang, S. (2007). RFID and operations management: Technology, value, and incentives. *Production and Operations Management, 16*(5), 646–655.

Edmondson, A. C. (1996). Learning from mistakes is easier said than done: Group and organizational influences on the detection and correction of human error. *The Journal of Applied Behavioral Science, 32*(1), 5–28.

Edmondson, A. C. (1999). Psychological safety and learning behavior in work teams. *Administrative Science Quarterly, 44*(2), 350–383.

Edmondson, A. C., & Lei, Z. (2014). Psychological safety: The history, renaissance, and future of an interpersonal construct. *Annual Review of Organizational Psychology and Organizational Behavior, 1*(1), 23–43.

Eisenhardt, K. M., & Martin, J. A. (2000). Dynamic capabilities: What are they? *Strategic Management Journal, 21*(10-11), 1105–1121.

Elmaghraby, W. (2007). Auctions within e-sourcing events. *Production and Operations Management, 16*(4), 409–422.

Ettlie, J. E., Bridges, W. P., & O'keefe, R. D. (1984). Organization strategy and structural differences for radical versus incremental innovation. *Management Science, 30*(6), 682–695.

Felin, T., Kauffman, S., Koppl, R., & Longo, G. (2014). Economic opportunity and evolution: Beyond landscapes and bounded rationality. *Strategic Entrepreneurship Journal, 8*(4), 269–282.

Fiet, J. O. (2007). A prescriptive analysis of search and discovery. *Journal of Management Studies, 44*(4), 592–611.

Fine, C., & Freund, R. (1990). Optimal investment in product flexible manufacturing capacity. *Management Science, 36*(4), 449–466.

Fleming, L., & Sorenson, O. (2004). Science as a map in technological research. *Strategic Management Journal, 25*(8-9), 909–928.

Foo, M. D., Uy, M. A., & Murnieks, C. (2015). Beyond affective valence: Untangling valence and activation influences on opportunity identification. *Entrepreneurship Theory and Practice, 39*(2), 407–431.

Forbes, D. P. (2005). Are some entrepreneurs more overconfident than others? *Journal of Business Venturing, 20*(5), 623–640.

Forgas, J. P. (2001). *Feeling and thinking: The role of affect in social cognition.* Cambridge: Cambridge University Press.

Fuchs, D., Fuchs, L. S., Mathes, P. G., & Simmons, D. C. (1997). Peer-assisted learning strategies: Making classrooms more responsive to diversity. *American Educational Research Journal, 34*(1), 174–206.

Gaimon, C. (1997). Planning information technology-knowledge worker systems. *Management Science, 43*(9), 1308–1328.

Gaimon, C. (2008). The management of technology: A production and operations management perspective. *Production and Operations Management, 17*(1), 1–11.

Gaimon, C., & Morton, A. (2005). Investment in facility changeover flexibility for early entry into high-tech markets. *Production and Operations Management, 14*(2), 159–174.

Galunic, D. C., & Eisenhardt, K. M. (2001). Architectural innovation and modular corporate forms. *Academy of Management journal, 44*(6), 1229–1249.

Gimeno, J., Folta, T. B., Cooper, A. C., & Woo, C. Y. (1997). Survival of the fittest? Entrepreneurial human capital and the persistence of underperforming firms. *Administrative Science Quarterly, 42*, 750–783.

Gong, Y., Cheung, S. Y., Wang, M., & Huang, J. C. (2012). Unfolding the proactive process for creativity integration of the employee proactivity, information exchange, and psychological safety perspectives. *Journal of Management, 38*(5), 1611–1633.

Grégoire, D. A., Barr, P. S., & Shepherd, D. A. (2010). Cognitive processes of opportunity recognition: The role of structural alignment. *Organization Science, 21*(2), 413–431.

Grégoire, D. A., & Shepherd, D. A. (2012). Technology-market combinations and the identification of entrepreneurial opportunities: An investigation of the opportunity-individual nexus. *Academy of Management Journal, 55*(4), 753–785.

Gunasekaran, A., & Ngai, E. W. T. (2007). Knowledge management in twenty-first century manufacturing. *International Journal of Production Research, 45*(11), 2391–2418.

Hart, S. L., & Milstein, M. B. (2003). Creating sustainable value. *Academy of Management Executive, 17*(2), 56–67.

Hartnell, C. A., & Walumbwa, F. O. (2011). Transformational leadership and organizational culture. In N. M. Ashkanasy, C. P. M. Wilderom, & M. F. Peterson (Eds.), *The handbook of organizational culture and climate* (pp. 225–248). Thousand Oaks, CA: Sage Publications.

Haynie, J. M., Shepherd, D. A., & McMullen, J. S. (2009). An opportunity for me? The role of resources in opportunity evaluation decisions. *Journal of Management Studies, 46*(3), 337–361.

Haynie, J. M., Shepherd, D. A., Mosakowski, E., & Earley, P. C. (2010). A situated metacognitive model of the entrepreneurial mindset. *Journal of Business Venturing, 25*(2), 217–229.

Haynie, J. M., Shepherd, D. A., & Patzelt, H. (2012). Cognitive adaptability and an entrepreneurial task: The role of metacognitive ability and feedback. *Entrepreneurship Theory and Practice, 36*(2), 237–265.

Helmuth, C. A., Craighead, C. W., Connelly, B. L., Collier, D. Y., & Hanna, J. B. (2015). Supply chain management research: Key elements of study design and statistical testing. *Journal of Operations Management, 36*, 178–186.

Henderson, R. M., & Clark, K. B. (1990). Architectural innovation: The reconfiguration of existing product technologies and the failure of established firms. *Administrative Science Quarterly, 35*(1), 9–30.

Hull, C. E., & Rothenberg, S. (2008). Firm performance: The interactions of corporate social performance with innovation and industry differentiation. *Strategic Management Journal, 29*(7), 781–789.

Hurley, R. F., & Hult, G. T. M. (1998). Innovation, market orientation, and organizational learning: An integration and empirical examination. *The Journal of Marketing, 62*(3), 42–54.

Kahneman, D., Treisman, A., & Gibbs, B. (1992). The reviewing of object files: Object-specific integration of information. *Cognitive Psychology, 24*(2), 175–219.

Kamp, M. T., Admiraal, W., Drie, J., & Rijlaarsdam, G. (2015). Enhancing divergent thinking in visual arts education: Effects of explicit instruction of metacognition. *British Journal of Educational Psychology, 85*(1), 47–58.

Kastalli, I. V., & Van Looy, B. (2013). Servitization: Disentangling the impact of service business model innovation on manufacturing firm performance. *Journal of Operations Management, 31*(4), 169–180.

Katz, J., & Gartner, W. B. (1988). Properties of emerging organizations. *Academy of Management Review, 13*(3), 429–441.

Kavadias, S., & Loch, C. H. (2003). Optimal project sequencing with recourse at a scarce resource. *Production and Operations Management, 12*(4), 433–444.

Kennedy, J. (1993). Debiasing audit judgment with accountability: A framework and experimental results. *Journal of Accounting Research, 31*(2), 231–245.

Khazanchi, S., Lewis, M. W., & Boyer, K. K. (2007). Innovation-supportive culture: The impact of organizational values on process innovation. *Journal of Operations Management, 25*(4), 871–884.

Kim, L. (1997a). The dynamics of Samsung's technological learning in semiconductors. *California Management Review, 39*(3), 86–100.

Kim, L. (1997b). *From imitation to innovation: The dynamics of Korea's technological learning.* Cambridge, MA: Harvard Business School Press.

Klaukien, A., Shepherd, D. A., & Patzelt, H. (2013). Passion for work, nonwork-related excitement, and innovation managers' decision to exploit new product opportunities. *Journal of Product Innovation Management, 30*(3), 574–588.

Klingebiel, R., & Rammer, C. (2014). Resource allocation strategy for innovation portfolio management. *Strategic Management Journal, 35*(2), 246–268.

Knight, F. H. (1921). *Risk, uncertainty and profit*. New York: Hart, Schaffner and Marx.

Kull, T., & Closs, D. (2008). The risk of second-tier supplier failures in serial supply chains: Implications for order policies and distributor autonomy. *European Journal of Operational Research, 186*(3), 1158–1174.

Kuo, R. J., Chi, S. C., & Kao, S. S. (2002). A decision support system for selecting convenience store location through integration of fuzzy AHP and artificial neural network. *Computers in Industry, 47*(2), 199–214.

Lai, H., & Chu, T. H. (2002). Knowledge management: A review of industrial cases. *Journal of Computer Information Systems, 42*(5), 26–39.

Lane, P. J., & Lubatkin, M. (1998). Relative absorptive capacity and interorganizational learning. *Strategic Management Journal, 19*(5), 461–477.

Leifer, R., McDermott, C. M., O'Connor, G. C., Peters, L. S., Rice, M. P., & Veryzer, R. W. (2000). *Radical innovation: How mature companies can outsmart upstarts*. Boston, MA: Harvard Business School Press.

Levinthal, D. A. (1997). Adaptation on rugged landscapes. *Management Science, 43*(7), 934–950.

Li, H., & Atuahene-Gima, K. (2001). Product innovation strategy and the performance of new technology ventures in China. *Academy of Management Journal, 44*(6), 1123–1134.

Lichtenstein, B. B., Dooley, K. J., & Lumpkin, G. T. (2006). Measuring emergence in the dynamics of new venture creation. *Journal of Business Venturing, 21*(2), 153–175.

Lofstrom, S. M. (2000). Absorptive capacity in strategic alliances: Investigating the effects of individuals' social and human capital on inter-firm learning. Paper presented at the Organization Science Winter Conference, Keystone, CO.

Lovejoy, W. S. (1998). Integrated operations: A proposal for operations management teaching and research. *Production and Operations Management, 7*(2), 106–124.

Lyles, M. A., & Schwenk, C. R. (1992). Top management, strategy and organizational knowledge structures. *Journal of Management Studies, 29*(2), 155–174.

Marroquín, B., Boyle, C. C., Nolen-Hoeksema, S., & Stanton, A. L. (2016). Using emotion as information in future-oriented cognition: Individual differences in the context of state negative affect. *Personality and Individual Differences, 95*, 121–126.

Mair, J., & Marti, I. (2006). Social entrepreneurship research: A source of explanation, prediction, and delight. *Journal of World Business, 41*(1), 36–44.

Matusik, S. F. (2000). Absorptive capacity and firm knowledge: Separating the effects of public knowledge, flexible firm boundaries, and firm absorptive abilities. Paper presented at the Organization Science Winter Conference, Keystone, CO.

Matusik, S. F., & Heeley, M. (2001). Absorptive capacity and firm knowledge: Separating the multiple components of the absorptive capacity construct. Paper presented at the annual meeting of the Academy of Management, Washington, DC.

McDermott, C. M., & O'Connor, G. C. (2002). Managing radical innovation: An overview of emergent strategy issues. *Journal of Product Innovation Management, 19*(6), 424–438.

McGrath, R. G. (1996). Options and the enterprise: Toward a strategic theory of entrepreneurial wealth creation. *Academy of Management Proceedings, 1*, 101–105.

McGrath, R. G. (1997). A real options logic for initiating technology positioning investments. *Academy of Management Review, 22*(4), 974–996.

McGrath, R. G. (1999). Falling forward: Real options reasoning and entrepreneurial failure. *Academy of Management Review, 24*(1), 13–30.

McGrath, R. G., & Keil, T. (2007). The value captor's process: Getting the most out of your new business ventures. *Harvard Business Review, 85*(5), 128–136.

McGrath, R. G., & MacMillan, I. C. (2000). *The entrepreneurial mindset: Strategies for continuously creating opportunity in an age of uncertainty* (Vol. 284). Boston, MA: Harvard Business Press.

McGrath, R. G., & Nerkar, A. (2004). Real options reasoning and a new look at the R&D investment strategies of pharmaceutical firms. *Strategic Management Journal, 25*(1), 1–21.

McMullen, J. S., Bagby, D., & Palich, L. E. (2008). Economic freedom and the motivation to engage in entrepreneurial action. *Entrepreneurship Theory and Practice, 32*(5), 875–895.

McMullen, J. S., & Shepherd, D. A. (2006). Entrepreneurial action and the role of uncertainty in the theory of the entrepreneur. *Academy of Management Review, 31*(1), 132–152.

Meyers, C., & Jones, T. B. (1993). *Promoting active learning: Strategies for the college classroom*. San Francisco, CA: Jossey-Bass Inc.

Miller, T. L., Grimes, M. G., McMullen, J. S., & Vogus, T. J. (2012). Venturing for others with heart and head: How compassion encourages social entrepreneurship. *Academy of Management Review, 37*(4), 616–640.

Mitchell, J. R., & Shepherd, D. A. (2010). To thine own self be true: Images of self, images of opportunity, and entrepreneurial action. *Journal of Business Venturing, 25*(1), 138–154.

Montes, G. M., Martin, E. P., Bayo, J. A., & Garcia, J. O. (2011). The applicability of computer simulation using Monte Carlo techniques in windfarm profitability analysis. *Renewable and Sustainable Energy Reviews, 15*(9), 4746–4755.

Morris, M. H., Kuratko, D. F., & Covin, J. G. (2010). *Corporate entrepreneurship & innovation*. Andover: Cengage Learning.

Morrison, E. W., Wheeler-Smith, S. L., & Kamdar, D. (2011). Speaking up in groups: A cross-level study of group voice climate and voice. *Journal of Applied Psychology, 96*(1), 183–191.

Mueller, W. F. (1962). The origins of the basic inventions underlying Du Pont's major product and process innovations, 1920 to 1950. In R. R. Nelson (Ed.), *The rate and direction of inventive activity: Economic and social factors* (pp. 323–358). Princeton: Princeton University Press.

Naumann, S. E., & Bennett, N. (2000). A case for procedural justice climate: Development and test of a multilevel model. *Academy of Management Journal, 43*(5), 881–889.

Nonaka, I., & Takeuchi, H. (1995). *The knowledge-creating company: How Japanese companies create the dynamics of innovation.* New York: Oxford University Press.

O'Connor, G. C. (1998). Market learning and radical innovation: A cross case comparison of eight radical innovation projects. *Journal of product innovation management, 15*(2), 151–166.

O'Connor, G. C., & Veryzer, R. W. (2001). The nature of market visioning for technology-based radical innovation. *Journal of Product Innovation Management, 18*(4), 231–246.

Ocasio, W. (1997). Towards an attention-based view of the firm. *Strategic Management Journal, 18*(S1), 187–206.

Patel, P. C., & Fiet, J. O. (2009). Systematic search and its relationship to firm founding. *Entrepreneurship Theory and Practice, 33*(2), 501–526.

Patzelt, H., & Shepherd, D. A. (2008). The decision to persist with underperforming alliances: The role of trust and control. *Journal of Management Studies, 45*(7), 1217–1243.

Patzelt, H., & Shepherd, D. A. (2010). Recognizing opportunities for sustainable development. *Entrepreneurship Theory and Practice, 35*(4), 631–652.

Peredo, A. M., & Chrisman, J. J. (2006). Toward a theory of community-based enterprise. *Academy of Management Review, 31*(2), 309–328.

Peteraf, M. A., & Bergen, M. E. (2003). Scanning dynamic competitive landscapes: A market-based and resource-based framework. *Strategic Management Journal, 24*(10), 1027–1041.

Pierce, J. L., Kostova, T., & Dirks, K. T. (2001). Toward a theory of psychological ownership in organizations. *Academy of Management Review, 26*(2), 298–310.

Pinson, S. D., Louçã, J. A., & Moraitis, P. (1997). A distributed decision support system for strategic planning. *Decision Support Systems, 20*(1), 35–51.

Rahmandad, H. (2008). Effect of delays on complexity of organizational learning. *Management Science, 54*(7), 1297–1312.

Reiss, S. (1991). Expectancy model of fear, anxiety, and panic. *Clinical Psychology Review, 11*(2), 141–153.

Riedl, D. F., Kaufmann, L., Zimmermann, C., & Perols, J. L. (2013). Reducing uncertainty in supplier selection decisions: Antecedents and outcomes of procedural rationality. *Journal of Operations Management, 31*(1), 24–36.

Rosenberg, N. (1982). *Inside the black box: Technology and economics.* Cambridge: Cambridge University Press.

Salomo, S., Talke, K., & Strecker, N. (2008). Innovation field orientation and its effect on innovativeness and firm performance. *Journal of Product Innovation Management, 25*(6), 560–576.

Sandberg, J., & Tsoukas, H. (2011). Grasping the logic of practice: Theorizing through practical rationality. *Academy of Management Review, 36*(2), 338–360.

Santos, F. M., & Eisenhardt, K. M. (2009). Constructing markets and shaping boundaries: Entrepreneurial power in nascent fields. *Academy of Management Journal, 52*(4), 643–671.

Schmidt, J. B., Sarangee, K. R., & Montoya, M. M. (2009). Exploring new product development project review practices. *Journal of Product Innovation Management, 26*(5), 520–535.

Schneider, B., Ehrhart, M. G., & Macey, W. H. (2013). Organizational climate and culture. *Annual Review of Psychology, 64*, 361–388.

Schultz, C., Salomo, S., Brentani, U., & Kleinschmidt, E. J. (2013). How formal control influences decision-making clarity and innovation performance. *Journal of Product Innovation Management, 30*(3), 430–447.

Seshadri, S., & Subrahmanyam, M. (2005). Introduction to the Special Issue on "Risk Management in Operations". *Production and Operations Management, 14*(1), 1–4.

Sethi, R., & Iqbal, Z. (2008). Stage-gate controls, learning failure, and adverse effect on novel new products. *Journal of Marketing, 72*(1), 118–134.

Shan, W., Walker, G., & Kogut, B. (1994). Interfirm cooperation and startup innovation in the biotechnology industry. *Strategic Management Journal, 15*(5), 387–394.

Shane, S. (2000). Prior knowledge and the discovery of entrepreneurial opportunities. *Organization Science, 11*(4), 448–469.

Shane, S., Locke, E. A., & Collins, C. J. (2003). Entrepreneurial motivation. *Human Resource Management Review, 13*(2), 257–279.

Shepherd, D. A. (2015). Party on! A call for entrepreneurship research that is more interactive, activity based, cognitively hot, compassionate, and prosocial. *Journal of Business Venturing, 30*(4), 489–507.

Shepherd, D. A., & DeTienne, D. R. (2005). Prior knowledge, potential financial reward, and opportunity identification. *Entrepreneurship Theory and Practice, 29*(1), 91–112.

Shepherd, D. A., McMullen, J. S., & Jennings, P. D. (2007). The formation of opportunity beliefs: Overcoming ignorance and reducing doubt. *Strategic Entrepreneurship Journal, 1*(1–2), 75–95.

Shepherd, D. A., McMullen, J. S., & Ocasio, W. (2016). Is that an opportunity? An attention model of top managers' opportunity beliefs for strategic action. *Strategic Management Journal.* doi:10.1002/smj.2499.

Shepherd, D. A., & Patzelt, H. (2011). The new field of sustainable entrepreneurship: Studying entrepreneurial action linking "what is to be sustained" with "what is to be developed". *Entrepreneurship Theory and Practice, 35*(1), 137–163.

Shepherd, D. A., & Patzelt, H. (2013). Operational entrepreneurship: How operations management research can advance entrepreneurship. *Production and Operations Management, 22*(6), 1416–1422.

Shepherd, D. A., & Sutcliffe, K. M. (2011). Inductive top-down theorizing: A source of new theories of organization. *Academy of Management Review, 36*(2), 361–380.

Shepherd, D. A., Wiklund, J., & Haynie, J. M. (2009). Moving forward: Balancing the financial and emotional costs of business failure. *Journal of Business Venturing, 24*(2), 134–148.

Simangunsong, E., Hendry, L. C., & Stevenson, M. (2016). Managing supply chain uncertainty with emerging ethical issues. *International Journal of Operations and Production Management, 36*(10), 1272–1307.

Smith, K. A., & DeGregorio, D. D. (2002). Biosocialization, discovery, and entrepreneurial action. In M. Hitt, D. Ireland, M. Camp, & D. Sexton (Eds.), *Strategic entrepreneurship: Creating an integrated mindset.* Oxford: Blackwell.

Sommer, S. C., & Loch, C. H. (2004). Selectionism and learning in projects with complexity and unforeseeable uncertainty. *Management Science, 50*(10), 1334–1347.

Song, J. D., & Kim, J. C. (2001). Is five too many? Simulation analysis of profitability and cost structure in the Korean mobile telephone industry. *Telecommunications Policy, 25*(1), 101–123.

Staw, B. M. (1981). The escalation of commitment to a course of action. *Academy of Management Review, 6*(4), 577–587.

Staw, B. M. (1997). The escalation of commitment: An update and appraisal. In Z. Shapira (Ed.), *Organizational decision making* (pp. 191–215). Cambridge: Cambridge University Press.

Staw, B. M., Barsade, S. G., & Koput, K. W. (1997). Escalation at the credit window: A longitudinal study of bank executives' recognition and write-off of problem loans. *Journal of Applied Psychology, 82*(1), 130–142.

Sterman, J. D. (2000a). *Business dynamics.* New York: McGraw-Hill.

Sterman, J. D. (2000b). Learning in and about complex systems. *Reflections, 1*(3), 24–51.

Sun, L., Hong, L. J., & Hu, Z. (2014). Balancing exploitation and exploration in discrete optimization via simulation through a Gaussian process-based search. *Operations Research, 62*(6), 1416–1438.

Szulanski, G. (1996). Exploring internal stickiness: Impediments to the transfer of best practice within the firm. *Strategic Management Journal, 17*, 27–43.

Talke, K., Salomo, S., & Rost, K. (2010). How top management team diversity affects innovativeness and performance via the strategic choice to focus on innovation fields. *Research Policy, 39*(7), 907–918.

Tatikonda, M. V., & Montoya-Weiss, M. M. (2001). Integrating operations and marketing perspectives of product innovation: The influence of organizational process factors and capabilities on development performance. *Management Science, 47*(1), 151–172.

Tatikonda, M. V., & Rosenthal, S. R. (2000). Successful execution of product development projects: Balancing firmness and flexibility in the innovation process. *Journal of Operations Management, 18*(4), 401–425.

Taylor, S. (2014). *Anxiety sensitivity: Theory, research, and treatment of the fear of anxiety.* New York: Routledge.

Teece, D. J. (1996). Firm organization, industrial structure, and technological innovation. *Journal of Economic Behavior & Organization, 31*(2), 193–224.

Teece, D. J., Pisano, G., & Shuen, A. (1997). Dynamic capabilities and strategic management. *Strategic Management Journal, 18*(7), 509–533.

Thornhill, S. (2006). Knowledge, innovation and firm performance in high-and low-technology regimes. *Journal of Business Venturing, 21*(5), 687–703.

Tilton, J. E. (1971). *International diffusion of technology: The case of semiconductors.* Washington, DC: Brookings Institution Press.

Tomlin, B. (2003). Capacity investments in supply chains: Sharing the gain rather than sharing the pain. *Manufacturing & Service Operations Management, 5*(4), 317–333.

Tornikoski, E. T., & Newbert, S. L. (2007). Exploring the determinants of organizational emergence: A legitimacy perspective. *Journal of Business Venturing, 22*(2), 311–335.

Tripsas, M., & Gavetti, G. (2000). Capabilities, cognition, and inertia: Evidence from digital imaging. *Strategic Management Journal, 21*(10-11), 1147–1161.

Tsai, W. (2001). Knowledge transfer in intraorganizational networks: Effects of network position and absorptive capacity on business unit innovation and performance. *Academy of Management Journal, 44*(5), 996–1004.

Tsai, K. H., Chang, H. C., & Peng, C. Y. (2016). Refining the linkage between perceived capability and entrepreneurial intention: Roles of perceived opportunity, fear of failure, and gender. *International Entrepreneurship and Management Journal.* doi:10.1007/s11365-016-0383-x.

Urban, G. L., & Hauser, J. R. (1993). *Designing and marketing of new products.* Englewood Cliffs, NJ: Prentice Hall.

Van de Vrande, V. (2013). Balancing your technology-sourcing portfolio: How sourcing mode diversity enhances innovative performance. *Strategic Management Journal, 34*(5), 610–621.

Van Wijk, R., Van den Bosch, F., & Volberda, H. (2001). The impact of knowledge depth and breadth of absorbed knowledge on levels of exploration and exploitation. Paper presented at the annual meeting of the Academy of Management, Washington, DC.

Vermeulen, F., & Barkema, H. (2001). Learning through acquisitions. *Academy of Management Journal, 44*(3), 457–476.

Veryzer, R. W. (1998). Discontinuous innovation and the new product development process. *Journal of Product Innovation Management, 15*(4), 304–321.

Vickery, S. K., Jayaram, J., Droge, C., & Calantone, R. (2003). The effects of an integrative supply chain strategy on customer service and financial performance: An analysis of direct versus indirect relationships. *Journal of Operations Management, 21*(5), 523–539.

Vivares, J. A., Sarache Castro, W. A., & Naranjo-Valencia, J. C. (2016). Impact of human resource management on performance in competitive priorities. *International Journal of Operations & Production Management, 36*(2), 114–134.

von Hippel, E. (1988). *The sources of innovation*. New York: Oxford University Press.

Walsh, J. P. (1995). Managerial and organizational cognition: Notes from a trip down memory lane. *Organization Science, 6*(3), 280–321.

Walsh, J. P., & Ungson, G. R. (1991). Organizational memory. *Academy of Management Review, 16*, 57–91.

Wagner, S. H., Parker, C. P., & Christiansen, N. D. (2003). Employees that think and act like owners: Effects of ownership beliefs and behaviors on organizational effectiveness. *Personnel Psychology, 56*(4), 847–871.

Weick, K. E. (1999). Theory construction as disciplined reflexivity: Tradeoffs in the 90s. *Academy of Management Review, 24*(4), 797–806.

Weinstein, N. D., & Klein, W. M. (1995). Resistance of personal risk perceptions to debiasing interventions. *Health Psychology, 14*(2), 132–140.

Wood, M. S., McKelvie, A., & Haynie, J. M. (2014). Making it personal: Opportunity individuation and the shaping of opportunity beliefs. *Journal of Business Venturing, 29*(2), 252–272.

Zahra, S. A., & Chaples, S. S. (1993). Blind spots in competitive analysis. *Academy of Management Executive, 7*(2), 7–28.

Zahra, S. A., & Covin, J. G. (1995). Contextual influences on the corporate entrepreneurship-performance relationship: A longitudinal analysis. *Journal of Business Venturing, 10*(1), 43–58.

Zahra, S. A., & George, G. (2002). Absorptive capacity: A review, reconceptualization, and extension. *Academy of Management Review, 27*(2), 185–203.

Zimmerman, B. J., & Pons, M. M. (1986). Development of a structured interview for assessing student use of self-regulated learning strategies. *American Educational Research Journal, 23*(4), 614–628.

Zohar, A., & Barzilai, S. (2013). A review of research on metacognition in science education: Current and future directions. *Studies in Science Education, 49*(2), 121–169.

Zohar, A., & Dori, Y. J. (2003). Higher order thinking skills and low-achieving students: Are they mutually exclusive? *The Journal Of The Learning Sciences, 12*(2), 145–181.

**Open Access** This chapter is distributed under the terms of the Creative Commons Attribution 4.0 International License (http://creativecommons.org/licenses/by/4.0/), which permits use, duplication, adaptation, distribution and reproduction in any medium or format, as long as you give appropriate credit to the original author(s) and the source, provide a link to the Creative Commons license and indicate if changes were made.

The images or other third party material in this chapter are included in the work's Creative Commons license, unless indicated otherwise in the credit line; if such material is not included in the work's Creative Commons license and the respective action is not permitted by statutory regulation, users will need to obtain permission from the license holder to duplicate, adapt or reproduce the material.

CHAPTER 5

# Researching Entrepreneurships' Role in Sustainable Development

## INTRODUCTION

Sustainable development is arguably the most significant issue of today. Each day, we hear accounts of ozone depletion, climate change, and the destruction of biodiversity as well as details about the detrimental and potentially lethal consequences these issues have for living species (e.g., IPCC, 2007; United Nations, 2004). Scholars have argued, however, that entrepreneurial action can help this dire situation by preserving ecosystems, neutralizing climate change, decreasing environmental degradation and deforestation, improving farming practices, providing more access to fresh water, and maintaining biodiversity (e.g., Cohen & Winn, 2007; Dean & McMullen, 2007). Furthermore, in developing countries in particular, such entrepreneurial actions can positively contribute to education, productivity, socioeconomic status, physical health, and self-reliance at both the individual and societal levels (e.g., Wheeler et al., 2005). Finally, while research has shown that entrepreneurial action creates economic gains for investors, entrepreneurs, and economies (e.g., Easterly, 2006), we need more sustainable entrepreneurship research investigating how entrepreneurial action can serve as a mechanism for preserving nature and ecosystems while also providing economic and non-economic gains for investors, entrepreneurs, and societies at large.

---

This chapter builds on Shepherd and Patzelt (2011).

When a community of scholars comes together with a shared research interest characterized by an agreed-upon set of assumptions (e.g., aim, central focus, research methods, and relevant literature streams) (Busenitz et al., 2003, pp. 287–288; Ogbor, 2000; Summer et al., 1990), an academic field emerges. Because the field of entrepreneurship itself is still emerging, it is unsurprising that scholars have failed to clearly define the sub-field of sustainable entrepreneurship and outline its core assumptions. Thus, the purpose of this chapter is to provide some clarity in this area. The framework we outline in this chapter is not meant to be a fully developed, conclusive scope of sustainable entrepreneurship, but we hope it contributes to the stream's continued development.

By creating a more meta-theoretical (as opposed to a purely theoretical) framework, we hope to attract scholars from different theoretical perspectives to be a part of this scholarly community. While our ultimate goal is to combine sustainable development and entrepreneurship to come to some agreement regarding a boundary distinguishing sustainable entrepreneurship from other fields, we also want to encourage scholarly diversity within this boundary (Cannella & Paetzold, 1994) as both aims are crucial for advancing the field. Consensus around a field's definition/boundary conditions is the foundation of knowledge generation and accumulation (Kuhn, 1974; Pfeffer, 1993), and diversity within those bounds enables scholars to make comparisons across theories (Feyerabend, 1980) that inspire creative visions (Gould, 1981) as well as allow those visions to be appraised as part of the continual discourse in the marketplace of ideas (Cannella & Paetzold, 1994). That is, a more transparent and precise definition of sustainable entrepreneurship will "set the scene" for a more diverse stream of theory-based research that—even with little (or no) overlap in dependent variables, independent variables, and theory—will at least have the chance to lead to knowledge accumulation because any study can be "located" within sustainable entrepreneurship (or not). For example, two separate studies may investigate different issues and be driven by distinct theoretical roots, but they can both contribute to the emergence of the field.

Our goal is to welcome numerous theoretical viewpoints to the sustainable entrepreneurship sub-field and embrace the significant variation in terminology, data, and methods instead of trying to focus on "the" definitive dependent and independent variables. While some scholars want to quickly come to agreement on these issues in new fields of study, it is our opinion that diversity within a broader framework is more beneficial—at least for the time being. Next, we lay the foundation for this broader sustainable entrepreneurship framework and then suggest some potential research avenues within it.

## A Definition of Sustainable Entrepreneurship

The literature on sustainable development contributes to a broader discussion of sustainability by describing what is to be sustained—namely, nature, life-support systems, and community (for a review, see Parris & Kates, 2003)—and what is to be developed—namely, individuals, the economy, and society (see Leiserowitz, Kates, & Parris, 2006; National Research Council, 1999).

### *What Is to Be Sustained in Sustainable Entrepreneurship?*

**Sustaining nature.** With intrinsic value above and beyond simply being a life-support system (see Muehlebach, 2001), nature encompasses all the phenomena of the physical world, including the *earth, biodiversity,* and *ecosystems* (Parris & Kates, 2003). Indeed, if these resources are not maintained, the survival of many species on the earth, including humans, is endangered. The destruction of the ozone layer, for example, has led to increased exposure to ultraviolet irradiation and thus higher rates of skin cancer (Slaper, Velders, Daniel, de Gruijl, & van der Leun, 1996). In contrast, research has shown that humans' health improves significantly with exposure to natural green places (Pretty, Hine, & Peacock, 2006). If individuals, organizations, and nations are proactive in preserving the earth, biodiversity, and ecosystems, nature can be sustained. One pathway to fulfilling this goal is through sustainable entrepreneurship. However, more research is needed to investigate entrepreneurial action's role as a mechanism for sustaining nature.

**Sustaining sources of life support.** Referring to the environment as "a source of resources and services for the utilitarian life support of humankind" (Parris & Kates, 2003, p. 560), sustaining life support involves preserving the *environment, natural resources,* and *ecosystem services.* In other words, life support for humans can be severely jeopardized if environmental systems are not sustained. For example, millions of deaths per year (particularly in third-world countries) are caused by the pollution of water with infectious agents, bacteria, and chemicals (Montgomery & Elimelech, 2007). In addition, the over-exploitation of natural resources over the last few decades has had severe consequences on life support for humans. The over-exploitation of minerals from mining, for instance, has caused large portions of land to become uninhabitable (Swanson, 1996), and over-fishing has resulted in reduced fish stocks and less marine biodiversity (Sala & Knowlton, 2006). Furthermore, declining ecosystem services directly impact human life support. For example, contamination has reduced the purification capacity of aquatic habitats, ultimately leading to a shortage of drinking water (Zedler & Kercher, 2005), and soil erosion has led to diminished soil fertility, which in turn has led to reduced crop yields (Schröter et al., 2005). More research is needed to gain a deeper understanding of entrepreneurial action as a mechanism for sustaining life support.

**Sustaining communities**. A community is made up of an intricate web of relationships between a set of people who share similar values, norms, meanings, histories, and identities (Etzioni, 1996). Communities' distinctive characteristics (and thus what makes them contribute to members' identities) are their *culture*, *groups*, and *places*, and when these factors are threatened, the community at hand may be lost. In terms of culture, it has been argued that "human beings have a right to culture—not just any culture, but to their own" (Margalit & Halbertal, 2004, p. 529). Being able to create and maintain cultures within larger societies enables humans to secure their personal identities, and the loss of a cultural identity can have significant negative impacts. For example, research has shown that the loss of cultural identity has led to increased alcoholism among American Indians (Spicer, 2001) and reduced physical health and life expectancy in Australian Aborigines (McDermott, O'Dea, Rowley, Knight, & Burgess, 1998). In addition to culture, families and other groups are also a source of personal identity and are often argued to be the foundation of well-developed communities (Miller, 2001). Research has shown that when the family breaks down, the disruption weakens individual well-being (Forste & Heaton, 2004). Finally, places are important to communities as they can represent important public symbols of culture and history (Borer, 2006), thus providing a sense of identity (Padua, 2007). Even though places are vital to communities, however, efforts to preserve places are not always effective. For example, tourism often threatens important community places, such as the Great Wall of China (du Cros, Bauer, Lo, & Rui, 2005), and air pollution continues to have harmful consequences for many places, such as cultural heritage sites in Florence (Monforti, Bellasio, Bianconi, Clai, & Zanini, 2004).

Research on how entrepreneurial action can contribute to sustaining communities has already begun. For instance, Peredo and Chrisman (2006) introduced the notion of community-based enterprise, describing how all individuals in a community can act as entrepreneurs. Because a community-based enterprise is "typically rooted in community culture, natural and social capital are integral and inseparable from economic considerations" (Peredo & Chrisman, 2006, p. 309), suggesting that in poorer regions of the world, communities' members acting as entrepreneurs can lessen poverty while preserving the natural environment. As another example, (O'Neill, Hershauer, & Golden, 2009) explained how the Navajo Nation, the largest Native American tribe in the USA, created an entrepreneurial venture (Navajo FlexCrete) that develops ecofriendly building supplies by recycling waste material. This venture not only builds economic, social, environmental, and cultural value for the Navajo Nation, but it also contributes to maintaining the native Navajo tribe's heritage. Future sustainable entrepreneurship research can add to the current body of knowledge by deepening our understanding of the entrepreneurial mechanisms for sustaining communities.

## *What Is to Be Developed in Sustainable Entrepreneurship?*

Generating economic gains is a central tenet of entrepreneurship (Venkataraman, 1997) and is thus also part of sustainable entrepreneurship. However, the literature on sustainable development argues that in addition to economic gains, non-economic outcomes (i.e., benefits to people and society) are also essential in development goals (National Research Council, 1999). Depending on their own characteristics and goals, individuals and organizations are likely to prioritize economic and non-economic gains in different ways. Some sustainable entrepreneurs, for instance, may believe it is sufficient to merely ensure their organization's financial viability, whereas others may want to earn economic profit for themselves.

**Developing economic gain**. An economics viewpoint focuses on the generation of economic gains for the actor and/or society, which also serve as an important development goal. For instance, economic gains can improve individuals' socioeconomic status (Oakes & Rossi, 2003) as well as result in enhanced emotional (Gallo & Matthews, 2003), psychological (Twenge & Campbell, 2002), and physical health (Hanson & Chen, 2007). These effects of economic gains go beyond generational boundaries because parents' increased socioeconomic status often leads to improved childhood well-being and enhanced socioeconomic status for their children when they become adults (Conger & Donnellan, 2007). In addition, individuals' subjective well-being (Diener et al., 1995) and physical health (Knowles & Owen, 1995) tend to increase with economic development in the countries in which they live. Individuals are likely to readily accept the development of these economic gains as an outcome of entrepreneurship. Therefore, when we combine these gains with a construct of what is to be sustained, the result is likely to be accepted as sustainable entrepreneurship.

**Developing non-economic gains for individuals.** In addition to the economic gains that can result from sustainable entrepreneurship, there are many non-economic gains, including increased child survival, life expectancy, education, equity, and equal opportunity (Board Sustainable Development, 1999; Parris & Kates, 2003). For example, in poor countries, one out of every ten children dies before the age of five (Millennium goals, United Nations), the primary causes of which are pneumonia, diarrhea, malaria, measles, and AIDS (www.childinfo.org). The main question of stakeholder research, for instance, appears to be "for whose benefit and at whose expense should the firm be managed?" (Freeman, 1994, p. 67). Past research has emphasized ways to ensure the gains generated by a business are distributed equitably between a firm and its stakeholders. When resources are not distributed fairly, the firm is exploiting its stakeholders.

Research in the budding field of social entrepreneurship and in the area of corporate social responsibility has argued that entrepreneurs can contribute significantly to providing non-economic gains to individuals. For example, Nobel Laureate Muhammad Yunus learned that impoverished people in Bangladesh were being exploited by loan providers who were charging more than 100% interest. These individuals had no choice but to accept these rates because they needed money to buy bamboo for the stools they built and sold to earn their living, and no one else provided loans. To help these individuals, Yunus founded Grameen Bank, a social enterprise aimed at offering the poor cheaper loans, which in turn enabled them to markedly improve their living situations (Yunus, 2005). Similarly, Victoria Hale, a social entrepreneur and former biopharmaceutical research scientist, founded OneWorld Health to provide people in low-income countries with medical treatment that would be unaffordable to them otherwise (Seelos & Mair, 2005). Innovative and entrepreneurial corporate social responsibility activities can also provide significant benefits to individuals. For example, McDonald's Ronald McDonald House Charities (McWilliams & Siegel, 2001) enables seriously ill children to stay with their parents when receiving medical treatment far from home. Future sustainable entrepreneurship research can contribute to our understanding of the entrepreneurial mechanisms for developing non-economic gains for individuals.

**Developing non-economic gains for society.** Gains to society include benefits for people living in that society; however, they are different from individual gains in that the latter may only go to a select few individuals whereas societal gains are accessible to all (or the vast majority of) societal members. For example, societies realize gains by developing the "well-being and security of national states, regions and institutions and, more recently, the valued social ties and community organizations" (Board of Sustainable Development, 1999, p. 25). The well-being of nations and regions encompasses inhabitants' satisfaction with life and happiness (Diener et al., 1995; Vemuri & Costanza, 2006), and security refers to defense against both outside threats (e.g., by other nations [e.g., Steinbruner, 1978]) and inside threats (e.g., through economic [Parkhe, 1992] or environmental [Porter, 1995] decay). Societies can also realize gains by developing social ties and inter-personal relationships between societal members. In poorer regions with decreased human well-being, weak social norms, low inter-personal trust, corruption, and violence tend to proliferate (Narayan & Petesch, 2002), representing significant impediments to societal development (Easterly, 2006).

Social entrepreneurship and corporate social responsibility studies have emphasized the importance of entrepreneurs in creating non-economic gains for society. For instance, Ibrahim Abouleish, a social entrepreneur, founded Sekem, an initiative that began by growing organic herbs for medicinal use in poor areas of Egypt. Not only did this initiative create jobs for locals, but it also improved the area's social structure and enhanced inhabitants' trust in society, thereby enabling people to escape poverty and regain control in their lives. By applying organic agriculture techniques, Sekem also helped preserve parts of the region's natural environment (Seelos & Mair, 2005). As Burton and Goldsby (2009) argued, entrepreneurs and small business owners are often driven less by profit than shareholders of larger publicly held organizations, thus enabling them to act in more socially responsible ways. For example, one way entrepreneurs can contribute to the development of their local society is by keeping employment locally instead of shifting their operations to less expensive production sites. By explaining these issues in more detail, sustainable entrepreneurship research can deepen our understanding of how, why, and under what circumstances entrepreneurial action can generate gains for society.

## What Is Sustainable Entrepreneurship?

**A definition of sustainable entrepreneurship.** So far in this chapter, we have outlined the constructs to be developed and constructs to be sustained. Now, we explain how the two are linked by entrepreneurial action, a topic informed by the entrepreneurship literature. According to Venkataraman (1997, p. 120), entrepreneurship as a scholarly field "seeks to understand how opportunities to bring into existence future goods and services are discovered, created and exploited, by whom and with what consequences." We offer the following definition for sustainable entrepreneurship, which builds on the shared affinity of a community of scholars interested in this topic and is informed by the sustainable development and entrepreneurship literatures:

> **Sustainable entrepreneurship** is focused on the preservation of nature, life support, and community in the pursuit of perceived opportunities to bring into existence future products, processes, and services for gain, where gain is broadly construed to include economic and non-economic gains to individuals, the economy, and society. (Shepherd & Patzelt, 2011, p. 137)

**What sustainable entrepreneurship is not.** If a definition tries to include everything, then it will end up representing nothing. Thus, in this section, we focus on research that—while likely very valuable—does not fit within the scope of sustainable entrepreneurship that we propose, thus delineating the boundaries of this sub-field. First, research that solely focuses on what is to be sustained without concurrently investigating what is to be developed does not qualify as sustainable entrepreneurship research. For example, sustainability-focused research, such as a study on climate change documenting a significant change in global temperatures over the last decade, is inarguably important; however, because it does not also consider the development of people, the economy, and/or society, it cannot be classified as sustainable entrepreneurship research. Second, research that solely focuses on development without concurrently investigating what is being sustained is not considered sustainable entrepreneurship research.

For example, research investigating child survival resulting from the creation of a new antibody for inoculation is very important but is not considered sustainable entrepreneurship research because it does not take into account sustainability. Third, research that concurrently addresses what is being sustained and what is being developed but does not connect the two with discussions related to the identification, creation, or exploitation of future goods, processes, or services is not sustainable entrepreneurship research (but may be considered sustainable development research). For example, government-funded programs and non-profit organizations may improve the sustainability of biodiversity while simultaneously developing people through education; however, this work is often done through actions that are not necessarily entrepreneurial in nature. Again, while exploring these topics is valuable research, it is not sustainable entrepreneurship. Finally, entrepreneurship research focusing entirely on the economic outcomes of entrepreneurial action (i.e., individuals, firms, and/or society) without simultaneous consideration of sustainability outcomes is not sustainable entrepreneurship research.

**Sustainable entrepreneurship and related concepts**. While we just outlined several research streams that are not a part of sustainable entrepreneurship, there are several research streams the field overlaps with and/or includes. First, our characterization of sustainable entrepreneurship encompasses studies on *ecopreneurship* (i.e., environmental entrepreneurship), a field exploring the ways entrepreneurial action can help preserve the natural environment, including the earth, biodiversity, and ecosystems (e.g., see Schaper, 2005; Pastakia, 1998). With this goal in mind, ecopreneurship is part of sustainable entrepreneurship, but the two are not identical because ecopreneurship does not overtly explore, for instance, sustaining communities or the creation of non-economic gains for individuals and societies. Second, our conceptualization of sustainable entrepreneurship intersects with the notion of *social entrepreneurship*, which "encompasses the activities and processes undertaken to discover, define, and exploit opportunities in order to enhance social wealth by creating new ventures or managing existing organizations in an innovative manner" (Zahra, Gedajlovic, Neubaum, & Shulman, 2009). While social entrepreneurship research explores the generation of (non-economic) gains for individuals and societies, it does not include preserving nature, sources of life support, or community. Finally, our definition of sustainable entrepreneurship embraces aspects of *corporate social responsibility*, which refers to firm actions that seem to promote some form of social good beyond firm interests and legal requirements (McWilliams & Siegel, 2001). However, corporate social responsibility does not necessarily involve entrepreneurial action or innovation; rather, it often involves organizations' societal engagements (e.g., funding a sports team or donating to social organizations).

The clearer definition of sustainable entrepreneurship that we developed serves as a foundation for investigating where and how future research can contribute to the field's development. Within the meta-theoretic framework this definition affords, we can start to uncover how entrepreneurial action can connect sustainability and development at both the individual and community levels—a topic to which we now turn.

## Entrepreneurial Action Linking Sustainability and Development at the Individual Level

Individuals' prior knowledge of the natural and communal environment is likely to be very important in terms of identifying potential opportunities that preserve the natural/communal environment and generate gains. For example, using their prior knowledge of aquatic chemistry and biology, individuals have uncovered opportunities to apply waste water treatment that decontaminates sewerage (Sonune & Ghate, 2004). Individuals with little or no knowledge about environmental issues (e.g., about ozone layer chemistry, pollution, mining techniques, and aquatic chemistry) or about cultures and places may not even recognize that changes occur in these areas and that such changes directly influence human life. As a result, individuals like these are unlikely to recognize opportunities for action to maintain the natural and communal environment.

Prior entrepreneurial knowledge also plays a role in one's ability to identify third-person opportunities. Shane (2000) outlined three types of entrepreneurial knowledge that influence individuals' ability to recognize opportunities: prior knowledge of markets, prior knowledge of ways to serve markets, and prior knowledge of customer problems. First, prior knowledge of markets impacts the entrepreneur's decision of which market to enter. For example, when an individual has prior knowledge of customers and suppliers in a particular market, he or she is better able to evaluate whether a new technology will be successful in that market and what potential gains may result (Roberts, 1991). Based on this evaluation, the individual is able to determine whether an opportunity for market entry exists. Second, prior knowledge of how to serve markets helps in the identification of opportunities because it enables entrepreneurs to evaluate (and perhaps attain) the skills needed for market entry (von Hippel, 1988). Finally, prior knowledge about customer problems with existing products or services can help individuals recognize opportunities to introduce new offerings that address customers' pain points and are thus accepted by the market (von Hippel, 1988).

Together with previous knowledge, motivation plays a significant role in individuals' ability to identify potential sustainable development opportunities (McMullen & Shepherd, 2006). Motivation likely points people and organizations toward signals of potential opportunities to preserve the natural and communal environment when they sense that their physical and psychological well-being is being threatened. These feelings trigger emotions, which in turn capture and direct attention to the problem at hand and instill the need to act. We explore some of these triggers.

First, individuals are often motivated to act on sustainable opportunities that enhance or uphold their own physical health. The decline of natural environment through pollution, for example, endangers many people's lives (Montgomery & Elimelech, 2007), and the over-exploitation of natural resources reduces humans' life support by decreasing food availability (Sala & Knowlton, 2006). In turn, these perceptions of threat and loss can lead to negative emotional reactions (Meijnders, Midden, & Wilke, 2001), which likely motivate individuals to act on opportunities that decrease pollution, improve natural resource–exploitation practices, decrease oppression of ethnic/cultural groups, and so on.

Second, it appears that when the natural and communal environment declines, individuals' psychological well-being can be negatively affected as well. As one example, research has shown that declining natural and communal environments can diminish individuals' needs for relatedness—namely, their desire to connect with other people (Ryan & Deci, 2000). For instance, declining communal environments can destroy important social relationships, such as ties between parents and children when families are dissolved. The dissatisfaction that results from psychological needs like these not being met or their fulfillment being thwarted can lead to intense negative emotions, such as fear, anger, frustration, loneliness, depression, and shame (Ryan & Deci, 2000; Wei, Shaffer, Young, & Zakalik, 2005), which then serve as an irritant that motivates action to remove its source (Foo, Uy, & Baron, 2009).

Therefore, the more individuals' physical and psychological health are endangered, the stronger their motivation will be to act on potential sustainable development opportunities to overcome these threats. That is, these types of threats (and potential opportunities) are more likely to lead to negative emotions that prompt the search for a solution (Mathews & MacLeod, 1994). After recognizing the threat and overcoming their primary fear response, motivated individuals methodically pursue opportunities to escape or overcome this threat (Beck & Clark, 1997). During this "elaborative strategic processing of [the] threat," individuals manage information slowly in an effortful and schema-driven way, but then a "secondary appraisal process occurs in which anxious individuals evaluate the availability and effectiveness of their coping resources to deal with the perceived threat" (Beck & Clark, 1997, p. 53). This discussion leads to several interesting questions: How do individuals whose physical and psychological health is threatened by the decline of the natural or communal environment evaluate opportunities to escape that threat? To what extent do these threatened individuals use information (i.e., knowledge) about the natural/communal environment and their entrepreneurial knowledge to create or recognize potential sustainable entrepreneurship opportunities?

In addition to the negative emotions arising from feelings of personal threat, altruism can also result in emotions that direct attention to potential sustainable development opportunities. This altruistic motivation occurs when people empathize with or sympathize for underprivileged others (Batson, 1991; Davis, 1996). Empathetic individuals are able to take the perspective of disadvantaged others and personally experience similar emotions to those in need (Eisenberg, 2000). For example, people who empathize with individuals in poverty-stricken societies are able to experience (at least partially) their disadvantaged counterparts' burdens in providing for their children. The higher individuals' empathy is for others, the more motivated they become to identify and act upon potential opportunities that counter these others' negative emotional experiences and sorrows because these feelings are partly their own. That is, highly empathetic individuals are driven to pursue sustainable development opportunities that transform disadvantaged people's situation because by doing so, they can also improve their own emotional state.

In contrast to those who are more empathetic, sympathetic individuals are able to think and feel themselves into disadvantaged others' position, but they have different emotions than those actually going through the experience at hand (Eisenberg, 2000). Individuals who sympathize with very impoverished people, for example, are able to understand these individuals' distress regarding their children's nutrition and health, yet they will not personally experience these sorrows; instead, they will pity them on account of the burdens they face. As an altruistic emotion, pity motivates individuals to ease others' suffering even when giving aid may lead to substantial personal costs (Dijker, 2001). That is, individuals who are sympathetic to the poor will be driven to assist them and act upon entrepreneurial opportunities that improve their situation.

Empathy and sympathy lead to different levels of motivation to act upon potential opportunities that help people and society depending on the amount of personal distress the individual feels. Empathetic or sympathetic over-arousal can lead to more severe forms of personal distress (Hoffman, 1982) that cause highly negative emotional states that compromise individuals' psychological well-being (Eisenberg, 2000). To avoid these feelings of distress, individuals may become less altruistic and focus more on themselves (e.g., Wood, Saltzberg, & Goldsamt, 1990), thus becoming less motivated to identify and act upon entrepreneurial opportunities that help others. However, individuals who are better at regulating their emotions and dealing with personal distress are more likely to avoid becoming overly distressed when empathizing with/sympathizing for disadvantaged others (Eisenberg, 1994; Eisenberg et al., 1998). Because these individuals' psychological and emotional well-being is threatened less from experiencing empathy and sympathy, they are likely to be more motivated to identify and act upon potential opportunities to develop society and help others with their problems.

## *Future Research*

In Fig. 5.1, we offer a sketch of the role of entrepreneurial action linking sustainable and development outcomes as a basis for guiding future research. Entrepreneurial action provides a link between sustainable outcomes—those that preserve nature, sources of life support, and/or communities—and development outcomes—those that provide (financial or non-financial) gain to the entrepreneur and/or others. Entrepreneurial action arises from the formation of (third- and first-person) opportunity beliefs, which are influenced by knowledge, motivation, and perceptions of threat. Both knowledge (of the natural and communal environment) and prosocial motivation can influence individuals' ability to notice threats

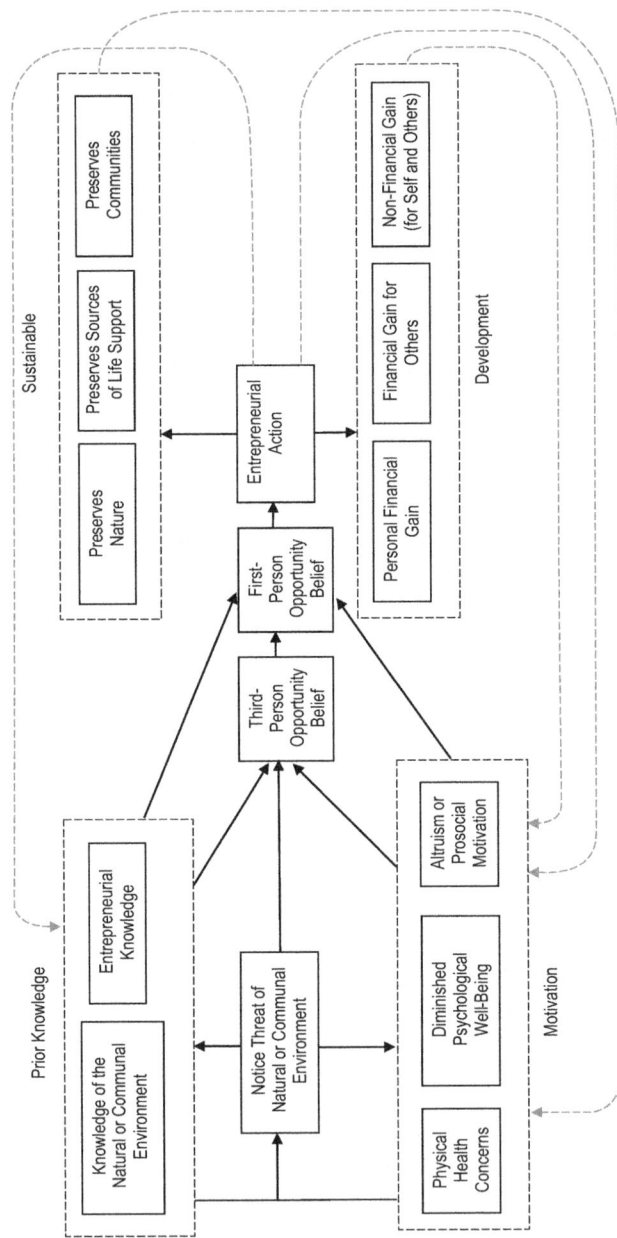

Fig. 5.1 A sketch of entrepreneurial action linking sustainability and development

to sustainability, and in turn, this ability to notice threats can generate new knowledge and influence motivation. Prime motivators include physical health concerns, diminished psychological well-being, and altruism or prosocial motivations. Entrepreneurial action can subsequently influence both knowledge and management, which in turn influence the appraisal of threat. Similarly, development and sustainability outcomes can influence motivation.

## Entrepreneurial Action Linking Sustainability and Development at the Community Level

Facilitating the transfer of research-based knowledge is one of the key steps toward sustainable development. The report of the World Summit for Sustainable Development held in Johannesburg in 2002 described "knowledge transfer to developing countries' as a key component of poverty eradication and frequently cites the importance of technology transfer for sustainable development" (Van Kerkhoof & Lebel, 2006, p. 451). Several approaches have already been attempted to foster this transfer process. For example, transfer may be aided by efforts to translate knowledge in the form of jargon-laden science into terms that can be understood by the laypeople (Rogers, 1995). Moreover, providing incentives for universities can enhance their patenting rate in certain scientific fields, which is a pre-requisite to making tacit knowledge explicit and legally transferring it to users of the private sector (Shane, 2004). The literature also describes measures specific to facilitating knowledge transfer in sustainable development. For example, effective coordination between private companies and public institutions, including universities and research institutes, contributed to the successful commercialization of wind turbine technology (Lewis & Wiser, 2007), and public-private partnerships between universities and firms have been described as an effective means to commercialize basic knowledge in the solar-energy sector (Mallett, 2007).

Although the above examples demonstrate that the transfer of research-based knowledge from the scientific community to the user community can be actively promoted, the effectiveness of this process in generating sustainable development—namely, sustainable development actions by users—appears to be limited. For example, Roux, Rogers, Biggs, Ashton, and Sergeant (2006) stated that there is misunderstanding and friction between researchers and practitioners; that is, there are fundamentally different operational working philosophies and operational cultures between the community that generates the knowledge and the community that uses it (Havens & Aumen, 2000). Van Kerkhoof and Lebel (2006, p. 451) concluded, "It is somewhat ironic that despite widespread evidence of the failure of transfer and translation models to achieve sustainability-oriented outcomes in agriculture, health, and other sectors, they still hold appeal in the imaginations of researchers and policy makers."

Although science has the potential of offering solutions to sustainable development issues, if its research-based knowledge remains unconnected to the "real world," then it remains a purely academic endeavor with little social relevance (Welp, de la Vega-Leinert, Stoll-Kleemann, & Jaeger, 2006, p. 170). A mechanism is required to make this connection (Ribot, 2006), and it must do so in a context characterized as "messy" (Kasperson, 2006). Entrepreneurial action represents a mechanism that operates in contexts of high uncertainty (Knight, 1921) and may serve to connect scientific and user communities. In this way, research-based knowledge may reveal potential entrepreneurial opportunities for sustainable development. In this section, we focus on entrepreneurial action as a mechanism that facilitates the transfer of research-based knowledge into users' sustainability behaviors and as a mechanism that facilitates feedback from users to scientists in the generation of further research that can impact the sustainability of development.

Although there may be a "race" to commercialize a sustainable development technology, research-based knowledge is unlikely to detail a fully formed version of such a technology. It is better thought of as a technology stimulus that triggers entrepreneurs to develop products, services, and/or processes that are eventually offered to the market. Given that research-based knowledge of sustainable development often represents a technology stimulus rather than a fully developed and packaged opportunity, it is not surprising that the success of technology-transfer efforts to end users is mixed (at best). Indeed, an implicit assumption of "trickle down" explanations of research-based knowledge is that this explanation assumes an objective truth that scientists pass on to users, who in turn either adopt or reject the technology (Thompson & Scoones, 1994). Information is assumed to "flow" one way—from scientist to users. However, users may be the originators of either technical knowledge or improved practice (Thompson & Scoones, 1994) that could inform scientific research on sustainable development (Lemos & Morehouse, 2005). For example, the formation of communities including both scientists and users facilitates their mutual communication and understanding and can facilitate the development of a sustainable natural resource–management strategy (Ewing, Grayson, & Argent, 2000), and feedback from users to scientists has been found to enhance the credibility, legitimacy, and relevance of scientific knowledge on air pollution (Tuinstra, Hordijk, & Kroeze, 2006). With respect to renewable energy technologies, close user involvement in the design and planning process of solar collectors and biomass heating systems has been found to yield improved and widely disseminated technologies (Ornetzeder & Rohracher, 2006).

Although the above examples illustrate that feedback from users to the scientific community may indeed be a critical component of the sustainable development process, it appears that effective feedback is difficult to achieve because fundamental differences exist in working philosophies and operational cultures between scientific and user communities. For example, Roux et al. (2006) reported that users view scientists as having an inward-looking and self-serving culture, having little regard for application contexts, and being incapable of contributing to the value-based debate that usually governs problem solving in the real world. On the other hand, scientists consider practitioners as being more interested in pursuing their own rather than the ecosystem's interests, having a poor understanding of scientific processes, and not being able to articulate their needs effectively. In line with these arguments, various studies have illustrated the obstacles of efficient communication between user and scientific communities in the context of sustainable development (Havens & Aumen, 2000).

Perhaps entrepreneurial actions can serve as an important link between scientific and user communities to facilitate these feedforward and feedback processes and thus impact the generation and adoption of sustainable development products and/or services.

### *Scientists Who Become Entrepreneurs*

Particularly in technology-based industries, entrepreneurs are often scientists who have left academia in order to exploit technological opportunities developed at university or public research institutes (Zucker, Darby, & Brewer, 1998). These entrepreneurs are able to "speak the language" of both the academic researchers from whom they acquire new technologies and the users of these technologies who are their customers. Entrepreneurs can receive direct verbal feedback from users about potential improvements and future development paths for their sustainable technologies (Ornetzeder & Rohracher, 2006), or they can receive indirect feedback by the market indicating which technologies users desire and which they do not. Both types of feedback can be passed on to the scientific community to suggest and motivate areas of research that reflect users' needs. These arguments are consistent with research indicating that the inclusion of individuals external to the scientific and user communities can facilitate the communication and transfer of knowledge on sustainable development (Bruckmeier, 2005). Entrepreneurs are likely very able and motivated to perform this role, but there is likely considerable heterogeneity in this motivation. We need to gain a deeper understanding of how entrepreneurs effectively link scientific and user communities to develop and refine sustainable development opportunities as well as gain insights into why some entrepreneurs are more motivated to provide this link and communicate with both communities, whereas others are reluctant to do so at all or prefer to communicate with only one community.

### *Entrepreneurial Action Generates Feedback*

In addition to serving as an information pathway, entrepreneurial action may also represent a signaling mechanism for the scientific community by indicating which research-based knowledge users accept and which they do not. Specifically, there is high variance in the performance of entrepreneurial firms, particularly in technology-based industries, for which the failure rates of new ventures are high (Bruno, McQuarrie, & Torgrimson, 1992). The success and failure of entrepreneurial ventures may indicate to the scientific community which type of research-based knowledge the user community values most and which type of research-based knowledge users are less likely to accept and adopt. For example, Jacobsson and Bergek (2004) found that successful firm entries in the wind- and solar-energy sectors have spurred the creation of new knowledge for these technologies.

Besides influencing the types of research-based knowledge created by scientists, entrepreneurs' pursuit of potential sustainable opportunities may also influence the amount of knowledge scientists create. Specifically, the results of sustainable entrepreneurial action can provide data and stimulus for the generation of new knowledge. For example, perhaps a technology developed by an entrepreneurial venture works but does so for an unexpected scientific reason. In attempting to understand why the technology works, scientific research may generate new research-based knowledge of sustainable development. To what extent does entrepreneurs' success in exploiting sustainable opportunities have on scientists' social, cultural, and/or organizational environments that motivates them to further advance research in that area of sustainable development? Perhaps, as Jobert, Laborgne, and Mimler (2007) reported, the success of entrepreneurial firms in the wind-energy sector and the population's participation in this success (e.g., by offering partial ownership of the technologies) changed social attitudes toward the technology in a favorable way, which motivated scientists to intensify their research in this area.

### *Entrepreneurs as Translators*

Entrepreneurship scholars have the chance to complement existing studies on science-based stakeholder dialogues. This literature has identified that there is insufficient interaction between scientists and users and that this is caused by differences between the two communities in terms of the way each frames environmental problems and perceives risk. To overcome these obstacles and induce action by users, studies on science-based stakeholder dialogue have highlighted the importance of communication-based methods, such as interviews, written reviews, workshops, interdisciplinary team work, and surveys (e.g., Lemos & Morehouse, 2005; Welp et al., 2006). Although these studies are important for understanding how communication between scientific and user communities can facilitate sustainability, there is an implicit assumption that better understanding of research-based knowledge by users will enhance the likelihood of user action. While this may be true in some cases, it appears that when finding solutions to sustainability problems via the market mechanism, both scientists and users often do not have the necessary motivation and knowledge for action. Specifically, they likely do not possess sufficient knowledge about market structures, economic environments, and the discovery and exploitation of opportunities and may not be motivated to act in the highly uncertain context associated with exploiting sustainability opportunities. The entrepreneurial community does possess knowledge of market specificities, the best ways to serve markets, and customer (user) problems (Shane, 2000). Moreover, entrepreneurs have the motivation to act based on this knowledge even if the outcomes of these actions are highly uncertain (Knight, 1921; McMullen & Shepherd, 2006). Thus, both communication and entrepreneurial action appear to be complementary mechanisms connecting scientific and user communities in order to achieve sustainability. Future research can explore how these mechanisms might be used together to enhance sustainable development.

In sum, achieving sustainable development is highly dependent upon the effective transfer of research-based knowledge to the user community. This process is difficult, and a variety of measures have been suggested to make it more effective; however, these efforts have often been met with limited success (Van Kerkhoof & Lebel, 2006). Perhaps entrepreneurial action can help bridge the scientific and user communities and facilitate knowledge transfer. What are the factors that enable entrepreneurial action to better transfer research-based knowledge to users and to communicate feedback from users to the scientific community? This entrepreneurial action–based feedback loop may become self-sustaining or self-enhancing—that is, the more positive feedback the scientific community receives from users, the better the created research-based knowledge will fit the needs of the user community. In turn, this will trigger users' feedback and so on.

### *Future Research*

In Fig. 5.2, we offer a sketch of the role of entrepreneurial action in linking scientific and user communities as a basis for guiding future sustainable entrepreneurship research at the community level. The scientific community and the user community face obstacles to effective communication. The scientific community—based on its members' knowledge and motivation—generates research-based knowledge of sustainability, which the community of entrepreneurs can translate (based on their scientific and entrepreneurial knowledge) into a potential sustainable development opportunity. This potential opportunity is tested with potential users who provide feedback, and the potential opportunity is refined, which provides feedback to the scientific community, thereby influencing the form, amount, and motivation of specific types of sustainability research. The new research-based knowledge further influences the community of entrepreneurs and their conception of the potential sustainable development opportunity.

## DISCUSSION AND CONCLUSION

In this chapter, our purpose was to offer a greater understanding of what constitutes the academic field of sustainable entrepreneurship and to offer some suggestions for moving it forward. We offered the following definition: sustainable entrepreneurship *is focused on the preservation of nature,*

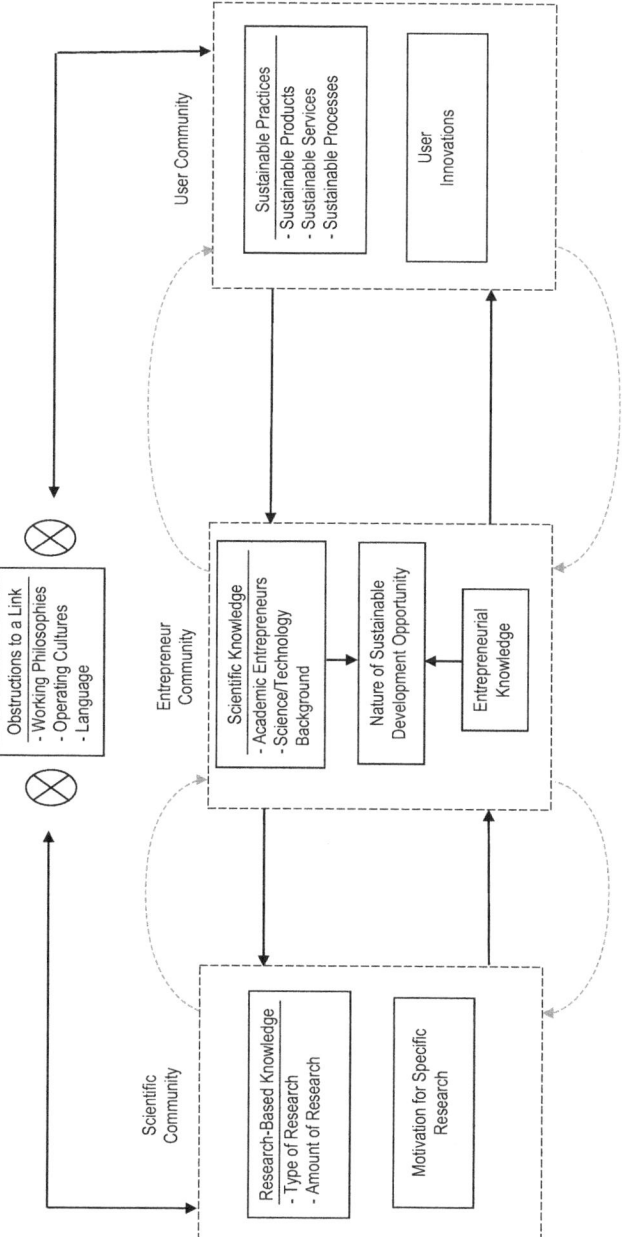

**Fig. 5.2** A sketch of entrepreneurial action linking scientific and user communities for sustainable development

*life support, and community in the pursuit of perceived opportunities to bring into existence future products, processes, and services for gain, where gain is broadly construed to include economic and non-economic gains to individuals, the economy, and society.* We believe that by defining sustainable entrepreneurship, this chapter provides a basis for exploring where and how future research can make a contribution to the development of the field. Indeed, our approach to defining the field of sustainable entrepreneurship is more meta-theoretical than theoretical because we propose that scholars from different theoretical perspectives can form part of this scholarly community and that such diversity is important for sustainable entrepreneurship's further development.

At the individual level of analysis, there appears to be ample room for theorizing from a psychological perspective capturing both individuals' cognitions and emotions. For example, theories on structural alignment (Grégoire, Barr, & Shepherd, 2010; Grégoire & Shepherd, 2012) and prototypes (Baron & Ensley, 2006) have been used to describe the cognitive processes underlying the recognition of entrepreneurial opportunity based on entrepreneurs' prior entrepreneurial knowledge, and they might also be helpful in explaining the identification of sustainable opportunities based on knowledge of a threat to the natural or communal environment as a starting point for (sustainable) entrepreneurial action. For example, basic needs theory as a theory of intrinsic motivation (Ryan & Deci, 2000) or the theory on prosocial behavior (Penner, Dovidio, Piliavin, & Schroeder, 2005) might help explain why some individuals engage in sustainable entrepreneurship and others do not. Recent work has also advocated an identity perspective to understand individuals' engagement in social (Wry & York, 2015) and environmental (York, Hargrave, & Pacheco, 2016) entrepreneurship. Further, Shepherd, Kuskova, and Patzelt (2009) published a psychometric scale that measures individuals' sustainability values; the "pro-environmental value" sub-scale has recently been used to explore why some entrepreneurs are more likely to exploit environmentally harmful opportunities than others (Shepherd, Patzelt, & Baron, 2013). Importantly, our discussion also offers a "reverse perspective" putting the outcome of sustainable entrepreneurial action first—to what extent do advancements toward sustainability (e.g., success in environmental-protection projects) impact individuals' subsequent motivation and/or knowledge to (continue to) act as sustainable entrepreneurs. There is more research required on the reverse perspective of entrepreneurship and sustainable development. With the individual as the level of analysis, we believe future research can make important contributions for both scholarship and the practice of sustainable development.

Second, we focused on the role of entrepreneurial actions in linking different communities in co-creating and refining a potential sustainable development opportunity. Such a community-level perspective involves—but ultimately goes beyond—the individual, suggesting that theories from, for example, sociology and economics can be informative. For instance, sociologists have a long tradition of studying the evolution of scientific communities (e.g., Collins, 1983; Shapin, 1995), and they have also studied entrepreneurial communities (e.g., Portes, 1995) and the sociological implications of new technologies (e.g., Pinch & Bijker, 1984). Similarly, scientific communities (e.g., Dasgupta & David, 1987; Partha & David, 1994), entrepreneurial communities (e.g., Lenzi, 1996; MacKenzie, 1992), and user communities (e.g., Lakhani & Von Hippel, 2003; Mazzoleni & Nelson, 2007) have been the focus of studies by economists. Further, recent studies (Pacheco, York, & Hargrave, 2014; York et al., 2016) have illustrated how the complex interactions between different communities ("fields") over time led to the emergence of an environmentally friendly sector (wind energy), suggesting that reciprocal interactions between different communities shape the development of sustainable entrepreneurship and its impact on economic and environmental development. Scholars can build on this work to study the concepts and relationships offered in our earlier discussion.

In conclusion, sustainability and sustainable development are among the most important topics of our time. Sustainable entrepreneurship can make important contributions to help preserve the natural and communal environment in which we live. However, research on sustainable entrepreneurship is still in its infancy. There are many interesting and important research questions both within and outside the topics we outlined in this chapter, including research using different theoretical lenses, levels of analysis, and/or research methods. Therefore, we hope that readers find our research suggestions interesting, but we also expect that readers, based on their different backgrounds and interests, will come up with different research questions and approaches that will advance the field of sustainable development.

# References

Baron, R. A., & Ensley, M. D. (2006). Opportunity recognition as the detection of meaningful patterns: Evidence from comparisons of novice and experienced entrepreneurs. *Management Science, 52*(9), 1331–1344.

Batson, C. D. (1991). *The altruism question: Toward a social-psychological answer.* Hillsdale, NJ: Erlbaum.

Beck, A. T., & Clark, D. A. (1997). An information processing model of anxiety: Automatic and strategic processes. *Behaviour Research and Therapy, 35*(1), 49–58.

Board Sustainable Development. (1999). *Our common journey: A transition toward sustainability.* Washington, DC: National Academy.

Borer, M. I. (2006). Important place and their public faces: Understanding Fenway Park as a public symbol. *The Journal of Popular Culture, 39*(2), 205–224.

Bruckmeier, K. (2005). Interdisciplinary conflict analysis and conflict mitigation in local resource management. *AMBIO: A Journal of the Human Environment, 34*(2), 65–73.

Bruno, A. V., McQuarrie, E. F., & Torgrimson, C. G. (1992). The evolution of new technology ventures over 20 years: Patterns of failure, merger, and survival. *Journal of Business Venturing, 7*(4), 291–302.

Burton, B. K., & Goldsby, M. (2009). Corporate social responsibility orientation, goals, and behavior a study of small business owners. *Business & Society, 48*(1), 88–104.

Busenitz, L. W., West III, G. P., Shepherd, D. A., Nelson, T., Chandler, G. N., & Zacharakis, A. (2003). Entrepreneurship research in emergence: Past trends and future directions. *Journal of Management, 29*(3), 285–308.

Cannella, A. A., & Paetzold, R. L. (1994). Pfeffer's barriers to the advance of organizational science: A rejoinder. *Academy of Management Review, 19*(2), 331–341.

Cohen, B., & Winn, M. I. (2007). Market imperfection, opportunity and sustainable entrepreneurship. *Journal of Business Venturing, 22*(1), 29–49.

Collins, H. M. (1983). The sociology of scientific knowledge: Studies of contemporary science. *Annual Review of Sociology, 9*, 265–285.

Conger, R. D., & Donnellan, M. B. (2007). An interactionist perspective on the socioeconomic context of human development. *Annual Review of Psychology, 58*, 175–199.

Dasgupta, P., & David, P. A. (1987). Information disclosure and the economics of science and technology. In G. R. Feiwel (Ed.), *Arrow and the ascent of modern economic theory* (pp. 519–542). London: Palgrave Macmillan.

Davis, M. H. (1996). *Empathy: A social psychological approach.* Madison, WI: Westview Press.

Dean, T. J., & McMullen, J. S. (2007). Toward a theory of sustainable entrepreneurship: Reducing environmental degradation through entrepreneurial action. *Journal of Business Venturing, 22*(1), 50–76.

Diener, E., Diener, M., & Diener, C. (1995). Factors predicting the subjective well-being of nations. *Journal of Personality and Social Psychology, 69*(5), 851–864.

Dijker, A. J. (2001). The influence of perceived suffering and vulnerability on the experience of pity. *European Journal of Social Psychology, 31*(6), 659–676.

du Cros, H., Bauer, T., Lo, C., & Rui, S. (2005). Cultural heritage assets in China as sustainable tourism products: Case studies of the Hutongs and the Huanghua section of the Great Wall. *Journal of Sustainable Tourism, 13*(2), 171–194.

Easterly, W. (2006). *The white man's burden. Why the west's efforts to aid the rest have done so much ill and so little good.* New York: Penguin Press.

Eisenberg, N. (1994). Empathy: A social-psychological approach. *Contemporary Psychology, 39*(11), 1026–1027.

Eisenberg, N. (2000). Emotion, regulation, and moral development. *Annual Review of Psychology, 51*(1), 665–697.

Eisenberg, N., Wentzel, M., & Harris, J. D. (1998). The role of emotionality and regulation in empathy-related responding. *School Psychology Review, 27*(4), 506–521.

Etzioni, A. (1996). *The golden rule.* New York: Basic Books.

Ewing, S. A., Grayson, R. B., & Argent, R. M. (2000). Science, citizens, and catchments: Decision support for catchment planning in Australia. *Society & Natural Resources, 13*(5), 443–459.

Feyerabend, P. (1980). *Against method.* London: Verso.

Foo, M.-D., Uy, M. A., & Baron, R. A. (2009). How do feelings influence effort? An empirical study of entrepreneurs' affect and venture effort. *Journal of Applied Psychology, 94*(4), 1086.

Forste, R., & Heaton, T. B. (2004). The divorce generation: Well-being, family attitudes, and socioeconomic consequences of marital disruption. *Journal of Divorce and Remarriage, 41*(1-2), 95–114.

Freeman, R. E. A. (1994). A stakeholder theory of the modern corporation. In T. L. Beauchamp & N. E. Bowie (Eds.), *Ethical theory and business* (pp. 66–76). Englewood Cliffs, NJ: Prentice-Hall.

Gallo, L. C., & Matthews, K. A. (2003). Understanding the association between socioeconomic status and physical health: Do negative emotions play a role? *Psychological Bulletin, 129*(1), 10–51.

Gould, S. J. (1981). *The mismeasure of man.* New York: Norton & Company.

Grégoire, D. A., Barr, P. S., & Shepherd, D. A. (2010). Cognitive processes of opportunity recognition: The role of structural alignment. *Organization Science, 21*(2), 413–431.

Grégoire, D. A., & Shepherd, D. A. (2012). Technology-market combinations and the identification of entrepreneurial opportunities: An investigation of the opportunity-individual nexus. *Academy of Management Journal, 55*(4), 753–785.

Hanson, M., & Chen, E. (2007). Socioeconomic status and health behaviors in adolescence: A review of the literature. *Journal of Behavioral Medicine, 30*(3), 263–285.

Havens, K. E., & Aumen, N. G. (2000). Hypothesis-driven experimental research is necessary for natural resource management. *Environmental Management, 25*(1), 1–7.

Hoffman, M. L. (1982). Development of prosocial motivation: Empathy and guilt. *The Development of Prosocial Behavior*, 281–313.

IPCC. (2007). *Intergovernmental panel on climate change*, IPCC Annual Report.

Jacobsson, S., & Bergek, A. (2004). Transforming the energy sector: The evolution of technological systems in renewable energy technology. *Industrial and Corporate Change, 13*(5), 815–849.

Jobert, A., Laborgne, P., & Mimler, S. (2007). Local acceptance of wind energy: Factors of success identified in French and German case studies. *Energy policy, 35*(5), 2751–2760.

Kasperson, R. E. (2006). Rerouting the stakeholder express. *Global Environmental Change, 16*(4), 320–322.

Knight, F. H. (1921). *Risk, uncertainty and profit*. New York: Hart, Schaffner and Marx.

Knowles, S., & Owen, P. D. (1995). Health capital and cross-country variation in income per capita in the Mankiw-Romer-Weil model. *Economics Letters, 48*(1), 99–106.

Kuhn, T. S. (1974). *The structure of scientific revolutions* (2nd ed.). Chicago: International Encyclopedia of Unified Science, University of Chicago.

Lakhani, K. R., & Von Hippel, E. (2003). How open source software works: "Free" user-to-user assistance. *Research Policy, 32*(6), 923–943.

Leiserowitz, A. A., Kates, R. W., & Parris, T. M. (2006). Sustainability values, attitudes, and behaviors: A review of multinational and global trends. *Annual Reviews of Environmental Resources, 31*, 413–444.

Lemos, M. C., & Morehouse, B. J. (2005). The co-production of science and policy in integrated climate assessments. *Global Environmental Change, 15*(1), 57–68.

Lenzi, R. C. (1996). The entrepreneurial community approach to community economic development. *Economic Development Review, 14*(2), 16–20.

Lewis, J. I., & Wiser, R. H. (2007). Fostering a renewable energy technology industry: An international comparison of wind industry policy support mechanisms. *Energy Policy, 35*(3), 1844–1857.

MacKenzie, L. R. (1992). Fostering entrepreneurship as a rural economic development strategy. *Economic Development Review, 10*(4), 38–44.

Mallett, A. (2007). Social acceptance of renewable energy innovations: The role of technology cooperation in urban Mexico. *Energy Policy, 35*(5), 2790–2798.

Margalit, M., & Halbertal, M. (2004). Liberalism and the right to culture. *Social Research, 71*(3), 529–548.

Mathews, A., & MacLeod, C. (1994). Cognitive approaches to emotion and emotional disorders. *Annual Review of Psychology, 45,* 25–50.

Mazzoleni, R., & Nelson, R. R. (2007). Public research institutions and economic catch-up. *Research Policy, 36*(10), 1512–1528.

McDermott, R., O'Dea, K., Rowley, K., Knight, S., & Burgess, P. (1998). Beneficial impact of the homeland movement on health outcomes in central Australian Aborigines. *Australian and New Zealand Journal of Public Health, 22,* 653–658.

McMullen, J. S., & Shepherd, D. A. (2006). Entrepreneurial action and the role of uncertainty in the theory of the entrepreneur. *Academy of Management Review, 31*(1), 132–152.

McWilliams, A., & Siegel, D. (2001). Corporate social responsibility: A theory of the firm perspective. *Academy of Management Review, 26*(1), 117–127.

Meijnders, A. L., Midden, C. J., & Wilke, H. A. (2001). Role of negative emotion in communication about $CO_2$ risks. *Risk Analysis, 21*(5), 955–955.

Miller, J. (2001). Family and community integrity. *Journal of Sociology and Social Welfare, 28,* 23–44.

Monforti, F., Bellasio, R., Bianconi, R., Clai, G., & Zanini, G. (2004). An evaluation of particle deposition fluxes to cultural heritage sites in Florence, Italy. *Science of the Total Environment, 334,* 61–72.

Montgomery, M. A., & Elimelech, M. (2007). Water and sanitation in developing countries: Including health in the equation. *Environmental Science and Technology, 41*(1), 17–24.

Muehlebach, A. (2001). Making place at the United Nations: Indigenous cultural politics at the U.N. working group on indigenous populations. *Cultural Anthropology, 16*(3), 415–448.

Narayan, D., & Petesch, P. (2002). *Voices of the poor.* Oxford: Oxford University Press.

National Research Council. (1999). *Our common journal. A transition toward sustainability.* Washington, DC: National Academy Press.

Oakes, J. M., & Rossi, P. H. (2003). The measurement of SES in health research: Current practice and steps toward a new approach. *Social Science & Medicine, 56*(4), 169–184.

Ogbor, J. O. (2000). Mythicizing and reification in entrepreneurial discourse: Ideology-critique of entrepreneurial studies. *Journal of Management Studies, 37*(5), 605–635.

O'Neill Jr., D. G., Hershauer, J. C., & Golden, J. S. (2009). The cultural context of sustainability entrepreneurship. *Greener Management International, 55,* 33–46.

Ornetzeder, M., & Rohracher, H. (2006). User-led innovations and participation processes: Lessons from sustainable energy technologies. *Energy Policy, 34*(2), 138–150.

Pacheco, D. F., York, J. G., & Hargrave, T. (2014). The co-evolution of industries, social movements, and institutions: The case of wind power. *Academy of Management Proceedings, 2011*(1), 1–6.

Padua, M. G. (2007). Designing an identity: The synthesis of a post-traditional landscape vocabulary in Hong Kong. *Landscape Research, 32*(2), 225–240.

Parkhe, A. (1992). U.S. national security export controls: Implications for global competitiveness of U.S. high-tech firms. *Strategic Management Journal, 13*(1), 47–66.

Parris, T. M., & Kates, R. W. (2003). Characterizing and measuring sustainable development. *Annual Review of Environment and Resources, 28*, 559–586.

Partha, D., & David, P. A. (1994). Toward a new economics of science. *Research Policy, 23*(5), 487–521.

Pastakia, A. (1998). Grassroots ecopreneurs: Change agents for a sustainable society. *Journal of Organizational Change Management, 11*(2), 157–173.

Penner, L. A., Dovidio, J. F., Piliavin, J. A., & Schroeder, D. A. (2005). Prosocial behavior: Multilevel perspectives. *Annual Review of Psychology, 56*, 365–392.

Peredo, A. M., & Chrisman, J. J. (2006). Toward a theory of community-based enterprise. *Academy of Management Review, 31*(2), 309–328.

Pfeffer, J. (1993). Barriers to the advance of organizational science: Paradigm development as a dependent variable. *Academy of Management Review, 18*(4), 599–620.

Pinch, T. J., & Bijker, W. E. (1984). The social construction of facts and artefacts: Or how the sociology of science and the sociology of technology might benefit each other. *Social Studies of Science, 14*(3), 399–441.

Porter, G. (1995). Environmental security as a national security issue. *Current History, 94*(592), 218–222.

Portes, A. (1995). *The economic sociology of immigration: Essays on networks, ethnicity, and entrepreneurship*. New York: Russell Sage Foundation.

Pretty, J., Hine, R., & Peacock, J. (2006). Green exercise: The benefits of activities in green places. *Biologist, 53*(3), 143–148.

Ribot, J. C. (2006). Choose democracy: Environmentalists' socio-political responsibility. *Global Environmental Change, 16*, 115–119.

Roberts, E. B. (1991). *Entrepreneurs in high technology: Lessons from MIT and beyond*. Oxford: Oxford University Press.

Rogers, E. M. (1995). Diffusion of innovations: Modifications of a model for telecommunications. In M. W. Stoetzer & A. Mahler (Eds.), *Die diffusion von innovationen in der telekommunikation* (pp. 25–38). Berlin and Heidelberg: Springer.

Roux, D. J., Rogers, K. H., Biggs, H., Ashton, P. J., & Sergeant, A. (2006). Bridging the science-management divide: Moving from unidirectional knowledge transfer to knowledge interfacing and sharing. *Ecology and Society, 11*(1), 4–23.

Ryan, R. M., & Deci, E. L. (2000). The darker and brighter sides of human existence: Basic psychological needs as a unifying concept. *Psychological Inquiry, 11*(4), 319–338.

Sala, E., & Knowlton, N. (2006). Global marine biodiversity trends. *Annual Review of Environment and Resources, 31*, 93–122.

Schaper, M. (2005). *Making ecopreneurs: Developing sustainable entrepreneurship* (pp. 61–70). Burlington, VT: Ashgate.

Schröter, D., Cramer, W., Leemans, R., Prentice, I. C., Araújo, M. B., Arnell, N. W., et al. (2005). Ecosystem service supply and vulnerability to global change in Europe. *Science, 310*, 1333–1337.

Seelos, C., & Mair, J. (2005). Social entrepreneurship: Creating new business models to serve the poor. *Business Horizons, 48*(3), 241–246.

Shane, S. (2000). Prior knowledge and the discovery of entrepreneurial opportunities. *Organization Science, 11*(4), 448–469.

Shane, S. A. (2004). *Academic entrepreneurship: University spinoffs and wealth creation*. Cheltenham, UK: Edward Elgar Publishing.

Shapin, S. (1995). Here and everywhere—Sociology of scientific knowledge. *Annual Review of Sociology, 21*, 289–321.

Shepherd, D. A., Kuskova, V., & Patzelt, H. (2009). Measuring the values that underlie sustainable development: The development of a valid scale. *Journal of Economic Psychology, 30*, 246–256.

Shepherd, D. A., & Patzelt, H. (2011). The new field of sustainable entrepreneurship: Studying entrepreneurial action linking "what is to be sustained" with "what is to be developed". *Entrepreneurship Theory and Practice, 35*(1), 137–163.

Shepherd, D. A., Patzelt, H., & Baron, R. A. (2013). "I care about nature, but …": Disengaging values in assessing opportunities that cause harm. *Academy of Management Journal, 56*(6), 1251–1273.

Slaper, H., Velders, G. J. M., Daniel, J. S., de Gruijl, F. R., & van der Leun, J. C. (1996). Estimates of ozone depletion and skin cancer incidence to examine the Vienna Convention achievements. *Nature, 384*(6606), 256–258.

Sonune, A., & Ghate, R. (2004). Developments in wastewater treatment methods. *Desalination, 167*, 55–63.

Spicer, P. (2001). Culture and the restoration of self among former American Indian drinkers. *Social Science and Medicine, 53*(2), 227–240.

Steinbruner, J. D. (1978). National security and the concept of strategic stability. *The Journal of Conflict Resolution, 22*(3), 411–428.

Summer, C. E., Bettis, R., Duhaime, I., Grant, J. H., Hambrick, D. C., Snow, C. C., et al. (1990). Doctoral education in the field of business policy and strategy. *Journal of Management, 16*(2), 361–391.

Swanson, T. N. (1996). *The economics of environmental degradation*. Cheltenham, UK: Edward Elgar.

Thompson, J., & Scoones, I. (1994). Challenging the populist perspective: Rural people's knowledge, agricultural research, and extension practice. *Agriculture and Human Values, 11*(2–3), 58–76.

Tuinstra, W., Hordijk, L., & Kroeze, C. (2006). Moving boundaries in transboundary air pollution co-production of science and policy under the convention on long range transboundary air pollution. *Global Environmental Change, 16*(4), 349–363.

Twenge, J. M., & Campbell, W. K. (2002). Self-esteem and socioeconomic status: A meta-analytic review. *Personality & Social Psychology Review, 6*, 59–71.

United Nations. (2004). UNEP 2004 Annual Report.

Van Kerkhoof, L., & Lebel, L. (2006). Linking knowledge and action for sustainable development. *Annual Review of Environmental Resources, 31*, 445–477.

Vemuri, A. W., & Costanza, R. (2006). The role of human, social, built and natural capital in explaining life satisfaction at the country level: Toward a national well-being Index. *Ecological Economics, 58*(1), 119–133.

Venkataraman, S. (1997). The distinctive domain of entrepreneurship research. In J. Katz (Ed.), *Advances in entrepreneurship, firm emergence, and growth* (pp. 119–138). Greenwich: JAI Press.

von Hippel, E. (1988). *The sources of innovation*. New York: Oxford University Press.

Wei, M., Shaffer, P. A., Young, S. K., & Zakalik, R. A. (2005). Adult attachment, shame, depression, and loneliness: The mediation role of basic psychological needs satisfaction. *Journal of Counseling Psychology, 52*(4), 591–601.

Welp, M., de la Vega-Leinert, A., Stoll-Kleemann, S., & Jaeger, C. C. (2006). Science-based stakeholder dialogues: Theories and tools. *Global Environmental Change, 16*(2), 170–181.

Wheeler, D., McKague, K., Thomson, J., Davies, R., Medalye, J., & Prada, M. (2005). Creating sustainable local enterprise networks. *Sloan Management Review, 47*(1), 33–40.

Wood, J. V., Saltzberg, J. A., & Goldsamt, L. A. (1990). Does affect induce self-focused attention? *Journal of Personality and Social psychology, 58*(5), 899–908.

Wry, T., & York, J. G. (2015). An identity based approach to social enterprise. *Academy of Management Review*. doi:10.5465/amr.2013.0506.

York, J. G., Hargrave, T. J., & Pacheco, D. F. (2016). Converging winds: Logic hybridization in the Colorado wind energy field. *Academy of Management Journal, 59*(2), 579–610.

Yunus, M. (2005). Grameen Bank's struggling (beggar) members programme. Retrieved from http://www.grameeninfo.org/index.php

Zahra, S. A., Gedajlovic, E., Neubaum, D. O., & Shulman, J. M. (2009). A typology of social entrepreneurs: Motives, search processes and ethical challenges. *Journal of Business Venturing, 24*(5), 519–532.

Zedler, J. B., & Kercher, S. (2005). Wetland resources: Status, trends, ecosystem services, and restorability. *Annual Review of Environment and Resources, 30*, 39–74.

Zucker, L. G., Darby, M. R., & Brewer, M. B. (1998). Intellectual human capital and the birth of US biotechnology enterprises. *American Economics Review, 88*(1), 290–306.

**Open Access** This chapter is distributed under the terms of the Creative Commons Attribution 4.0 International License (http://creativecommons.org/licenses/by/4.0/), which permits use, duplication, adaptation, distribution and reproduction in any medium or format, as long as you give appropriate credit to the original author(s) and the source, provide a link to the Creative Commons license and indicate if changes were made.

The images or other third party material in this chapter are included in the work's Creative Commons license, unless indicated otherwise in the credit line; if such material is not included in the work's Creative Commons license and the respective action is not permitted by statutory regulation, users will need to obtain permission from the license holder to duplicate, adapt or reproduce the material.

CHAPTER 6

# Researching at the Intersection of Family Business and Entrepreneurship

## INTRODUCTION

The family business and entrepreneurship literatures have had some exchange in the past; however, this exchange has been largely limited in scope (e.g., the addition of a variable from one field into the other), borrowing in nature (e.g., the transferred variable maintains its initial meaning, form, and measurement), and uni-directional (i.e., contributing minimally back to the source literature). Nevertheless, studies combining these two literatures have made important contributions to both fields. For example, researchers have contributed to our understanding of family firms' performance by exploring firms' entrepreneurial orientation (e.g., Casillas, Moreno, & Barbero, 2009; Cruz & Nordqvist, 2012; Lumpkin, Brigham, & Moss, 2010; Naldi, Nordqvist, Sjöberg, & Wiklund, 2007; Short, Payne, Brigham, Lumpkin, & Broberg, 2009). Even with these important contributions, however, research could go further, investigating the possibility of a different level and form of exchange, one that has a broad scope and involves blending (Oswick, Fleming, & Hanlon, 2011) and bricolage (Boxenbaum & Rouleau, 2011). Importantly, this new exchange should provide the opportunity to contribute to both the family business and entrepreneurship literatures.

---

This chapter builds on Shepherd (2016)

The goal of this chapter is to start to build such a framework. Specifically, we begin with issues of vitality in entrepreneurship, compare them to topics in family business, and then begin to blend and recombine constructs and relationships to create research opportunities that will contribute to both the family business and entrepreneurship fields. We focus on three specific sources of vitality at the intersection of family business and entrepreneurship for several reasons. First, each source of vitality aligns with a recent framework describing sources of vitality for entrepreneurship (i.e., Shepherd, 2015; see also Chap. 2). Additionally, each source moves past the strategic-management perspective that is often used in family business research (Sharma, De Massis, & Gagne, 2014; for reviews, see De Massis, Frattini, & Lichtenthaler, 2012; James, Jennings, & Breitkreuz, 2012), instead taking a psychological perspective, which has become increasingly popular in entrepreneurship research (e.g., Baron, 1998; Cardon, Foo, Shepherd, & Wiklund, 2012; Shepherd, 2015) and has substantial potential in family business research (Gagné, Sharma, & De Massis, 2014; Miller & Le Breton-Miller, 2014; Sharma et al., 2014). Next, by focusing on these sources of vitality, we are able shift the level of analysis from the firm to the individual in order to further move beyond the strategic-management perspective. Finally, this approach has solid theoretical grounding in established literatures, thus providing the foundation for research to significantly contribute to these "source" literatures by pushing theories' boundaries given the extreme context of family business and entrepreneurial action these theories need to accommodate. By focusing the discussion in this way, we hope this chapter (and, ultimately, the discourse and actions that follow) makes several important contributions.

First, family business research has a strong tradition of exploring social interactions (Kellermanns & Eddleston, 2004; Morris, Williams, Allen, & Avila, 1997) largely focused on the relationship between principals and agents of family businesses (Chrisman, Chua, & Litz, 2004; Gomez-Mejia, Nunez-Nickel, & Gutierrez, 2001; Schulze, Lubatkin, & Dino, 2003; Siebels & zu Knyphausen-Aufseß, 2012; Vilaseca, 2002). Although this research has made important contributions to our understanding of management and governance, we lack a sufficient understanding of other commercial relationships involving the family firm (Gagné et al., 2014). In this chapter, we begin to address the call in Chap. 2 (see also Shepherd, 2015) for more research on the inter-relationship between the actor and a community of inquiry in developing and refining a potential opportunity in order to explore how the family business context can help challenge and extend the boundaries of an emerging social interaction theory of opportunity generation and refinement. Specifically, by considering the role of the family, theorizing needs to consider the nature of a "collective mind" forming opportunity beliefs; consider at least two communities of inquiry internal to the firm refining an opportunity and, in doing so, being transformed themselves; and consider how the family, through a potential opportunity, can transform the business (as a community of inquiry) and communities of inquiry external to the firm.

Second, family business research has put great effort into exploring the impact emotion has on decision making and action (e.g., Astrachan & Jaskiewicz, 2008; Berrone, Cruz, Gomez-Mejia, & Larraza-Kintana, 2010; Harrell, 1997; Kellermanns, Eddleston, & Zellweger, 2012; Zellweger & Dehlen, 2011), focusing a considerable subset of that research on socio-emotional wealth (Berrone, Cruz, & Gomez-Mejia, 2012; Berrone et al., 2010; Gómez-Mejía, Haynes, Núñez-Nickel, Jacobson, & Moyano-Fuentes, 2007; Kellermanns et al., 2012). Along these lines, it is highly likely that contributions to both the entrepreneurship and family business literatures will result from exploring (1) *opportunities to gain* socio-emotional wealth rather than threats to this wealth, (2) the *flow* of socio-emotional wealth rather than a sole focus on its stock; and, consistent with these principles, and (3) the development of a micro-foundation process model of socio-emotional wealth.

Lastly, family business researchers have often been trailblazers in exploring and acknowledging firm-management practices to reap benefits that go beyond purely economic gains, such as benefits associated with supporting family members' psychological and social well-being (Lubatkin, 2007; Schulze, Lubatkin, Dino, & Buchholtz, 2001; Schulze et al., 2003), offering valuable career paths (Dyer & Handler, 1994), and protecting socio-emotional wealth (Cruz, Gomez-Mejia, & Becerra, 2010; Gomez-Mejia, Cruz, Berrone, & De Castro, 2011; Gomez-Mejia, Makri, & Kintana, 2010; Gómez-Mejía et al., 2007; Jones, Makri, & Gomez-Mejia, 2008). Extending these concepts to prosocial behavior, in this chapter, we begin to investigate how family firms could use their unique position to identify, organize, and develop opportunities to alleviate suffering in- or outside the family or the business.

The chapter proceeds by highlighting each of the areas of vitality and the ways research in those areas can make important contributions to both the family business and entrepreneurship fields.

## An Interactions Perspective of Entrepreneurial Opportunities and Family Businesses

Family business research has a strong tradition of exploring social interactions (e.g., Kellermanns & Eddleston, 2004; Morris et al., 1997). Specifically, because family firms often have both family and non-family owners, considerable attention has been paid to the interaction between principals and agents for issues related to conflicts of interest and asymmetric information (Chrisman et al., 2004; Gomez-Mejia et al., 2001; Schulze et al., 2003; Siebels & zu Knyphausen-Aufseß, 2012; Vilaseca, 2002). For example, Schulze (2001) highlighted the agency costs of altruism—parents acting generously toward their children when running the business (Kets de Vries, 1993; Schulze et al., 2003b)—and management entrenchment—family members having secure positions in management through neutralized internal control mechanisms (Gomez-Mejia et al., 2001; Siebels & zu Knyphausen-Aufseß, 2012; Villalonga & Amit, 2006). Whereas research based on stewardship theory explains how agents act in the best interest of the principles (Davis, Schoorman, & Donaldson, 1997; Donaldson & Davis, 1991; Siebels & zu Knyphausen-Aufseß, 2012), family members tend to place the well-being of the firm over their own well-being (Cabrera-Suárez, De Saá-Pérez, & García-Almeida, 2001; Corbetta & Salvato, 2004; Zahra, 2003). For example, the managers (i.e., stewards) engage in pro-organizational behaviors that enhance family firm performance (Corbetta & Salvato, 2004; Kellermanns & Eddleston, 2004) and create a sense of community (Arregle, Hitt, Sirmon, & Very, 2007; Guzzo & Abbott, 1990; Miller & Le Breton-Miller, 2006).

Despite knowledge about the economic and social exchange from the family to others, there is little understanding of other commercial relationships in family firms (Gagné et al., 2014). Indeed, research on the inter-relationships between the community and the actor over potential opportunities provides a basis for an important contribution to entrepreneurship (Chap. 2; see also Shepherd, 2015), and, as we explore below, this contribution can be achieved through family business research.

A potential opportunity represents both a vehicle and an outcome of interaction, the exploration of which in the family business context can provide the basis for important contributions to both fields. Individuals can form a belief that a situation represents an opportunity for someone (Cornelissen & Clarke, 2010; Grégoire & Shepherd, 2012) and an opportunity for them specifically (Autio, Dahlander, & Frederiksen, 2013;

Haynie, Shepherd, & McMullen, 2009; Mitchell & Shepherd, 2010)—that is, third- and first-person opportunity beliefs (McMullen & Shepherd, 2006), respectively. By acting on this potential opportunity, the individual engages with a community to test (e.g., talk, probe, and exploit) the veracity of the potential opportunity; in turn, a community of inquiry (e.g., customers, suppliers, and financers) provides feedback about the potential opportunity (Autio et al., 2013; Shepherd, 2015; see also Chap. 2). This feedback can transform the mind of the individual, which can then transform the nature of the potential opportunity and, through interactions with the manifestations of the potential opportunity, transform the community of inquiry. This notion of mutual adjustment between the mind and the world (Dewey, 1939) through testing and refining a potential opportunity can inform (and be informed by) family business research.

From the social interactive perspective of the identification and refinement of a potential opportunity, the "mind" refers to an individual (implicitly independent of the firm context), and the "world" is external to the individual (implicitly independent of the individual). The family firm context requires us to begin to question these implicit assumptions and thereby raise opportunities for future research to make important contributions.

### *The Mutual Adjustment of the Family and the Potential Opportunity*

Although we have an understanding of how individuals identify (Fiet, 2007; Grégoire, Barr, & Shepherd, 2010; Shane, 2000) and form beliefs about opportunities (McMullen & Shepherd, 2006), we do not have a good idea of how groups come to form opportunity beliefs. Because family members are (to varying degrees) in tune with each other's emotional and cognitive states (Morris, Silk, Steinberg, Myers, & Robinson, 2007), have similar values (Aronoff, 2004), and have established communication patterns (Fitzpatrick & Ritchie, 1994), the family business context is ideal to begin to explore the role of the "collective mind" as an input and an outcome of the refinement of potential opportunities. For example, to what extent does the community of inquiry, through refining a potential opportunity, transform the family of a family business? At first, this seems like a stretch because we often think of the family as relatively stable and enduring. However, despite the initial assumption that the identity of individuals and organizations are relatively stable and enduring (Albert

& Whetten, 1985), recent research has acknowledged that identity is mutable (Gioia, Patvardhan, Hamilton, & Corley, 2013; Gioia, Schultz, & Corley, 2000). Although we are not going to resolve the debate about the endurance of identity here, we can begin to think about when, how, and in what way the family can be transformed by a community of inquiry through interactions over a potential opportunity. In many ways, this can add new insights into our understanding of mutual adjustment. It is not just conflict over business issues that influences the family (Carr & Hmieleski, 2015; Shepherd & Haynie, 2009) or conflict within the family that influences the business (Dyer, 1994; Kellermanns & Eddleston, 2004; Lee & Rogoff, 1996; Schulze et al., 2003; Sorenson, 1999), but interactions with a community of inquiry over a potential opportunity have the potential to transform the family.

Moreover, the transformed family refines the potential opportunity, which in turn influences the community. It is interesting to follow the logic of this theorizing further. This process of mutual adjustment potentially drives the family firm and the community of inquiry closer together, and while this might be a profitable outcome for the business, it may fundamentally transform the family "mind" in a way that perhaps none of its individual members would prefer. Can family firms resist or cease the interactive effect of a particular potential opportunity that is transforming the family in an undesirable way? What are the processes of recognizing a family transformation as undesirable, and what are the processes for terminating (and even reversing) this mutual adjustment of family and community of inquiry via opportunity refinement or opportunity termination (despite its high-profit potential)? It could be that the transformation of the family from the pursuit of an emerging potential opportunity creates a slippery slope (or path dependence) that is difficult to redirect or stop.

### *Communities of Inquiry Within the Family Business*

While research has typically considered the community of inquiry to be external and somewhat independent of the individual identifying and refining the opportunity (Shepherd, 2015), a shift to the family business context offers a different perspective on the community of inquiry. For example, a community of inquiry could be considered more internal when it involves other members of the business and/or other members of the family. Given that a potential opportunity can be refined through interaction with a community of inquiry, what happens when there are multiple communities of inquiry and each provides different feedback? The different feedback provides a basis for refining the opportunity in different ways—a fork in the road. Which path is chosen, why, and with what consequence? Perhaps it is less about consciously choosing a path but choosing the community of inquiry with which to remain engaged. Indeed, by pursuing one of the directions for refining the potential opportunity, both communities of inquiry may be transformed but in different ways. Therefore, the process of refining a potential opportunity may lead to the transformation of the business (as a community of inquiry) and the family (as a community of inquiry) in ways that create divergence between the family and the business where there once was convergence. This notion has implications for future research on the generation, evaluation, and refinement of potential opportunities in the family business context.

If a potential opportunity is a source of transformation that creates divergence between the family and the business in some family businesses, then perhaps it can also be a source of convergence in other family businesses. That is, for family firms with little congruence between the family and business sub-systems, the identification and refinement of a potential opportunity may be a vehicle for transforming the communities such that there is more overlap between the two, thereby resolving the "disconnect"—namely, putting them both on the same page. Rather than creating two immovable yet opposing "mindsets," a potential opportunity can represent a vehicle for interaction through which the potential opportunity is refined. In so doing, the communities of inquiry are transformed, thus closing the "mindset" gap. Future research can determine whether this process of convergence leads to a compromise of tradeoffs or a win-win situation.

### *Family Members' Choices of Internal Communities of Inquiry*

Over and above the interaction with the external community of inquiry and between the family and the business communities of inquiry, the process of refining a potential opportunity will likely have an impact at the inter-personal level within both of the family firm's sub-systems. Here, we can focus on the unique aspect of the family business context—the family. When a member of the family forms an opportunity belief, how does he or she "test" it with other family members, change his or her conceptualization of the potential opportunity (in line with feedback), and reflect that changed conceptualization in refinements to the nature of the potential opportunity? How do these refinements then transform the group of family members acting as a community of inquiry? Perhaps the individual with the initial idea of a potential opportunity can choose or create this first community of inquiry. Perhaps the family is used first as a community of inquiry because they are proximal and vested. Alternatively, the first community of inquiry could be a smaller sub-group within the family, a smaller sub-group of non-family business members, or an external (i.e., outside the family business) community of inquiry before the family is approached as a whole. As alluded to in the previous paragraph, the differential transformation of communities through a potential opportunity's refinement may complicate a sequential process of advancing from one community to the next. Indeed, although the generation of a potential opportunity likely starts with one community or the other, this opportunity process likely continues in a highly iterative process by which opportunity refinement occurs through interactions within and between these different communities, which are themselves being transformed by the process.

In sum, we can learn a great deal about the process of opportunity identification and refinement by exploring social interactions in the family business context and thereby make important contributions to theory. We can also learn a great deal about transformations of the family and the business by exploring the identification and refinement of opportunities.

## Summary

In Fig. 6.1, we offer a sketch of an example of a more opportunity-based perspective of family business interactions as a basis for guiding future research. Although there are likely many potential future research contributions arising from studies of the interactions occurring in the family business context, we propose that important avenues for future research include addressing the following questions: (1) How does testing the veracity of a family business's potential opportunity in a community of inquiry transform the family, business, and/or external community? (2) How does the transformation of the family community of inquiry and/or the business community of inquiry refine the nature of the potential opportunity? (3) How does the transformation of the business community of inquiry (through the refinement of a potential opportunity) transform the family community of inquiry and vice versa? (4) How and when does the refinement of a potential opportunity lead to convergence of the family and business (or convergence within either sub-system)? (5) How and

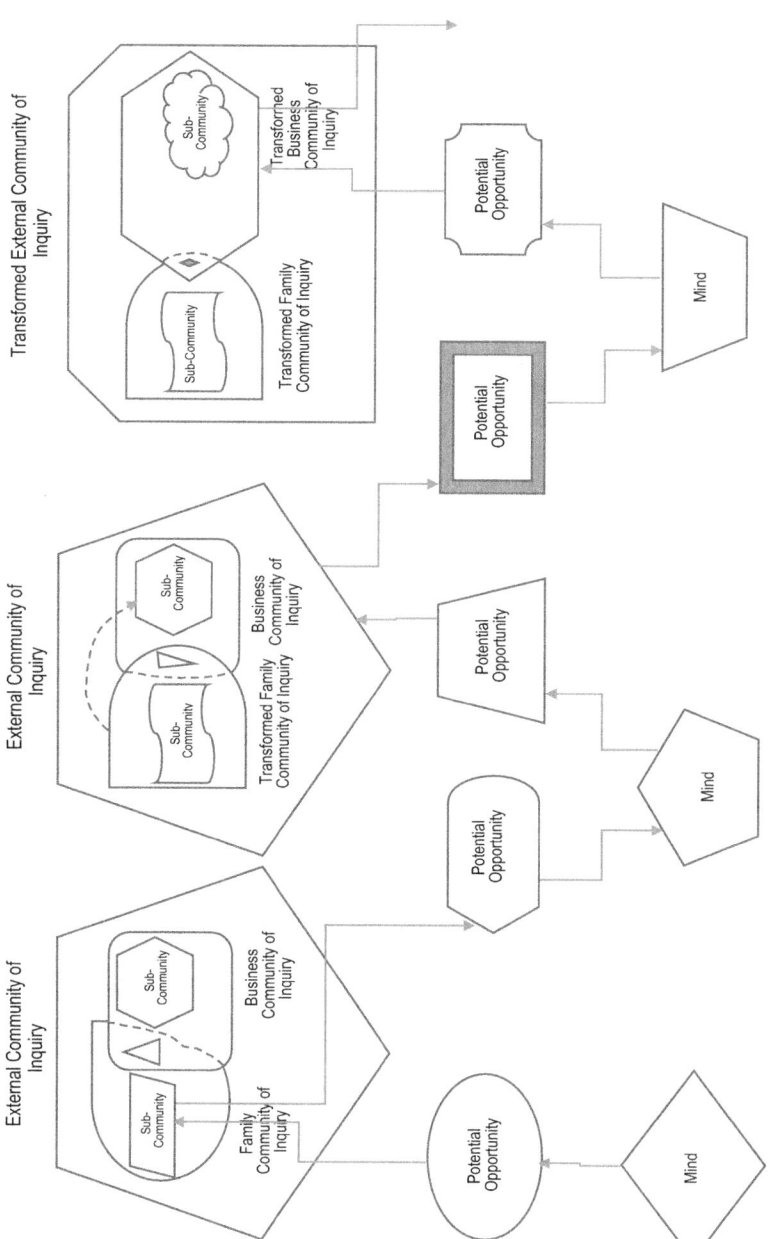

Fig. 6.1 A sketch of an opportunity-based perspective of family business interactions

when does the refinement of a potential opportunity lead to divergence of the family and the business (or divergence within either sub-system)? (6) Finally, how does the sequence of engaging different communities of inquiry impact the evolution of the potential opportunity and the mind of the originator of the idea?

## Emotions, Entrepreneurship, and Family Businesses[1]

Our initial arguments are grounded in socio-emotional wealth (as represented in the family business literature) but also reflect a broader thinking in regard to the more general role emotion plays at the intersection of family business and entrepreneurship. In this context, emotion refers to subjective feeling states with a clear cause or object, a short duration, and a focus on a specific target (adapted from Frijda, 1994). We believe future research can make substantial contributions to the family business and entrepreneurship fields (and beyond) by exploring the different roles emotion plays. To begin this process, in the remainder of this chapter, we briefly introduce potential contributions

### *Building of a Firm's Stock of Emotion Resources*

Because most family business research takes a strategic-management perspective (Sharma, Chrisman, & Chua, 1997), it is unsurprising that studies of socio-emotional wealth usually start by focusing on an established firm and its endowment of socio-emotional wealth (Chua, Chrisman, & De Massis, 2015; Gómez-Mejía et al., 2007; Kellermanns et al., 2012). Given the nature of entrepreneurship research, however, an important topic of study is new venture creation and organizational emergence (Delmar & Davidsson, 2000; Katz & Gartner, 1988). Through a more in-depth investigation of organizational emergence, we can start to understand how this endowment of socio-emotional wealth is created and, perhaps, what "imprinting effect" it has. How do emerging organizations develop an emotion-related endowment, why do some new organizations have stronger emotion-related endowments than others, and how does this endowment (or lack thereof) influence the other nascent activities in the organizational-emergence process?

Research exploring the connections between activities of building emotion stocks and those of building an organization is likely to shed new light on our understanding of not only the entrepreneurial process as a whole but also the beginning phases of family firms. For example, through such research, we could gain a deeper understanding of how an emerging organization's current emotion-related endowment affects the type, timing, and/or sequence of the nascent activities associated with organizational emergence (for nascent activities, see Lichtenstein, Dooley, & Lumpkin, 2006). Perhaps there is a different pattern of organizational emergence for firms starting with a greater emotion-related endowment than for organizations with a weaker emotion-related endowment and/or for firms trying to grow their emotional endowment (although, this likely depends greatly on the type of emotional endowment under investigation). For instance, as firms engage in organizational-emergence activities, such as member selection for family businesses or activities that build stronger connections between founding team members, they are likely to uncover or begin to build a socio-emotional endowment. Thus, firms may be able to influence and actively manage the creation of an emotional endowment around the family or some other kinship group.

### *Micro-Foundations of a Firm's Stock of Emotion Resources*

Unsurprisingly, many family business scholars of socio-emotional wealth have focused on the firm level of analysis primarily due to their interest in the performance of family firms (Cruz et al., 2010; Gómez-Mejía et al., 2007). However, by shifting the level of analysis to individuals, dyads, and sub-groups within the firm (including within the family), many new research opportunities arise to investigate the micro-foundations of firms' stocks of emotions (see Miller & Le Breton-Miller, 2014; Schulze & Kellermanns, 2015). In particular, by disaggregating firm-level socio-emotional wealth, research has the potential to reveal how and why the stocks and flows of emotions (specifically those related to kinship ties) influence entrepreneurial activities. Further, this approach will allow us to explain the degree and characteristics of firms' entrepreneurial actions as well as the outcomes of those actions for not only family and/or business members but also firm performance.[2] A promising first step may be to study the emotion stocks (type and level) of sub-groups within the firm as well as within the family. More specifically, it is probable that sub-groups within the family (e.g., husband and wife, siblings, in-laws, grandchildren) form different perceptions regarding various aspects of the business (e.g., the value of current family control of the business), thereby resulting in different levels of socio-emotional wealth. By exploring sub-groups' emotion stocks in general and their emotion-related values more specifically (and emotions flows), future research can clarify how and why families with different sub-groups make different decisions and/or have different performance outcomes.[3]

Indeed, to the extent that these differences in emotion stocks across sub-groups affect entrepreneurial activities and thus entrepreneurial action, the importance of this research will be heightened. It could be that differences in emotion-related values among sub-groups create tension among firm members over which opportunities the firm should pursue. If this is the case, how do firm members overcome conflicts? It could be that tension among sub-groups could be functional (i.e., task conflict) if the different sub-groups serve as a "check" for other groups' opportunity proposals, thus maintaining some form of "emotional" balance in the firm. It is also likely that differences in sub-group emotional stocks help firms identify and/or generate more opportunities from which to choose (for more on the advantages of a larger opportunity set, see Gruber, MacMillan, & Thompson, 2008) or from which to create a portfolio of ventures (see Bakker & Shepherd, 2017).

### *Stocks and Flows of Emotion Resources*

Researchers can improve theory on the stock of emotion-related values (e.g., socio-emotional wealth) by studying the flow of such stock (Chua et al., 2015) as well as variations in flow across family members (Miller & Le Breton-Miller, 2014). Such research will enable the creation of a more dynamic, finer-grained process model (e.g., the stock and flow of knowledge [Dierickx & Cool, 1989]) detailing how collective emotions affect decision making within family and/or entrepreneurial businesses. More specifically, as the firm, family, family members, and/or founders move through the entrepreneurial process, the firm's stock of socio-emotional wealth and other forms of emotion-related values will likely change (and perhaps ebb and flow). For example, for some parts of the entrepreneurial process (e.g., developing the business), the perceived value of family control and influence (Berrone et al., 2010; Gómez-Mejía et al., 2007) may be more desirable than for other parts (e.g., inventing). Similarly, given their different interests, skills, and preferences, family members are likely to identify with and be attracted to (Dyer & Whetten, 2006) different parts and activities of the firm (e.g., identifying more with the marketing department than with the manufacturing department). By pursuing opportunities with which they identify, family members are likely to generate positive emotions, whereas they are likely to generate negative emotions by pursuing opportunities with which they do not identify.

Kinship ties also play an interesting role in family businesses, with some ties likely being stronger among some sub-groups than others (e.g., Discua-Cruz, Howorth, & Hamilton, 2013). Additionally, kinship ties may "switch" for different tasks associated with the entrepreneurial process: ties with one's sister, for example, may be stronger for creative endeavors, whereas ties with one's brother are stronger for opportunity exploitation. Furthermore, because most individuals are emotionally attached to at least some parts of their work (Eddleston & Kellermanns, 2007), entrepreneurial project failure may negatively impact emotional attachments (Shepherd, Patzelt, & Wolfe, 2011) between kin but may also open up the possibility for other attachments to develop (e.g., a new project or an addition to the family). However, while kinship ties are generally discussed in the context of family firms, researchers can also consider investigating the development of stocks of emotions in non-family kinship groups. Socio-emotional wealth theory may no longer apply when the focal group is not the family, but socio-emotional wealth scholars do seem to be open to the possibility: "non-family principles and managers might experience some of this [socio-emotional wealth]" (Berrone et al., 2012, pp. 259–260).

Acknowledging that stocks of emotions can be affected by firm members' entrepreneurial activities, researchers can begin to explore the reciprocal relationship between stocks of emotions and entrepreneurial action. There could be an emotion stock–entrepreneurial action spiral, for example, if a stock of emotions (e.g., collective emotion–related values) affects a firm's decision to undertake entrepreneurial action and then the entrepreneurial process impacts that stock of emotions. This spiral could be positive, with a higher stock of emotions leading to more entrepreneurial action and the increased entrepreneurial action contributing to the emotion stock. The spiral could also be negative, with a drop in the emotion stock (or a threat of a loss in stock) resulting in decreased entrepreneurial action and this reduced entrepreneurial action leading to a further decrease in the emotion stock.

*Emotional Reactions to Failure*

Family business researchers have spent considerable time investigating the negative effects of the loss (or threatened loss) of socio-emotional wealth on decision making (Cruz et al., 2010; Gómez-Mejía et al., 2007), and entrepreneurship researchers have studied the negative effects of the loss of an entrepreneurial endeavor (i.e., a project [Shepherd et al., 2011] or a business [Shepherd, 2003]) on decision making; however, surprisingly, there has been little overlap between the two fields. Given their similar interests, cross-fertilization will likely benefit both fields. In particular, higher stocks of emotions could lead firm members to persist in business endeavors despite poor performance. However, such persistence may make failure more costly if it does occur, which is likely to have an adverse effect on the family's (and its members') well-being. Moreover, as the family invests greater emotion stocks in the business, the firm is likely to grow in importance among family members, thus generating more grief if failure does occur. This resulting grief could cause family members to suffer longer, learn less, and be less motivated to try again after failure. On the other hand, some of the emotion stocks that led to persistence could also serve as a means to cope with grief. Namely, when faced with grief over entrepreneurial failure, firms with higher emotion stocks may be able to help family members more quickly reduce grief, learn from the failure, and try again. However, firm failure could also ruin or dramatically alter the family's (and family members') set of emotion-related values. These conjectures are all speculations at this point. Further research is needed on the emotion stocks of the family (and/or the individuals and groups within the family) and on the failing and/or failure of entrepreneurial endeavors (i.e., projects or firms).

## Summary

In Fig. 6.2, we offer a sketch of an emotion-based entrepreneurial process in a family business as a basis for guiding future research. The creation of a family business begins with the family and some level of organizing (a nascent organization) and includes an emotional endowment that influences the extent of entrepreneurial action. Entrepreneurial action, at the project level, can lead to success or failure, and these project outcomes influence the overall performance of the family business. The family business's emotional endowment is made up of the emotional endowment of

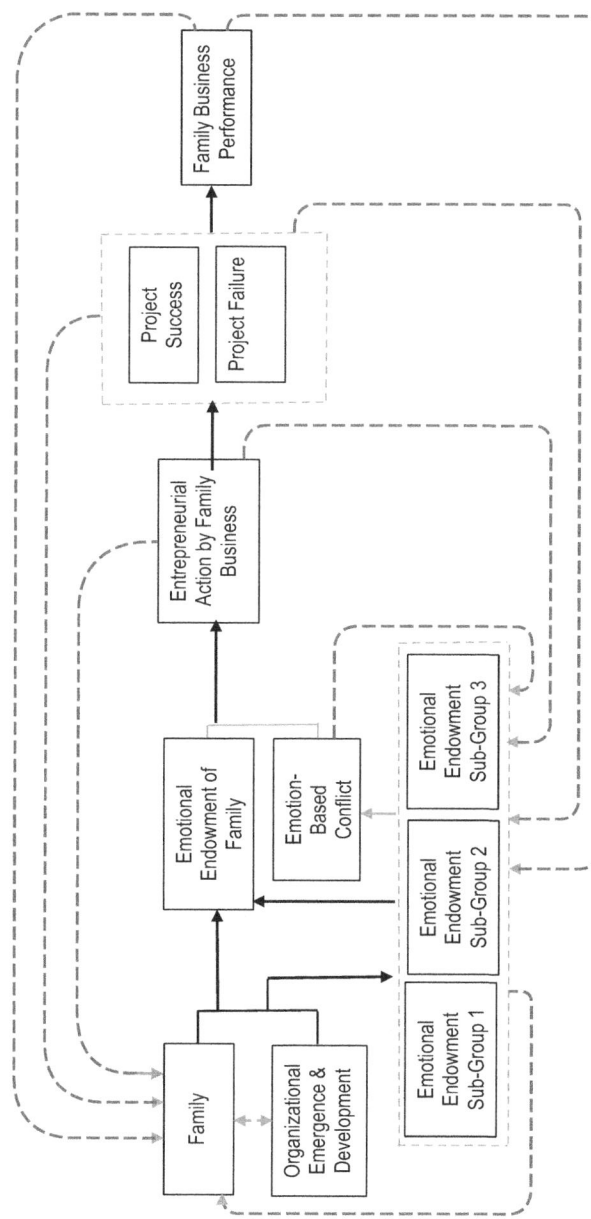

**Fig. 6.2** A sketch of an emotion-based entrepreneurial process in a family business

its various sub-groups. Differences in emotional endowments can lead to conflict, which can in turn influence entrepreneurial action and the sub-groups' emotional endowment from which the conflict originally arose. Indeed, the emotional endowment of the family's sub-groups is influenced by the family business's entrepreneurial action, project outcomes, and performance. Similarly, the nature of the family business itself can be influenced by the family business's entrepreneurial action, project outcomes, and performance.

## EMOTIONAL RESPONSES TO OTHERS' SUFFERING, ENTREPRENEURSHIP, AND FAMILY BUSINESSES[4]

Researchers have found that when the family has influence in managing the business, resulting business decisions are generally more socially responsible and reflect stronger notions of community citizenship (Berrone et al., 2010; Dyer & Whetten, 2006). The driving force of such "socially responsible" behavior is likely *prosocial motivation*—an individual's desire to expend effort to assist (i.e., protect or promote the welfare of) other people (Batson, 1998; Grant, 2007). In addition, firms can engage in prosocial behavior through compassion organizing: "a collective response to a particular incident of human suffering that entails the coordination of individual compassion" (Dutton, Worline, Frost, & Lilius, 2006, p. 62). Compassion organizing refers to organizations' repurposing and redirecting routines used for normal work to quickly respond to employees in need to help alleviate their suffering, such as the University of Michigan's response to the suffering caused to students by a fire on campus (Dutton et al., 2006).

However, there are times when the firm's current routines and processes do not align with the needs associated with a member's suffering. In such cases, the family within (and perhaps reaching beyond) the boundaries of the firm may be able to offer the routines and processes necessary to ease the organizational member's suffering. That is, the family can serve as the foundation for organizing the identification and exploitation of a potential opportunity to alleviate the member's suffering. As with any business task, it is likely that some families are better at compassion organizing than others. For instance, families that faced suffering in the past could have stronger compassion-organizing capabilities in the family business context than families without such experience.

As opposed to the "normal" routines of an established firm being used to alleviate suffering, Shepherd and Williams found that new ventures were spontaneously created (within hours and days) to ease people's suffering in the aftermath of the Black Saturday bushfires (Shepherd & Williams, 2014; Williams & Shepherd, 2016) and the Haiti earthquake (Williams & Shepherd, 2017), both of which were natural disasters that caused extensive damage. It usually takes months and even years for an organization to emerge, so it is remarkable how rapidly these ventures were created and acted to ease suffering (within days and weeks). Interestingly, many of these ventures involved family. In this context, families may have been uniquely positioned to provide the routines and processes necessary to speed up the venture-creation process in order to quickly deliver customized solutions for the alleviation of suffering. While the Black Saturday bushfire and Haiti earthquake are extreme examples of compassion organizing, it is through extreme cases like these that we can extend and build theory (Eisenhardt, 1989). Shepherd and Williams's work highlights that our understanding of the role of family in the venture-creation process is incomplete (over and above the "family" from "fools, family, and friends" as sources of capital [Aldrich & Cliff, 2003]), especially in regard to alleviating suffering through venture creation. It could be that responding compassionately to others' suffering strengthens prosocial motivation, enables the development of new routines (within the family and/or firm) to alleviate subsequent suffering (by family and/or organizational members), and builds individuals' capacity to rapidly create new ventures.

Contingencies—rather than global predictions about family firms' (or even one specific family firm's) entrepreneurial actions—are likely to be important in fully understanding behavior. The nature of a potential opportunity is one such contingency. This particular contingency is important because a potential opportunity's non-economic value can vary significantly across family businesses for a host of family and non-family reasons. For instance, the concept of family values often underpins the notion of community (Arregle et al., 2007; Miller & Le Breton-Miller, 2006). As such, it could be that family-run businesses act more prosocially toward the communities in which they are located (e.g., local neighborhood and/or family-oriented groups), which may or may not lead them to act less prosocially toward "outside" groups. In an entrepreneurial context, this prosocial behavior is significant as prosocial motivation could help explain why some family firms identify and exploit specific opportunities to "do good" for some individuals/groups while foregoing opportunities to help others. That is, we can learn more about the fundamental elements of social and sustainable entrepreneurship research by gaining a deeper understanding of the family's role in firm decision making. For instance, investigating differences among families and the influence such differences have on firm decision making is likely to lead to a richer understanding of firm actions that enable (or hinder) specific social and/or environmental outcomes.

While research has shown that family firm managers take action to promote and/or protect other family members' welfare (Kellermanns & Eddleston, 2004; Schulze et al., 2001), it is unclear whether these same managers are driven to promote and/or protect the natural environment. For instance, entrepreneurs have been found to disengage their pro-environmental values to pursue opportunities that harm the natural environment when they have high entrepreneurial self-efficacy and face conditions of low munificence (Shepherd, Patzelt, & Baron, 2013). As this example shows, even people who have strong pro-environmental values (and who are thus expected to be good stewards of the environment) are occasionally confronted with situations that cause them to disengage their values, leading them to serve as poor environmental stewards. While many studies in the family business field have focused on the notion of stewardship, it remains uncertain what stewardship theory would predict when family business members are confronted with conflicting stewardship scenarios. On the one hand, maintaining a positive external image of the family would require family stewards to make ethical decisions (e.g., not exploiting opportunities that harm the environment). On the other hand, however, if stewardship of the firm comes into direct conflict with stewardship of the environment, the entrepreneur may decide to disengage his or her pro-environmental values to pursue an opportunity that protects the family's interests but harms nature. Alternatively, when presented with this type of stewardship conflict, the entrepreneur (or other key decision maker) may decide to disengage his or her family values to avoid damaging the natural environment. Future research is needed to fully understand the role family plays in firm members' disengagement of values to exploit potentially harmful opportunities as well as the conditions under which family values are disengaged to exploit certain opportunities.

## Summary

In Fig. 6.3, we offer a sketch of a prosocially based entrepreneurial process in a family business as a basis for guiding future research. The family business is at the intersection of the family and the business and, through its prosocial motivation, can form a belief about a potential opportunity to alleviate suffering. This compassionate response can be organized through its normal routines or through compassion venturing—the creation of either a de novo or de alio new venture. The suffering alleviated can be inside the family business (i.e., family employees and/or non-family employees) or outside the family business (i.e., non-employee members of the family or others unrelated to the business or the family). In turn, the alleviation of suffering can influence the family business and/or its prosocial motivation.

## Discussion and Conclusion

Although there are many research opportunities at the intersection of the entrepreneurship and family business fields (see Goel & Jones, 2016; Kellermanns & Eddleston, 2006; Zellweger, Kellermanns, Chrisman, & Chua, 2012), in this chapter, we offered three potential future areas that we believe can considerably advance both fields by combining and blending constructs and relationships specific to one field with those of the other field.

First, we proposed that an entrepreneurial-opportunities perspective can be a fruitful avenue to study interactions within family businesses as well as interactions between these families and associated communities of inquiry. In addition, this perspective can shed light on how both the family business and the communities of inquiry are shaped by and shape the potential opportunities being developed. An important aspect of this research stream is that it needs to be dynamic. It seems that longitudinal data would offer great benefits for addressing the research questions outlined earlier. For example, inductive case studies may be able to provide in-depth insight into the co-evolution of families, opportunities, and communities of inquiry as well as mutual adjustments (e.g., see Gioia and colleagues' work on identity as potential exemplars [Gioia, Price, Hamilton, & Thomas, 2010; Patvardhan, Gioia, & Hamilton, 2015]). Furthermore, since the formation of opportunity beliefs is a cognitive process that takes place in family members' minds, experimental approaches like conjoint

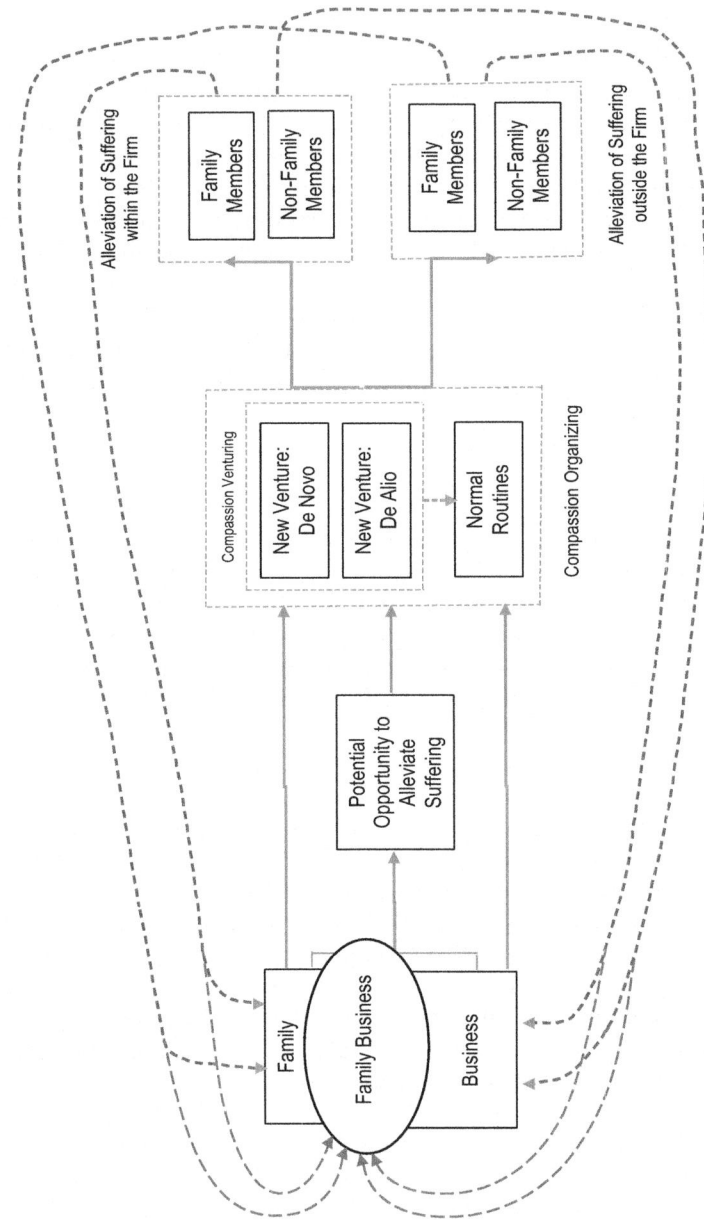

Fig. 6.3 A sketch of a prosocially based entrepreneurial process in a family business

studies and verbal protocol analysis, which have been used previously to study opportunity evaluations (Grégoire et al., 2010; Shepherd et al., 2013, respectively), might provide new insights into family members' decisions to adjust potential opportunities based on the characteristics and feedback of the community of inquiry.

In addition, we believe that future research opportunities on the topic of emotion could offer important contributions to knowledge. While both fields acknowledge the importance of emotion and have explored it in a variety of ways, blending the two fields' diverse knowledge on the topic is likely to provide the foundation for new insights. In particular, the speculations we made regarding future research on emotional responding and on decisions to do good and/or cause harm are the most uncertain. In many ways, however, this uncertainty makes these topics so exciting. Through this future research, we have the opportunity to venture into the unknown to explore an area that could have positive implications not only for individuals, families, and organizations but also for societies at large. We hope this chapter leads to fruitful thought, discussion, and action and are eager about the possible contributions for research in the family business and entrepreneurship fields as well as at the intersection of the two.

## Notes

1. The content of this section relies largely on Shepherd (2016).
2. We are in no way criticizing previous work on socio-emotional wealth when we suggest that nuances are lost when individuals' and groups' emotions are aggregated to the firm level; this occurs with most (if not all) psychological variables at the firm level, and we do not deny that there are benefits of investigating phenomena at the firm level. Shifting levels of analysis, however, is likely to enable new theoretical insights (Hedström & Swedberg, 1998).
3. As this research unfolds, new labels for emotion stocks at different levels of analysis may be needed. For example, if research reveals that socio-emotional wealth exists only at the firm level, we may need different labels for socio-emotional wealth at the individual, dyad, and within-firm group levels. Of course, we need more theorizing for this construct at different levels. For instance, does the socio-economic wealth of a sub-group within the family (e.g., a husband and wife) indicate that sub-group's overall perceptions of, for example, the value of current family control or the value of their (i.e., the

husband and wife's) control of the family firm? Unanswered questions like these represent important research opportunities. To fully understand the micro-foundations of socio-emotional wealth, research will likely have to reveal how differences in perceived value by family sub-units aggregate to become a firm-level construct.
4. The content of this section relies largely on Shepherd (2016).

## REFERENCES

Albert, S., & Whetten, D. A. (1985). Organizational identity. *Research in Organizational Behavior, 7*, 263–295.

Aldrich, H. E., & Cliff, J. E. (2003). The pervasive effects of family on entrepreneurship: Towards a family embeddedness perspective. *Journal of Business Venturing, 18*(5), 573–596.

Aronoff, C. (2004). Self-perpetuation family organization built on values: Necessary condition for long-term family business survival. *Family Business Review, 17*(1), 55–59.

Arregle, J. L., Hitt, M. A., Sirmon, D. G., & Very, P. (2007). The development of organizational social capital: Attributes of family firms. *Journal of Management Studies, 44*(1), 73–95.

Astrachan, J. H., & Jaskiewicz, P. (2008). Emotional returns and emotional costs in privately held family businesses: Advancing traditional business valuation. *Family Business Review, 21*(2), 139–149.

Autio, E., Dahlander, L., & Frederiksen, L. (2013). Information exposure, opportunity evaluation, and entrepreneurial action: An investigation of an online user community. *Academy of Management Journal, 56*(5), 1348–1371.

Bakker, R. M., & Shepherd, D. A. (2017). Pull the plug or take the plunge: Multiple opportunities and the speed of venturing decisions in the australian mining industry. *Academy of Management Journal*, amj-2013.

Baron, R. A. (1998). Cognitive mechanisms in entrepreneurship: Why and when enterpreneurs think differently than other people. *Journal of Business Venturing, 13*(4), 275–294.

Batson, C. (1998). Altruism and prosocial behavior. In D. T. Gilbert, S. T. Fiske, & G. Lindzey (Eds.), *The handbook of social psychology* (pp. 463–484). New York, NY: McGraw-Hill.

Berrone, P., Cruz, C., Gomez-Mejia, L. R., & Larraza-Kintana, M. (2010). Socioemotional wealth and corporate responses to institutional pressures: Do family-controlled firms pollute less? *Administrative Science Quarterly, 55*(1), 82–113.

Berrone, P., Cruz, C., & Gomez-Mejia, L. R. (2012). Socioemotional wealth in family firms theoretical dimensions, assessment approaches, and agenda for future research. *Family Business Review, 25*(3), 258–279.

Boxenbaum, E., & Rouleau, L. (2011). New knowledge products as bricolage: Metaphors and scripts in organizational theory. *Academy of Management Review, 36*(2), 272–296.

Cabrera-Suárez, K., De Saá-Pérez, P., & García-Almeida, D. (2001). The succession process from a resource-and knowledge-based view of the family firm. *Family Business Review, 14*(1), 37–46.

Cardon, M. S., Foo, M. D., Shepherd, D., & Wiklund, J. (2012). Exploring the heart: Entrepreneurial emotion is a hot topic. *Entrepreneurship Theory and Practice, 36*(1), 1–10.

Carr, J. C., & Hmieleski, K. M. (2015). Differences in the outcomes of work and family conflict between family-and nonfamily businesses: An examination of business founders. *Entrepreneurship Theory and Practice, 39*(6), 1413–1432.

Casillas, J. C., Moreno, A. M., & Barbero, J. L. (2009). A configurational approach of the relationship between entrepreneurial orientation and growth of family firms. *Family Business Review*. Advance online publication.

Chua, J. H., Chrisman, J. J., & De Massis, A. (2015). A closer look at socioemotional wealth: Its flows, stocks, and prospects for moving forward. *Entrepreneurship Theory & Practice, 39*(2), 173–182.

Chrisman, J. J., Chua, J. H., & Litz, R. A. (2004). Comparing the agency costs of family and non-family firms: Conceptual issues and exploratory evidence. *Entrepreneurship Theory and Practice, 28*(4), 335–354.

Corbetta, G., & Salvato, C. (2004). Self-serving or self-actualizing? Models of man and agency costs in different types of family firms: A commentary on "comparing the agency costs of family and non-family firms: Conceptual issues and exploratory evidence". *Entrepreneurship Theory and Practice, 28*(4), 355–362.

Cornelissen, J. P., & Clarke, J. S. (2010). Imagining and rationalizing opportunities: Inductive reasoning and the creation and justification of new ventures. *Academy of Management Review, 35*(4), 539–557.

Cruz, C. C., Gomez-Mejia, L. R., & Becerra, M. (2010). Perceptions of benevolence and the design of agency contracts: CEO-TMT relationships in family firms. *Academy of Management Journal, 53*(1), 69–89.

Cruz, C. C., & Nordqvist, M. (2012). Entrepreneurial orientation in family firms: A generational perspective. *Small Business Economics, 38*(1), 33–49.

Davis, J. H., Schoorman, F. D., & Donaldson, L. (1997). Toward a stewardship theory of management. *Academy of Management review, 22*(1), 20–47.

Delmar, F., & Davidsson, P. (2000). Where do they come from? Prevalence and characteristics of nascent entrepreneurs. *Entrepreneurship & Regional Development, 12*(1), 1–23.

De Massis, A., Frattini, F., & Lichtenthaler, U. (2012). Research on technological innovation in family firms: Present debates and future directions. *Family Business Review*. Advance online publication.

Dewey, J. (1939). Theory of valuation. *International Encyclopedia of Unified Science, 2*(4), vii–v67.

Dierickx, I., & Cool, K. (1989). Asset stock accumulation and sustainability of competitive advantage. *Management Science, 35*(12), 1504–1511.

Discua-Cruz, A., Howorth, C., & Hamilton, E. (2013). Intrafamily entrepreneurship: The formation and membership of family entrepreneurial teams. *Entrepreneurship Theory and Practice, 37*(1), 17–46.

Donaldson, L., & Davis, J. H. (1991). Stewardship theory or agency theory: CEO governance and shareholder returns. *Australian Journal of Management, 16*(1), 49–64.

Dutton, J. E., Worline, M. C., Frost, P. J., & Lilius, J. (2006). Explaining compassion organizing. *Administrative Science Quarterly, 51*(1), 59–96.

Dyer, W. G. (1994). Potential contributions of organizational behavior to the study of family-owned businesses. *Family Business Review, 7*(2), 109–131.

Dyer, W. G., & Handler, W. (1994). Entrepreneurship and family business: Exploring the connections. *Entrepreneurship Theory and Practice, 19*, 71–71.

Dyer, W. G., & Whetten, D. A. (2006). Family firms and social responsibility: Preliminary evidence from the S&P 500. *Entrepreneurship Theory and Practice, 30*(6), 785–802.

Eddleston, K. A., & Kellermanns, F. W. (2007). Destructive and productive family relationships: A stewardship theory perspective. *Journal of Business Venturing, 22*(4), 545–565.

Eisenhardt, K. M. (1989). Making fast strategic decisions in high-velocity environments. *Academy of Management Journal, 32*(3), 543–576.

Fiet, J. O. (2007). A prescriptive analysis of search and discovery. *Journal of Management Studies, 44*(4), 592–611.

Fitzpatrick, M. A., & Ritchie, L. D. (1994). Communication schemata within the family. *Human Communication Research, 20*(3), 275–301.

Frijda, N. H. (1994). Varieties of affect: Emotions and episodes, moods, and sentiments. In P. Ekman & R. Davison (Eds.), *The nature of emotions: Fundamental questions* (pp. 197–202). New York: Oxford University Press.

Gagné, M., Sharma, P., & De Massis, A. (2014). The study of organizational behaviour in family business. *European Journal of Work and Organizational Psychology, 23*(5), 643–656.

Gioia, D. A., Patvardhan, S. D., Hamilton, A. L., & Corley, K. G. (2013). Organizational identity formation and change. *The Academy of Management Annals, 7*(1), 123–193.

Gioia, D. A., Price, K. N., Hamilton, A. L., & Thomas, J. B. (2010). Forging an identity: An insider-outsider study of processes involved in the formation of organizational identity. *Administrative Science Quarterly, 55*(1), 1–46.

Gioia, D. A., Schultz, M., & Corley, K. G. (2000). Organizational identity, image, and adaptive instability. *Academy of Management Review, 25*(1), 63–81.

Goel, S., & Jones, R. J. (2016). Entrepreneurial exploration and exploitation in family business: A systematic review and future directions. *Family Business Review, 29*(1), 94–120.

Gomez-Mejia, L. R., Cruz, C., Berrone, P., & De Castro, J. (2011). The bind that ties: Socioemotional wealth preservation in family firms. *The Academy of Management Annals, 5*(1), 653–707.

Gómez-Mejía, L. R., Haynes, K. T., Núñez-Nickel, M., Jacobson, K. J., & Moyano-Fuentes, J. (2007). Socioemotional wealth and business risks in family-controlled firms: Evidence from Spanish olive oil mills. *Administrative Science Quarterly, 52*(1), 106–137.

Gomez-Mejia, L. R., Makri, M., & Kintana, M. L. (2010). Diversification decisions in family-controlled firms. *Journal of Management Studies, 47*(2), 223–252.

Gomez-Mejia, L. R., Nunez-Nickel, M., & Gutierrez, I. (2001). The role of family ties in agency contracts. *Academy of Management Journal, 44*(1), 81–95.

Grant, A. M. (2007). Relational design and the motivation to make a prosocial difference. *Academy of Management Review, 32*, 393–417.

Grégoire, D. A., Barr, P. S., & Shepherd, D. A. (2010). Cognitive processes of opportunity recognition: The role of structural alignment. *Organization Science, 21*(2), 413–431.

Grégoire, D. A., & Shepherd, D. A. (2012). Technology-market combinations and the identification of entrepreneurial opportunities: An investigation of the opportunity-individual nexus. *Academy of Management Journal, 55*(4), 753–785.

Gruber, M., MacMillan, I. C., & Thompson, J. D. (2008). Look before you leap: Market opportunity identification in emerging technology firms. *Management Science, 54*(9), 1652–1665.

Guzzo, R. A., & Abbott, S. (1990). Family firms as utopian organizations. *Family Business Review, 3*(1), 23–33.

Harrell, S. (1997). *Human families*. Boulder, CO: Westview.

Haynie, J. M., Shepherd, D. A., & McMullen, J. S. (2009). An opportunity for me? The role of resources in opportunity evaluation decisions. *Journal of Management Studies, 46*(3), 337–361.

Hedström, P., & Swedberg, R. (1998). *Social mechanisms: An analytical approach to social theory*. Cambridge: Cambridge University Press.

James, A. E., Jennings, J. E., & Breitkreuz, R. S. (2012). Worlds apart? Rebridging the distance between family science and family business research. *Family Business Review, 25*(1), 87–108.

Jones, C. D., Makri, M., & Gomez-Mejia, L. R. (2008). Affiliate directors and perceived risk bearing in publicly traded, family-controlled firms: The case of diversification. *Entrepreneurship Theory and Practice, 32*(6), 1007–1026.

Katz, J., & Gartner, W. B. (1988). Properties of emerging organizations. *Academy of Management Review, 13*(3), 429–441.

Kellermanns, F. W., & Eddleston, K. A. (2004). Feuding families: When conflict does a family firm good. *Entrepreneurship Theory and Practice, 28*(3), 209–228.

Kellermanns, F. W., & Eddleston, K. A. (2006). Corporate entrepreneurship in family firms: A family perspective. *Entrepreneurship Theory and Practice, 30*(6), 809–830.

Kellermanns, F. W., Eddleston, K. A., & Zellweger, T. M. (2012). Extending the socioemotional wealth perspective: A look at the dark side. *Entrepreneurship Theory and Practice, 36*(6), 1175–1182.

Kets de Vries, M. F. (1993). *Leaders, fools and imposters: Essays on the psychology of leadership*. San Francisco: Jossey Bass.

Lee, M. S., & Rogoff, E. G. (1996). Research note: Comparison of small businesses with family participation versus small businesses without family participation: An investigation of differences in goals, attitudes, and family/business conflict. *Family Business Review, 9*(4), 423–437.

Lichtenstein, B. B., Dooley, K. J., & Lumpkin, G. T. (2006). Measuring emergence in the dynamics of new venture creation. *Journal of Business Venturing, 21*(2), 153–175.

Lubatkin, M. (2007). One more time: What is a realistic theory of corporate governance? *Journal of Organizational Behavior, 28*(1), 59–67.

Lumpkin, G. T., Brigham, K. H., & Moss, T. W. (2010). Long-term orientation: Implications for the entrepreneurial orientation and performance of family businesses. *Entrepreneurship and Regional Development, 22*(3–4), 241–264.

McMullen, J. S., & Shepherd, D. A. (2006). Entrepreneurial action and the role of uncertainty in the theory of the entrepreneur. *Academy of Management Review, 31*(1), 132–152.

Miller, D., & Le Breton-Miller, L. (2006). Family governance and firm performance: Agency, stewardship, and capabilities. *Family Business Review, 19*(1), 73–87.

Miller, D., & Le Breton-Miller, L. (2014). Deconstructing socioemotional wealth. *Entrepreneurship Theory and Practice, 38*(4), 713–720.

Mitchell, J. R., & Shepherd, D. A. (2010). To thine own self be true: Images of self, images of opportunity, and entrepreneurial action. *Journal of Business Venturing, 25*(1), 138–154.

Morris, A. S., Silk, J. S., Steinberg, L., Myers, S. S., & Robinson, L. R. (2007). The role of the family context in the development of emotion regulation. *Social Development, 16*(2), 361–388.

Morris, M. H., Williams, R. O., Allen, J. A., & Avila, R. A. (1997). Correlates of success in family business transitions. *Journal of Business Venturing, 12*(5), 385–401.

Naldi, L., Nordqvist, M., Sjöberg, K., & Wiklund, J. (2007). Entrepreneurial orientation, risk taking, and performance in family firms. *Family Business Review, 20*(1), 33–47.

Oswick, C., Fleming, P., & Hanlon, G. (2011). From borrowing to blending: Rethinking the processes of organizational theory building. *Academy of Management Review, 36*(2), 318–337.

Patvardhan, S. D., Gioia, D. A., & Hamilton, A. L. (2015). Weathering a meta-level identity crisis: Forging a coherent collective identity for an emerging field. *Academy of Management Journal, 58*(2), 405–435.

Schulze, B., & Kellermanns, F. W. (2015). Reifying socioemotional wealth. *Entrepreneurship Theory & Practice, 39*(3), 447–459.

Schulze, W. S., Lubatkin, M. H., & Dino, R. N. (2003). Toward a theory of agency and altruism in family firms. *Journal of Business Venturing, 18*(4), 473–490.

Schulze, W. S., Lubatkin, M. H., Dino, R. N., & Buchholtz, A. K. (2001). Agency relationships in family firms: Theory and evidence. *Organization Science, 12*(2), 99–116.

Shane, S. (2000). Prior knowledge and the discovery of entrepreneurial opportunities. *Organization Science, 11*(4), 448–469.

Sharma, P., De Massis, A., & Gagne, M. (2014). Family business: A fertile ground for research on time, teams and positive organizational study. *European Journal of Work and Organizational Psychology, 23*(5), 674–679.

Sharma, P., Chrisman, J. J., & Chua, J. H. (1997). Strategic management of the family business: Past research and future challenges. *Family Business Review, 10*(1), 1–35.

Shepherd, D. A. (2003). Learning from business failure: Propositions about the grief recovery process for the self-employed. *Academy of Management Review, 28*(2), 318–329.

Shepherd, D. A. (2015). Party on! A call for entrepreneurship research that is more interactive, activity based, cognitively hot, compassionate, and prosocial. *Journal of Business Venturing, 30*(4), 489–507.

Shepherd, D., & Haynie, J. M. (2009). Family business, identity conflict, and an expedited entrepreneurial process: A process of resolving identity conflict. *Entrepreneurship Theory and Practice, 33*(6), 1245–1264.

Shepherd, D. A., Patzelt, H., & Baron, R. A. (2013). "I care about nature, but …": Disengaging values in assessing opportunities that cause harm. *Academy of Management Journal, 56*(5), 1251–1273.

Shepherd, D. A., Patzelt, H., & Wolfe, M. (2011). Moving forward from project failure: Negative emotions, affective commitment, and learning from the experience. *Academy of Management Journal, 54*(6), 1229–1259.

Shepherd, D. A., & Williams, T. A. (2014). Local venturing as compassion organizing in the aftermath of a natural disaster: The role of localness and community in reducing suffering. *Journal of Management Studies, 51*(6), 952–994.

Shepherd, D. A. (2016). An emotions perspective for advancing the fields of family business and entrepreneurship stocks, flows, reactions, and responses. Family Business Review, 29, 151–158

Short, J. C., Payne, G. T., Brigham, K. H., Lumpkin, G. T., & Broberg, J. C. (2009). Family firms and entrepreneurial orientation in publicly traded firms A comparative analysis of the S&P 500. *Family Business Review, 22*(1), 9–24.

Siebels, J. F., & zu Knyphausen-Aufseß, D. (2012). A review of theory in family business research: The implications for corporate governance. *International Journal of Management Reviews, 14*(3), 280–304.

Sorenson, R. L. (1999). Conflict management strategies used by successful family businesses. *Family Business Review, 12*(4), 325–339.

Vilaseca, A. (2002). The shareholder role in the family business: Conflict of interests and objectives between nonemployed shareholders and top management team. *Family Business Review, 15*(4), 299–320.

Villalonga, B., & Amit, R. (2006). Benefits and costs of control-enhancing mechanisms in US family firms. *ECGI WP Series in Finance*, 209.

Williams, T. A., & Shepherd, D. A. (2016). Victim entrepreneurs doing well by doing good: Venture creation and well-being in the aftermath of a resource shock. *Journal of Business Venturing, 31*(4), 365–387.

Williams, T., & Shepherd, D. (2017). Building resilience or providing sustenance: Different paths of emergent ventures in the aftermath of the haiti earthquake. *Academy of Management Journal*. Forthcoming.

Zahra, S. A. (2003). International expansion of US manufacturing family businesses: The effect of ownership and involvement. *Journal of Business Venturing, 18*(4), 495–512.

Zellweger, T. M., & Dehlen, T. (2011). Value is in the eye of the owner: Affect infusion and socioemotional wealth among family firm owners. *Family Business Review, 25*, 280–297.

Zellweger, T. M., Kellermanns, F. W., Chrisman, J. J., & Chua, J. H. (2012). Family control and family firm valuation by family CEOs: The importance of intentions for transgenerational control. *Organization Science, 23*(3), 851–868.

**Open Access** This chapter is distributed under the terms of the Creative Commons Attribution 4.0 International License (http://creativecommons.org/licenses/by/4.0/), which permits use, duplication, adaptation, distribution and reproduction in any medium or format, as long as you give appropriate credit to the original author(s) and the source, provide a link to the Creative Commons license and indicate if changes were made.

The images or other third party material in this chapter are included in the work's Creative Commons license, unless indicated otherwise in the credit line; if such material is not included in the work's Creative Commons license and the respective action is not permitted by statutory regulation, users will need to obtain permission from the license holder to duplicate, adapt or reproduce the material.

CHAPTER 7

# Researching the Inter-Relationship of Health and Entrepreneurship

## INTRODUCTION

Health is inarguably a significant topic in people's everyday lives, and unsurprisingly, scholars have taken great interest in exploring this issue. For example, marketing scholars have explored the health implications of "supersizing" food purchases (Haws & Winterich, 2013), the impact of health claims on product preference (Aschemann-Witzel & Hamm, 2010), and price sensitivity to healthy versus unhealthy food (Talukdar & Lindsey, 2013); operations scholars have explored capacity expansion in outpatient clinics (LaGanga, 2011), quality management practices and processes in hospitals (Goldstein & Iossifova, 2012), and the performance of health information technology (Queenan, Angst, & Devaraj, 2011); management scholars have explored the relationship between employee stress and health (Bono et al., 2013), the effects of sleep deprivation on workplace deviance (Christian & Ellis, 2011), and learning by surgical teams (Vashdi, Bamberger, & Erez, 2012); and strategy scholars have explored multinational firms' responses to disasters (Oh & Oetzel, 2011), the effects of diversification in the medical-device industry (Wu, 2013), and the effect of board characteristics on firms' strategic change in the healthcare industry (Goodstein, Gautam, & Boeker, 1994).

---

This chapter is based on Shepherd and Patzelt (2015).

Although there is some entrepreneurship research exploring the topic of health (e.g., work on how an entrepreneurial career impacts individuals' psychological [e.g., Kets de Vries, 1980; Tetrick, Slack, Da Silva, & Sinclair, 2000] and physical [Boyd & Gumpert, 1983; Buttner, 1992] well-being or work on biotechnology ventures developing new therapeutic treatments [e.g., Deeds, DeCarolis, & Coombs, 1999; Evans & Varaiya, 2003; Patzelt, Shepherd, Deeds, & Bradley, 2008]), there are still numerous opportunities for scholars to expand this body of knowledge and, by doing so, not only make significant contributions to people's lives but also deepen our understanding of entrepreneurial phenomena. When we refer to health, we mean both physical health—"the physiological and physical status of the body"—and mental health—"the state of the mind, including basic intellectual functions" (Shepherd & Patzelt, 2015, p. 22; Ware, Brook, Davies, & Lohr, 1981). To limit the scope of this chapter and make the topic a bit more manageable, we restrict our focus to an *individual's* health as these specific aspects of health have an obvious boundary—namely, they "end at the skin" (Shepherd & Patzelt, 2015, p. 22; Ware et al., 1981). Drawing on multiple health-related streams of research from different disciplines, we identify potential linkages between entrepreneurship and both the health of the entrepreneur and the health of others. From these linkages, we develop sets of research questions and suggest potential points of departure and trajectories for future research projects. We believe this chapter makes an important contribution and can stimulate fruitful future research for a number of reasons.

First, our proposed research agenda reflects our belief that the community of entrepreneurship scholars has the research capabilities to generate new insights that enhance our understanding of health, which in turn may lead to knowledge on how to better protect and improve people's health (World Health Organization, 2000). By better understanding the health of those who select an entrepreneurial career (and why) and the health consequences of pursuing entrepreneurship, we are a step closer to the lofty goal of helping protect and improve entrepreneurs' health.

Second, the continuously increasing number of research projects on environmental, social, developmental, and sustainable entrepreneurship (see also Chap. 5) provides evidence of many entrepreneurship scholars' desire to "do good" by providing a deeper understanding of the processes by which entrepreneurship can help alleviate social problems. Scholars can continue this focus on doing good by exploring the antecedents of entrepreneurial actions that improve others' health. Thus, we expect that many members of the entrepreneurship scholarly community show a strong motivation to expand their research into studying the relationship between entrepreneurship and health.

Third, entrepreneurship research will hopefully contribute to knowledge that enhances the health of individuals (entrepreneurs and others). Although we take a psycho-social perspective as a basis for making conjectures on the relationship between entrepreneurship and an individual's health, we hope that we pique the interest of a broad range of scholars to further explore this topic beyond the individual level of analysis. Since one of the strengths of the entrepreneurship research community is its interdisciplinary composition, we hope that this chapter can inspire scholars focusing on other levels of analysis (e.g., teams, organizations, institutions, and regions) and draw on other theoretical perspectives (e.g., institutional entrepreneurship).

To develop our research agenda, we first explore how entrepreneurship might impact the entrepreneur's health. Specifically, we speculate on how entrepreneurship generates stress and both positive and negative emotions, which impact the entrepreneur's health, and we speculate on how entrepreneurship can improve the entrepreneur's health through enhancing socioeconomic status. Second, we explore how entrepreneurial action might impact the health of others. We explore the ways particular personal experiences, professional knowledge, and prosocial motivation can result in entrepreneurial action that improves the health outcomes of people aside from the entrepreneur him- or herself.

## Entrepreneurship and the Health of the Entrepreneur

An entrepreneurial career differs from a career as an employee in an established organization in multiple ways. For example, while entrepreneurs usually enjoy more decision autonomy (Shane, Locke, & Collins, 2003) and freedom in arranging their work environment (Forbes, Borchert, Zellmer-Bruhn, & Sapienza, 2006), their job demands are typically more complex (Lazear, 2005) and uncertain (Teoh & Foo, 1997) than those of employees. Further, research indicates that entrepreneurs are often subject to more occupational stress than non-entrepreneurs (Buttner, 1992; Stoner, Hartman, & Arora, 1990; Teoh & Foo, 1997; Williams, 1984) but that they nevertheless tend to experience fewer negative (Patzelt & Shepherd, 2011) and more positive (Baum & Locke, 2004; Cardon, Wincent, Shigh,

& Drnovsek, 2009; Cardon, Zietsma, Saparito, Matherne, & Davis, 2005; Smilor, 1997) emotions from work than employees. Finally, there is evidence that entrepreneurship can help achieve better financial income than other careers (Carter, 2011; Lazear, 2005; Nanda, 2008; Quadrini, 2000; for an exception, see Blanchflower & Shadforth, 2007). Based on these findings and specific characteristics of an entrepreneurial career, we now explore (1) the role of an individual's health status in his or her decision to pursue entrepreneurship as a career option and the ways the pursuit of an entrepreneurial career impacts the individual's health by influencing his or her (2) stress levels, (3) emotions, and (4) socioeconomic status.

### *Health and the Pursuit of an Entrepreneurial Career*

There is evidence that people with health-related restrictions select into an entrepreneurial career. For example, groups who perceive obstacles to advancement in traditional employment roles are likely drawn to an entrepreneurial career (Callahan, Shumpert, & Mast, 2002; Kendall, Buys, Charker, & MacMillan, 2006). Specifically, people with disabilities are frequently drawn to an entrepreneurial career because it can provide greater accommodations for aspects of their work (Arnold and Seekins, Arnold & Seekins, 2002; Hagner & Davies, 2002), such as flexibility to manage work around visits to doctors and hospitals and days when poor health could negatively impact performance. Although accommodations related to physical access are generally made in the workplace for employees (Batavia & Schriner, 2001), people with disabilities desire other accommodations; they desire (and often require) flexibility to arrange work time around health problems and treatment, and they highly value autonomy (Arnold & Seekins, 2002; Hagner & Davies, 2002). Indeed, statistics demonstrate that people with disabilities are more than twice as likely to become self-employed than people without disabilities (US Census Bureau, 2002). Therefore, limitations caused by health-related problems appear to motivate such people to pursue an entrepreneurial career. In turn, an entrepreneurial career provides the flexibility to allow these individuals to accommodate their health needs and treatment, which likely has a positive impact on their health. These aspects and findings represent a number of research opportunities.

**Flexibility and health.** While entrepreneurial careers generally provide more flexibility than traditional employment, each entrepreneurial career path is different in terms of the amount and type of flexibility it offers.

For example, founders who seek and obtain external capital to grow their business often realize they must give up more decision-making authority and control in running their business compared to those who restrict business growth to activities that can be funded by internal sources, such as additional owner equity or funding acquired through bootstrapping (Wasserman, 2008). Furthermore, long-time and dominant alliance partners can limit founders' strategic flexibility in developing their venture's network in new directions (Maurer & Ebers, 2006). Indeed, different health problems may require different work-related flexibility. What are the different flexibility requirements stemming from major health problems, and how do they motivate an entrepreneurial career? How do these entrepreneurs use flexibility to enhance health or reduce health problems? Perhaps for entrepreneurs with specific health problems, there is a level of flexibility offered by an entrepreneurial career beyond which further increases are actually detrimental to health. For instance, some psychological disorders, such as attention deficit/hyperactivity disorder, are associated with high levels of impulsivity, and entrepreneurs suffering from these disorders might not be able to control themselves and function well under highly flexible conditions. That is, it is important to understand the activities, processes, and other mechanisms that entrepreneurs use to attain the types of flexibility that accommodates their health requirements and/or enhances their state of health because as we gain a deeper understanding of the "how," we can also begin to gain a deeper understanding of which mechanisms are most effective at managing health. Understanding the effectiveness of specific "flexibility mechanisms" in enhancing health through an entrepreneurial career would represent an important step toward providing advice to those considering such a career move. Perhaps training and education programs, especially for those with health-related problems, can one day provide concrete steps outlining how such people can pursue a rewarding entrepreneurial career that offers the appropriate types and levels of flexibility needed to also benefit their health.

The above discussion focuses on individuals drawn to the flexibility of an entrepreneurial career to cope with *health problems*, but perhaps other entrepreneurs (motivated by other reasons) can also use the flexibility of this career to pursue personal *health opportunities*. Perhaps the flexibility of an entrepreneurial career enables individuals to pursue their sporting or recreational activities. For example, Goldsby, Kuratko, and Bishop (2005) showed how small business owners' engagement in physical activities (e.g., running and weight-lifting) is positively associated with the intrinsic and extrinsic rewards from entrepreneurship as well as increased firm sales. How do entrepreneurs use flexibility to enhance personal health? Again, we are interested in the activities, processes, and other mechanisms that entrepreneurs use to pursue these health opportunities as well as which are more effective in doing so. However, as we explore below, this is not a one-way street—the flexibility of an entrepreneurial career facilitates health, but health can also generate flexibility in an entrepreneurial career. For example, as an individual begins to overcome health-related problems, there are fewer constraints on entrepreneurial action. Similarly, the health opportunities, such as recreational activities, the entrepreneur pursues may help entrepreneurial action. Indeed, physical activity (associated with sporting, recreational, and leisure activities) is associated with enhanced cognitive functioning in terms of, for example, selective attention, working memory, and cognitive flexibility (in their review of the literature, Prakash, Voss, Ericvkson, and Kramer [2015] noted that while the results are quite strong for children, there are few studies of adults and that the results for adults are somewhat mixed); psychological functioning, such as higher self-esteem (Sonstroem & Morgan, 1989), reduced anxiety (Anderson & Shivakumar, 2015), decreased likelihood of depression (Camacho, Roberts, Lazarus, Kaplan, & Cohen, 1991), and reduced likelihood of mortality (Kampert, Blair, Barlow, & Kohl, 1996; Katzmarzyk, Janssen, & Ardern, 2003). Future research can explore the nature of this reciprocal relationship between time used for enhancing health and performance in an entrepreneurial career (perhaps even vis-à-vis a career as an employee). Obviously, there are likely limits to time spent enhancing health in terms of its positive impact on entrepreneurial performance—if an individual dedicates most of his or her time to surfing, then his or her personal health is likely enhanced but not necessarily the firm's financial health.

**Autonomy and health.** Self-determination theory (Deci & Ryan, 1985; Ryan & Deci, 2000) proposes that individuals have a basic need for autonomy, and people often pursue an entrepreneurial career because it provides more autonomy than working as an employee. However, different entrepreneurial ventures are likely to provide varying levels of autonomy, and entrepreneurs themselves are likely to desire more or less autonomy depending on their personal characteristics. Future research has an opportunity to more deeply explore the relationship between health-related problems and the desire for autonomy. Why are some health-related problems associated with a greater desire for autonomy than other health-related problems, and how do these manifest in the entrepreneurial ventures formed? It could be that the desire for autonomy is associated with obtaining the flexibility to deal with health-related issues or opportunities (described above), but autonomy may provide additional psychological benefits. Haynie and Shepherd's (2011) research offered some initial insight; they found that people who were injured after obeying orders on the battlefield wanted more autonomy as did individuals who required a long period of hospitalization due to their health problems, during which they had to follow others' (e.g., nurses, doctors, therapists) instructions. These findings indicate that the more a health-related problem is associated with a loss of personal control (either directly causing the health problem or being caused by the health problem), the more the individual desires autonomy in an entrepreneurial career. Therefore, while the need for autonomy is considered a basic psychological need (Ryan & Deci, 2000), the weight and the nature of this need for autonomy likely vary across (potential) entrepreneurs and the amount offered by the careers they pursue. The key then becomes obtaining a fit between the level of autonomy needed and the entrepreneurial career (created or chosen). How do individuals achieve such a fit? Future research looking to address this question about fit may want to begin with the career literature, particularly the research on identity work discussing how individuals can modify themselves to achieve fit, modify the nature of the task to achieve fit, or both (e.g., Ibarra & Barbulescu, 2010; Nicholson, 1984; Pratt, Rockmann, & Kaufmann, 2006). This career literature has typically been developed such that changes to the task are relatively modest given a focus on employment; more research is needed exploring substantial changes to the task (e.g., an entrepreneurial career) (see Shepherd & Williams, 2017). To what extent have individuals created and changed the nature of their entrepreneurial role to satisfy their health-related needs for autonomy? It is likely that such accommodations have implications for the nature of the opportunities identified and pursued.

**Competence and health.** Over and above physical accommodations, flexibility, and autonomy, what other requirements do people with health problems seek when deciding whether to pursue an entrepreneurial career or deciding between different entrepreneurial career alternatives? According to self-determination theory, people also need to satisfy the psychological needs for competence and belonging (Deci & Ryan, 1985; Ryan & Deci, 2000). It appears that when poor health prevents one from doing tasks, there is an even greater desire to pursue an entrepreneurial career in which the individual can build and use his or her competencies (Haynie & Shepherd, 2011). To the extent that an entrepreneurial career enables people who have lost confidence in their ability to rebuild that confidence, then there are likely health benefits (especially benefits arising from improved psychological well-being). How does poor health impact the need for competence, and how does this need for competence impact the choice and pursuit of an entrepreneurial career? It would seem that an entrepreneurial career provides the opportunity for an individual to best utilize his or her competences (Sarasvathy, 2001) and therefore satisfy the psychological need for competence caused by health-related problems. However, an entrepreneurial career also provides feedback on that competence. Even negative feedback can help satisfy the need for competence if that feedback allows the individual to further enhance his or her competences. However, receivers do not always interpret negative feedback as an unambiguous blessing (i.e., as a way to improve their competences); rather, they may interpret it as a signal of incompetence that cannot be overcome. Future research can investigate why some people who receive negative feedback interpret it in a way that satisfies their need for competence while others interpret in a way that thwarts their need for competence. Of particular interest to this chapter is how the health problem underlying the need for competence impacts (if at all) how individuals interpret negative feedback from an entrepreneurial career. Perhaps health problems caused by a traumatic injury—an injury that shatters the individual's assumptions about him- or herself, others, and the nature of the world—may result in a more negative interpretation of negative feedback from entrepreneurial action than non-traumatic health problems. On the flip side, perhaps positive feedback from entrepreneurial action is interpreted as more positive by those who experienced traumatic injuries than those with non-traumatic health problems. There is much to explore in terms of the psychological need for competence, the nature of individuals' health, and the continued pursuit of an entrepreneurial career.

**Belongingness and health.** In addition to needs for autonomy and competence, people also strive to fulfill a need for belongingness to a social group (Deci & Ryan, 1985; Ryan & Deci, 2000). However, poor health can lead to loneliness (Molloy, McGee, O'Neill, & Conroy, 2010), including active avoidance of people who are healthy (Hazer & Boylu, 2010). Loneliness is an emotional state caused by feeling alienated and/or misunderstood by others, thereby leading individuals to feel a lack of social integration and/or emotional intimacy (Donaldson & Watson, 1996; Rook, 1984). Loneliness is not the same as being alone, which individuals occasionally seek out for their own enjoyment. Due to its characteristics, loneliness can sometimes make health problems worse (Hawkley & Cacioppo, 2010; Sugisawa, Liang, & Liu, 1994; Thurston & Kubzansky, 2009). For example, Holt-Lunstad, Smith, and Layton (2010) found that the mortality rate among lonely individuals is 45% higher than among individuals who are not lonely. What influence does pursuing an entrepreneurial career have on health-related loneliness? On the one hand, entrepreneurs are often seen as "lone wolves," and "being the boss" separates them from their employees, which can result in feelings of loneliness and isolation (Akande, 1994; Gumpert & Boyd, 1984; Hannafey, 2003). However, on the other hand, entrepreneurs are often able to choose with whom they want to work (Forbes et al., 2006), and many ventures are created by founding teams instead of one individual (Ucbasaran, Lockett, Wright, & Westhead, 2003), thus leading to strong friendships that can ease feelings of loneliness (Deborah & William, 2000). Future research can further contribute by investigating the extent to which health-related problems caused by loneliness are exacerbated or minimized by the pursuit of an entrepreneurial career. More than likely, the answer is going to be "it depends," and it will likely be more productive to explore the following questions: why are some individuals able to avoid loneliness when having an entrepreneurial career (and the subsequent negative health consequences) and others are not, and why are some entrepreneurs with health problems able to use their entrepreneurial career to avoid or overcome loneliness while others are unable to do so?

Some possible answers to these questions may come from exploring the entrepreneurial venture (e.g., number of employees, industry, and location); the venture's human-resource management approach (e.g., selecting people who "fit" in the venture, developing a supportive organizational culture, having a participative management style, sharing venture equity); and/or the venture's network with suppliers, customers, investors, and other stakeholders. While some entrepreneurs may structure (deliberately or not) their business to avoid loneliness, others may satisfy their need for belongingness (and thus reduce loneliness and its negative health consequences) through their non-work–related identity. An entrepreneur may feel completely comfortable with the isolation of his or her entrepreneurial career and not feel lonely because his or her non-work life involves active engagement in a sporting team, a large family, an online gaming community, or membership in any other form of community. Therefore, future research can explore not only how an entrepreneurial career impacts loneliness and/or how entrepreneurs' non-work lives are structured to avoid loneliness but also why some entrepreneurs focus on internal structures (i.e., social contacts within the venture) whereas others focus on structuring social aspects external to their entrepreneurial venture.

**Finances and health.** Although for the reasons stated above, individuals with health-related problems may find an entrepreneurial career more desirable, the costs associated with their health-related problems may make an entrepreneurial career less viable. For example, poor health is often expensive, leading to out-of-pocket costs, lost earnings, and a reduction in household assets (Poterba, Venti, & Wise, 2010). In turn, such expenses may decrease the personal financial resources one has free to start an entrepreneurial venture. However, when entrepreneurship is viewed as the pursuit of opportunity *beyond* the resources one currently controls (Baker & Nelson, 2005; Brown, Davidsson, & Wiklund, 2001; Stevenson, 1983) and considering the recent work on effectual reasoning that stresses the means an entrepreneur currently has as a starting point (Sarasvathy, 2001), entrepreneurial action is still conceivable even with limited available resources. Indeed, some health-related problems might not only restrict the financial resources available to the entrepreneur but also impact his or her potential to capitalize on the few resources available, for example, by diminishing the creativity needed to identify opportunities or ways to exploit them with few resources at hand. Thus, the question remains: how do health-related financial costs influence individuals' decision to start an entrepreneurial venture?

It might be that financial resources constrain the search for potential opportunities to those based on the combination and recombination of local resources (i.e., the resources at hand). However, we do not yet have a good understanding of how the "resource situation" impacts the nature of potential opportunities identified or, for that matter, the nature of this opportunity pursuit itself. For example, perhaps the resource slack necessary for distant search provides a basis for opportunities to generate radical or discontinuous innovations (Benner & Tushman, 2007), whereas a resource-constrained local search (e.g., bricolage and effectuation) may lead to potential opportunities that are more incremental in nature (Rosenkopf & Nerkar, 2001). Therefore, those with health problems that cause financial constraints may generate and pursue potential opportunities of a fundamentally different nature than those with health problems that do not cause financial constraints (or do so to a lesser extent). However, it could be that health problems lead to financial constraints related to search depth—"how frequently the firm re-uses its existing knowledge"—and search scope—"how widely the firm explores new knowledge" (Katila & Ahuja, 2002, p. 1183)—but also provide a source of knowledge that facilitates search depth and scope. Future research can explore the multi-dimensional implications of health problems on the nature of search and the resulting potential opportunities.

Over and above differences in the nature of the opportunity, the financial costs of health-related issues may impact the scale of the venture founded to exploit the potential opportunity. The greater the financial burden from health problems, the more likely the entrepreneur will begin with a smaller-scale venture unless he or she is able to raise additional equity from a business angel or venture capital firm. How do potential investors assess entrepreneurs with health-related problems? When engaging with potential investors (and even potential stakeholders for that matter), entrepreneurs may use impression-management strategies (Bird & Jelinek, 1988; Zott & Huy, 2007) to compensate for their health-related problems, which could include keeping them hidden or minimizing their effects.

**Time and health.** Not only can health-related problems drain resources, they can also be costly in terms of lost time (Stewart, Ricci, Chee, Morganstein, & Lipton, 2003; Weiss, Sullivan, & Lyttle, 2000) and energy from work-related tasks. How do entrepreneurs with health-related problems manage their time differently from others (if at all), and why are some better at time management than others? However, research has shown that time-management behaviors (e.g., goal and priority setting) can be associated with higher employee stress (Macan, 1994). As such, can entrepreneurs' time-management practices to overcome the time costs associated with poor health lead to additional health issues? Alternatively, the additional stress created by time management may be more than offset by the time dedicated to addressing (and hopefully solving) the health problem. Indeed, when engaging in health-entrepreneurship research, we need to be careful not to assume that the nature of people's health problems is static; rather, such problems could be highly dynamic and fluctuate with changes in the entrepreneurial process. Although a static perspective might suggest that poor health will suck energy out of an entrepreneurial venture, a more dynamic perspective allows us to consider whether and how the individual's investment of energy into the entrepreneurial venture transforms the health issue. Thus, future research should investigate the generation, reduction, and flow of energy in the relationship between health and entrepreneurial actions.

While we previously proposed that poor health might motivate some to pursue an entrepreneurial career in the first place, there is also some evidence that an entrepreneurial career path can impact the health of the entrepreneur over time. Specifically, the existing literature has emphasized that entrepreneurship is often stressful (Buttner, 1992; Stoner et al., 1990; Teoh & Foo, 1997; Williams, 1984) and highly emotional (Baron, 2008; Shepherd, 2003), both of which can lead to health-related problems, to which we now turn.

### *Pursuit of an Entrepreneurial Career, Stress, and Health*

Stress occurs in the relationship between a person and his or her environment (Lazarus & Folkman, 1984, 1987) when the requirements of a particular situation require more resources than the person has on hand and the person appraises the situation as involving harm, threats of harm, or (more positively) a challenge (Lazarus, 1990). While some stress can provide positive motivation for individuals to engage in some sort of action and some stress can enhance health, the health literature has established a clear link between high levels of stress over extended periods and poor health outcomes (DeLongis, Folkman, & Lazarus, 1988; for a review, see Schneiderman, Ironson, & Siegel, 2005), such as depression (see Hammen, 2005; Kendler, Karkowski, & Prescott, 1999), anxiety disorders (Faravelli & Pallanti, 1989; Finlay-Jones & Brown, 1981), and cardiovascular disease (Brownley, Hurwitz, & Schneiderman, 2000; for a review, see Hemingway & Marmot, 1999).

There is some research connecting entrepreneurs to high levels of stress (Buttner, 1992; Stoner et al., 1990; Teoh & Foo, 1997; Williams, 1984). For example, researchers have shown that compared to employees, entrepreneurs tend to have heavier workloads (Eden, 1975; Harris, Saltstone, & Fraboni, 1999; Lewin-Epstein & Yuchtman-Yaar, 1991), face greater business risk, and ultimately experience greater job stress (Harris et al., 1999; Jamal & Badawi, 1995). However, the direct link between an entrepreneurial career and stress may not be so clear. A number of studies have found no significant difference between entrepreneurs and employees in terms of strain (Rahim, 1996), life stress (Parasuraman & Simmers, 2001), and depression/anxiety (Grzywacz & Bass, 2003), and some have even found that entrepreneurs experience less stress (Eden, 1975; Tetrick et al., 2000) than employees. Although these mixed findings on the relationship between entrepreneurship and stress muddy the waters somewhat, they also represent a number of research opportunities.

**Individual differences and stress.** Perhaps the differences in findings in research on entrepreneurial stress are due to heterogeneity in individual differences in the appraisal of and reaction to events as potential stressors. These individual differences could be due to differences in resilience. When confronted with difficulty, loss, and/or trauma, resilient individuals are able to maintain relatively normal psychological and physical functioning, and their capacity for positive emotions and personal growth remains intact (Bonanno, 2004; Bonanno, Papa, & O'Neill, 2001; see also Sutcliffe & Vogus, 2003; Williams & Shepherd, 2016). Are resilient people more likely to select into an entrepreneurial career (and/or non-resilient individuals select out)? Alternatively, it could be that people who pursue an entrepreneurial career develop psychological and emotional capabilities that are the foundations for resilience. This notion of building the resources and capabilities for resilience is particularly important in entrepreneurship as entrepreneurs generally face uncertain environments and often some form of adversity. Why do some entrepreneurs develop resilience while others do not or are slow in doing so? Positive psychology research (Seligman, Steen, Park, & Peterson, 2005), including that on positive emotions (Fredrickson, 2001), hardiness (Florian, Mikulincer, & Taubman, 1995), and optimism (Seligman, 2011), may provide some insights into why some individuals are more resilient than others. However, to understand why some are able to become more resilient may involve a different set of factors. For example, perhaps those who have experienced a negative health event and have learned to deal with (i.e., live with or reduce) a health problem have built up the resources and capabilities of resilience that are useful in the pursuit of an entrepreneurial career. It could also be that in pursuing an entrepreneurial career, the individual builds resources and capabilities of resilience that are useful in functioning in the face of a health problem. It is important that we gain a deeper understanding of resilience in the health-entrepreneurship context.

**Differences in tasks and the level of stress.** Perhaps the mixed findings on the relationship between entrepreneurship and stress reflect substantial variation in entrepreneurial tasks and roles and/or in the entrepreneur's fit with those tasks and roles. The entrepreneurial process often involves the identity roles of inventor, founder, and developer, and just as entrepreneurs likely differ in their passion across these different roles (Cardon et al., 2009), they also likely differ in the stress they experience from these different roles. For example, an individual who is passionate about the inventor role may feel more stress from the founder and/or developer roles. Underlying this passion-based conjecture of stress is an implicit assumption that people are less stressed in domains about which they are passionate—an assumption worthy of further theorizing and empirical testing. Indeed, Brigham, De Castro, and Shepherd (2007) showed that entrepreneurs tend to be more satisfied when their primary decision-making style complements their firm's formalization and structure. Therefore, because entrepreneurs and ventures are heterogeneous, it is likely that the fit between the two will help clarify an entrepreneur's level of stress. While we are starting to gain a firmer grasp on the many tasks an entrepreneurial role requires (Chen, Greene, & Crick, 1998) and the ways these tasks change as a venture matures (Fichman & Levinthal, 1991; Shepherd, Douglas, & Shanley, 2000) and grows (Wasserman, 2008; Zimmerman & Zeitz, 2002) and as the entrepreneur prepares for exit (DeTienne, 2010; Wennberg, Wiklund, DeTienne, & Cardon, 2010), numerous opportunities still exist to learn more about how stress links to these entrepreneurial micro-tasks and multiple and changing roles.

Third, although time may reveal a pattern for how entrepreneurial tasks and roles change over time, sometimes the change is less predictable. For example, in dynamic environments—for instance, markets that are unstable as a result of continuing changes (Keats & Hitt, 1988)—the nature of tasks can transform and involves considerable role ambiguity. Role ambiguity has been shown to be a source of stress (Caplan & Jones, 1975; Rizzo, House, & Lirtzman, 1970), and these possible stressors are likely to be exacerbated in highly complex environments. Eisenhardt and Brown (1998) referred to managing entrepreneurial ventures in dynamic and complex environments (i.e., high-velocity environments) as managing on the edge of chaos. Entrepreneurs can face other environmental events, such as severe economic downturns (Bradley, Aldrich, Shepherd, & Wiklund, 2011), disruptive technologies (Carayannopoulos, 2009; Christensen, 1997), and emerging markets (George & Prabhu, 2000; Venkataraman, 2004). Future research can further explore the effect that competitive and natural environments have on entrepreneurs' stress, the mechanisms they use to effectively manage this stress, and the impact this stress has on the nature of entrepreneurial action (and the interesting feedback loops).

**Level of stress and its health consequences.** The above discussions are relevant to the extent that entrepreneurial stress causes health outcomes. Although this link is well established at high levels of stress, future research can deepen our understanding of this relationship. As we mentioned, lower levels of stress can actually improve health (Quick, Horn, &

Quick, 1987). As such, at what level does stress become unhealthy, and what explains differences among entrepreneurs in terms of the "optimal" level of stress? Further, when certain events do cause high levels of stress, it could be that some entrepreneurs are able to quickly cope with that stress, thereby reducing or eliminating any detrimental health consequences. We know, for example, that entrepreneurs utilize different strategies to cope with stress (Patzelt & Shepherd, 2011). However, is there a less negative relationship between initial stress and health for entrepreneurs with highly refined coping skills compared to those with less developed coping skills? In addition, physical exercise may have a direct positive influence on entrepreneurs' health as well as an indirect positive impact on health, with physical exercise reducing stress (Nabkasorn et al., 2006; Salmon, 2001). Do entrepreneurs who are more physically fit (or engage in more physical exercise) experience less stress, or do they experience fewer of the health-related implications of a given level of stress or both? Future research can add to this body of knowledge in important ways by theorizing on and empirically testing mediators and moderators of the relationship between stress and health in the entrepreneurial context.

### *Pursuit of an Entrepreneurial Career, Emotion, and Health*

Health has also been linked to emotions. Positive emotions have been found to be associated with optimal health and well-being and negative emotions with anxiety, depression, and stress-related health problems (Fredrickson, 2000; Tugade, Fredrickson, & Feldman Barrett, 2004). Further, research has linked entrepreneurial careers with positive emotional outcomes (Baum & Locke, 2004; Cardon et al., 2005, 2009; Smilor, 1997). For example, self-employment can lead to experiences of passion, "a consciously accessible, intense positive feeling" (Cardon et al., 2009, p. 7); excitement; happiness; flow (Komisar, 2000; Rai, 2008; Schindehutte, Morris, & Allen, 2006); and job satisfaction (Blanchflower, Oswald, & Stutzer, 2001; Bradley & Roberts, 2004; Thompson, Kopelman, & Schriesheim, 1992). Along with being linked to positive emotions, entrepreneurial action has also been linked to negative emotions, such as fear and anxiety (Boyd & Gumpert, 1983), loneliness and social isolation (Akande, 1994; Hannafey, 2003), frustrations (Du Toit, 1980), and grief (Byrne & Shepherd, 2015; Jenkins, Wiklund, & Brundin, 2014; Shepherd, 2003), as well as the co-existence of highly positive and highly negative emotions (see Fong, 2006; Fong & Tiedens,

2002; Larsen, McGraw, & Cacioppo, 2001; Larsen, McGraw, Mellers, & Cacioppo, 2004). While it seems that entrepreneurial action can generate positive and negative emotions, there is insufficient theorizing and empirical research on the links between the emotions generated throughout the entrepreneurial process and their health consequences.

**Positive emotions.** First, a fine-grained investigation of the relationship between positive emotions and health might contribute to the literature by linking the generation of specific emotions to specific health outcomes in an entrepreneurial context (i.e., both positive emotions and health are multi-dimensional constructs). Furthermore, there are some questions about whether more is always better. For example, Cardon et al. (2009) proposed that there is an inverse U-shaped relationship between entrepreneurial passion and creative problem solving. Indeed, Vallerand et al. (2003) argued that the possible obsessiveness resulting from high levels of passion can result in negative health outcomes. Do continually increasing positive emotions have diminishing returns for an entrepreneur's health (or is there an optimal level of emotions after which further increases diminish health)? For example, at extremely high levels of passion, perhaps entrepreneurs do not allocate sufficient time for sleeping; exercise; or preventative actions, such as receiving regular doctor checkups and eating healthy foods. Therefore, it is interesting to explore why some entrepreneurs' health benefits from positive emotions, such as passion, more than other entrepreneurs and why some may experience health problems from their highly positive emotional state. Perhaps these effects are different for different types of entrepreneurial passion (for more on the different types of entrepreneurial passion, see Cardon et al., 2009).

Second, although entrepreneurship can generate positive emotions, we assume there is heterogeneity in the extent of those positive emotions. Why do some entrepreneurs experience more positive emotions than others? Perhaps some entrepreneurs have a stronger "fit" with their ventures and thus generate more positive emotions from performing venture-related tasks. Perhaps in building and managing their ventures, some entrepreneurs use techniques that facilitate positive emotions, such as reflecting on (or engaging in) helping others (Seligman et al., 2005), undertaking cognitive reframing (Seligman, Rashid, & Parks, 2006), performing loving-kindness meditation (Fredrickson, Cohn, Coffey, Pek, & Finkel, 2008), and/or using humor (Folkman & Moskowitz, 2000; Menninger, 1963). If positive emotions are associated with improved health, it is important that future research explore how entrepreneurs are able to generate positive emotions to improve health, whether there are indeed negative health outcomes for high levels of positive emotions and/or passion, and how entrepreneurs regulate positive emotions to avoid health problems.

Third, over and above the notion of fit, it is likely that entrepreneurs who do good for others, such as those who pursue potential opportunities to preserve the natural environmental (Dean & McMullen, 2007), help maintain community and customs (Peredo & Chrisman, 2006), improve people's lives (Shepherd & Patzelt, 2011), and alleviate suffering (Shepherd & Williams, 2014; Williams & Shepherd, 2016, 2017), feel more positive emotions than those who create neutral or negative value for others. Research has found that acts of kindness toward others generate positive emotions in the giver (Buchanan & Bardi, 2010; Seligman et al., 2005). As we detail below, entrepreneurs can pursue opportunities that enhance the health of others. In doing so, the entrepreneur is doing good, which can generate positive emotions that enhance his or her health. That is, in helping to improve others' (or the natural environment's) health through their actions, entrepreneurs may be improving their own health. Such a relationship provides the basis for a virtuous prosocial spiral. Future research can provide explanations for what starts, perpetuates, and stops these prosocial spirals of entrepreneurship and health.

**Negative emotions.** First, the most severe negative emotional response in the entrepreneurial context appears to stem from business failure. The stream of research on this topic explores how the failure of an entrepreneurial project or business characterizes the loss of something important to the entrepreneur and thus causes a negative emotional reaction—namely, grief—which can inhibit learning from failure (Byrne & Shepherd, 2015; Shepherd, 2003). Although the psychology literature has established a strong link between grief and depression (Bruce, Kim, Leaf, & Jacobs, 1990; Clayton, 1990), anxiety-related disorders (Parkes & Weiss, 1983), increased doctor visits (Mor, McHorney, & Sherwood, 1986), poor physical health (Kaprio, Koskenvuo, & Rita, 1987), and higher risk of mortality (Kraus & Lilienfeld, 1959), research to date has failed to explore the health-related outcomes of entrepreneurial failure. This lack of research is surprising given the significant number of entrepreneurial businesses that fail every year. For example, 914,015 businesses filed for Chap. 7 bankruptcy in the USA in the year ending June 30, 2012 (uscourts.gov/FederalCourts/Bankruptcy.aspx). This number even understates failure because it ignores those businesses that simply closed or were forced into an acquisition or merger to avoid legal bankruptcy. What are the health-related costs to entrepreneurs of failed business? If we find and can explain variance in grief and/or the relationship between grief and health, we might be a step closer toward helping a large number of entrepreneurs reduce the negative health implications of business failure. For example, perhaps the oscillation between a loss and a restoration orientation that reduces grief (Shepherd, 2003; Shepherd, Patzelt, & Wolfe, 2011) also reduces the negative health consequences of business or project failure. Although we have assumed that grief from failure is the most extreme negative emotion, such an assumption requires investigation. It could be that fear, loneliness, and concern can also have a substantial impact on entrepreneurial health. Again, to the extent researchers can unpack the construct of negative emotions (and, for that matter, grief) to enable a finer-grained investigation of how these different emotions have different health consequences, future research can make important contributions to the literature. As this is done, advances in emotion regulation may be found to have an important outcome in terms of entrepreneurs' health. Specifically, we could teach emotion regulation in entrepreneurship classes to help individuals maintain health during negative entrepreneurial events.

Second, while positive and negative emotions can co-exist (Fong, 2006; Fong & Tiedens, 2002; Larsen et al., 2001, 2004), positive emotions seem to be able to "undo" negative emotions as well as extend and build lasting personal resources (Fredrickson, 1998, 2001). Therefore, the negative health outcomes caused by negative emotions may be short lived in the presence of positive emotions because if the source of the health problem is eliminated, then so might its effect—the health problem. Therefore, the health consequences of a negative emotional reaction likely depend on how quickly those negative emotions can be reduced, which likely partly depends on the entrepreneur's experience of positive emotions. However, the undoing effect of positive emotions might not reverse some health problems, which may, once started, perpetuate or magnify even in the absence of the trigger—the negative emotional reaction. Future research can make a valuable contribution by exploring the generation of negative emotions throughout the entrepreneurial process, the type and extent of health problems arising from those negative emotions, and the ways the cause (i.e., negative emotions) or the consequence (i.e., health problems) can be reduced.

Finally, there is an opportunity for future research to explore how the entrepreneurial context facilitates (or constrains) the undoing effect of positive emotions on negative emotions. Why is this undoing effect stronger for some entrepreneurs than others, in some ventures than in others, and in some environments than in others? For example, entrepreneurs with more emotional intelligence (Sonstroem & Morgan, 1989) may be more capable of using positive emotions to control and reduce negative emotions, or perhaps entrepreneurs in organizations (Huy, 1999) or families (Shepherd, 2009) that are more emotionally capable receive help in using positive emotions to undo negative emotions. Similarly, entrepreneurs in fast-moving environments (e.g., high-velocity markets [Eisenhardt & Brown, 1998]) may be more capable of using positive emotions to *rapidly* undo negative emotions. Future research is needed to explore the dynamic relationship between positive and negative emotions and its impact on health throughout the entrepreneurial process.

## *Pursuit of an Entrepreneurial Career, Socioeconomic Status, and Health*

Individuals with low socioeconomic status are known to have, on average, worse health than those with high socioeconomic status in terms of minor ailments, such as headaches, and major health problems, including life-threatening disease and mortality (Matthews & Gallo, 2011). Indeed, there is a substantial health disparity between high and low socioeconomic groups (Chen & Miller, 2013; U.S. Department of Health and Human Services, 2012). Those from the lowest socioeconomic groups are two to seven times more likely to have repeat hospitalizations in one year (National Center for Health statistics) and three to five times more likely to face disease-related activity limitations (Braveman, Cubbin, Egerter, Williams, & Pamuk, 2010). Further, individuals of low socioeconomic status have fewer financial resources (in reserve or access to them) to reduce the stress from negative events (Cohen, Janicki-Deverts, & Miller, 2007; Everson-Rose & Lewis, 2005; Matthews & Gallo, 2011). They also have a diminished belief in their ability to master or control important aspects of their lives, low self-esteem, and low optimism about the future (Gallo & Matthews, 2003; Rasmussen, Scheier, & Greenhouse, 2009; Uchino, 2006), all of which together represent a diminished endowment of resilience resources for preventing health problems (Bosma, Schrijvers, & Mackenbach, 1999; Matthews, Gallo, & Taylor, 2010). Over and above an individual's socioeconomic status, the socioeconomic status of his or her neighborhood impacts that individual's health (Pickett & Pearl, 2001). For example, individuals in low socioeconomic neighborhoods face greater asthma problems (Sternthal, Jun, Earls, & Wright, 2010; Wright et al., 2004), risk of cardiovascular disease (Sundquist et al., 2006), and disability and chronic pain (Coker, Smith, Bethea, King, & McKeown, 2000) and are more likely to witness violence (Buka, Stichick, Birdthistle, & Earls, 2001; Crouch, Hanson, Saunders, Kilpatrick, & Resnick, 2000; Margolin & Gordis, 2000). A consequence of violence in the neighborhood is fewer safe places to exercise, which has negative health consequences (Lovasi, Hutson, Guerra, & Neckerman, 2009). This is exacerbated by the limited access to healthy food in these neighborhoods (Lovasi et al., 2009) and greater noise pollution, air pollution, second-hand smoke, and crowding, all of which elevate health risks (Matthews & Gallo, 2011). These neighborhoods are also characterized by low social capital and an unwillingness to formulate and contribute to common goals (Coleman, 1988; Putnam, 2001; Sampson, Raudenbush, & Earls, 1997), which are in turn associated with cardiovascular disease (Chaix, Lindström, Rosvall, & Merlo, 2008; Sundquist et al., 2006), higher mortality risk (Lochner, Kawachi, Brennan, & Buka, 2003), and lower self-reported health (Kawachi, Kennedy, & Glass, 1999). Moreover, poorer families face greater financial stress that can negatively impact the quality of relationships among family members (Conger & Elder, 1994). This conflict and dysfunction have been found to be linked to negative health outcomes (Repetti, Taylor, & Seeman, 2002; Troxel & Matthews, 2004), including increased risk of asthma (Klinnert et al., 2001), diabetes (Miller-Johnson et al., 1994), and illness and mortality (Lundberg, 1993).[1] We propose that entrepreneurship may play a role in the relationship between health and socioeconomic status.

**Pursuing an entrepreneurial career is not highly dependent on socioeconomic status.** There are substantial institutional constraints to enhancing one's economic position. With low education, it is difficult (but not impossible) to climb the corporate ladder (Hartog & Oosterbeek, 2007; Pfeffer, 1977). Indeed, some high-paying jobs, such as those in medicine, architecture, law, and the sciences, require graduate degrees. Such education is financially expensive and time consuming (Nemetz & Cameron, 2006). Although entrepreneurship may be advanced by a university degree, people are less constrained by the lack of a (prestigious university) degree in achieving success in an entrepreneurial career than in employment (Van der Sluis, Van Praag, & Vijverberg, 2008). That is, an entrepreneurial career is based more on the value created for customers than on the symbols of status that are useful in the political environment of employment (for such signals, see Spence, 1973), requires different criteria than those used for selection into university programs (Shepherd, Douglas, & Fitzsimmons, 2008), and benefits less from the static knowledge taught in some business schools (Ghoshal, 2005). Indeed, people facing career constraints, such as disability (Arnold & Seekins, 2002; Kendall et al., 2006) or discrimination (Kets de Vries, 1977; Scase & Goffee, 1987; Stanworth & Curran, 1976), often seek an entrepreneurial career (as discussed above).

**An entrepreneurial career to change socioeconomic status.** Second, although some studies have indicated that income, on average, drops moving from employment to self-employment (Blanchflower, 2004; Blanchflower & Shadforth, 2007), others have shown that entrepreneurs are wealthier than those in employment (Cagetti & De Nardi, 2006; Lazear, 2005; Nanda, 2008; Quadrini, 2000). Indeed, Carter (2011, pp. 44–45) argued that when we move from focusing on one individual's income to focusing on household wealth, we find a "tight relationship between being an 'entrepreneur' and being rich" (Cagetti & De Nardi, 2006, p. 838). Therefore, while employment can provide incremental adjustments to salary (based on performance or otherwise), entrepreneurship provides an opportunity to make a substantial shift in income (Cagetti & De Nardi, 2006; Lazear, 2005; Nanda, 2008; Quadrini, 2000). Although there is ample evidence of a link between socioeconomic status and health (as detailed above), many of the issues that Carter (2011) raised about capturing the economic implications of entrepreneurship apply to the socioeconomic status construct, and this indicates the need for "new multi-dimensional measures of economic well-being that provide a broader perspective on the variety of reward mechanisms available to the entrepreneur" (Carter, 2011, p. 46). Developing such measures and linking them to health are important challenges for future research.

**A finer-grained understanding of socioeconomic status.** As we conceptualize the economic well-being of individuals more broadly (e.g., "earnings, wealth, assets, savings, and pensions as well as highly subjective and individualized measures of consumption, lifestyle and living standards" [Carter, 2011, pp. 46–47] in the context of their household), we not only gain a deeper understanding of the impact of entrepreneurial action but also provide a basis for research on entrepreneurship and health. While an overarching measure of economic well-being is likely to be useful, there are many opportunities for future research on health and entrepreneurship arising from a fine-grained analysis based on the underlying dimensions of socioeconomic status. That is, which dimensions of socioeconomic status are influenced (positively and negatively) by pursuing an entrepreneurial career (versus salaried employment), and what are the different health consequences of these different paths? For example, if becoming an entrepreneur lowers earnings but increases wealth, what is the likely overall impact on health? Specifically, which health problems are exacerbated by reduced income, and which problems are alleviated by increased wealth?

**The irregularity of entrepreneurial income and health consequences.** The irregularity of income from entrepreneurship may lead to decisions and actions that have health consequences. For example, we detailed above how the socioeconomic status of the community in which people live has health implications. Purchasing a house in a region with a higher socioeconomic status requires a larger mortgage (holding savings constant), and obtaining a larger mortgage is more difficult when future income is uncertain and irregular. Similarly, regular health insurance payments may also be more difficult with an uncertain, irregular income. Despite having a potentially higher mean income than those in employment (Cagetti & De Nardi, 2006; Lazear, 2005; Nanda, 2008; Qudrini, Quadrini, 2000), entrepreneurs may have highly variable and/or uncertain incomes. What are the health implications of the greater uncertainty and irregularity of entrepreneurs' income (and thereby socioeconomic status)?

Counter-intuitively, perhaps when it comes to entrepreneurial income, greater uncertainty and irregularity of socioeconomic status can even generate health benefits. For example, it appears that entrepreneurial households more readily adjust consumption (i.e., expenditure) in tough economic times and temper consumption in good times to save for a "rainy day" (Cagetti & De Nardi, 2006; Carter, 2011; Quadrini, 2000). One form of rainy day could be swiftly dealing with a health problem that would otherwise deteriorate without such savings.

**The entrepreneurial process and socioeconomic status.** The extent and nature of socioeconomic status derived from entrepreneurship may depend on where in the entrepreneurial process economic well-being is captured. For example, entrepreneurial income from creating a new venture is likely to be low, highly uncertain, and highly irregular early in the venture's life but high, certain, and regular once the business becomes established. That is, the positive link between entrepreneurship and health from enhanced socioeconomic status will likely strengthen over time. However, even this more dynamic perspective requires a finer-grained analysis. More specifically, the uncertainty of income generated early in the entrepreneurial process may have a differential effect on different aspects of socioeconomic status, which can then affect different aspects of health. Also, as the venture ages, so too does the entrepreneur, meaning that some potential health problems may become more problematic. Future research can investigate the direct and indirect effects of time on the relationship between entrepreneurial action, socioeconomic status, and health.

**Future research**. In Fig.7.1, we offer a sketch of a model on the role of health in the pursuit of an entrepreneurial career as the basis for future research. The choice to pursue an entrepreneurial career can be influenced by an individual's health and health-related issues at least partly due to the flexibility it offers. The choice to pursue an entrepreneurial career can directly impact the individual's psychological, emotional, and socioeconomic status, or this impact can be indirect through psychological well-being and/or personal resources. An entrepreneurial career influences the individual's satisfaction of his or her needs for autonomy, belongingness, and competence, which can influence the entrepreneur's psychological and emotional states. An entrepreneurial career can also influence the

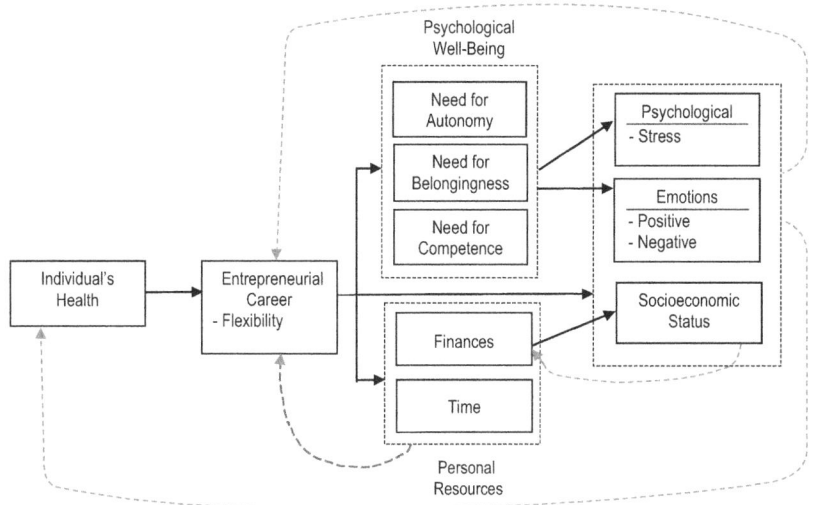

**Fig. 7.1** A sketch of the role of health in the pursuit of an entrepreneurial career

individual's personal financial resources (which can impact socioeconomic status) and time resources. In turn, a change in socioeconomic status can influence personal finances, and personal resources (i.e., financial and time) can influence the pursuit of an entrepreneurial career. Indeed, all outcomes—psychological, emotional, and socioeconomic—can influence both the entrepreneur's health and his or her entrepreneurial career.

## ENTREPRENEURSHIP AND THE HEALTH OF OTHERS

Entrepreneurs can impact the health of others through the opportunities they identify and exploit. To do so, entrepreneurs must believe that there is an opportunity for someone (third-person opportunity) to improve the health of others and that this identified opportunity is one that they personally want to pursue (first-person opportunity). Knowledge and motivation influence both the identification of opportunities and the evaluation that the identified opportunity is a personal opportunity (McMullen & Shepherd, 2006). Although the process of opportunity identification and exploitation to enhance health can be similar to the processes for all other opportunities that provide economic gain for the entrepreneur, we focus on aspects of the process specific to health. That is, entrepreneurs who identify and act on opportunities to enhance others' health likely attend to (at least some) different aspects of the environment and are motivated differently than entrepreneurs solely focused on economic gain (or other non-health–related outcomes). In the sections that follow, we explore the role of (1) personal experiences, (2) professional knowledge, and (3) prosocial motivation on the identification, evaluation, and exploitation of opportunities to enhance others' health.

### *Knowledge, Entrepreneurship, and Others' Health*

Recognizing which individuals have prior knowledge of health problems in the community will likely point to the individuals who are best able to identify and act upon opportunities that improve others' health. While some people are fortunate enough to have good health and do not have to deal with health-related issues, other individuals are not as fortunate. Some individuals have health issues of their own, while others become acquainted with community health problems through their loved ones' medical issues. By either directly or indirectly experiencing health problems, individuals are not only able to more deeply understand the nuances of these problems but also obtain more knowledge of current solutions and the ways these solutions fail to fully solve the problems at hand. This deeper understanding of community health problems and solutions can in turn lead to increased insight into latent demand. For example, after fleeing Vietnam in the 1980s, Han Pham got a bacterial infection from an accident with a "dirty" vaccination needle. When immigrating to Denmark, she entered a graduate program in design and came up with a solution for needle-stick injuries by developing the YellowOne Needle Cap design, a yellow plastic cap that fits on soft drink cans to accept discarded needles without letting them come out (www.designtoimprovelife.dk/antivirus).

**Personally experiencing a health problem impacts the opportunity-identification process.** First, personally experiencing a health problem likely provides deeper knowledge of the cause of the problem, the interrelated parts of the problem, and the inadequacy of current solutions. Second, does experiencing health problems motivate the sort of cognitive processes (e.g., analogical thinking [Grégoire & Shepherd, 2012]) and/or perseverance necessary for identifying potential opportunities? Perhaps high levels of motivation (from experiencing a health problem) generate an urgency that focuses attention on potentially rapid but superficial features (e.g., threatening symptoms of the health problem) rather than the deeper structural thinking often associated with opportunity identification (e.g., the underlying causes of and solutions to the health problem) (Grégoire, Barr, & Shepherd, 2010). Finally, do the consequences of experiencing health problems (e.g., pain, discomfort, distraction) obstruct opportunity identification? For example, is experiencing a health problem similar to dealing with negative emotions (Fredrickson, 1998) or appraised threats (Staw, Sandelands, & Dutton, 1981) in that it constricts thinking in a way that reduces creativity and encourages reliance on tried-and-tested current approaches? That is, some health problems may obstruct the knowledge and motivation usually gained from experiencing health problems, thereby preventing opportunity identification.

While it is likely that someone who either directly or indirectly experiences health problems is both knowledgeable and motivated to identify an opportunity for someone (i.e., have a third-person opportunity belief), that individual may not be adequately knowledgeable and motivated to act on the opportunity him- or herself (i.e., have a first-person opportunity belief). For example, exploiting an opportunity to introduce a product to solve people's health problems likely necessitates knowledge of sector-specific production, marketing, and management as well as the resources to go to market. For example, the invention of the YellowOne Needle Cap was based on Pham's knowledge about design gained at a design graduate school. An individual who creates a solution to overcome his or her own health-related problem and then uses that innovation may initiate (perhaps unintentionally) a process that results in the adoption, technical enhancement, and full-scale exploitation of the potential health opportunity. Indeed, research on this type of process could contribute to the stream of work building on user innovation research (Shah & Tripsas, 2007; von Hippel, 1988) to investigate health entrepreneurship. Since user innovation is likely a significant source of entrepreneurial actions that improve health, we argue that future research investigating this process among users of health-related technologies, products, and services is likely to make important contributions to the user innovation literature as well as to the (hopefully) emerging health-entrepreneurship literature.

**Building on sources of knowledge other than health-related experiences.** People who do not personally have health-related problems can still have the knowledge to first identify and then exploit opportunities that enhance health. Some individuals might have considerable knowledge of technologies that could be fashioned into health solutions. For example, engineer Dean Kamien realized that there was a lack of safe drinking water for many people in developing countries. He set out to, in his opinion, solve the biggest world problem because poor-quality drinking water is a major source of microbial pathogens, which, along with poor sanitation and hygiene, account for 1.7 million deaths per year (Ashbolt, 2004). Building on his knowledge of engineering and inventing things, Kamien came up with the Slingshot—a portable low-power water-purification system.[2] Future research can explore how people apply their knowledge of technology to a health problem that they have not personally experienced (including vicariously experienced health problems through loved ones). That is, how do individuals (e.g., engineers, technologists, inventors) find a health problem to solve? Perhaps they take an analytical approach of finding the biggest problem and setting out to solve it (as Dean Kamien did with the Slingshot), or maybe it involves some other selection process, such as perspective taking to develop a deep knowledge of the nature of the health problems people face. Indeed, it could be that not personally experiencing the health problem provides the level of detached perspective taking necessary to take the creative mental leaps for opportunity identification.

In particular, most medical professionals have developed in-depth knowledge of health problems from treating numerous patients, which could facilitate opportunity identification (Simmons, 2002). For instance, using patent data from the American Medical Association, Chatterji, Fabrizio, Mitchell, and Schulman (2008) demonstrated that doctors filed nearly 20% of all medical-device patents in the USA from 1990 to 1996. However, many medical professionals may be reluctant to act upon the potential opportunities they identify for reasons related to decreased desirability and/or a lack of apparent feasibility. There are likely to be high opportunity costs for doctors who choose to exploit opportunities (i.e., entrepreneurial action is less desirable), or they may believe they lack the personal knowledge needed to fully exploit an opportunity (i.e., entrepreneurial action is seen as infeasible). This type of scenario opens up numerous paths for future research.

**Combining the identification of a health opportunity identified with its exploitation.** When an opportunity to improve health is identified but not exploited, it represents a potentially wasted resource (and, worse, people may continue to suffer who otherwise would have benefited from the exploitation of the opportunity). Therefore, it is vital for researchers to question and empirically investigate our initial premise: do medical professionals detect health opportunities (third-person opportunities) that they do not end up personally acting upon? If so, why not? In the end, what happens to these potentially valuable opportunities that are recognized but not exploited? Perhaps the medical professionals who initially identify these ideas share them with their colleagues, who in turn ultimately agree that they do represent opportunities for someone but not for them due to their lack of knowledge and/or motivation to act upon them. However, some individuals do end up acting upon the opportunities they identify to improve health. Why do only some individuals do this and not others? Entrepreneurship programs could be a useful addition to medical professionals' education and training. Future research should investigate the characteristics and benefits (if any) of such entrepreneurship programs for medical professionals.

While researchers often view the entrepreneurial process as involving only one actor (e.g., one individual, team, and/or venture), this assumption is an artificial limitation to our conceptualization of the practice of entrepreneurship, especially when others' health is the outcome of that practice. When a medical professional identifies an opportunity but does not believe it represents a personally desirable or feasible opportunity, can he or she "pass" the opportunity on to someone else with the knowledge and motivation needed to successfully exploit it? If we are able to gain deeper insights into the mechanisms behind a successful exchange of this type, we could uncover important practical implications for the ways organizations manage and reward medical professionals. In addition, new doctors who are educated about health problems but lack experience with current solutions could be important sources of new health-related innovations. Indeed, as research has shown, new entrants into an industry frequently introduce radical innovations (Anderson & Tushman, 1990; Christensen, 1997) because of their higher tendency to challenge the status quo. Do new medical professionals also do this? Again, although being a new entrant into the medical field may result in the identification of potential opportunities to solve health-related problems, the difficulties associated with exploitation could be even greater (yet different) for this group. For instance, new medical professionals generally spend their time and energy on learning and adapting their knowledge and expectations to fit their new roles (Pratt et al., 2006) and thus will have less time to consider an entrepreneurial endeavor "on the side."

## *Motivation, Entrepreneurship, and Others' Health*

As we mentioned earlier, an individual does not need to personally have health problems to identify and act on opportunities to improve others' health.

**Prosocial motivation and the identification and exploitation of potential health-related opportunities.** Some people naturally have prosocial motivations—"the desire to expend effort based on a concern for helping or contributing to other people" (Grant & Berry, 2011, p. 77)—which can in turn shape their cognitive processing (Kunda, 1990; Nickerson, 1998). For instance, Grant and Berry (2011) showed that prosocial motivation often leads to perspective taking that helps individuals become more creative in generalizing useful ideas. Perspective taking is "a cognitive process in which individuals adopt others' viewpoints in an attempt to understand their preferences, values, and needs" (Grant & Berry, 2011, p. 79), which provides insights into health problems that are needed to identify solutions to these problems. For example, although prosocial motivation does not exclude self-interested actions, to a certain extent, the "rubber meets the road" with patents (i.e., to what extent is the intellectual property protection–strategy consistent with a prosocial motivation). For instance, in explaining why he did not seek patents for his Solar Ear (i.e., a hearing aid that was cheap, durable, and powered by solar energy), the founder Howard Weinstein explained that the cost of intellectual property protection would drive up the costs of the product and that he wanted the product to be copied and widely spread to address the health problem on the largest scale possible (https://www.ashoka.org/fellow/howard-weinstein). Therefore, prosocial motivation not only molds individuals' cognitions to provide knowledge about potentially valuable solutions to health problems but also motivates individuals to exploit these identified opportunities and informs the means and scope by which these potential opportunities are exploited.

**Making a difference by acting entrepreneurially to solve health problems.** Although prosocial motivation has been found to lead to perspective taking and ultimately useful innovations in employees (Grant & Berry, 2011), there is an opportunity to extend this research to better understand the nature of the relationship between entrepreneurship and health. Prosocially motivated individuals are likely drawn to those with health problems because such problems can cause considerable suffering. It is important to note that prosocial motivation does not preclude benefits accruing to the actor, only that the actor has a desire to (and hopefully creates outcomes that) help or contribute to other people (Grant, 2007; Grant & Berry, 2011). In a similar way, we propose that health entrepreneurship can generate profit for the entrepreneur but emphasize that it has the potential to enhance the health of others. Scholars can also investigate a phenomenon that can "make a difference"—with health as the dependent variable—while at the same time advancing their career by publishing high-quality highly impactful research. We hope that scholars will be prosocially motivated in their choice of research topics.

**Differences across entrepreneurs in prosocial motivation.** There is likely to be considerable heterogeneity among entrepreneurs in their prosocial motivation. What is the impact of heterogeneity in prosocial motivation on health entrepreneurship? Perhaps only highly prosocially motivated individuals identify and exploit health opportunities. Due to the high likelihood of financial success in this sector, however, it is more probable that a wide variety of entrepreneurs enter this sector. Thus, more fruitful research may come from trying to understand heterogeneity in the potential opportunities exploited in terms of entrepreneurs' prosocial motivation. For instance, do entrepreneurs with higher prosocial motivation act on health opportunities that are more radical compared to those with lower prosocial motivation? If so, is it because these entrepreneurs tend to conduct more perspective taking to identify opportunities that are better at overcoming health problems (consistent with Grant & Berry, 2011), and/or does being prosocially motivated enhance entrepreneurs' willingness to accept uncertainty in order to exploit more radical potential opportunities? It could be that individuals who are more prosocially motivated are more interested in exploiting opportunities with the highest probability of relieving suffering. Scholars can also explore why some prosocially motivated entrepreneurs are attracted to opportunities that improve others' health problems while other prosocially motivated entrepreneurs are attracted to opportunities that help others' in non-health–related ways.

**A potential dark side of prosocially motivated pursuits of potential health-related opportunities.** The pursuit of potential opportunities that enhance the health of others can have a dark side—or at least research can explore this potential dark side: (1) Pursuing opportunities that improve others' health can itself lead to negative health consequences for entrepreneurs. While entrepreneurs are likely to gain some benefits to their psychological well-being from assisting others, doing so may also come with health costs (as discussed above). (2) As with all potential opportunities, potential health opportunities are characterized by uncertainty, and pursuing what one believes represents an opportunity may ultimately end in failure. What influence does such failure have on health? Does it negatively impact the health of those the entrepreneur was trying to assist (e.g., through false hope and early commitments) and/or the entrepreneur him- or herself? Maybe entrepreneurial grief is most severe when the business failure also means that others' suffering will persist because the business can no longer alleviate it. In this context, entrepreneurs are likely to be a vital source of health assistance to others, thus making the implications for their own health resulting from entrepreneurial actions even more important.

**Future Research.** In Fig. 7.2, we offer a sketch of a model of the impact of entrepreneurial action on others' health as the basis for future research. Knowledge of health, such as experience with a health problem (directly or indirectly) or from education and experience as a medical professional provides a basis for the identification and exploitation of potential opportunities to enhance health. However, this relationship is magnified by knowledge of technology and/or entrepreneurial knowledge, both of which facilitate finding a (technically and commercially appropriate)

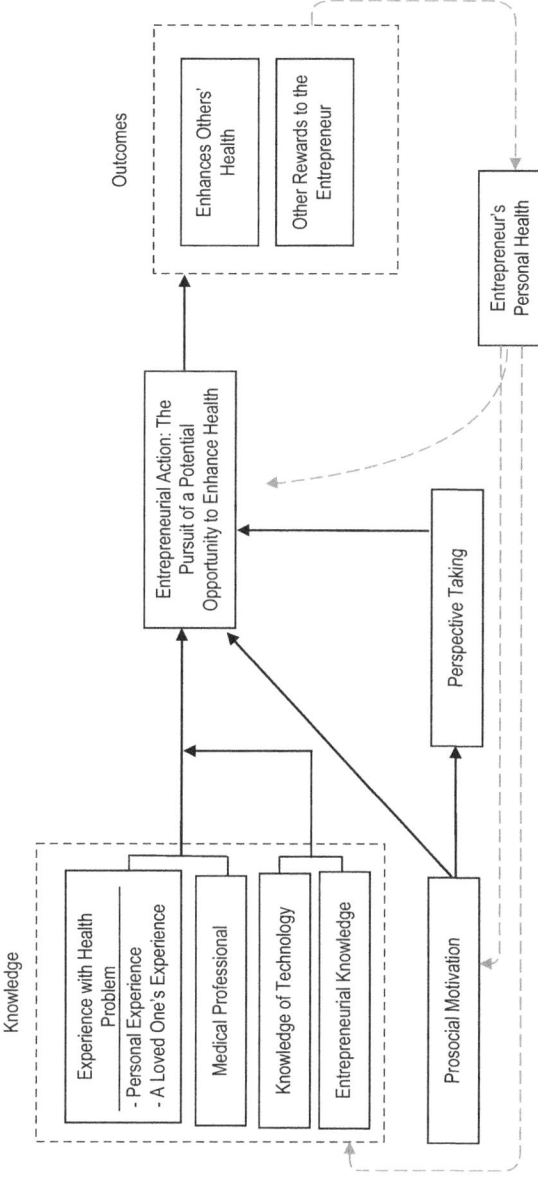

**Fig. 7.2** A sketch of the role of entrepreneurial action in enhancing others' health

solution to health problems. Prosocial motivation can directly impact the pursuit of a potential opportunity to enhance others' health as well as indirectly impact this pursuit by facilitating perspective taking. The pursuit of such potential opportunities may not only enhance others' health but also generate (intrinsic and extrinsic) rewards for the entrepreneur. As indicated in the previous section (and illustrated in this figure), the outcomes of entrepreneurial action can impact the entrepreneur's personal health, which can impact his or her knowledge, personal motivation, and subsequent entrepreneurial action.

## Discussion and Conclusion

Health is an important topic as health problems cause suffering. In this chapter, we propose that an entrepreneurial career can impact the entrepreneur's health and that a person who acts entrepreneurially can enhance others' health. Entrepreneurship scholars have a good idea of how entrepreneurial action generates economic benefits for the entrepreneur (Cagetti & De Nardi, 2006; Lazear, 2005; Nanda, 2008; Quadrini, 2000) and the local economy (Audretsch & Feldman, 2004; Audretsch & Thurik, 2001), and there is growing understanding of how entrepreneurship can impact the natural environment (Dean & McMullen, 2007; Patzelt & Shepherd, 2011) and communities (Peredo & Chrisman, 2006; Shepherd & Williams, 2014; see also Chap. 5). We provide a first step and a roadmap for ways entrepreneurship scholars can extend current research efforts to build a better understanding of how entrepreneurship impacts health (of the entrepreneur and others) and how health impacts entrepreneurship.

In the face of criticism that a threat to entrepreneurship as a field is that it lacks a "unifying" dependent variable, we interpret this as a rich opportunity throughout this book in general and in this chapter specifically. Indeed, entrepreneurship as the nexus of opportunity and individuals provides entrepreneurship scholars the chance to apply and extend our trade to society's most important problems—such as health—at varying levels of analysis. Although social entrepreneurship primarily focuses on developing economies, health problems exist locally in all economies. That is, entrepreneurship scholars can do research in their local community and make a difference. Many health problems appear to vary across regions. Rather than focus on some omnibus measure of health, we have the opportunity to exploit specific health problems (e.g., visual problems, obesity, and childhood asthma). However, which problems should entrepreneurship scholars research first? Similar to an individual who experiences a health problem (directly through his or her personal health or indirectly through an unhealthy family member) identifying and pursuing a potential opportunity, entrepreneurship scholars may draw on their idiosyncratic knowledge of health problems and their personal motivations to identify potential research opportunities to deepen our understanding of the relationship between entrepreneurial action and specific health outcomes.

As we develop this deeper understanding of the role that entrepreneurship plays in enhancing health outcomes, we complement the body of research on health innovation in large established organizations. We are not saying that research on large established organizations' health innovations is not important—clearly it is—but that the actions of entrepreneurial individuals and teams also generate positive health outcomes and require researchers' attention. We hope that this chapter's proposed research agenda inspires scholars to develop this important research stream and, in doing so, contribute to both enhancing scholarship and improving people's lives.

## Notes

1. We also acknowledge that poor health can reduce socioeconomic status. For example, poor health can be costly in terms of money and time (Poterba, Venti, & Wise, 2013) and negatively impact salary increases and promotion.
2. The system is called the Slingshot based on the story of David taking down the giant Goliath with his slingshot. Kamen views bad water as the Goliath of the current century, with little villages (Davids) having to fight it with the Slingshot (http://www.wired.com/2008/03/colbert-and-kam).

## References

Akande, A. (1994). Coping with entrepreneurial stress: Evidence from Nigeria. *Journal of Small Business Management, 32*(1), 83–87.

Anderson, E., & Shivakumar, G. (2015). Effects of exercise and physical activity on anxiety. In F. B. Schuch, N. Rocha, & E. L. Cadore (Eds.), *Progress in physical activity and exercise and affective and anxiety disorders: Translational studies, perspectives and future directions* (pp. 46–49. [Frontiers in Psychiatry]).

Anderson, P., & Tushman, M. L. (1990). Technological discontinuities and dominant designs: A cyclical model of technological change. *Administrative Science Quarterly, 35*(4), 604–633.

Arnold, N. L., & Seekins, T. (2002). Self-employment: A process for use by vocational rehabilitation agencies. *Journal of Vocational Rehabilitation, 17*(2), 107–113.

Aschemann-Witzel, J., & Hamm, U. (2010). Do consumers prefer foods with nutrition and health claims? Results of a purchase simulation. *Journal of Marketing Communications, 16*(1–2), 47–58.

Ashbolt, N. J. (2004). Microbial contamination of drinking water and disease outcomes in developing regions. *Toxicology, 198*(1), 229–238.

Audretsch, D. B., & Thurik, A. R. (2001). What's new about the new economy? Sources of growth in the managed and entrepreneurial economies. *Industrial and Corporate Change, 10*(1), 267–315.

Audretsch, D. B., & Feldman, M. P. (2004). Knowledge spillovers and the geography of innovation. In J. V. Henderson & J.-F. Thisse (Eds.), *Handbook of regional and urban economics* (Vol. 4, pp. 2713–2739). San Diego, CA: Elsevier.

Baker, T., & Nelson, R. E. (2005). Creating something from nothing: Resource construction through entrepreneurial bricolage. *Administrative Science Quarterly, 50*(3), 329–366.

Baron, R. A. (2008). The role of affect in the entrepreneurial process. *Academy of Management Review, 33*(2), 328–340.

Batavia, A. I., & Schriner, K. (2001). The Americans with disabilities act as engine of social change: Models of disability and the potential of a civil rights approach. *Policy Studies Journal, 29*(4), 690–702.

Baum, J. R., & Locke, E. A. (2004). The relationship of entrepreneurial traits, skill, and motivation to subsequent venture growth. *Journal of Applied Psychology, 89*(4), 587–598.

Benner, M. J., & Tushman, M. (2007). Process management, technological innovation, and organizational adaptation. In V. Grover & M. L. Markus (Eds.), *Business process transformation* (pp. 317–326). New York: Routledge.

Bird, B., & Jelinek, M. (1988). The operation of entrepreneurial intentions. *Entrepreneurship Theory and Practice, 13*(2), 21–29.

Blanchflower, D. G. (2004). Self-employment: More may not be better. National Bureau of Economic Research.

Blanchflower, D. G., Oswald, A., & Stutzer, A. (2001). Latent entrepreneurship across nations. *European Economic Review, 45*(4), 680–691.

Blanchflower, D., & Shadforth, C. (2007). Entrepreneurship in the UK. *Foundations and Trends in Entrepreneurship, 3*(4), 257–364.

Bonanno, G. A. (2004). Loss, trauma, and human resilience. *American Psychologist, 59*(1), 20–28.

Bonanno, G. A., Papa, A., & O'Neill, K. (2001). Loss and human resilience. *Applied and Preventive Psychology, 10*(3), 193–206.

Bono, J., Glomb, T., Shen, W., Kim, E., & Koch, A. (2013). Building positive resources: Effects of positive events and positive reflection on work-stress and health. *Academy of Management Journal, 56*(6), 1601–1627.

Bosma, H., Schrijvers, C., & Mackenbach, J. P. (1999). Socioeconomic inequalities in mortality and importance of perceived control: Cohort study. *British Medical Journal, 319*(7223), 1469–1470.

Boyd, D. P., & Gumpert, D. E. (1983). Coping with entrepreneurial stress. *Harvard Business Review, 61*(2), 44–64.

Bradley, S. W., Aldrich, H. E., Shepherd, D. A., & Wiklund, J. (2011). Resources, environmental change, and survival: Asymmetric paths of young independent and subsidiary organizations. *Strategic Management Journal, 32*(5), 486–509.

Bradley, D. E., & Roberts, J. A. (2004). Self-Employment and job satisfaction: Investigating the role of self-efficacy, depression, and seniority. *Journal of Small Business Management, 42*(1), 37–58.

Braveman, P. A., Cubbin, C., Egerter, S., Williams, D. R., & Pamuk, E. (2010). Socioeconomic disparities in health in the United States: What the patterns tell us. *American Journal of Public Health, 100*(S1), S186–S196.

Brigham, K. H., De Castro, J. O., & Shepherd, D. A. (2007). A person-organization fit model of owner-managers' cognitive style and organizational demands. *Entrepreneurship Theory and Practice, 31*(1), 29–51.

Brown, T. E., Davidsson, P., & Wiklund, J. (2001). An operationalization of Stevenson's conceptualization of entrepreneurship as opportunity-based firm behavior. *Strategic Management Journal, 22*(10), 953–968.

Brownley, K., Hurwitz, B., & Schneiderman, N. (2000). Cardiovascular psychophysiology. In J. Cacioppo, L. Tassinary, & G. Berntson (Eds.), *Handbook of psychophysiology* (2nd ed., pp. 224–264). New York: Cambridge University.

Bruce, M. L., Kim, K., Leaf, P. J., & Jacobs, S. (1990). Depressive episodes and dysphoria resulting from conjugal bereavement in a prospective community sample. *American Journal of Psychiatry, 147*(5), 608–611.

Buchanan, K. E., & Bardi, A. (2010). Acts of kindness and acts of novelty affect life satisfaction. *Journal of Social Psychology, 150*(3), 235–237.

Buka, S. L., Stichick, T. L., Birdthistle, I., & Earls, F. J. (2001). Youth exposure to violence: Prevalence, risks, and consequences. *American Journal of Orthopsychiatry, 71*(3), 298–310.

Buttner, E. H. (1992). Entrepreneurial stress: Is it hazardous to your health. *Journal of Managerial Issues, 4*(3), 223–240.

Byrne, O., & Shepherd, D. A. (2015). Different strokes for different folks: Entrepreneurial narratives of emotion, cognition, and making sense of business failure. *Entrepreneurship Theory and Practice, 39*(2), 375–405.

Cagetti, M., & De Nardi, M. (2006). Entrepreneurship, frictions, and wealth. *Journal of Political Economy, 114*(5), 835–870.

Callahan, M., Shumpert, N., & Mast, M. (2002). Self-employment, choice and self-determination. *Journal of Vocational Rehabilitation, 17*(2), 75–85.

Camacho, T. C., Roberts, R. E., Lazarus, N. B., Kaplan, G. A., & Cohen, R. D. (1991). Physical activity and depression: Evidence from the Alameda county study. *American Journal of Epidemiology, 134*(2), 220–231.

Caplan, R. D., & Jones, K. W. (1975). Effects of work load, role ambiguity, and type A personality on anxiety, depression, and heart rate. *Journal of Applied Psychology, 60*(6), 713.

Carayannopoulos, S. (2009). How technology-based new firms leverage newness and smallness to commercialize disruptive technologies. *Entrepreneurship Theory and Practice, 33*(2), 419–438.

Cardon, M. S., Zietsma, C., Saparito, P., Matherne, B. P., & Davis, C. (2005). A tale of passion: New insights into entrepreneurship from a parenthood metaphor. *Journal of Business Venturing, 20*(1), 23–45.

Cardon, M. S., Wincent, J., Shigh, J., & Drnovsek, M. (2009). The nature and experience of entrepreneurial passion. *Academy of Management Review, 34*(3), 511–532.

Carter, S. (2011). The rewards of entrepreneurship: Exploring the incomes, wealth, and economic well-being of entrepreneurial households. *Entrepreneurship Theory and Practice, 35*(1), 39–55.

Chaix, B., Lindström, M., Rosvall, M., & Merlo, J. (2008). Neighbourhood social interactions and risk of acute myocardial infarction. *Journal of Epidemiology and Community Health, 62*(1), 62–68.

Chatterji, A. K., Fabrizio, K. R., Mitchell, W., & Schulman, K. A. (2008). Physician-industry cooperation in the medical device industry. *Health Affairs, 27*(6), 1532–1543.

Chen, C. C., Greene, P. G., & Crick, A. (1998). Does entrepreneurial self-efficacy distinguish entrepreneurs from managers? *Journal of Business Venturing, 13*(4), 295–316.

Chen, E., & Miller, G. E. (2013). Socioeconomic status and health: Mediating and moderating factors. *Annual Review of Clinical Psychology, 9*, 723–749.

Christensen, C. (1997). *The innovator's dilemma: When new technologies cause great firms to fail*. Boston, MA: Harvard Business Press.

Christian, M. S., & Ellis, A. P. (2011). Examining the effects of sleep deprivation on workplace deviance: A self-regulatory perspective. *Academy of Management Journal, 54*(5), 913–934.

Clayton, P. J. (1990). Bereavement and depression. *Journal of Clinical Psychiatry, 51*, S34–S40.

Cohen, S., Janicki-Deverts, D., & Miller, G. E. (2007). Psychological stress and disease. *Journal of the American Medical Association, 298*(14), 1685–1687.

Coker, A. L., Smith, P. H., Bethea, L., King, M. R., & McKeown, R. E. (2000). Physical health consequences of physical and psychological intimate partner violence. *Archives of Family Medicine, 9*(5), 451–457.

Coleman, J. S. (1988). Social capital in the creation of human capital. *American Journal of Sociology, 94*, 95–120.

Conger, R., & Elder, G. H. (1994). *Families in troubled times.* Hawthorne, NY: Aldine de Gruyter.

Crouch, J. L., Hanson, R. F., Saunders, B. E., Kilpatrick, D. G., & Resnick, H. S. (2000). Income, race/ethnicity, and exposure to violence in youth: Results from the national survey of adolescents. *Journal of Community Psychology, 28*(6), 625–641.

Dean, T. J., & McMullen, J. S. (2007). Toward a theory of sustainable entrepreneurship: Reducing environmental degradation through entrepreneurial action. *Journal of Business Venturing, 22*(1), 50–76.

Deborah, H. F., & William, R. S. (2000). Friendship within entrepreneurial teams and its association with team and venture performance. *Entrepreneurship Theory and Practice, 25*(2), 5–21.

Deci, E. L., & Ryan, R. M. (1985). *Intrinsic motivation and self-determination in human behavior.* New York: Plenum.

Deeds, D. L., Decarolis, D., & Coombs, J. E. (1999). The impact of firm-specific capabilities on the amount of capital raised in an initial public offering: An empirical investigation of the biotechnology industry. Strategic Management Journal, 20, 953–968.

DeLongis, A., Folkman, S., & Lazarus, R. S. (1988). The impact of daily stress on health and mood: Psychological and social resources as mediators. *Journal of Personality and Social Psychology, 54*(3), 486–495.

DeTienne, D. R. (2010). Entrepreneurial exit as a critical component of the entrepreneurial process: Theoretical development. *Journal of Business Venturing, 25*(2), 203–215.

Donaldson, J. M., & Watson, R. (1996). Loneliness in elderly people: An important area for nursing research. *Journal of Advanced Nursing, 24*(5), 952–959.

Du Toit, D. F. (1980). Confessions of a successful entrepreneur. *Harvard Business Review, 58*(6), 44–58.

Eden, D. (1975). Organizational membership vs. self-employment: Another blow to the American dream. *Organizational Behavior and Human Performance, 13*(1), 79–94.

Eisenhardt, K. M., & Brown, S. L. (1998). Competing on the edge: Strategy as structured chaos. *Long Range Planning, 31*(5), 786–789.

Evans, A. G., & Varaiya, N. P. (2003). Assessment of a biotech market opportunity. *Entrepreneurship Theory and Practice, 28*(1), 87–105.

Everson-Rose, S. A., & Lewis, T. T. (2005). Psychosocial factors and cardiovascular diseases. *Annual Review of Public Health, 26*, 469–500.

Faravelli, C., & Pallanti, S. (1989). Recent life events and panic disorder. *American Journal of Psychiatry, 146*(5), 622–626.

Fichman, M., & Levinthal, D. A. (1991). Honeymoons and the liability of adolescence: A new perspective of duration dependence in social and organizational relationships. *Academy of Management Review, 16*(2), 442–468.

Finlay-Jones, R., & Brown, G. W. (1981). Types of stressful life event and the onset of anxiety and depressive disorders. *Psychological Medicine, 11*(4), 803–815.

Florian, V., Mikulincer, M., & Taubman, O. (1995). Does hardiness contribute to mental health during a stressful real-life situation? The roles of appraisal and coping. *Journal of Personality and Social Psychology, 68*(4), 687.

Folkman, S., & Moskowitz, J. T. (2000). Stress, positive emotion, and coping. *Current Directions in Psychological Science, 9*(4), 115–118.

Fong, C. T. (2006). The effects of emotional ambivalence on creativity. *Academy of Management Journal, 49*(5), 1016–1030.

Fong, C. T., & Tiedens, L. Z. (2002). Dueling experiences and dual ambivalences: Emotional and motivational ambivalence of women in high status positions. *Motivation and Emotion, 26*(1), 105–121.

Forbes, D. P., Borchert, P. S., Zellmer-Bruhn, M. E., & Sapienza, H. J. (2006). Entrepreneurial team formation: An exploration of new member addition. *Entrepreneurship Theory and Practice, 30*(2), 225–248.

Fredrickson, B. L. (1998). What good are positive emotions? *Review of General Psychology, 2*(3), 300–319.

Fredrickson, B. L. (2000). Cultivating positive emotions to optimize health and well-being. *Prevention and Treatment, 3*(1), 1–25.

Fredrickson, B. L. (2001). The role of positive emotions in positive psychology: The broaden-and-build theory of positive emotions. *American Psychologist, 56*(3), 218–226.

Fredrickson, B. L., Cohn, M. A., Coffey, K. A., Pek, J., & Finkel, S. M. (2008). Open hearts build lives: Positive emotions, induced through loving-kindness meditation, build consequential personal resources. *Journal of Personality and Social Psychology, 95*(5), 1045.

Gallo, L. C., & Matthews, K. A. (2003). Understanding the association between socioeconomic status and physical health: Do negative emotions play a role? *Psychological Bulletin, 129*(1), 10.

George, G., & Prabhu, G. N. (2000). Developmental financial institutions as catalysts of entrepreneurship in emerging economies. *Academy of Management Review, 25*(3), 620–629.

Ghoshal, S. (2005). Bad management theories are destroying good management practices. *Academy of Management Learning and Education, 4*(1), 75–91.

Goldsby, M. G., Kuratko, D. F., & Bishop, J. W. (2005). Entrepreneurship and fitness: An examination of rigorous exercise and goal attainment among small business owners. *Journal of Small Business Management, 43*(1), 78–92.

Goldstein, S. M., & Iossifova, A. R. (2012). Ten years after: Interference of hospital slack in process performance benefits of quality practices. *Journal of Operations Management, 30*(1), 44–54.

Goodstein, J., Gautam, K., & Boeker, W. (1994). The effects of board size and diversity on strategic change. *Strategic Management Journal, 15*(3), 241–250.

Grant, A. M. (2007). Relational job design and the motivation to make a prosocial difference. *Academy of Management Review, 32*(2), 393–417.

Grant, A. M., & Berry, J. W. (2011). The necessity of others is the mother of invention: Intrinsic and prosocial motivations, perspective taking, and creativity. *Academy of Management Journal, 54*(1), 73–96.

Grégoire, D. A., Barr, P. S., & Shepherd, D. A. (2010). Cognitive processes of opportunity recognition: The role of structural alignment. *Organization Science, 21*(2), 413–431.

Grégoire, D. A., & Shepherd, D. A. (2012). Technology-market combinations and the identification of entrepreneurial opportunities: An investigation of the opportunity-individual nexus. *Academy of Management Journal, 55*(4), 753–785.

Grzywacz, J. G., & Bass, B. L. (2003). Work, family, and mental health: Testing different models of work-family fit. *Journal of Marriage and Family, 65*(1), 248–261.

Gumpert, D. E., & Boyd, D. P. (1984). The loneliness of the small business owner. In H. Levinson (Ed.), *Designing and managing your career*. Boston, MA: Harvard Business School Publishing.

Hagner, D., & Davies, T. (2002). "Doing my own thing": Supported self-employment for individuals with cognitive disabilities. *Journal of Vocational Rehabilitation, 17*(2), 65–74.

Hammen, C. (2005). Stress and depression. *Annual Review of Clinical Psychology, 1*, 293–319.

Hannafey, F. T. (2003). Entrepreneurship and ethics: A literature review. *Journal of Business Ethics, 46*(2), 99–110.

Harris, J. A., Saltstone, R., & Fraboni, M. (1999). An evaluation of the job stress questionnaire with a sample of entrepreneurs. *Journal of Business and Psychology, 13*(3), 447–455.

Hartog, J., & Oosterbeek, H. (2007). What should you know about private returns to education. In J. Hartog & H. M. v. d. Brink (Eds.), *Human capital: Moving the Frontier*. Cambridge, UK: Cambridge University Press.

Hawkley, L. C., & Cacioppo, J. T. (2010). Loneliness matters: A theoretical and empirical review of consequences and mechanisms. *Annals of Behavioral Medicine, 40*(2), 218–227.

Haws, K., & Winterich, K. (2013). When value trumps health in a supersized world. *Journal of Marketing, 77*(3), 48.

Haynie, J. M., & Shepherd, D. A. (2011). Toward a theory of discontinuous career transition: Investigating career transitions necessitated by traumatic life events. *Journal of Applied Psychology, 96*(3), 501–524.

Hazer, O., & Boylu, A. A. (2010). The examination of the factors affecting the feeling of loneliness of the elderly. *Procedia-Social and Behavioral Sciences, 9*, 2083–2089.

Hemingway, H., & Marmot, M. (1999). Evidence based cardiology-psychosocial factors in the aetiology and prognosis of coronary heart disease: Systematic review of prospective cohort studies. *British Medical Journal, 318*(7196), 1460–1467.

Holt-Lunstad, J., Smith, T. B., & Layton, J. B. (2010). Social relationships and mortality risk: A meta-analytic review. *PLoS Medicine, 7*(7), e1000316.

Huy, Q. N. (1999). Emotional capability, emotional intelligence, and radical change. *Academy of Management Review, 24*(2), 325–345.

Ibarra, H., & Barbulescu, R. (2010). Identity as narrative: Prevalence, effectiveness, and consequences of narrative identity work in macro work role transitions. *Academy of Management Review, 35*(1), 135–154.

Jamal, M., & Badawi, J. A. (1995). Job stress and quality of working life of self-employed immigrants: A study in workforce diversity. *Journal of Small Business & Entrepreneurship, 12*(1), 55–63.

Jenkins, A. S., Wiklund, J., & Brundin, E. (2014). Individual responses to firm failure: Appraisals, grief, and the influence of prior failure experience. *Journal of Business Venturing, 29*(1), 17–33.

Kampert, J. B., Blair, S. N., Barlow, C. E., & Kohl, H. W. (1996). Physical activity, physical fitness, and all-cause and cancer mortality: A prospective study of men and women. *Annals of Epidemiology, 6*(5), 452–457.

Kaprio, J., Koskenvuo, M., & Rita, H. (1987). Mortality after bereavement: A prospective study of 95,647 widowed persons. *American Journal of Public Health, 77*(3), 283–287.

Katila, R., & Ahuja, G. (2002). Something old, something new: A longitudinal study of search behavior and new product introduction. *Academy of Management Journal, 45*(6), 1183–1194.

Katzmarzyk, P. T., Janssen, I., & Ardern, C. I. (2003). Physical inactivity, excess adiposity and premature mortality. *Obesity Reviews, 4*(4), 257–290.

Kawachi, I., Kennedy, B. P., & Glass, R. (1999). Social capital and self-rated health: A contextual analysis. *American Journal of Public Health, 89*(8), 1187–1193.

Keats, B. W., & Hitt, M. A. (1988). A causal model of linkages among environmental dimensions, macro organizational characteristics, and performance. *Academy of Management Journal, 31*(3), 570–598.

Kendall, E., Buys, N., Charker, J., & MacMillan, S. (2006). Self employment: An underutilized rehabilitation strategy. *Journal of Vocational Rehabilitation, 25*, 197–205.

Kendler, K. S., Karkowski, L. M., & Prescott, C. A. (1999). Causal relationship between stressful life events and the onset of major depression. *American Journal of Psychiatry, 156*(6), 837–841.

Kets De Vries, M. (1977). The entrepreneurial personality: A person at the crossroads. *Journal of Management Studies, 14*(1), 34–57.

Kets de Vries, M. (1980). Stress and the entrepreneur. In C. L. Cooper & R. Payne (Eds.), *Current concerns in occupational stress.* New York: John Wiley and Sons.

Klinnert, M. D., Nelson, H. S., Price, M. R., Adinoff, A. D., Leung, D. Y., & Mrazek, D. A. (2001). Onset and persistence of childhood asthma: Predictors from infancy. *Pediatrics, 108*(4), e69–e69.

Komisar, R. (2000). Goodbye career, hello success. *Harvard Business Review, 78*(2), 160–174.

Kraus, A. S., & Lilienfeld, A. M. (1959). Some epidemiologic aspects of the high mortality rate in the young widowed group. *Journal of Chronic Diseases, 10*(3), 207–217.

Kunda, Z. (1990). The case for motivated reasoning. *Psychological Bulletin, 108*(3), 480–498.

LaGanga, L. R. (2011). Lean service operations: Reflections and new directions for capacity expansion in outpatient clinics. *Journal of Operations Management, 29*(5), 422–433.

Larsen, J. T., McGraw, A. P., & Cacioppo, J. T. (2001). Can people feel happy and sad at the same time? *Journal of Personality and Social Psychology, 81*(4), 684–696.

Larsen, J. T., McGraw, A. P., Mellers, B. A., & Cacioppo, J. T. (2004). The agony of victory and thrill of defeat mixed emotional reactions to disappointing wins and relieving losses. *Psychological Science, 15*(5), 325–330.

Lazarus, R. S. (1990). Theory-based stress measurement. *Psychological Inquiry, 1*(1), 3–13.

Lazarus, R. S., & Folkman, S. (1984). *Stress, appraisal, and coping.* New York: Springer.

Lazarus, R. S., & Folkman, S. (1987). Transactional theory and research on emotions and coping. *European Journal of Personality, 1*(3), 141–169.

Lazear, E. M. (2005). Entrepreneurship. *Journal of Labor Economics, 23*(4), 649–680.

Lewin-Epstein, N., & Yuchtman-Yaar, E. (1991). Health risks of self-employment. *Work and Occupations, 18*(3), 291–312.

Lochner, K. A., Kawachi, I., Brennan, R. T., & Buka, S. L. (2003). Social capital and neighborhood mortality rates in Chicago. *Social Science & Medicine, 56*(8), 1797–1805.

Lovasi, G. S., Hutson, M. A., Guerra, M., & Neckerman, K. M. (2009). Built environments and obesity in disadvantaged populations. *Epidemiologic Reviews, 31*(1), 7–20.

Lundberg, O. (1993). The impact of childhood living conditions on illness and mortality in adulthood. *Social Science & Medicine, 36*(8), 1047–1052.

Macan, T. H. (1994). Time management: Test of a process model. *Journal of Applied Psychology, 79*(3), 381–391.

Margolin, G., & Gordis, E. B. (2000). The effects of family and community violence on children. *Annual Review of Psychology, 51*(1), 445–479.

Matthews, K. A., Gallo, L. C., & Taylor, S. E. (2010). Are psychosocial factors mediators of socioeconomic status and health connections? In N. E. Adler & J. Stewart (Eds.), *Annals of the New York academy of sciences* (Vol. 1186, pp. 146–173). New York: Wiley.

Matthews, K. A., & Gallo, L. C. (2011). Psychological perspectives on pathways linking socioeconomic status and physical health. *Annual Review of Psychology, 62*, 501.

Maurer, I., & Ebers, M. (2006). Dynamics of social capital and their performance implications: Lessons from biotechnology start-ups. *Administrative Science Quarterly, 51*(2), 262–292.

McMullen, J. S., & Shepherd, D. A. (2006). Entrepreneurial action and the role of uncertainty in the theory of the entrepreneur. *Academy of Management Review, 31*(1), 132–152.

Menninger, K. (1963). *The vital balance: The life process in mental health and illness.* New York: Viking.

Miller-Johnson, S., Emery, R. E., Marvin, R. S., Clarke, W., Lovinger, R., & Martin, M. (1994). Parent-chld relationships and the management of insulin-dependent diabetes mellitus. *Journal of Consulting and Clinical Psychology, 62*(3), 603–610.

Molloy, G. J., McGee, H. M., O'Neill, D., & Conroy, R. M. (2010). Loneliness and emergency and planned hospitalizations in a community sample of older adults. *Journal of the American Geriatrics Society, 58*(8), 1538–1541.

Mor, V., McHorney, C., & Sherwood, S. (1986). Secondary morbidity among the recently bereaved. *The American Journal of Psychiatry, 143*, 158–163.

Nabkasorn, C., Miyai, N., Sootmongkol, A., Junprasert, S., Yamamoto, H., Arita, M., & Miyashita, K. (2006). Effects of physical exercise on depression, neuroendocrine stress hormones and physiological fitness in adolescent females with depressive symptoms. *The European Journal of Public Health, 16*(2), 179–184.

Nanda, R. (2008). Cost of external finance and selection into entrepreneurship. *Harvard Business School Entrepreneurial Management Working Paper.* Cambridge, MA: Harvard Business School.

Nemetz, P. L., & Cameron, A. (2006). Higher education out of control: Regaining strategic focus in an age of diminishing resources. *Academy of Management Learning & Education, 5*(1), 38–51.

Nicholson, N. (1984). A theory of work role transitions. *Administrative Science Quarterly, 29*(2), 172–191.

Nickerson, R. S. (1998). Confirmation bias: A ubiquitous phenomenon in many guises. *Review of General Psychology, 2*(2), 175–220.

Oh, C. H., & Oetzel, J. (2011). Multinationals' response to major disasters: How does subsidiary investment vary in response to the type of disaster and

the quality of country governance? *Strategic Management Journal, 32*(6), 658–681.
Parasuraman, S., & Simmers, C. A. (2001). Type of employment, work–family conflict and well-being: A comparative study. *Journal of Organizational Behavior, 22*(5), 551–568.
Parkes, C. M., & Weiss, R. S. (1983). *Recovery from bereavement.* New York: Basic Books.
Patzelt, H., & Shepherd, D. A. (2011). Negative emotions of an entrepreneurial career: Self-employment and regulatory coping behaviors. *Journal of Business Venturing, 26*(2), 226–238.
Patzelt, H., Shepherd, D. A., Deeds, D., & Bradley, S. W. (2008). Financial slack and venture managers' decisions to seek a new alliance. *Journal of Business Venturing, 23*(4), 465–481.
Peredo, A. M., & Chrisman, J. J. (2006). Toward a theory of community-based enterprise. *Academy of Management Review, 31*(2), 309–328.
Pfeffer, J. (1977). Effects of an MBA and socioeconomic origins on business school graduates' salaries. *Journal of Applied Psychology, 62*(6), 698–705.
Pickett, K. E., & Pearl, M. (2001). Multilevel analyses of neighbourhood socio-economic context and health outcomes: A critical review. *Journal of Epidemiology and Community Health, 55*(2), 111–122.
Poterba, J. M., Venti, S. F., & Wise, D. A. (2013). *Health, education, and the post-retirement evolution of household assets* (No. w18695). National Bureau of Economic Research.
Poterba, J. M., Venti, S. F., & Wise, D. A. (2010). *The asset cost of poor health* (No. w16389). National Bureau of Economic Research.
Prakash, R. S., Voss, M. W., Erickson, K. I., & Kramer, A. F. (2015). Physical activity and cognitive vitality. *Annual Review of Psychology, 66,* 769–797.
Pratt, M. G., Rockmann, K. W., & Kaufmann, J. B. (2006). Constructing professional identity: The role of work and identity learning cycles in the customization of identity among medical residents. *Academy of Management Journal, 49*(2), 235–262.
Putnam, R. D. (2001). *Bowling alone: The collapse and revival of American community.* New York: Simon and Schuster.
Quadrini, V. (2000). Entrepreneurship, saving, and social mobility. *Review of Economic Dynamics, 3*(1), 1–40.
Queenan, C. C., Angst, C. M., & Devaraj, S. (2011). Doctors' orders—If they're electronic, do they improve patient satisfaction? A complements/substitutes perspective. *Journal of Operations Management, 29*(7), 639–649.
Quick, J. D., Horn, R. S., & Quick, J. C. (1987). Health consequences of stress. *Journal of Organizational Behavior Management, 8*(2), 19–36.
Rahim, A. (1996). Stress, strain, and their moderators: An empirical comparison of entrepreneurs and managers. *Journal of Small Business Management, 34*(1), 46–58.

Rai, S. K. (2008). Indian entrepreneurs: An empirical investigation of entrepreneur's age and firm entry, type of ownership and risk behaviour. *Journal of Services Research, 8*(1), 213–228.

Rasmussen, H. N., Scheier, M. F., & Greenhouse, J. B. (2009). Optimism and physical health: A meta-analytic review. *Annals of Behavioral Medicine, 37*(3), 239–256.

Repetti, R. L., Taylor, S. E., & Seeman, T. E. (2002). Risky families: Family social environments and the mental and physical health of offspring. *Psychological Bulletin, 128*(2), 330–366.

Rizzo, J. R., House, R. J., & Lirtzman, S. I. (1970). Role conflict and ambiguity in complex organizations. *Administrative Science Quarterly, 15*(2), 150–163.

Rook, K. S. (1984). The negative side of social interaction: Impact on psychological well-being. *Journal of Personality and Social Psychology, 46*(5), 1097–1108.

Rosenkopf, L., & Nerkar, A. (2001). Beyond local search: Boundary-spanning, exploration, and impact in the optical disk industry. *Strategic Management Journal, 22*(4), 287–306.

Ryan, R. M., & Deci, E. L. (2000). Self-determination theory and the facilitation of intrinsic motivation, social development, and well-being. *American Psychologist, 55*, 68–78.

Salmon, P. (2001). Effects of physical exercise on anxiety, depression, and sensitivity to stress: A unifying theory. *Clinical Psychology Review, 21*(1), 33–61.

Sampson, R. J., Raudenbush, S. W., & Earls, F. (1997). Neighborhoods and violent crime: A multilevel study of collective efficacy. *Science, 277*(5328), 918–924.

Sarasvathy, S. D. (2001). Causation and effectuation: Toward a theoretical shift from economic inevitability to entrepreneurial contingency. *Academy of Management Review, 26*(2), 243–263.

Scase, R., & Goffee, R. (1987). *The real world of the small business owner.* London: Croom Helm.

Schindehutte, M., Morris, M., & Allen, J. (2006). Beyond achievement: Entrepreneurship as extreme experience. *Small Business Economics, 27*(4–5), 349–368.

Schneiderman, N., Ironson, G., & Siegel, S. D. (2005). Stress and health: Psychological, behavioral, and biological determinants. *Annual Review of Clinical Psychology, 1*, 607–628.

Seligman, M. E. (2011). *Learned optimism: How to change your mind and your life.* New York: Random House.

Seligman, M. E., Rashid, T., & Parks, A. C. (2006). Positive psychotherapy. *American Psychologist, 61*(8), 774–788.

Seligman, M. E., Steen, T. A., Park, N., & Peterson, C. (2005). Positive psychology progress: Empirical validation of interventions. *American Psychologist, 60*(5), 410–421.

Shah, S. K., & Tripsas, M. (2007). The accidental entrepreneur: The emergent and collective process of user entrepreneurship. *Strategic Entrepreneurship Journal, 1*(1–2), 123–140.

Shane, S., Locke, E. A., & Collins, C. J. (2003). Entrepreneurial motivation. *Human Resource Management Review, 13*(2), 257–279.

Shepherd, D. A. (2003). Learning from business failure: Propositions of grief recovery for the self-employed. *Academy of Management Review, 28*(2), 318–328.

Shepherd, D. A. (2009). Grief recovery from the loss of a family business: A multi- and meso-level theory. *Journal of Business Venturing, 24*(1), 81–97.

Shepherd, D. A., Douglas, E. J., & Fitzsimmons, J. R. (2008). MBA admission criteria and an entrepreneurial mind-set: Evidence from "Western" style MBAs in India and Thailand. *Academy of Management Learning & Education, 7*(2), 158–172.

Shepherd, D. A., Douglas, E. J., & Shanley, M. (2000). New venture survival: Ignorance, external shocks, and risk reduction strategies. *Journal of Business Venturing, 15*(5–6), 393–410.

Shepherd, D. A., & Patzelt, H. (2011). The new field of sustainable entrepreneurship: Studying entrepreneurial action linking "what is to be sustained" with "what is to be developed". *Entrepreneurship Theory and Practice, 35*(1), 137–163.

Shepherd, D. A., & Patzelt, H. (2015). Harsh evaluations of entrepreneurs who fail: The role of sexual orientation, use of environmentally friendly technologies, and observers' perspective taking. *Journal of Management Studies, 52*(2), 253–284.

Shepherd, D. A., Patzelt, H., & Wolfe, M. (2011). Moving forward from project failure: Negative emotions, affective commitment, and learning from the experience. *Academy of Management Journal, 54*(6), 1229–1259.

Shepherd, D. A., & Williams, T. A. (2014). Local venturing as compassion organizing in the aftermath of a natural disaster: The role of localness and community in reducing suffering. *Journal of Management Studies, 51*(6), 952–994.

Shepherd, D. A., & Williams, T. (2017). Hitting rock bottom after job loss: Bouncing back to create a new positive work identity. *Academy of Management Review*. doi:10.5465/amr.2015.0102.

Simmons, J. G. (2002). *Doctors and discoveries: Lives that created today's medicine*. Boston: Houghton Mifflin.

Smilor, R. W. (1997). Entrepreneurship: Reflections on a subversive activity. *Journal of Business Venturing, 12*(5), 341–346.

Spence, A. M. (1973). *Market signaling: Information transfer in hiring and related processes*. Cambridge, MA: Harvard University Press.

Sonstroem, R. J., & Morgan, W. P. (1989). Exercise and self-esteem: Rationale and model. *Medicine & Science in Sports & Exercise., 21*(3), 329–337.

Stanworth, M., & Curran, J. (1976). Growth and the small firm: An alternative view. *Journal of Management Studies, 13*(2), 95–110.

Staw, B. M., Sandelands, L. E., & Dutton, J. E. (1981). Threat-rigidity effects in organizational behavior: A multilevel analysis. *Administrative Science Quarterly, 26*(4), 501–524.

Sternthal, M., Jun, H., Earls, F., & Wright, R. J. (2010). Community violence and urban childhood asthma: A multilevel analysis. *European Respiratory Journal, 36*(6), 1400–1409.

Stevenson, H. H. (1983). *A perspective on entrepreneurship*. Cambridge, MA: Harvard Business School.

Stewart, W. F., Ricci, J. A., Chee, E., Morganstein, D., & Lipton, R. (2003). Lost productive time and cost due to common pain conditions in the US workforce. *The Journal of the American Medical Association, 290*(18), 2443–2454.

Stoner, C. R., Hartman, R. I., & Arora, R. (1990). Work-home role conflict in female owners of small businesses: An exploratory study. *Journal of Small Business Management, 28*(1), 30–38.

Sugisawa, H., Liang, J., & Liu, X. (1994). Social networks, social support, and mortality among older people in Japan. *Journal of Gerontology, 49*(1), S3–S13.

Sundquist, K., Theobald, H., Yang, M., Li, X., Johansson, S.-E., & Sundquist, J. (2006). Neighborhood violent crime and unemployment increase the risk of coronary heart disease: A multilevel study in an urban setting. *Social Science & Medicine, 62*(8), 2061–2071.

Sutcliffe, K. M., & Vogus, T. J. (2003). Organizing for resilience. In K. S. Cameron, J. E. Dutton, & R. E. Quinn (Eds.), *Positive organizational scholarship: Foundations of a new discipline* (pp. 94–110). San Francisco, CA: Berrett-Koehler.

Talukdar, D., & Lindsey, C. (2013). To buy or not to buy: Consumers' demand response patterns for healthy versus unhealthy food. *Journal of Marketing, 77*(2), 124–138.

Teoh, H. Y., & Foo, S. L. (1997). Moderating effects of tolerance for ambiguity and risktaking propensity on the role conflict-perceived performance relationship: Evidence from Singaporean entrepreneurs. *Journal of Business Venturing, 12*(1), 67–81.

Tetrick, L. E., Slack, K. J., Da Silva, N., & Sinclair, R. R. (2000). A comparison of the stress–strain process for business owners and nonowners: Differences in job demands, emotional exhaustion, satisfaction, and social support. *Journal of Occupational Health Psychology, 5*(4), 464–476.

Thompson, C. A., Kopelman, R. E., & Schriesheim, C. A. (1992). Putting all one's eggs in the same basket: A comparison of commitment and satisfaction among self-and organizationally employed men. *Journal of Applied Psychology, 77*(5), 738–743.

Thurston, R. C., & Kubzansky, L. D. (2009). Women, loneliness, and incident coronary heart disease. *Psychosomatic Medicine, 71*(8), 836–842.

Troxel, W. M., & Matthews, K. A. (2004). What are the costs of marital conflict and dissolution to children's physical health? *Clinical Child and Family Psychology Review, 7*(1), 29–57.

Tugade, M. M., Fredrickson, B. L., & Feldman Barrett, L. (2004). Psychological resilience and positive emotional granularity: Examining the benefits of positive emotions on coping and health. *Journal of Personality, 72*(6), 1161–1190.

Ucbasaran, D., Lockett, A., Wright, M., & Westhead, P. (2003). Entrepreneurial founder teams: Factors associated with member entry and exit. *Entrepreneurship Theory and Practice, 28*(2), 107–127.

Uchino, B. N. (2006). Social support and health: A review of physiological processes potentially underlying links to disease outcomes. *Journal of Behavioral Medicine, 29*(4), 377–387.

U.S. Census Bureau. (2002). Census 2000 summary file. Retrieved from http://www.factfinder.census.gov

U.S. Department of Health and Human Services. (2012). *Healthy people 2010*. Washington, DC: Office of Disease and Preventative Healthcare Promotion, US Dep. Health Human Services.

Vallerand, R. J., Blanchard, C., Mageau, G. A., Koestner, R., Ratelle, C., Léonard, M., et al. (2003). Les passions de l'ame: On obsessive and harmonious passion. *Journal of Personality and Social Psychology, 85*(4), 756–767.

Van der Sluis, J., Van Praag, M., & Vijverberg, W. (2008). Education and entrepreneurship selection and performance: A review of the empirical literature. *Journal of Economic Surveys, 22*(5), 795–841.

Vashdi, D., Bamberger, P., & Erez, M. (2012). Can surgical teams ever learn? Towards a theory of transitive team learning in action teams. *Academy of Management Journal*. Advance online publication.

Venkataraman, S. (2004). Regional transformation through technological entrepreneurship. *Journal of Business Venturing, 19*(1), 153–167.

von Hippel, E. (1988). *The sources of innovation*. New York: Oxford University Press.

Ware Jr., J. E., Brook, R. H., Davies, A. R., & Lohr, K. N. (1981). Choosing measures of health status for individuals in general populations. *American Journal of Public Health, 71*(6), 620–625.

Wasserman, N. (2008). The founder's dilemma. *Harvard Business Review, 86*(2), 102–109.

Weiss, K. B., Sullivan, S. D., & Lyttle, C. S. (2000). Trends in the cost of illness for asthma in the United States, 1985–1994. *Journal of Allergy and Clinical Immunology, 106*(3), 493–499.

Wennberg, K., Wiklund, J., DeTienne, D. R., & Cardon, M. S. (2010). Reconceptualizing entrepreneurial exit: Divergent exit routes and their drivers. *Journal of Business Venturing, 25*(4), 361–375.

World Health Organization. (2000). The world health report 2000: Health systems: Improving performance. WHO.

Williams, A. (1984). Stress and the entrepreneur role. *International Small Business Journal, 3*, 11–25.

Williams, T. A., & Shepherd, D. A. (2016). Victim entrepreneurs doing well by doing good: Venture creation and well-being in the aftermath of a resource shock. *Journal of Business Venturing, 31*(4), 365–387.

Williams, T., & Shepherd, D. (2017). Building resilience or providing sustenance: Different paths of emergent ventures in the aftermath of the haiti earthquake. *Academy of Management Journal*. Forthcoming.

Wright, R. J., Mitchell, H., Visness, C. M., Cohen, S., Stout, J., Evans, R., & Gold, D. R. (2004). Community violence and asthma morbidity: The inner-city asthma study. *American Journal of Public Health, 94*(4), 625–632.

Wu, B. (2013). Opportunity costs, industry dynamics, and corporate diversification: Evidence from the cardiovascular medical device industry, 1976–2004. *Strategic Management Journal, 34*(11), 1265–1287.

Zimmerman, M. A., & Zeitz, G. J. (2002). Beyond survival: Achieving new venture growth by building legitimacy. *Academy of Management Review, 27*(3), 414–431.

Zott, C., & Huy, Q. N. (2007). How entrepreneurs use symbolic management to acquire resources. *Administrative Science Quarterly, 52*(1), 70–105.

**Open Access** This chapter is distributed under the terms of the Creative Commons Attribution 4.0 International License (http://creativecommons.org/licenses/by/4.0/), which permits use, duplication, adaptation, distribution and reproduction in any medium or format, as long as you give appropriate credit to the original author(s) and the source, provide a link to the Creative Commons license and indicate if changes were made.

The images or other third party material in this chapter are included in the work's Creative Commons license, unless indicated otherwise in the credit line; if such material is not included in the work's Creative Commons license and the respective action is not permitted by statutory regulation, users will need to obtain permission from the license holder to duplicate, adapt or reproduce the material.

CHAPTER 8

# Researching Entrepreneurial Decision Making

## INTRODUCTION

Entrepreneurship scholars have dedicated substantial time to exploring how and why entrepreneurs think differently from both non-entrepreneurs (e.g., Busenitz & Barney, 1997; Mitchell, 1994; Mitchell et al., 2002) and other entrepreneurs (e.g., Baron, 2004, 2006; Mitchell et al., 2007). Studies have also emphasized that the entrepreneurial context is characterized by high uncertainty, ambiguity, time pressure, emotional intensity, and high risk, which can have substantial impact on how entrepreneurs evaluate specific situations and make decisions (e.g., Baron, 2008; Busenitz & Barney, 1997; Mullins & Forlani, 2005). This literature on entrepreneurial decision making is important because the strategic decisions firm leaders make have a major impact on the firm's future direction and performance (Carpenter, Geletkanycz, & Sanders, 2004; Hambrick & Mason, 1984).

However, despite the theoretical progress in understanding how entrepreneurs make different types of decisions and decisions in different contexts, including, for example, the decision to become an entrepreneur (Bates, 1995; Douglas & Shepherd, 2000; Robinson & Sexton, 1994), opportunity exploitation decisions (e.g., Choi & Shepherd, 2004; Shepherd, Patzelt, & Baron, 2013), alliance decisions (Patzelt, Shepherd, Deeds, & Bradley, 2008), internationalization decisions (e.g., Domurath & Patzelt,

---

This chapter is based on Shepherd (2011) and Shepherd, Williams, and Patzelt (2015).

2016; Williams & Grégoire, 2014), and exit decisions for both entrepreneurial ventures (e.g., DeTienne, 2010; Shepherd, Wiklund, & Haynie, 2009; Wennberg & DeTienne, 2014; Wennberg, Wiklund, DeTienne, & Cardon, 2010) and projects (e.g., Behrens & Patzelt, 2017; Shepherd & Cardon, 2009; Shepherd, Patzelt, Williams, & Warnecke, 2014; Shepherd, Patzelt, & Wolfe, 2011), the existing literature is far from fully capturing the complexity and dynamics of entrepreneurial decisions (Shepherd, Williams, & Patzelt, 2015). In this chapter, our aim is to make several contributions to advance an agenda for research on entrepreneurial decision making.

First, entrepreneurial decision-making research has explored how individual experiences (e.g., entrepreneurial experience [Baron & Ensley, 2006; Ucbasaran et al., 2009] and failure experience [Behrens & Patzelt, 2017]) and characteristics (e.g., entrepreneurial self-efficacy [Shepherd et al., 2013] and emotions [Klaukien, Shepherd, & Patzelt, 2013; Mitchell & Shepherd, 2010]) impact entrepreneurs' decision policies. By emphasizing the dynamic nature of entrepreneurial contexts and entrepreneurial decision making, we hope to open up new research avenues that acknowledge how the experiences and characteristics of individuals as well as their ventures and external contexts (e.g., industries, technologies) change over time, which likely has a substantial impact on how entrepreneurs make decisions. Such a dynamic perspective addresses the call for more research on the inter-relationship between the entrepreneur and the (changing) social context in the development of entrepreneurial opportunities and ventures (see Chap. 2 and Shepherd, 2015).

Second, research on decision making in entrepreneurship has often focused on decision cues based on established theoretical concepts (e.g., characteristics of venture resources [Mitchell & Shepherd, 2010] or types of environmental uncertainty [McKelvie et al., 2010]) and known players of the entrepreneurial process (e.g., entrepreneurs, venture capitalists, and bankers). However, with quickly changing technologies in a global world, new phenomena not well captured by existing theoretical concepts (e.g., crowdfunding) and new players (e.g., crowd investors) play an increasingly important role in entrepreneurship. We discuss several ways future studies can advance entrepreneurship theory by exploring the impact of new phenomena on entrepreneurial decision making.

Finally, a considerable part of decision-making research in entrepreneurship has been based on experimental methodology, specifically conjoint analysis (Shepherd & Zacharakis, 1997; for a review, see Lohrke, Holloway, & Woolley, 2010), which creates hierarchically nested data—

namely, multiple decisions made by the same individual. Although the nested nature in these studies has been exploited in existing research to some extent, we suggest a number of novel ways that multi-level analyses can further enhance our understanding of entrepreneurial decision making.

In the next section, we begin by outlining the types of entrepreneurial decisions and then investigate the role of context in the entrepreneurial decision-making process.

## Types of Entrepreneurial Decisions

### Opportunity-Assessment Decisions

Central to entrepreneurship is the identification and pursuit of opportunities (Shane & Venkataraman, 2000; a point also made throughout this book, at least in terms of "potential" opportunities). Before an individual pursues or acts upon a potential opportunity, he or she must assess it (Bakker & Shepherd, 2017; McMullen & Shepherd, 2006). There are numerous research opportunities to build on our current knowledge of entrepreneurial thinking to make important contributions to the field.

**The impact of changes in the individual on entrepreneurial decision making.** Although prior research has provided insights into the ways entrepreneurs assess opportunities and make opportunity-related decisions (Choi & Shepherd, 2004; Haynie, Shepherd, & McMullen, 2009; Mitchell & Shepherd, 2010; Westhead, Ucbasaran, Wright, & Binks, 2005), thus far, researchers have tended to take a static view, largely disregarding the possibility that entrepreneurs' opportunity-related decision policies could vary over time. Studies have shown, for instance, novice entrepreneurs' opportunity-related assessments and decisions are different than those of more experienced entrepreneurs (Baron & Ensley, 2006; Westhead et al., 2005). Nevertheless, we know little about *how* changes in the individual over time influence the nature of the decisions they make. Specifically, by acting entrepreneurially, an individual may increase his or her knowledge, skills, and experience, which may in turn impact entrepreneurial self-efficacy. How do these changes in the decision maker influence assessments of subsequent potential opportunities vis-à-vis the previous (or first) opportunity assessment? Indeed, research on effectuation (Sarasvathy, 2001) proposes that the development and pursuit of a potential opportunity depend on the entrepreneur's assessment of "who

I am," "what I know," and "whom I know." However, entrepreneurial action itself could lead to a change in one, two, or all of these inputs such that not only does the environment, venture, and opportunity change but so too does the individual making the assessments and taking the actions. This notion suggests an even more dynamic decision-making process than has been investigated to date. Research that explores the type, amount, and rate of change in decision-making inputs and the corresponding change in the type, amount, and rate of change in decision policies (and their effects) is likely to provide important new insights into our understanding of opportunity assessment.

**The role of non-financial decision criteria.** The majority of entrepreneurship studies have focused on the financial aspects of entrepreneurs' assessments of potential opportunities, including whether a potential opportunity is likely to provide the entrepreneur's firm a sustainable competitive advantage (Choi & Shepherd, 2004; Haynie et al., 2009). Research on social and environmental entrepreneurship, however, has shown that non-economic motivations drive many entrepreneurs, yet research has not adequately investigated whether and how economic and non-economic (e.g., social and environmental) factors influence opportunity-related decisions and whether there are tradeoffs between the two. For instance, if an opportunity's positive social or environmental effect is large, will the entrepreneur being more willing to accept lower financial return (or greater uncertainty, potential downside loss, and/or personal toll)? Perhaps there are other factors that lower the performance threshold for starting a sustainable development venture (consistent with the notion of a lower performance threshold that encourages persistence [Gimeno, Folta, Cooper, & Woo, 1997]). Indeed, in Chap. 5, we described how knowledge of the natural or communal environment likely increases the identification of potential sustainable development opportunities, but perhaps this knowledge (and/or the act of identifying an opportunity) lowers the financial desirability necessary for opportunity exploitation. This simple illustration highlights the need for future research to gain a deep understanding of the inter-relationship between the financial and non-financial inputs to opportunity assessments and the ways these different decision policies manifest themselves in financial and non-financial development outcomes.

**User innovation and entrepreneurial action.** Some research has revealed that users (i.e., entrepreneurs who commercialize a product and are also users of that product) are a significant source of entrepreneurship.

However, more work is needed on this topic. How do these *user entrepreneurs* (Shah & Tripsas, 2007) identify, assess, and decide to act on an opportunity stemming from a product they invented for their own personal use? What effect does the user entrepreneur's human and social capital (e.g., knowledge of and participation in user communities, knowledge of and interaction with markets) have in this process? At what point do users choose to share their idea with others and then decide to obtain economic income from their idea (alone or with others from the user community), and what prompts them to take such action? The answers to these questions likely depend on the characteristics of the specific opportunity and the user community. For instance, perhaps users who invented a product to solve their own medical problem are more likely to share their invention with others compared to users who invented a product with a lower social impact. Do those who invent medical products have different opportunity decision policies than others? For example, perhaps such individuals focus less on their own economic gains and more on the potential benefits for others who suffer more.

## *Entrepreneurial Career Decisions*

Entrepreneurship scholars have long explored people's decision to become self-employed (Bates, 1995; Douglas & Shepherd, 2000; Robinson & Sexton, 1994) and to create a new organization (Gartner, 1985; Katz & Gartner, 1988; Shaver & Scott, 1991). Future research can build on this body of literature to make important contributions to the field.

**How entrepreneurial action impacts individual attributes.** Although research has increased our understanding of how an individual's attributes (e.g., attitudes [Douglas & Shepherd, 2002], aspirations [Herron & Sapienza, 1992], and human capital [Davidsson and Honig]) explain his or her decision to become an entrepreneur, there is considerably less research on how the decision to become an entrepreneur impacts the individual (in terms of the same types of attributes). Perhaps acting entrepreneurially "clarifies" the individual's perception of him- or herself. Alternatively, entrepreneurial action may lead to learning something new about oneself, thus increasing self-knowledge (see Cardon, Wincent, Shigh, & Drnovsek, 2009; Wilson, Marlino, & Kickul, 2004), which may inform subsequent decisions, including, perhaps, exiting an entrepreneurial career, "doubling down" on the current venture's course of action, or refining (or substantially changing) the nature of the opportunity underlying the venture.

How is self-knowledge built, and what impact does its changes have on subsequent entrepreneurial decisions? Importantly, learning that enhances individuals' self-knowledge may lead to the conclusion that an entrepreneurial career is not for them. This could have implications for research on entrepreneurship education. Specifically, rather than aspiring to increase students' entrepreneurial knowledge and then motivating them to pursue an entrepreneurial career, as educators, we may need to focus on educational tools that build self-knowledge in the entrepreneurial context that informs and motivates career decisions, which may be careers that are not entrepreneurial. Perhaps ironically, for some students, an entrepreneurship course that builds self-knowledge such that they are deterred from pursuing an entrepreneurial career could be considered successful. We need more research on this topic before we can make such determinations.

**Entrepreneurial careers as a series of steps.** Studies of entrepreneurial careers often have an implicit assumption that an entrepreneurial career is a destination for some individuals—an optimal outcome (e.g., Douglas & Shepherd, 2000; Eisenhauer, 1995; Kolvereid & Isaksen, 2006). Instead of seeing self-employment as a one-time decision, scholars should investigate this career option in the context of *a series of career decisions*. Viewing self-employment as a series of career decisions, we begin to gain some insight into re-entry (e.g., Carroll & Mosakowski, 1987), including more knowledge on serial entrepreneurs (Westhead & Wright, 1998; Westhead et al., 2005) and multiple exits. How is the "one-time" decision perspective different from the focal decision in the context of thinking about careers as a series of decisions? Such research is critical, especially as we consider the changes in people over their life course (Levesque & Minniti, 2006; Levesque, Shepherd, & Douglas, 2002) and especially given the aging population (Lévesque & Minniti, 2011). How are the decision policies for a graduating student different from a mid-career employee or someone nearing retirement? It seems that we know quite a lot about the first, a little bit about the second, and not much about the third. We believe (hope) that this will soon be rectified.

**Progression along the steps of an entrepreneurial career.** Related to the previous point, there is a considerable literature about how competences (Davidsson & Honig, 2003), beliefs (Shaver & Scott, 1991), and motivations (Herron & Sapienza, 1992) influence the decision to start of a new venture, but in many ways, the creation of a new venture involves a series of activities (e.g., Lichtenstein, Dooley, & Lumpkin, 2006) that themselves require a series of decisions (perhaps as a sequence of nested decisions). What are these decision points, and how are these decisions made? Consistent with the notion that individuals can change as a result of acting entrepreneurially, the decision-making process of new venture emergence is likely highly dynamic. Although quite a challenge, researchers can make an important contribution to the field by exploring how progression through the nascent steps toward venture emergence presents choices among alternatives in the context of a changing environment that is internal in terms of the entrepreneurs' self-knowledge and the extent of venture emergence and external in terms of the market and industry. Some individuals, for instance, remain nascent entrepreneurs for long periods of time, engaging in numerous preparations to start their venture but eventually choosing not to. How and why do various motivations related to the venture-creation decision change throughout the nascent phase? As nascent entrepreneurs learn increasingly more about the different tasks and demands that go along with starting and running a venture, their views of their own skills and abilities are likely to change. In turn, these changes may affect their ultimate desire to continue or cease their venture. As individuals decide to start a new venture, does their confidence in their ability to complete some tasks (e.g., find customers) make up for their lack of confidence in their ability to complete other tasks (e.g., find investors)? Since motivation focuses attention on specific elements of available information (Ocasio, 1997; Shepherd, McMullen, & Ocasio, 2016), how do the various motivations (e.g., economic, prosocial, autonomy, and intrinsic) of nascent entrepreneurs influence the attention they pay to and the way they interpret information in venture-creation decisions? Moreover, failure occurs often in entrepreneurial undertakings and has been shown to result in both sensemaking and negative emotions (Shepherd, 2003; Shepherd et al., 2011), both of which affect motivation and decision making. How do previous failures alter entrepreneurs' perceptions of themselves and the environment and their use of decision-making tools when deciding to start a new venture?

**Deciding to exit an entrepreneurial venture.** Recent research has begun to complement the substantial literature on entry by exploring the decision to exit a business (DeTienne, 2010; Shepherd et al., 2009; Wennberg & DeTienne, 2014; Wennberg et al., 2010) and the decision to exit a project (Shepherd & Cardon, 2009; Shepherd et al., 2011, 2014). We have already discussed future research opportunities related to exit in terms of advancing knowledge on stage gates (Chap. 4) and the emotional antecedents and consequences of the termination of a project or a firm

(Chap. 3). Here, we focus on an entrepreneur's decision to voluntarily exit his or her business and the process of assessing and choosing between sources of exit. For instance, what decision-making process does the entrepreneur go through when deciding whether to exit a successful venture? It is likely that venture success and other venture traits (e.g., number of employees, benefits created for other stakeholders, links to personal identity, and presence of a family member successor) impact the exit mode. Furthermore, entrepreneurs likely have diverse reasons for deciding to exit as well as different career/lifestyle possibilities after exit, both of which could influence their likelihood of exit, their timing for doing so, and/or their exit mode. Researchers could also explore the emotional outcomes (i.e., type and intensity of emotions) associated with the various modes of entrepreneurial exit. What emotional outcomes come from a successful exit? Does the entrepreneur experience positive emotions (which he or she likely assumes will occur) and/or negative emotions from ending a (successful) business? Do emotional reactions after exit vary in intensity, and if so, does such variance effect later outcomes (e.g., decisions to start another venture, and enter corporate life)? Perhaps feelings of grief are more intense for those who exit successful businesses as opposed to failing businesses or for those who had more control over when to exit than those with less control. We hope researchers further investigate these important relationships.

### *Decisions on Funding Entrepreneurial Actions*

Although entrepreneurship has a long tradition of investigating the decision making of venture capitalists (Fried & Hisrich, 1994; Shepherd, 1999; Zacharakis & Shepherd, 2001) and to a lesser extent the decision making of business angels (Maula, Autio, & Arenius, 2005; Maxwell, Jeffrey, & Leveque, 2011), recent research on funding entrepreneurial endeavors has begun to focus on crowdfunding (e.g., Belleflamme, Lambert, & Schwienbacher, 2014; Mollick, 2014). According to Mollick (2014, p. 1), "crowdfunding allows founders of for-profit, artistic, and cultural ventures to fund their efforts by drawing on relatively small contributions from a relatively large number of individuals using the internet, without standard financial intermediaries." Although crowdfunding research could be a new fad, we doubt it—we think it has "legs." We believe that the phenomenon of crowdfunding itself will rapidly change over the next few years, but future research that moves beyond descriptive statements of crowdfunding is likely to still make a contribution that has longevity by deeply theorizing on the topic.

**Crowdfunding as a source of entrepreneurial capital.** Researchers can add to our understanding of entrepreneurial decision making by exploring entrepreneurs' consideration of crowdfunding as a possible capital source. When do individuals prefer crowdfunding over more customary equity (or even debt) funding sources? While it seems likely that entrepreneurs who are younger, more computer literate, and more connected will find crowdfunding attractive, the nature of entrepreneurs' networks is also likely to be an important factor in funding decisions. More specifically, entrepreneurs who have larger virtual networks through their social media presence are better able to evaluate the crowd needed for funding and are more likely to take on the risks inherent in this funding source compared to those with weaker virtual networks or those with stronger "traditional" networks. In addition, researchers can investigate how obtaining crowdfunding influences later entrepreneurial decision making. For instance, completing a successful crowdfunding campaign may affect the entrepreneur's future funding decisions, including how much money can be raised and how quickly, which could be biased by the entrepreneur's positive but relatively limited prior experience. Prior crowdfunding success may also influence the entrepreneur's perceptions of the appeal of starting a new venture and decisions regarding what type of venture to pursue based on his or her knowledge of the crowd's interests. In turn, these choices could impact the individual's decision to become a portfolio or serial entrepreneur. On the one hand, the speed of crowdfunding, for instance, may foster a faster type of serial entrepreneurship or alter the scope and configuration of individuals' entrepreneurial business portfolios. On the other hand, does unsuccessful crowdfunding experience influence entrepreneurial decision making? In this context, the entrepreneur may choose to focus on traditional funding sources or to use negative input from the crowd to inform his or her decision to end the venture or to reconfigure the potential opportunity. Further still, certain conventional considerations, including the amount of, timing of, and control "given away" through fundraising, are likely to have different effects for crowdfunding. However, not all the changes occur on the entrepreneur's side—how does the crowd change as a result of different campaigns? This is an exciting new area with many opportunities for future research.

**Bootstrapping entrepreneurial ventures.** Given that the entrepreneurship literature has acknowledged the importance of resourcefulness (e.g., Baker & Nelson, 2005; Powell & Baker, 2015; Shepherd & Williams, 2014), it is somewhat surprising that so little research has investigated the role of bootstrapping in new and otherwise entrepreneurial firms. Entrepreneurs use bootstrapping, which refers to "finding creative ways to avoid the need for external financing through reducing overall cost of operation, improving cash flow, or using financial sources internal to the company" (Ebben & Johnson, 2006, p. 851), as another funding source. However, research on the decision making associated with tapping into bootstrapping as a source of resources is scarce (for exceptions, see Harrison, Mason, & Girling, 2004; Jonsson & Lindbergh, 2013). Future studies can investigate why and how entrepreneurs choose to pursue bootstrapping instead of external funding sources as well as what decision making is involved in lessening operation costs, enhancing cash flow, and generating other internal funding sources. We believe that accounting scholars are particularly well qualified to address these questions and, more importantly, to begin to ask additional questions about entrepreneurial firms' internal funding.

**The role of business plans in funding entrepreneurial ventures.** A discussion of funding decisions would be incomplete without also considering the business plan. Although the pros and cons of strategic planning have been well litigated (Brinckmann, Grichnik, & Kapsa, 2010; Chwolka & Raith, 2012; Karlsson & Honig, 2009) and somewhat settled, the discussion of the benefits of business plans and business planning still generates a lot of heat. This indicates that people hold opposing views and hold those views strongly. Although it is difficult to challenge people's strongly held views, we suspect that future research will be able to reconcile these previously contrasting perspectives. For example, researchers can build on the idea that planning is an important activity regardless of whether the venture has a formal business plan. However, some planning processes may be better than others. For instance, planning that is more comprehensive may lead to more in-depth thinking and more educated decisions. However, such intense planning could also result in the planning fallacy or drawn-out decision making, in which case windows of opportunity may close or entrepreneurs may be discouraged from changing their decision making. These latter possibilities are likely to be especially harmful in environments that are highly dynamic, such as the micro-computer industry in the early 1990s and social media over the last decade.

**Balancing financial and social missions.** Recent research has begun to explore the role of hybrid organizations—those "organizations that combine institutional logics in unprecedented ways" (Battilana & Dorado, 2010, p. 1419; see also Battilana & Lee, 2014)—particularly those pursuing both an economic and social mission. For instance, research has frequently stressed the need for socially motivated entrepreneurs to offset their venture's financial needs with their desire to help others. However, we know less about how these entrepreneurs balance financial and social concerns in the decision-making process (e.g., for decisions on what market to enter, which products or services to develop, which employees to bring onboard). Additionally, it is likely that organizational context influences entrepreneurs' decisions to "do good." For example, what effect do firms' economic performance, organizational members' culture and norms, and organizational structure have on entrepreneurs' decisions to do good? Further, how does venture environment impact entrepreneurs' decisions to do good? It could be that entrepreneurs in hostile and dynamic environments feel greater managerial burden and experience less resource slack and are therefore less likely to engage in social entrepreneurship than those in benign or stable environments. Lastly, do these effects vary over time (e.g., after the entrepreneur gains more venture or industry experience or when the venture becomes older), and if so, how do they change? We believe that theories and existing research on prosocial motivation (Grant, 2007; Grant & Mayer, 2009) and values disengagement (Bandura, 1999; Shepherd et al., 2013) can contribute to this research stream.

## Biases and Heuristics in Entrepreneurial Decision Making

The literature clearly indicates that entrepreneurs, as all people, have biased decision making (Busenitz & Barney, 1997; e.g., Hayward, Shepherd, & Griffin, 2006; Simon, Houghton, & Aquino, 2000), especially under conditions consistent with the entrepreneurial context (Baron, 1998). This body of knowledge becomes particularly useful if future research further investigates when these biases are beneficial and when they are particularly detrimental. We normally refer to the positive side of mental shortcuts (i.e., those that also lead to biases) as heuristics. Heuristics are "efficient cognitive processes, conscious or unconscious, that ignore part of the information" (Gigerenzer & Gaissmaier, 2011, p. 451). It is important that future research details the type (based on content) of entrepreneurs' heuristics; the way in which they are formed, updated, and triggered; and the benefits arising from their use. For instance, researchers can examine the ways heuristics impact decision-making speed and the circumstances under which speed is vital (perhaps even more so than accuracy). If future research is able to uncover benefits arising from the use of heuristics, we can be less concerned about biases and concentrate more on when to utilize heuristics and how individuals can learn, develop, alter, and communicate heuristics. Moreover, future research could also explore the benefits resulting from biases while also recognizing their costs. After business failure, for example, an individual's over-confidence may have ego-protective effects and may foster initial sensemaking efforts and emotional recovery, all of which could outweigh the costs of being over-confident.

In terms of eliminating bias or otherwise reducing its negative effects, future research can begin by exploring heterogeneity across individuals. Why are some individuals less susceptible to biases than others? Perhaps there is something about an entrepreneur's experiences that makes him or her less susceptible to a particular bias. For instance, recent experience with a project failure may reduce over-confidence with other venture-related decisions. It could be that the entrepreneur (with less bias) engages metacognition when facing a novel environment, which improves his or her adaptation to a dynamic environment. Perhaps those who can withhold their expectations of a situation or can take another's perspective of the situation are less likely to be biased. The nature of the context is also likely to make the focal individual more or less biased. How can entrepreneurs recognize and perhaps adjust their context or thinking to diminish their biases? Decision aids may serve as an important tool. We realize that given the nature of the entrepreneurial task, there is considerable difficulty in creating such decision aids, but the difficulty is likely more than offset by the benefits from somewhat de-biasing specific decisions. For example, educators could develop training on the circumstances under which individuals are more vulnerable to a bias; on the creation and use of decision aids; on team participation in the decision-making process (however, we acknowledge that the team environment can create different biases); and/or on ways to capture, interpret, and communicate decision input.

Above, we explored the content of research opportunities to advance the field of entrepreneurship. We know turn to how this can be done in the hope that it might help scholars methodologically open up new conceptual domains. The next section proceeds as follows: First, using findings from multi-level research on decisions, we explain how individuals make choices while completing an entrepreneurial task (i.e., weighting specific criteria of a decision or evaluation). Second, we investigate other potential paths for cross-level research that explains variation in people's decision policies resulting from individual differences. Third, in line with the conceptualization of interactions across three levels of analysis, we explore potential research avenues that could connect the levels of the decision, the individual, and the context in which they are situated. Finally, we examine whether and how various situational contexts explain within-individual (i.e., intra-individual) variation in decision policies.

## Entrepreneurs' Decision Policies

### Entrepreneurs' Common Decision Policy

In this section, our goal is to build on multi-level decision-making research in the entrepreneurial context to suggest future contributions to this research stream. The majority of studies in this research stream have used conjoint analysis, which involves participants' evaluating a series of profiles and making judgments in order to capture their decision processes and decompose them into their underlying structure (Shepherd & Zacharakis, 1997). Metric conjoint analysis and policy capturing are the most common forms of conjoint analysis (for a review of the types of conjoint analysis, see Priem & Harrison, 1994).[1] By design, conjoint analysis necessitates that each respondent within a sample make a series of decisions. As such, subsequent data analysis must consider that these decisions are not independent of one another across the entire sample. Mitchell and Shepherd (2010), for instance, explored 1936 decisions about hypothetical entrepreneurial opportunities made by 121 high-tech firm executives (each executive made 16 decisions).

Random coefficient modeling (e.g., hierarchical linear modeling software package) enables researchers to empirically determine which criteria participants use most often in the decisions they make when completing entrepreneurial tasks. That is, by accounting for variance between respondents, researchers can develop and test a decision policy for the entire sample (i.e., based on the commonality among the decision policies of all the individuals in the sample). For instance, Choi and Shepherd (2004) studied entrepreneurs with ventures within incubators, finding that entrepreneurs are more likely to act upon opportunities when they feel there is more information about customer demand, the required technology is developed enough, and there is strong managerial capabilities and stakeholder support. Further, they revealed that these positive relationships are stronger when the new product's anticipated lead time is longer. Numerous opportunities exist for researchers to explore common decision policies among individuals in the entrepreneurial context. Studies in this area could explore the decision policies entrepreneurs use during various nascent activities that eventually lead to firm emergence, the onboarding of key employees, the selection of venture capitalists and other important stakeholders, the identification of early adopters, and the development of reputation-building strategies. Research could also expand the corporate entrepreneurship and organization literatures to gain deeper insights into internal entrepreneurs' decision policies. For instance, researchers could theorize on and empirically test how organizational members' evaluations of the corporate environment inform their decisions regarding the level of commitment they will dedicate to entrepreneurial initiatives, how team members evaluate product champions and exit champions, and how product champions judge mentors within the organization (and vice versa).

While there is a strong body of knowledge on venture capitalists' decision making (e.g., Muzyka, Birley, & Leleux, 1996; Shepherd, 1999; Zacharakis & Meyer, 2000), additional entrepreneurial research opportunities exist to explore the decision making of other individuals immersed in or influenced by the entrepreneurial process. For instance, how do managers evaluate their alliances' entrepreneurial actions, how do employees evaluate the challenges stemming from rapid firm growth, and how do entrepreneurs' spouses feel about their partner's work-life balance? These questions represent the most basic form of multi-level research—namely, controlling for one level (i.e., individual differences) while exploring a different level (i.e., the decision). However, we are likely to gain a deeper understanding of entrepreneurial phenomena by studying the various decisions that serve as inputs to or outputs of the entrepreneurial process and help explain heterogeneity across groups of people.

### *Individual Differences in Entrepreneurs' Decision Policies*

While the decision policies among individuals in a particular sample are likely to have similarities, variance is also likely to exist. In other words, there is likely variance in the weights individuals assign to certain criteria when making choices in an entrepreneurial task. Researchers have begun to explore and theorize on these individual differences to delineate variance in people's decision policies. DeTienne, Shepherd, and De Castro (2008), for instance, built on escalation of commitment theory and the literature on motivation to explain variance in the decision policies of entrepreneurs who persist in poorly performing ventures. Their theoretical model first hypothesized a common decision policy and then hypothesized the moderating role of an individual's extrinsic motivation on that decision policy. The authors revealed that extrinsic motivation has a moderating effect on the negative relationships between dynamism and persistence, complexity and persistence, and personal opportunities and persistence. That is, entrepreneurs with high extrinsic motivation weight these criteria less when making venture-persistence decisions compared to those with low extrinsic motivation. The study also showed that extrinsic motivation has a moderating effect on the positive relationship between personal sunk costs and persistence. In other words, entrepreneurs with high extrinsic motivation weight this particular criterion (i.e., the amount of sunk costs) more when making venture-persistence decisions compared to those with low extrinsic motivation.

The theoretical and empirical exploration of individual variance in decision policies opens up some interesting pathways for future research.

**Building on existing studies of common decision policies from a new theoretical perspective.** Researchers could focus theory, hypotheses, and analyses to explain variance in decision policies across individuals using results from existing conjoint studies capturing individuals' decision policies during entrepreneurial tasks. This approach is advantageous because the initial conjoint studies have already theoretically and empirically established the importance of the decision policies, thus enabling subsequent research to dig deeper into the decision by exploring why certain individuals (and not others) are likely to weight specific criteria more or less heavily. For example, the following moderators could aid in explaining variance in individuals' decision policies to act upon an opportunity: (1) positions toward the various errors stemming from decision making in highly uncertain environments (e.g., informed by regret theory [Zeelenberg, 1999] and/or norm theory [Zeelenberg, Van Dijk, Van Den Bos, & Pieters, 2002]); (2) the level of positive affect, negative affect, and a combination of both (e.g., informed by the psychology literature related to emotion and cognition [Izard, 2009]); (3) the intrinsic motivation to take action (e.g., informed by self-determination theory [Deci & Ryan, 2000; Ryan & Deci, 2000]); (4) the level of previous knowledge (e.g., informed by the literatures on Austrian economics [Shane, 2000], opportunity identification [Baron & Ensley, 2006; Grégoire, Barr, & Shepherd,

2010], or entrepreneurial action [McMullen & Shepherd, 2006]); (5) perceptions of how the world operates, the nature of people, and the nature of oneself (e.g., informed by the literatures on values [Schwartz, 1994; for an example, see Holland & Shepherd, 2013], resilience [Bonanno, 2004; Sutcliffe & Vogus, 2003], and identity [Brewer, 1991; Tajfel & Turner, 1979]); and (6) links to the business and social communities (e.g., informed by literatures on social networks [Granovetter, 1995] and social capital [Walker, Kogut, & Shan, 1997]). Furthermore, future research could extend entrepreneurship research on the influence of gender (Brush, Carter, Gatewood, Greene, & Hart, 2006) to explore whether and how gender explains variation in individuals' decision policies.

**Investigating moderators by theoretically sampling groups.** For instance, Zacharakis, McMullen, and Shepherd (2007) proposed that institutional differences would result in variation in venture capitalists' evaluations of entrepreneurial ventures. The authors analyzed 119 venture capitalists' decision policies across three countries representing unique economic institutions: the USA, which represents a mature market economy; South Korea, which represents an emerging economy; and China, which represents a transitional economy. The study revealed that venture capitalists in rules-based market economies depend on market information more heavily than those in emerging economies and that venture capitalists in China weight human capital factors more heavily than their US or Korean counterparts. Differences in decision policies are also likely to occur between, for example, entrepreneurs and venture capitalists; between entrepreneurs from the USA and those from China, India, and Sweden; and between entrepreneurs from high-tech companies and those from low-tech companies as well as across stakeholder groups.

**Building on individual difference constructs to explore variation in decisions.** For instances, researchers have shown that extrinsic motivation explains variation in entrepreneurs' decisions to persist with poorly performing firms (DeTienne et al., 2008), that human capital can explain variation in decisions regarding the allocation of small business loans (Bruns, Holland, Shepherd, & Wiklund, 2008), and that fear of failure can explain variation in individuals' opportunity-assessment policies (Mitchell & Shepherd, 2010). It could be that extrinsic motivation, human capital, and fear of failure are all individual difference constructs that serve as important moderators (depending on theory) for other decisions within the entrepreneurial process (e.g., those outlined throughout this chapter). Again, using recognized decision-policy moderators could enable researchers to accrue knowledge across the numerous decisions in the entrepreneurial process. For instance, studies independently exploring human capital's moderating effect on the decision to pursue an opportunity, on nascent activities aimed at starting a venture, on firm-growth strategies, and on the termination of a poorly performing firm are likely to contribute to our understanding of the role human capital plays in the different tasks of the entrepreneurial process.

Finally, researchers have the opportunity to contribute to this line of research by combining the above ideas—that is, by investigating decisions for entrepreneurial tasks that have not been explored yet and to explain variation in those decision policies with moderators that have not been explored yet.

### *Decisions of Individual Entrepreneurs Within Contexts*

In the previous section, we outlined a multi- and cross-level model of individual differences to explain variance in decisions. However, individuals are also likely to be embedded in particular contexts, (e.g., entrepreneurs embedded in different countries, such as the USA, China, India, and Sweden). Additionally, there are likely to be individual differences within each group that help explain variance in decisions (e.g., entrepreneurial experience). Theorizing about entrepreneurial tasks at three levels—for instance, decisions (Level 1), individual experience (Level 2), and country (Level 3)—leads to fascinating research questions. Continuing with the previous example, for instance, research could explore the relationships described above beyond focusing exclusively on shared decision policies or explaining individual differences in those decision policies.

**Within-Context Variance.** First, does the entrepreneur's nationality explain variance in his or her decision policies, and if so, to what extent? In light of institutional theory (North, 2005) and the literature on national cultures (Hofstede, 1980), we may assume that entrepreneurs from certain countries weight the criteria for evaluating an opportunity differently compared to entrepreneurs from other countries. For instance, weak intellectual property protection in China could lead Chinese entrepreneurs to focus less on patenting their ideas than entrepreneurs from the UK, a country with strong intellectual property rights. Perhaps entrepreneurs from risk-averse countries emphasize the possible downside loss of opportunity exploitation (i.e., the costs of being wrong), but entrepreneurs from less risk-averse countries emphasize the upside of opportunity exploitation (i.e., the benefits of being right). Researchers could test these relationships (and others) by controlling for individual differences, such as experience.

Second, nationality can also be included in this three-level model to explain variance in how individuals' entrepreneurial experience impacts decision policies. For example, during an entrepreneurial task, a more experienced entrepreneur may emphasize competition more when evaluating an opportunity's attractiveness compared to a less experienced entrepreneur, but this difference will likely be stronger in economies that are less regulated. This scenario characterizes a three-way interaction that involves all three levels. Finally, nationality may also explain entrepreneurs' propensity to find opportunities more or less attractive beyond the information they have about each of the decision criteria and the effects of entrepreneurial experience.

**Within-Individual Variance.** In the previous section, we highlighted the potential of considering the context in which an individual is embedded when he or she makes decisions in an entrepreneurial task. However, the same individual is likely to be presented with a variety of situations at different points in time that impact his or her decision policies in entrepreneurial tasks. Again, these tasks have a nested data structure with three levels of analysis: in this case, decisions (Level 1), situations/time (Level 2), and the individual (Level 3). Researchers have the opportunity to gain deeper insights into within-individual (i.e., intra-individual) variance by exploring situational differences. For instance, an individual's decision policy for evaluating an opportunity's appeal may vary when he or she has a promotion focus compared to a prevention focus, when he or she is in a gain situation compared to a loss situation, when he or she is in a positive emotional state compared to a negative emotional state, when there is great time pressure compared to minimal time pressure, and so on.

First, using the strong established literature on decision making in general and entrepreneurial decision making in particular, researchers can build models of within-individual variation in decision policies as well as develop valid situational contexts. Such studies will likely contribute substantially to the literatures on entrepreneurship, management, and decision making by providing a greater understanding of the influence situational contexts have on decision making. For instance, studies have shown that researchers sometimes manipulate situations to prime a regulatory focus (Halamish, Liberman, Higgins, & Idson, 2008), emotion

(Bradley & Lang, 1999), and feedback (Leung & Trotman, 2008). Do situational contexts like these also impact entrepreneurs' decision policies? If they do, in what ways?

Second, researchers also have the opportunity to study the role individual differences play in explaining variance in the way situational contexts affect decision policies. While experience, knowledge, and motivation all likely help explain variance in situational contexts' influence on decision policies, numerous opportunities exist for researchers to learn more about this element of decision making in entrepreneurial tasks. For instance, compared to those with low emotional intelligence, differences in the decision policy regarding opportunity appeal across emotional states (i.e., high negative versus low negative) may not be as substantial for individuals high in emotional intelligence. It could be that differences in individuals' decision policies to try again (e.g., act upon a later opportunity) across feedback conditions (e.g., success with a prior opportunity vs. failure) are not as strong for highly resilient people or those with extensive coping skills compared to less resilient individuals or those with weaker coping skills.

Finally, future research can explore situational contexts' role in the decision-making process. For example, in highly positive emotional states, entrepreneurs may consider opportunities to be more attractive compared to when they are in more negative emotional states (keeping the nature of the opportunity and individual differences constant).

**Summary.** Figure 8.1 offers a sketch of hierarchically nested concepts that researchers can use to explore entrepreneurial decision making. In Fig. A, individual entrepreneurs are nested within different contexts (i.e., nation, industry, organization), and there are several decisions each entrepreneur must make as part of his or her experimental tasks. Hierarchical linear modeling analysis of such nested data allows researchers to focus on one level while controlling for influences of all other levels (e.g., explaining decision-level variance while controlling for the characteristics of the entrepreneur and his or her industry). Alternatively, researchers can explore effects covering multiple levels of analysis (e.g., explaining how industry influences decisions while controlling for the characteristics of the entrepreneur). In Fig. B, decisions are nested within different situations/time points, which are nested within entrepreneurs. In such settings, researchers can explore, for example, how decisions vary over different time points while controlling for (or testing the moderating effects of) the characteristics of the entrepreneur.

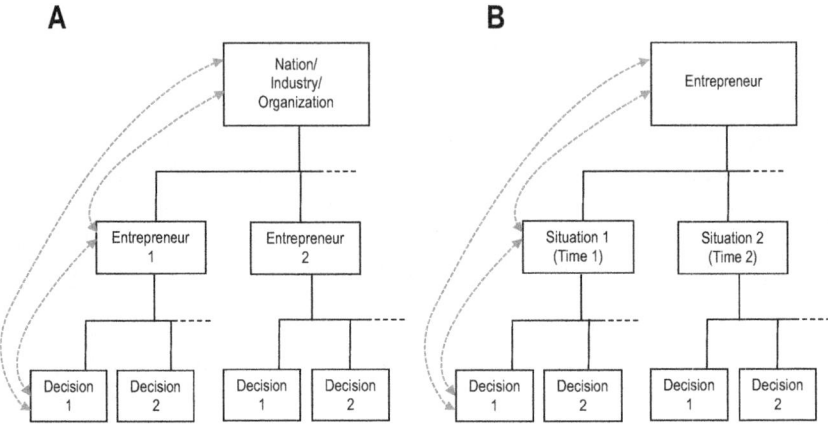

**Fig. 8.1** A sketch of a model of the nested nature of data captured by conjoint analysis (and other experimental techniques); cross-level effects in dashed arrows

## Discussion and Conclusion

Although there is a substantial body of research on entrepreneurial decision making (for a review, see Shepherd et al., 2015), in this chapter, we offered multiple ways to tap into unknown territory. First, we discussed several ways to explore different types of entrepreneurial decisions as well as biases and heuristics in these decisions. To pursue some of these research opportunities and find others that advance our understanding of entrepreneurial decision making will likely require us, as scholars, to be more entrepreneurial in our methods. For example, adopting new methods to explore new empirical terrain can help trigger theorizing about entrepreneurial decision making and lead to interesting contributions. By combining established methods in new ways, we can also stimulate new theorizing. For example, we expect future research will begin to more frequently combine surveys with experiments, experiments with secondary data, inductive content analysis of secondary data to create panel datasets, and so on. Not only do we hope scholars are entrepreneurial in using methods to generate new insights, but we also hope that reviewers and editors are "open" to this sort of novelty because this is where (we believe) the greatest future contributions will come on the entrepreneurial decision-making topic. These contributions will not only be to the entrepreneurship and management literatures but will be more far-reaching. Because the context in which entrepreneurial decisions are made is so extreme in a number of ways (e.g., high consequences, emotional anticipation and reactions, time pressures, and ambiguity), this provides us the opportunity to extend the boundaries of current theories of decision making and thus make a more general contribution to the psychology and behavioral economics literatures. In particular, conjoint analysis allows entrepreneurship researchers to explore and empirically test multi-level decision-making studies.

Second, we hope we have opened up some stimulating pathways for future research by conceptualizing decision making in entrepreneurial tasks using a hierarchical multi-level framework. By theorizing on and empirically testing cross-level models of decision making in entrepreneurial tasks, research in this area can add significantly to the literature on entrepreneurship. Regardless of whether studies use conjoint analysis to explore decision making or use another method to explore a different topic, multi-level research has the potential to make substantial contributions to the entrepreneurship field.

In conclusion, we are convinced that while prior studies have created a strong body of knowledge on entrepreneurial decision making, these studies have only paved the ground for more work on this important subject. We hope that this chapter inspires scholars to advance this important stream of literature in the multiple ways described here and beyond.

## Note

1. There are several differences between metric conjoint analysis and policy capturing, including (but not limited to) the following: First, metric conjoint analysis generally represents attributes at two (i.e., high and low) or three (i.e., high, medium, and low) discrete levels. Policy capturing, on the other hand, generally presents attributes along a continuum. Second, metric conjoint analysis employs experimental designs to reveal the attribute combinations for each profile in a sample as well as the number of total profiles, and it usually entails completely duplicating the initial set of profiles. Policy capturing generally does not use an experimental design and only duplicates a small subset of the original profiles.

## References

Baker, T., & Nelson, R. E. (2005). Creating something from nothing: Resource construction through entrepreneurial bricolage. *Administrative Science Quarterly, 50*(3), 329–366.

Bakker, R. M., & Shepherd, D. A. (2017). Pull the plug or take the plunge: Multiple opportunities and the speed of venturing decisions in the Australian mining industry. *Academy of Management Journal*. Forthcoming.

Bandura, A. (1999). Social cognitive theory of personality. In L. Pervin & O. P. John (Eds.), *Handbook of personality: Theory and research* (pp. 154–196). New York: Guilford Publications.

Baron, R. A. (1998). Cognitive mechanisms in entrepreneurship: Why and when enterpreneurs think differently than other people. *Journal of Business venturing, 13*(4), 275–294.

Baron, R. A. (2004). The cognitive perspective: A valuable tool for answering entrepreneurship's basic "why" questions. *Journal of Business Venturing, 19*(2), 221–239.

Baron, R. A. (2006). Opportunity recognition as pattern recognition: How entrepreneurs "connect the dots" to identify new business opportunities. *Academy of Management Perspectives, 20*(1), 104–119.

Baron, R. A. (2008). The role of affect in the entrepreneurial process. *Academy of Management Review, 33*(2), 328–340.

Baron, R. A., & Ensley, M. D. (2006). Opportunity recognition as the detection of meaningful patterns: Evidence from comparisons of novice and experienced entrepreneurs. *Management Science, 52*(9), 1331–1344.

Bates, T. (1995). Self-employment entry across industry groups. *Journal of Business Venturing, 10*(2), 143–156.

Battilana, J., & Dorado, S. (2010). Building sustainable hybrid organizations: The case of commercial microfinance organizations. *Academy of Management Journal, 53*(6), 1419–1440.

Battilana, J., & Lee, M. (2014). Advancing research on hybrid organizing—Insights from the study of social enterprises. *The Academy of Management Annals, 8*(1), 397–441.

Behrens, J., & Patzelt, H. (2017). Corporate entrepreneurship managers' project terminations: Integrating portfolio-level, individual-level, and firm-level effects. *Entrepreneurship Theory and Practice*.

Belleflamme, P., Lambert, T., & Schwienbacher, A. (2014). Crowdfunding: Tapping the right crowd. *Journal of Business Venturing, 29*(5), 585–609.

Bonanno, G. A. (2004). Loss, trauma, and human resilience: Have we underestimated the human capacity to thrive after extremely aversive events? *American Psychologist, 59*, 20–28.

Bradley, M. M., & Lang, P. J. (1999). Fearfulness and affective evaluations of pictures. *Motivation and Emotion, 23*(1), 1–13.

Brewer, M. B. (1991). The social self: On being the same and different at the same time. *Personality and Social Psychology Bulletin, 17*(5), 475–482.

Brinckmann, J., Grichnik, D., & Kapsa, D. (2010). Should entrepreneurs plan or just storm the castle? A meta-analysis on contextual factors impacting the business planning–performance relationship in small firms. *Journal of Business Venturing, 25*(1), 24–40.

Bruns, V., Holland, D. V., Shepherd, D., & Wiklund, J. (2008). The role of human capital in loan officers' decision policies. *Entrepreneurship Theory & Practice, 32*(3), 485–506.

Brush, C. G., Carter, N. M., Gatewood, E. J., Greene, P. G., & Hart, M. M. (2006). *Growth-oriented women entrepreneurs and their businesses: A global research perspective.* London: Edward Elgar.

Busenitz, L. W., & Barney, J. B. (1997). Differences between entrepreneurs and managers in large organizations: Biases and heuristics in strategic decision-making. *Journal of Business Venturing, 12*(1), 9–30.

Cardon, M. S., Wincent, J., Shigh, J., & Drnovsek, M. (2009). The nature and experience of entrepreneurial passion. *Academy of Management Review, 34*(3), 511–532.

Carpenter, M. A., Geletkanycz, M. A., & Sanders, W. G. (2004). Upper echelons research revisited: Antecedents, elements, and consequences of top management team composition. *Journal of Management, 30*(6), 749–778.

Carroll, G. R., & Mosakowski, E. (1987). The career dynamics of self-employment. *Administrative Science Quarterly, 32*(4), 570–589.

Choi, Y. R., & Shepherd, D. A. (2004). Entrepreneurs' decisions to exploit opportunities. *Journal of Management, 30*(3), 377–395.

Chwolka, A., & Raith, M. G. (2012). The value of business planning before start-up—A decision-theoretical perspective. *Journal of Business Venturing, 27*(3), 385–399.

Davidsson, P., & Honig, B. (2003). The role of social and human capital among nascent entrepreneurs. *Journal of Business Venturing, 18*(3), 301–331.

Deci, E. L., & Ryan, R. M. (2000). The "what" and "why" of goal pursuits: Human needs and the self-determination of behavior. *Psychological Inquiry, 11*(4), 227–268.

DeTienne, D. R. (2010). Entrepreneurial exit as a critical component of the entrepreneurial process: Theoretical development. *Journal of Business Venturing, 25*(2), 203–215.

DeTienne, D. R., Shepherd, D. A., & De Castro, J. O. (2008). The fallacy of "only the strong survive": The effects of extrinsic motivation on the persistence decisions for under-performing firms. *Journal of Business Venturing, 23*(5), 528–546.

Domurath, A., & Patzelt, H. (2016). Entrepreneurs' assessments of early international entry: The role of foreign social ties, venture absorptive capacity, and generalized trust in others. *Entrepreneurship Theory & Practice, 40*(5), 1149–1177.

Douglas, E. J., & Shepherd, D. A. (2000). Entrepreneurship as a utility maximizing response. *Journal of Business Venturing, 15*(3), 231–251.

Douglas, E. J., & Shepherd, D. A. (2002). Self-employment as a career choice: Attitudes, entrepreneurial intentions, and utility maximization. *Entrepreneurship Theory and Practice, 26*(3), 81–90.

Ebben, J., & Johnson, A. (2006). Bootstrapping in small firms: An empirical analysis of change over time. *Journal of Business Venturing, 21*(6), 851–865.

Eisenhauer, J. G. (1995). The entrepreneurial decision: Economic theory and empirical evidence. *Entrepreneurship: Theory and Practice, 19*(4), 67–80.

Fried, V. H., & Hisrich, R. D. (1994). Toward a model of venture capital investment decision making. *Financial Management, 23*(3), 28–37.

Gartner, W. B. (1985). A conceptual framework for describing the phenomenon of new venture creation. *Academy of Management Review, 10*(4), 696–706.

Gigerenzer, G., & Gaissmaier, W. (2011). Heuristic decision making. *Annual Review of Psychology, 62*, 451–482.

Gimeno, J., Folta, T. B., Cooper, A. C., & Woo, C. Y. (1997). Survival of the fittest? Entrepreneurial human capital and the persistence of underperforming firms. *Administrative Science Quarterly, 42*, 750–783.

Grant, A. M. (2007). Relational design and the motivation to make a prosocial difference. *Academy of Management Review, 32*, 393–417.

Grant, A. M., & Mayer, D. M. (2009). Good soldiers and good actors: Prosocial and impression management motives as interactive predictors of affiliative citizenship behaviors. *Journal of Applied Psychology, 94*(4), 900–912.

Grégoire, D. A., Barr, P. S., & Shepherd, D. A. (2010). Cognitive processes of opportunity recognition: The role of structural alignment. *Organization Science, 21*(2), 413–431.

Halamish, V., Liberman, N., Higgins, E. T., & Idson, L. C. (2008). Regulatory focus effects on discounting over uncertainty for losses vs. gains. *Journal of Economic Psychology, 29*(5), 654–666.

Hambrick, D. C., & Mason, P. A. (1984). Upper echelons: The organization as a reflection of its top managers. *Academy of Management Review, 9*(2), 193–206.

Harrison, R. T., Mason, C. M., & Girling, P. (2004). Financial bootstrapping and venture development in the software industry. *Entrepreneurship & Regional Development, 16*(4), 307–333.

Haynie, J. M., Shepherd, D. A., & McMullen, J. S. (2009). An opportunity for me? The role of resources in opportunity evaluation decisions. *Journal of Management Studies, 46*(3), 337–361.

Hayward, M. L., Shepherd, D. A., & Griffin, D. (2006). A hubris theory of entrepreneurship. *Management Science, 52*(2), 160–172.

Herron, L., & Sapienza, H. J. (1992). The entrepreneur and the initiation of new venture launch activities. *Entrepreneurship Theory and Practice, 17*(1), 49–55.

Hofstede, G. H. (1980). *Culture's consequences: International differences in work-related values.* Beverly Hills, CA: Sage Publications.

Holland, D. V., & Shepherd, D. A. (2013). Deciding to persist: Adversity, values, and entrepreneurs' decision policies. *Entrepreneurship Theory and Practice, 37*(2), 331–358.

Izard, C. E. (2009). Emotion theory and research: Highlights, unanswered questions, and emerging issues. *Annual Review of Psychology, 60,* 1–25.

Jonsson, S., & Lindbergh, J. (2013). The development of social capital and financing of entrepreneurial firms: From financial bootstrapping to bank funding. *Entrepreneurship Theory and Practice, 37*(4), 661–686.

Karlsson, T., & Honig, B. (2009). Judging a business by its cover: An institutional perspective on new ventures and the business plan. *Journal of Business Venturing, 24*(1), 27–45.

Katz, J., & Gartner, W. B. (1988). Properties of emerging organizations. *Academy of Management Review, 13*(3), 429–441.

Kolvereid, L., & Isaksen, E. (2006). New business start-up and subsequent entry into self-employment. *Journal of Business Venturing, 21*(6), 866–885.

Klaukien, A., Shepherd, D. A., & Patzelt, H. (2013). Passion for work, nonwork-related excitement, and innovation managers' decision to exploit new product opportunities. *Journal of Product Innovation Management, 30*(3), 574–588.

Leung, P. W., & Trotman, K. T. (2008). Effect of different types of feedback on the level of auditors' configural information processing. *Accounting & Finance, 48,* 301–318.

Levesque, M., & Minniti, M. (2006). The effect of aging on entrepreneurial behavior. *Journal of Business Venturing, 21*(2), 177–194.

Lévesque, M., & Minniti, M. (2011). Age matters: How demographics influence aggregate entrepreneurship. *Strategic Entrepreneurship Journal, 5*(3), 269–284.

Levesque, M., Shepherd, D. A., & Douglas, E. J. (2002). Employment or self-employment: A dynamic utility-maximizing model. *Journal of Business Venturing, 17*(3), 189–210.

Lichtenstein, B. B., Dooley, K. J., & Lumpkin, G. T. (2006). Measuring emergence in the dynamics of new venture creation. *Journal of Business Venturing, 21*(2), 153–175.

Lohrke, F. T., Holloway, B. B., & Woolley, T. W. (2010). Conjoint analysis in entrepreneurship research a review and research agenda. *Organizational Research Methods, 13*(1), 16–30.

Maula, M., Autio, E., & Arenius, P. (2005). What drives micro-angel investments? *Small Business Economics, 25*(5), 459–475.

McMullen, J. S., & Shepherd, D. A. (2006). Entrepreneurial action and the role of uncertainty in the theory of the entrepreneur. *Academy of Management Review, 31*(1), 132–152.

Mitchell, R. K. (1994). *The composition, classification, and creation of new venture formation expertise.* Doctoral dissertation, University of Utah.

Mitchell, R. K., Busenitz, L. W., Bird, B., Marie Gaglio, C., McMullen, J. S., Morse, E. A., et al. (2007). The central question in entrepreneurial cognition research 2007. *Entrepreneurship Theory and Practice, 31*(1), 1–27.

Mitchell, R. K., Busenitz, L., Lant, T., McDougall, P. P., Morse, E. A., & Smith, J. B. (2002). Toward a theory of entrepreneurial cognition: Rethinking the people side of entrepreneurship research. *Entrepreneurship Theory and Practice, 27*(2), 93–104.

Mitchell, J. R., & Shepherd, D. A. (2010). To thine own self be true: Images of self, images of opportunity, and entrepreneurial action. *Journal of Business Venturing, 25*(1), 138–154.

Mollick, E. (2014). The dynamics of crowdfunding: An exploratory study. *Journal of Business Venturing, 29*(1), 1–16.

Mullins, J. W., & Forlani, D. (2005). Missing the boat or sinking the boat: A study of new venture decision making. *Journal of Business Venturing, 20*(1), 47–69.

Muzyka, D., Birley, S., & Leleux, B. (1996). Trade-offs in the investment decisions of European venture capitalists. *Journal of Business Venturing, 11*(4), 273–288.

North, D. (2005). *Understanding the process of economic change.* Princeton, NJ: Princeton University Press.

Ocasio, W. (1997). Towards an attention-based view of the firm. *Strategic Management Journal, 18*(Special), 187–206.

Patzelt, H., Shepherd, D. A., Deeds, D., & Bradley, S. W. (2008). Financial slack and venture managers' decisions to seek a new alliance. *Journal of Business Venturing, 23*(4), 465–481.

Priem, R. L., & Harrison, D. A. (1994). Exploring strategic judgment: Methods for testing the assumptions of prescriptive contingency theories. *Strategic Management Journal, 15*(4), 311–324.

Robinson, P. B., & Sexton, E. A. (1994). The effect of education and experience on self-employment success. *Journal of Business Venturing, 9*(2), 141–156.

Ryan, R. M., & Deci, E. L. (2000). Self-determination theory and the facilitation of intrinsic motivation, social development, and well-being. *American Psychologist, 55*, 68–78.

Sarasvathy, S. D. (2001). Causation and effectuation: Toward a theoretical shift from economic inevitability to entrepreneurial contingency. *Academy of Management Review, 26*(2), 243–263.

Schwartz, S. H. (1994). Are there universal aspects in the structure and contents of human values? *Journal of Social Issues, 50*(4), 19–45.

Shah, S. K., & Tripsas, M. (2007). The accidental entrepreneur: The emergent and collective process of user entrepreneurship. *Strategic Entrepreneurship Journal, 1*(1–2), 123–140.

Shane, S. A. (2000). Prior knowledge and the discovery of entrepreneurial opportunities. *Organization Science, 11*(4), 448–469.

Shane, S., & Venkataraman, S. (2000). The promise of entrepreneurship as a field of research. *Academy of Management Review, 25*(1), 217–226.

Shaver, K. G., & Scott, L. R. (1991). Person, process, choice: The psychology of new venture creation. *Entrepreneurship Theory and Practice, 16*(2), 23–45.

Shepherd, D. A. (1999). Venture capitalists' assessment of new venture survival. *Management Science, 45*(5), 621–632.

Shepherd, D. A. (2003). Learning from business failure: Propositions of grief recovery for the self-employed. *Academy of Management Review, 28*(2), 318–328.

Shepherd, D. A. (2011). Multilevel entrepreneurship research: Opportunities for studying entrepreneurial decision making. *Journal of Management, 37*(2), 412–420.

Shepherd, D. A. (2015). Party On! A call for entrepreneurship research that is more interactive, activity based, cognitively hot, compassionate, and prosocial. *Journal of Business Venturing, 30*(4), 489–507.

Shepherd, D. A., & Cardon, M. S. (2009). Negative emotional reactions to project failure and the self-compassion to learn from the experience. *Journal of Management Studies, 46*(6), 923–949.

Shepherd, D. A., McMullen, J. S., & Ocasio, W. (2017). Is that an opportunity? An attention model of top managers' opportunity beliefs for strategic action. *Strategic Management Journal.* Forthcoming.

Shepherd, D., Patzelt, H., & Baron, R. (2013). "I care about nature, but ...": Disengaging values in assessing opportunities that cause harm. *Academy of Management Journal, 56*(5), 1251–1273.

Shepherd, D. A., Patzelt, H., Williams, T. A., & Warnecke, D. (2014). How does project termination impact project team members? Rapid termination, 'creeping death', and learning from failure. *Journal of Management Studies, 51*(4), 513–546.

Shepherd, D. A., Patzelt, H., & Wolfe, M. (2011). Moving forward from project failure: Negative emotions, affective commitment, and learning from the experience. *Academy of Management Journal, 54*(6), 1229–1259.

Shepherd, D. A., Wiklund, J., & Haynie, J. M. (2009). Moving forward: Balancing the financial and emotional costs of business failure. *Journal of Business Venturing, 24*(2), 134–148.

Shepherd, D. A., & Williams, T. A. (2014). Local venturing as compassion organizing in the aftermath of a natural disaster: The role of localness and community in reducing suffering. *Journal of Management Studies, 51*(6), 952–994.

Shepherd, D. A., Williams, T. A., & Patzelt, H. (2015). Thinking about entrepreneurial decision making: Review and research agenda. *Journal of Management*, 41(1), 11–46.
Shepherd, D. A., & Zacharakis, A. (1997). Conjoint analysis: A window of opportunity for entrepreneurship research. In J. Katz (Ed.), *Advances in entrepreneurship, firm emergence and growth* (Vol. 3, pp. 203–248). Greenwich, CT: JAI Press.
Simon, M., Houghton, S. M., & Aquino, K. (2000). Cognitive biases, risk perception, and venture formation: How individuals decide to start companies. *Journal of Business Venturing*, 15(2), 113–134.
Sutcliffe, K. M., & Vogus, T. J. (2003). Organizing for resilience. In K. S. Cameron, J. E. Dutton, & R. E. Quinn (Eds.), *Positive organizational scholarship* (pp. 94–110). San Francisco: Berrett-Koehler Publishers.
Tajfel, H., & Turner, J. C. (1979). An integrative theory of intergroup conflict. In W. Austin & S. Worchel (Eds.), *The social psychology of intergroup relations* (pp. 33–48). Pacific Grove, CA: Brooks/Cole.
Walker, G., Kogut, B., & Shan, W. (1997). Social capital, structural holes and the formation of an industry network. *Organization Science*, 8(2), 109–125.
Wennberg, K., & DeTienne, D. R. (2014). What do we really mean when we talk about 'exit'? A critical review of research on entrepreneurial exit. *International Small Business Journal*, 32(1), 4–16.
Wennberg, K., Wiklund, J., DeTienne, D. R., & Cardon, M. S. (2010). Reconceptualizing entrepreneurial exit: Divergent exit routes and their drivers. *Journal of Business Venturing*, 25(4), 361–375.
Westhead, P., Ucbasaran, D., Wright, M., & Binks, M. (2005). Novice, serial and portfolio entrepreneur behaviour and contributions. *Small Business Economics*, 25(2), 109–132.
Westhead, P., & Wright, M. (1998). Novice, portfolio, and serial founders: Are they different? *Journal of Business Venturing*, 13(3), 173–204.
Williams, D. W., & Grégoire, D. A. (2014). Seeking commonalities or avoiding differences [quest] Re-conceptualizing distance and its effects on internationalization decisions. *Journal of International Business Studies*, 46(3), 253–284.
Wilson, F., Marlino, D., & Kickul, J. (2004). Our entrepreneurial future: Examining the diverse attitudes and motivations of teens across gender and ethnic identity. *Journal of Developmental Entrepreneurship*, 9(3), 177–197.
Zacharakis, A., McMullen, J., & Shepherd, D. A. (2007). VC decision making across three countries: An institutional theory perspective. *Journal of International Business Studies*, 38(5), 691–708.
Zacharakis, A., & Meyer, D. G. (2000). The potential of actuarial decision models: Can they improve the venture capital investment decision? *Journal of Business Venturing*, 15(4), 323–346.

Zacharakis, A. L., & Shepherd, D. A. (2001). The nature of information and overconfidence on venture capitalists' decision making. *Journal of Business Venturing, 16*(4), 311–332.

Zeelenberg, M. (1999). Anticipated regret, expected feedback and behavioral decision making. *Journal of Behavioral Decision Making, 12*(2), 93–106.

Zeelenberg, M., Van Dijk, E., Van Den Bos, K., & Pieters, R. (2002). The inaction effect in the psychology of regret. *Journal of Personality and Social Psychology, 82*(3), 314–328.

**Open Access** This chapter is distributed under the terms of the Creative Commons Attribution 4.0 International License (http://creativecommons.org/licenses/by/4.0/), which permits use, duplication, adaptation, distribution and reproduction in any medium or format, as long as you give appropriate credit to the original author(s) and the source, provide a link to the Creative Commons license and indicate if changes were made.

The images or other third party material in this chapter are included in the work's Creative Commons license, unless indicated otherwise in the credit line; if such material is not included in the work's Creative Commons license and the respective action is not permitted by statutory regulation, users will need to obtain permission from the license holder to duplicate, adapt or reproduce the material.

# CHAPTER 9

# Conclusion

We are excited about the state of entrepreneurship research. The community of entrepreneurship researchers has grown rapidly over the last couple of decades, there has been a dramatic increase in the quality and variety of entrepreneurship research as well as a dramatic increase in the number of entrepreneurship-specific journals, and entrepreneurship research now has greater prominence in disciplinary and functional journals (e.g., the *Academy of Management Journal*). As a result, there has been a boom in the generation of knowledge about entrepreneurial phenomena. This is all great news. Although we, as a community, can bask in the glory of this relatively recently acquired prominence, this is not the approach recommended in this book. Rather, we can apply the saying "dance with the one who brung you" to suggest that being entrepreneurial in our research is what has led to the field's successes and that we need to continue to do so to maintain (or increase) the current trajectory. It is not a time to rest on our laurels but to push ahead. As March (1991) noted, after a period of time, exploration begins to drown out exploitation, which creates an unproductive imbalance for the entity. We hope this book provides a counterbalance to the tendency toward exploitation in entrepreneurship research by providing what we believe are some interesting research explorations.

While we are excited about the past achievements and the current state of entrepreneurship research, we are even more excited about the trailblazing opportunities that are ahead of us to develop the field in the future. Indeed, in this book, we have hopefully established a number of trailheads (based on current state-of-the-art knowledge about important aspects of the entrepreneurial process) and then offered some insights into possible trails that can be blazed from these trailheads. The proposed trailblazing has largely focused on the notion of individuals' thinking, feeling, and acting in relation to potential opportunities embedded in communities and often extreme contexts. This is not to say that there are not important trails to be blazed at the entrepreneurial team, firm, institutional, regional, and other levels of analysis. These levels of analysis are not within our area of expertise, so it is more difficult for us personally to highlight potential trails at these levels of analysis even though we believe that they exist. We look forward to seeing advancements at these levels of analysis as well.

Regardless of the level of analysis (or across levels of analysis), maintaining an open mind to novelty is critical. We need to have an open mind about the philosophical approach. This does not mean that an author should use a different philosophical perspective for each paper (although he or she certainly could) but that we should be open enough to allow others to have a different philosophical perspective underlying their research. If we converge on a specific philosophical perspective, perhaps as the result of more closed-minded editors, reviewers, and authors, then we discourage trailblazing and "kill off" an important source of potential new insights. We are not advocating an approach of "anything goes," but we, as scholars, should (should is a strong word, but it emphasizes our strong belief) judge research based on the traditions and expectations in which it is embedded.

In a similar way, it is important that entrepreneurship scholars remain open-minded to different theoretical lenses and ways of generating new theory. Indeed, to the extent that people can apply new theories to entrepreneurship research, there is an increased chance of uncovering new insights into entrepreneurial phenomena as well as making contributions back to the literatures from which these "borrowed" theories come. Therefore, while we can borrow theories to understand entrepreneurial phenomena, it is important to go one step further and look toward "blending" to make a contribution back to the solutions' origins. That is, in applying a specific theory (from outside the entrepreneurship domain), what adaptions to that theory are required to apply it to an aspect of the entrepreneurial context? Exploring this question provides a basis for blending (see Oswick, Fleming, & Hanlon, 2011) and/or bricolage (see Boxenbaum & Rouleau, 2011). Theorizing using blending and/or bricolage provides a strong basis for blazing new trails that contribute to knowledge and perhaps widen the entrepreneurial tent to include more diverse others.

Although we have largely focused on the content as the basis for blazing new trails, we want to acknowledge that method likely also plays an important role. Indeed, content and method are often closely intertwined. The empirical testing of new theories may require the adaption of existing techniques from other fields or the creation of new methods altogether, and the use of new (to entrepreneurship) methods has the potential of opening up our theorizing by encouraging us to think about research questions not normally conceived or rapidly dismissed because they were thought to be untestable. It seems that the community of entrepreneurship scholars has been very welcoming of new methods, used these new methods to open new research themes, and improved upon existing measures to further explore entrepreneurial phenomena. We encourage this interest in new methods for future studies as well.

The flipside to the same coin is that there is a very real danger to the future of the field if we collectively (but especially the gatekeepers—namely, editors and reviewers) become closed-minded. Signs of closed-mindedness are when the entrepreneurship field converges on a dominant philosophical approach, a dominant theoretical lens, a few preferred methodological techniques, and a narrow definition of the field. Although such outcomes may provide the field of entrepreneurship even greater legitimacy, our major concern is not so much with establishing legitimacy (this is largely already established) but with the generation of new knowledge about entrepreneurial phenomena. We believe that the entrepreneurship field will prosper more from blazing new trails than relying too heavily on well-established trails. Our hope is that this book provided the reader with some starting points for future trailblazing entrepreneurship research.

## References

Boxenbaum, E., & Rouleau, L. (2011). New knowledge products as bricolage: Metaphors and scripts in organizational theory. *Academy of Management Review, 36*(2), 272–296.

March, J. G. (1991). Exploration and exploitation in organizational learning. *Organization Science, 2*(1), 71–87.
Oswick, C., Fleming, P., & Hanlon, G. (2011). From borrowing to blending: Rethinking the processes of organizational theory building. *Academy of Management Review, 36*(2), 318–337.

**Open Access**  This chapter is distributed under the terms of the Creative Commons Attribution 4.0 International License (http://creativecommons.org/licenses/by/4.0/), which permits use, duplication, adaptation, distribution and reproduction in any medium or format, as long as you give appropriate credit to the original author(s) and the source, provide a link to the Creative Commons license and indicate if changes were made.

The images or other third party material in this chapter are included in the work's Creative Commons license, unless indicated otherwise in the credit line; if such material is not included in the work's Creative Commons license and the respective action is not permitted by statutory regulation, users will need to obtain permission from the license holder to duplicate, adapt or reproduce the material.

# Index

**A**
abducting (abduction), 27
absorptive capacity, 12, 104–6, 112
action (entrepreneurial action), 8, 9, 11–14, 17–19, 28–30, 32, 33, 35, 40, 43–9, 68, 69, 73, 85, 86, 88, 90, 108, 114, 126–8, 132, 149, 151–3, 156–8, 161–71, 182, 191–7, 210, 211, 214, 216, 218, 219, 222, 224, 229, 231, 234, 235, 238–41, 260, 261, 264, 270, 272
activity, 18, 19, 28–39, 47, 67–9, 71, 72, 121, 213, 214, 227, 266
alleviation of suffering, 43, 197, 199, 200
anomaly, 27, 107, 108, 110
assessment, 13, 20, 33, 113, 123, 126, 259–61, 272
attention, 4, 7, 25, 32, 36–9, 41, 67, 69, 75, 76, 78, 86, 91, 107, 111, 118, 123, 124, 129–31, 159, 160, 184, 213, 214, 233, 241, 263
autonomy, 88, 89, 211, 212, 214–16, 231, 263

**B**
belief, 18, 21, 22, 27, 31–3, 78, 83, 85, 119, 130, 162, 184, 187, 199, 210, 227, 233, 288
belongingness, 216, 217, 231
biases, 6, 87, 115, 116, 120, 126, 132, 267, 268, 276
boundaries, 3, 4, 42–4, 47, 86, 126, 133, 154, 156, 182, 183, 196, 277

**C**
career (entrepreneurial career), 13, 66, 210–21, 223–32, 240, 261–4
cognition (cognitive), 11, 17–21, 32, 34–8, 40, 50, 68, 76–8, 80, 82, 84, 86, 107, 116, 118, 119, 170, 185, 199, 214, 224, 233, 236, 267, 271

Note: Page numbers with "n" denote endnotes.

© The Author(s) 2017
D.A. Shepherd, H. Patzelt, *Trailblazing in Entrepreneurship*,
DOI 10.1007/978-3-319-48701-4

community of Inquiry, 18, 22–5, 28–31, 48, 108–11, 122, 182, 183, 185–9, 201
compassion (compassion organizing), 13, 19, 42–4, 196, 197, 200
competence, 67, 88, 89, 215, 216, 231
conjoint analysis, 5, 13, 258, 269, 276, 277, 277n1
creation (new venture creation), 30, 31, 50, 190
cross level, 269, 273, 276, 277, 288
culture, 28, 66, 71, 81, 84, 88, 89, 120, 126, 152, 153, 155, 158, 164, 165, 169, 217, 267, 273

## D

decision making, 10, 11, 13, 80, 84, 90, 117, 118, 132, 183, 192, 194, 198, 213, 222, 257–77
desirability, 33, 235, 260
development, 4, 7, 9, 12, 19, 24, 26, 27, 30, 31, 35, 47, 64, 85, 87, 105, 111, 113, 116, 117, 119, 128, 130, 132, 133, 149–71, 183, 193, 195, 197, 258–60, 270
do good, 40, 48–50, 198, 201, 210, 225, 267
doubt, 22, 27–9, 31, 33, 68, 130, 264

## E

emotion, 11, 19, 34, 39, 50, 77, 82, 119, 161, 183, 190–5, 201, 223–7, 271, 274
end-user, 12
endowment, 111, 190, 191, 194–6, 227
exploitation, 7, 9, 10, 14, 17–50, 67, 104–6, 108–13, 122–4, 126, 128, 129, 133, 151, 152, 157, 159, 167, 193, 196, 232, 234–6, 238, 257, 260, 273, 274, 287
extrinsic motivation, 48, 49, 271, 272

## F

failure, 7, 38, 63–91, 116, 164, 193, 225, 258
family business, 10, 12, 181–202
feasibility, 31, 33, 235
field, 2–9, 11, 12, 14, 14n1, 17, 19, 20, 25, 26, 29, 30, 34, 42, 43, 48, 104, 150, 154, 156, 157, 168, 170, 171, 181, 198, 199, 236, 240, 259, 261, 263, 268, 277, 287, 289
first-person opportunity, 20, 31–3, 48, 49, 128, 130, 131, 161, 162, 185, 232, 233
funding, 13, 37, 68, 158, 213, 264–6

## G

generation (of a potential opportunity), 188
go (no go), 115
grief, 39, 75–9, 82, 88, 89, 119, 194, 223, 225, 226, 238, 264

## H

health, 10, 11, 13, 116, 149, 151–4, 159–64, 209–41
heuristics, 13, 21, 267–9, 276

## I

identification, 21–2, 36, 38, 72, 104, 105, 111, 112, 123–8, 130, 133, 157, 159, 170, 185, 187, 188, 196, 232–6, 238, 259, 260, 270, 271

innovation, 9, 10, 12, 25, 64, 103–33, 158, 234, 241, 260
intrinsic motivation, 47, 49, 170, 271

## M

micro-foundation (of entrepreneurial action), 11, 30, 33, 50, 85, 90, 183
mind, 7, 17, 18, 22–7, 29, 48, 50, 107–11, 116, 157, 183, 185, 186, 189, 190, 210, 288
multi-level, 13, 83, 84, 259, 268–70, 277
mutual adjustment, 11, 18, 21, 23, 25, 26, 48, 108–10, 185–6

## N

nature (natural environment), 8, 10, 11, 28, 40, 43, 123, 153, 155, 157, 159, 198, 240
needs, 26, 44, 69, 76, 83, 88, 89, 105, 116, 119, 125, 128, 159, 165, 166, 168, 170, 183, 196, 199, 212, 215, 216, 231, 236, 267
negative emotion, 39, 77, 226
nested (nested data; nested decisions), 258, 259, 262, 274–6
non-economic gains, 12, 149, 153–7, 170

## O

operations (operations management), 12, 103–33
option, 117, 121, 122, 212, 262

## P

paradigm, 3, 4, 14
perspective taking, 234, 236–40

plausible (plausible stories), 11, 85–7
positive emotion(s), 34–9, 41, 75, 78, 79, 88, 89, 193, 221, 223–7, 264
preservation (preserves), 49, 156, 168
prosocial motivation, 8, 19, 46–8, 161, 162, 196, 197, 199, 211, 232, 236–40, 267
psychological well-being, 159, 161–3, 216, 231, 238

## R

refinement (of a potential opportunity), 12, 21–2, 26, 110, 111, 185, 187, 188, 190
relationship, 7, 13, 19, 23, 24, 26, 31, 34, 37, 39, 71, 72, 74, 80–5, 88–90, 113, 182, 193, 209–41, 258, 260, 271
resilience, 46, 70, 73, 74, 78, 80, 88, 89, 221, 227, 272

## S

scientific (science; scientists), 12, 129, 163–9, 171
search, 4, 5, 23, 123, 129–31, 160, 218, 219
sensemaking, 11, 64, 84–9, 263, 268
socioeconomic status, 13, 149, 153, 154, 211, 212, 227–32, 241n1
socio-emotional wealth, 12, 183, 190–4, 201–2n3
stage gates, 12, 91, 104, 113–20, 132, 263
stress, 13, 45, 71, 81, 209, 211, 212, 219–23, 227, 228, 231
suffering, 8, 13, 19, 42–9, 69, 161, 183, 196–200, 213, 225, 237, 238, 240
sustainable (sustainable entrepreneurship; sustainability),

10–12, 19, 35, 40, 42, 48, 127, 149–71, 198, 210

## T

terminate, 27, 68, 91, 120
third-person opportunity, 20, 33, 49, 123, 128, 130, 131, 162, 232
threat, 159–63, 170, 193, 240
trailblazing (trailblazers), 1–14, 287–9
transformed (transformation), 12, 22, 24, 26, 72, 106, 108–13, 122, 183, 186–9

## U

uncertainty, 3, 8, 11, 13, 17, 28, 31, 63, 78, 90, 104, 113, 114, 116–24, 127, 128, 130–2, 164, 201, 230, 231, 238, 257, 258, 260
users, 12, 25, 115, 122, 163–8, 234, 260, 261

The manufacturer's authorised representative in the EU is Springer Nature Customer Service Centre GmbH, Europaplatz 3, 69115 Heidelberg, Germany. If you have any concerns regarding our products, please contact ProductSafety@springernature.com

Printed and bound by CPI Group (UK) Ltd, Croydon, CR0 4YY

23/03/2026

02076663-0009